T0312164

Also by Geri Sullivan and Saffi Crawford

The Power of Birthdays, Stars, & Numbers
The Power of Attraction

THE
POWER OF
PLAYING CARDS

An Ancient System for
Understanding Yourself,
Your Destiny
& Your Relationships

GERI SULLIVAN
and
SAFFI CRAWFORD

A FIRESIDE BOOK
Published by Simon & Schuster
New York London Toronto Sydney

FIRESIDE
Rockefeller Center
1230 Avenue of the Americas
New York, NY 10020

FIRESIDE and colophon are registered trademarks
of Simon & Schuster, Inc.

For information regarding special discounts for bulk purchases,
please contact Simon & Schuster Special Sales at
1-800-456-6798 or business@simonandschuster.com

Designed by Katy Riegel

Manufactured in the United States of America

3   5   7   9   10   8   6   4   2

Library of Congress Cataloging-in-Publication Data
Sullivan, Geri
The power of playing cards: an ancient system for understanding yourself,
your destiny & your relationships / Geri Sullivan and Saffi Crawford.
p. cm.
1. Fortune-telling by cards.
I. Crawford, Saffi.   II. Title.
BF1878.C73   2004
133.3'242—dc22   2004053341

ISBN-13: 978-0-7432-5057-3
ISBN-10:   0-7432-5057-5

ACKNOWLEDGMENTS

WE WOULD LIKE to thank all those who made this book possible, in particular Andy Fletcher, Julie Castiglia, Marcela Landres, Allyson Edelhertz-Peltier, Cleo Foulcer, Melissa Crawford, Ricky Foulcer, Margaret Sullivan, Darren Dickson, Sara Kristina Grushko, David James, Hazel Aldred, and Liz Bevilacqua.

Contents

PREFACE

As an astrologer and numerologist I was very interested in this system when I came upon it over fifteen years ago, as it seemed to combine astrology and numerology and come up with something extra. I soon learned the cards of all my friends and family members and started to find patterns in my life and theirs. For example, there was a period in my life when the majority of my friends were 2s of Diamonds. As statistically the odds were way beyond this being a coincidence I had to look at what the 2 of Diamonds was telling me. As this card had a Mars influence on me I quickly realized that I admired their drive, courage, and desire for action. This energy was definitely something I desired or wanted to be associated with at that time.

Soon I could no longer think of people I knew without also associating them with their card. I can, for example, no longer think of John Lennon without thinking of him as the King of Clubs and Paul McCartney as the Queen of Clubs. Madonna and Nelson Mandela are both 10 of Clubs, a card usually associated with leaders. Besides famous figures, knowing the cards of those close to you can

help give you greater insight into their talents and foibles. For instance, if your husband is a 4 of Diamonds you must realize that his work is of major importance in his learning or life blueprint, and you may need to respond accordingly.

In my many years of research I have studied thousands of people and their cards, often comparing them with their astrological charts. In some instances this simple card system can give nearly as much information as a basic horoscope reading. Since astrology takes many years of concentrated study, this system is a wonderful way to obtain quick access to information about yourself and others.

As well as the deeper spiritual insight you can gain from studying the cards, they can also prove to be a fun influence in your life. Bob Dylan, an 8 of Clubs who knows the system, used it creatively and wrote a song about the Jack of Hearts. Alternatively, you may start to find playing cards in the street. My writing partner, Saffi, and I found a 2 of Spades in the subway on our way to meet our first publisher. Since the 2 of Spades Card emphasizes working in partnership, this card was most appropriate for both our writing together and the partnership we were just about to form with our publisher. Realizing how appropriate the card's meaning was for us at that moment, we then turned the card over and saw that the back was marked "The Lucky Silver Mine"—a fortuitous sign! Symbols can definitely be fun as well as profound.

Studying dreams shows us that the subconscious and superconscious work with symbols in many different ways. As well as using humor and puns dreams can provide us with premonitions or more serious insights. As you work with the card system you will find the symbolic language of the cards an equally useful tool to access that same deeper knowledge that puts us in touch with our greatest good.

—Geri Sullivan

Although in our world the confused usually lead the misguided, occasionally you can find knowledge that can be both truthful and inspiring such as the Ancient Card System. Akin to the esoteric belief of *as above so below,* this system reveals that *everything counts and is accounted for* in two unique tables called the Early and Spiritual Spreads. The orderly layout in the Spiritual Spread signifies heavenly perfection, while the random setting of the Earthly Spread corresponds to the irregularity of everyday life. During my early years of research into astrology and numerology, I have found the card system invaluable. It offers simple yet defined insight into the destiny, personal life, and relationships of each and every one of us. There are many personal symbols and messages hidden in the cards. By studying the links of different cards within the system, you can also expand and deepen your perceptions of yourself and those who play important roles in your life. In fact, this card system is second to none when it comes to understanding human relationships. Although these are found through the planetary links, there are other important factors to look out for, such as the links of governing and Replacement Cards. On many occasions I have found that strong relationships include more than one link and that relatives fit within the card system in ways similar to a family tree.

—Saffi Crawford, M.A.

Introduction

THIS IS A MODERN interpretation of an ancient system that uses playing cards to represent a synthesis of astrology and numerology in a unique way. The origins of playing cards can be traced back to early times, and some argue even to the lost civilization of Atlantis. As some variation of playing cards can be found all over the world the mystery of their creation and meaning has been investigated over many centuries in order to reveal their hidden knowledge.

Although most people nowadays see playing cards as objects of games or gambling, due to their universal use and timeless symbolism, people can also feel an affinity with them on a subconscious level. In every culture they have crept into the language and have been used as metaphors. People use sayings such as "this person is an Ace," "the whole thing could fall down like a pack of cards," or "he's a Joker." In literature, Lewis Carroll used the Queen of Hearts as a character in *Alice in Wonderland,* while Princess Diana was called the Queen of Hearts by the British press. Even though people regularly try to change the basic designs of the cards or put famous faces on them, the mystical power of the cards and their symbolism ensures that their original depictions retain their longevity and popularity.

Although through the ages mystics kept this remarkable card system alive, its knowledge has been kept secret. The Rosicrucians brought it back to light by publishing a book about it in 1893 called *The Mystic Test Book* by Olney H. Richmond. The mystical order to which he belonged had decided to make known part of the hidden wisdom of the cards to the general public.

This card system was further developed many years ago in two other books called *Sacred Symbols of the Ancients* by Edith Randall and Florence Campbell and *What's Your Card?* by Arne Lein. More recent books by Robert Camp also explore aspects of the system. All these books provide excellent interpretations on how this card system works.

In this extraordinary system each card carries its own special message through the suits, planets, and numbers. Not only can your card reveal your life purpose and unique characteristics, but since the cards are linked, they interact with one another. Knowing a person's card can reveal a great deal about their personality and also provide you with accurate information about the type of relationship you could have. Working with the cards enables you to reach different levels of understanding. The only limitation is how much time you want to put into learning the system.

It has been suggested that the Minor Arcana of the Tarot also derives from this ancient card system. There is evidence from the fifteenth century that the Major and Minor cards were seen as two distinct types of cards that may have been incorporated into one deck at a later date. Unlike Tarot cards, however, where you need to develop your psychic abilities and the cards are laid out at random, this simple card system has a definite structure. Nevertheless, if you are learning the Tarot cards, this system can give you valuable insight and a much greater understanding of the Minor Arcana. The information you can gain from this card system can also enhance your knowledge of astrology and numerology as well as increase your insight into your life lessons and personal relationships. Whether you just want to learn about your card and those of your friends for fun, or want to explore the deeper, more mystical side of the system, you will find it equally intriguing and enjoyable.

HOW TO USE THIS BOOK

- Discover what card you are by looking up your birth date in the table on the following page.
- After finding your card in the Contents section, go directly to Part II of the book (page 39) for a full interpretation of your card.
- Once you familiarize yourself with your card, go to Part I of the book (page 5) to learn not only the system itself but more about your relationships.
- After learning how this card system works, you can use Part III of the book (page 305) to find a card that symbolizes each year of your life, from birthday to birthday.

HOW TO FIND YOUR CARD AT A GLANCE
Birthday Timetable
To find what card you are, go to the birthday timetable below
and look for the card in the box for your birth date.

	Jan	Feb	Mar	Apr	May	Jun	Jul	Aug	Sept	Oct	Nov	Dec
1	K♠	J♠	9♠	7♠	5♠	3♠	A♠	Q♦	10♦	8♦	6♦	4♦
2	Q♠	10♠	8♠	6♠	4♠	2♠	K♦	J♦	9♦	7♦	5♦	3♦
3	J♠	9♠	7♠	5♠	3♠	A♠	Q♦	10♦	8♦	6♦	4♦	2♦
4	10♠	8♠	6♠	4♠	2♠	K♦	J♦	9♦	7♦	5♦	3♦	A♦
5	9♠	7♠	5♠	3♠	A♠	Q♦	10♦	8♦	6♦	4♦	2♦	K♣
6	8♠	6♠	4♠	2♠	K♦	J♦	9♦	7♦	5♦	3♦	A♦	Q♣
7	7♠	5♠	3♠	A♠	Q♦	10♦	8♦	6♦	4♦	2♦	K♣	J♣
8	6♠	4♠	2♠	K♦	J♦	9♦	7♦	5♦	3♦	A♦	Q♣	10♣
9	5♠	3♠	A♠	Q♦	10♦	8♦	6♦	4♦	2♦	K♣	J♣	9♣
10	4♠	2♠	K♦	J♦	9♦	7♦	5♦	3♦	A♦	Q♣	10♣	8♣
11	3♠	A♠	Q♦	10♦	8♦	6♦	4♦	2♦	K♣	J♣	9♣	7♣
12	2♠	K♦	J♦	9♦	7♦	5♦	3♦	A♦	Q♣	10♣	8♣	6♣
13	A♠	Q♦	10♦	8♦	6♦	4♦	2♦	K♣	J♣	9♣	7♣	5♣
14	K♦	J♦	9♦	7♦	5♦	3♦	A♦	Q♣	10♣	8♣	6♣	4♣
15	Q♦	10♦	8♦	6♦	4♦	2♦	K♣	J♣	9♣	7♣	5♣	3♣
16	J♦	9♦	7♦	5♦	3♦	A♦	Q♣	10♣	8♣	6♣	4♣	2♣
17	10♦	8♦	6♦	4♦	2♦	K♣	J♣	9♣	7♣	5♣	3♣	A♣
18	9♦	7♦	5♦	3♦	A♦	Q♣	10♣	8♣	6♣	4♣	2♣	K♥
19	8♦	6♦	4♦	2♦	K♣	J♣	9♣	7♣	5♣	3♣	A♣	Q♥
20	7♦	5♦	3♦	A♦	Q♣	10♣	8♣	6♣	4♣	2♣	K♥	J♥
21	6♦	4♦	2♦	K♣	J♣	9♣	7♣	5♣	3♣	A♣	Q♥	10♥
22	5♦	3♦	A♦	Q♣	10♣	8♣	6♣	4♣	2♣	K♥	J♥	9♥
23	4♦	2♦	K♣	J♣	9♣	7♣	5♣	3♣	A♣	Q♥	10♥	8♥
24	3♦	A♦	Q♣	10♣	8♣	6♣	4♣	2♣	K♥	J♥	9♥	7♥
25	2♦	K♣	J♣	9♣	7♣	5♣	3♣	A♣	Q♥	10♥	8♥	6♥
26	A♦	Q♣	10♣	8♣	6♣	4♣	2♣	K♥	J♥	9♥	7♥	5♥
27	K♣	J♣	9♣	7♣	5♣	3♣	A♣	Q♥	10♥	8♥	6♥	4♥
28	Q♣	10♣	8♣	6♣	4♣	2♣	K♥	J♥	9♥	7♥	5♥	3♥
29	J♣	8♣	7♣	5♣	3♣	A♣	Q♥	10♥	8♥	6♥	4♥	2♥
30	10♣		6♣	4♣	2♣	K♥	J♥	9♥	7♥	5♥	3♥	A♥
31	9♣		5♣		A♣		10♥	8♥		4♥		Joker

To find the interpretation for your card go to Part II,
Descriptions of the Cards, page 41

Part I

The Playing Card System

I

The Playing Card System

THE BEAUTY OF this card system is in its symbolic simplicity. The cycles of thirteen cards and the four suits—Hearts, Clubs, Diamonds, and Spades—that represent the four elements or seasons, fall neatly into the fifty-two weeks of the year in a definite order. The twelve Court Cards—Kings, Queens, Jacks—symbolize the months of the year. The two colors (black and red) represent positive and negative, male and female, and each of the fifty-two playing cards is linked to a particular birthday of the year.

The card system is based on two tables, the Earthly Spread and the Spiritual Spread. It is in the Earthly Spread that our day-to-day existence takes place, and where we can read about most of our personality traits, life challenges, and external happenings. Although this book focuses mainly on the Earthly Spread, where we can find information about our everyday lives, the Spiritual Spread is significant, as it represents the superconscious level. Superconsciousness includes the intuitive or soul level, so in the Spiritual Spread we can find further hidden symbols and karmic links that shed light on a deeper level of understanding. For example, the astrological links to a card in the Spiritual Spread can often point to our life mission.

Each card has its positive and negative attributes, and it is up to the person to live up to the highest potential indicated by their card. A highly successful person can be a "2 card" and an individual can be a nonachiever even though he or she is a King or a Queen. The key question is, what can your card reveal about you? Once you become familiar with your card and its hidden knowledge you will be able to improve your life by utilizing your natural attributes, transforming your weaknesses, and making the most of your potential.

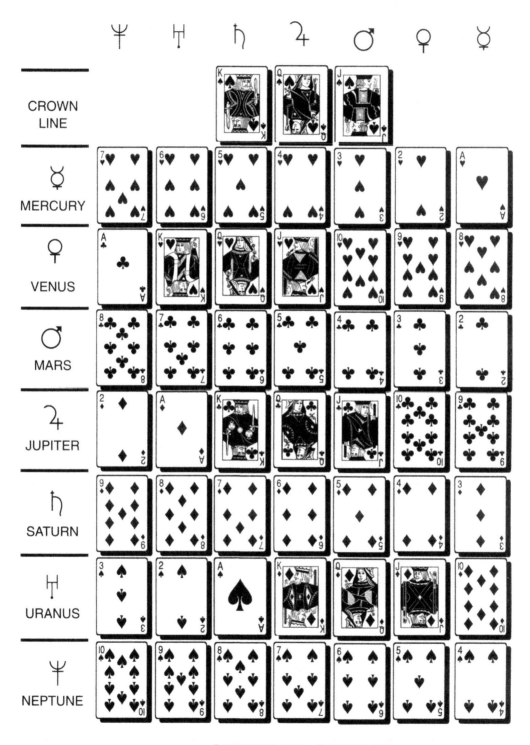

SPIRITUAL SPREAD

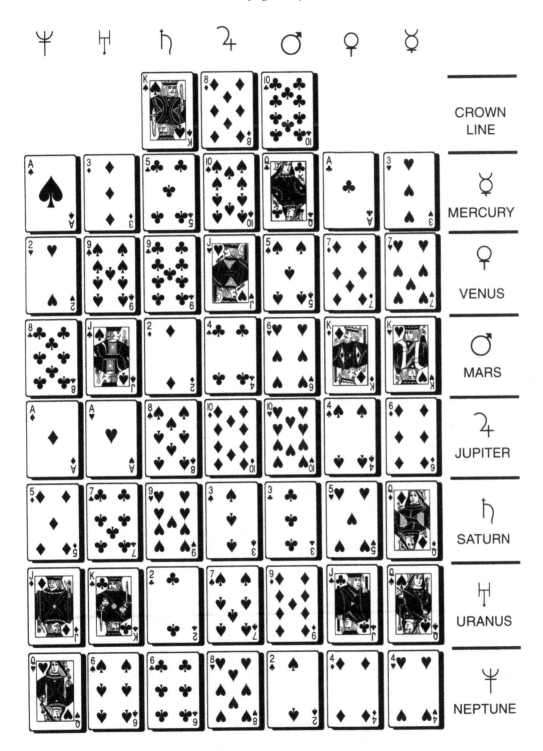

EARTHLY SPREAD

2

The Symbols of the Cards

THE SYMBOLS OF the cards are expressed through the suits, astrological signs, numbers, and planets that are linked to each card.

THE SUITS

♥ The Hearts

Individuals belonging to the Hearts suit usually possess sensitive yet strong emotions. Generally, they enhance life with their ability to give love and support or show affection and compassion. Caring and sensual, they are often loving partners and loyal friends. Their natural charm and excellent people skills signify that they can succeed in careers dealing with the public or working in the community. Alternatively, they can express themselves through their innate talents, creativity, and idealism. Those who belong to the Hearts suit need to learn how to best utilize their emotions and recognize that with the power of love they can achieve great results. The challenge of the Hearts suit is not to succumb to emotional impulsiveness or fears that can evoke negative feelings such as selfishness, hatred, or jealousy. In the Tarot, Hearts are Cups.

♣ The Clubs

Individuals who belong to the Clubs suit are usually rational and intelligent, with an inquiring or curious mind. If they pay attention to their inner voice they can also develop their intuitive abilities and unique gifts. Mentally quick and often enthusiastic about their favorite subjects, they usually succeed when they recognize that their cerebral power is their principal asset. Often freethinking and communicative, these people are keen to acquire knowledge, express their thoughts, or join debates and discussions. A tendency to talk rather than listen may also stimulate their inclination to argue. Nevertheless, astute and well informed, they can benefit greatly from early education or special training. They often choose a profession that requires mental agility, such as commerce, administration, law, or teaching and counseling. Alternatively, a natural gift of the gab may lead them to sales and promotion.

They can also express their mental creativity through writing, problem solving, and designing. In the Tarot, Clubs are Wands.

♦ The Diamonds

Diamonds represent practicality, sensation, money, and the ability to evaluate. In highly developed Diamonds individuals this ability to evaluate goes beyond money, as they can assess personality qualities or spiritual values astutely. In the less developed person, however, a Diamonds card places much more emphasis on materialism. Nevertheless, most Diamonds cards have a shrewd assessment of material opportunities that usually works well for them. It helps them understand how to commercialize their skills and talents or those of others. More importantly, it provides a strong inner system to understand life. Every experience and every piece of new information is evaluated as to whether it is useful. Although at first this evaluation system is used to merely obtain money, property, or material security, eventually a Diamonds' values become clearer as to what produces happiness. Positive Diamonds individuals work on themselves by constantly updating and upgrading their value systems. This leads them to want wealth so they can do good with it and become more generous and philanthropic. In the Tarot, Diamonds are Pentacles.

♠ The Spades

Spades represent the need to work to make theories a reality and thus produce wisdom. A highly developed Spades individual is self-disciplined and industrious, with the ability to sacrifice for the greater good of all. A less developed Spades individual also can work but may be caught in the "rat race" of life, continually repeating their mistakes and never focusing on obtaining wisdom from their experiences. Their attitudes toward work can thus become extra-important to people who are Spades cards. If working on themselves Spades people are willing to discipline themselves for self-improvement. Through their experiences and self-mastery they often become students of highly specialized knowledge or even disciples of Mystery Schools, where they can further develop their sharp insights. They learn to offer their services for humanity and relinquish personal ambition. If operating negatively, however, they may force discipline and their strong will onto others through misuse of personal power. In the Tarot, Spades are Swords.

THE NUMBERS

Each of the cards is affiliated with a number. This number has a symbolic message and is therefore highly significant. For example, if your birthday indicates that you are a 2 card you are more likely to focus on your relationships and gain knowledge and experience from dealing with others. This card number also suggests that your people skills are particularly enhanced. To find out more about the number of your card, look at the list of keywords for all the numbers following.

Key Words for the Numbers

1 (Ace)
POSITIVE: natural leader, ambitious, energetic, motivated, dynamic, creative, progressive, powerful will, optimistic, strong convictions, competitive, independent, strong desires, gregarious
NEGATIVE: demanding, jealous, loner, overbearing, egotistical, too proud, tyrannical,

antagonistic, lacks restraint, selfish, weak, unstable, vacillating, impatient

2

Positive: creates good partnerships, considerate, gentle, tactful, receptive, intuitive, harmonious, agreeable, ambassador of goodwill, objective, sociable, balanced, cooperative, sensitive
Negative: suspicious, lack of confidence, codependent, gets discouraged too easily, subservient, timid, oversensitive, selfish, easily hurt, too subjective, crafty, deceitful

3

Positive: creative, friendly, happy, humorous, productive, artistic, freedom loving, has a gift with words, versatile, charming, sensitive, multitalented, fun loving, expressive
Negative: indecisive, self-doubting, worried, scattered, feels unprepared, exaggerates, jealous, intolerant, boastful, extravagant, self-indulgent, lazy, hypocritical, insecure

4

Positive: practical, honest, determined, hardworking, loyal, self-disciplined, steady, organized, methodical, skilled at crafts, dexterous, patient, orderly, pragmatic, trusting, exact
Negative: stubborn, uncommunicative, rebellious, unstable, destructive, emotionally repressed, rigid, prone to excesses, unfeeling, too frugal, bossy, hides affections, resentful, too strict

5

Positive: strong instincts, freedom loving, daring, adaptable, enterprising, progressive, magnetic, lucky, quick, witty, curious, mystical, versatile, enthusiastic, fond of travel, sociable
Negative: unreliable, impatient, changeable, inconsistent, drifting, irresponsible, lustful,

easily bored, too outspoken, overconfident, restless, impulsive, headstrong

6

Positive: worldly, responsible, friendly, home loving, caring, compassionate, dependable, sympathetic, idealistic, creative, universal, comfort loving, humanitarian, artistic, balanced, harmonious
Negative: discontented, overcritical, anxious, unreasonable, stubborn, outspoken, domineering, irresponsible, inert, selfish, suspicious, snobbish, self-centered

7

Positive: thoughtful, analytical, fine mind, very sensitive, has much faith, perfectionist, original, strong intuition, spontaneous, meticulous, spiritual, idealistic, trusting, technical, rational, sense of melody, reflective
Negative: cold, skeptical, overcritical, gets lost in detail, overrationalizes, overly sensitive, withdraws, uncommunicative, cynical, suspicious, confused, feels misunderstood, self-absorbed

8

Positive: determined, practical, natural leader, thorough, hardworking, authoritative, protective, powerful, good with money, has executive or organizational abilities, ambitious, dependable, capable, is good judge of values, goal-oriented, self-confident, realistic
Negative: impatient, intolerant, materialistic, domineering, miserly, workaholic, bullying, plays power games, controlling, stubborn

9

Positive: generous, compassionate, idealistic, objective, kind, intuitive, sentimental, spiritual, tolerant, intelligent, romantic, philanthropic, helpful, good with people, creative, sympathetic, selfless, humanitarian, broad-minded

NEGATIVE: frustrated, selfish, too detached, disappointed, miserly, inferiority complex, overly sentimental, nervous, escapist

10

POSITIVE: self-confident, strong willpower, ambitious, progressive, success-oriented, natural leader, creative, has executive skills, forceful, excellent mind, original, practical, strong convictions, energetic, competitive, strong, gregarious, independent

NEGATIVE: demanding, arrogant, dominating, egotistical, doesn't use opportunities, dictatorial streak, too proud, selfish, unstable, impatient

COURT CARDS

Keywords for the Court Cards

Jacks

POSITIVE: clever, sociable, creative, dramatic, natural leader, inspirational, has good people skills, enthusiastic, strong willpower, noble, playful, responsible, talented, intuitive, humanitarian, confident, inventive, charismatic, entertaining

NEGATIVE: too proud, immature, overly emotional, has superiority complex, high strung, irresponsible, selfish, superficial, aimless, stubborn, frivolous, easily hurt

Queens

POSITIVE: natural leader, receptive, intelligent, confident, intuitive, has good people skills, strong willpower, ambitious, independent, creative, teacher, dramatic, inspired, progressive, has executive or organizational skills, intuitive, original

NEGATIVE: selfish, drama queen, uncooperative, too passive, doesn't use opportunities for service, overly sensitive, stubborn

Kings

POSITIVE: has strong will, freedom loving, shows initiative, natural leader, clever, has organizational or executive abilities, creative, confident, ambitious, dramatic, original, independent

NEGATIVE: bossy, stubborn, doesn't use opportunities for service, arrogant, too proud, impatient, impulsive, indecisive, unemotional, rebellious

THE TWELVE ASTROLOGICAL SUN SIGNS & THEIR ARCHETYPES

Each zodiac Sun sign has a particular role that enables it to manifest its power in the act of creation. We can also associate a number of archetypes with each of the Sun signs.

ARIES

March 21–April 20

Ruling Planet: Mars ♂

Keywords: energy, activity, leadership

Aries is governed by the element of fire and is the first sign of the zodiac. Ruled by Mars, Aries individuals are often action-oriented and full of vitality. Daring and assertive, they rarely sit around or wait for others. Since they are keen to take the initiative they prefer leadership positions and are often pioneers. Not known for their patience, Arians are often direct and bold. Arians may, however, sometimes need to resist being self-centered or bullying. Nevertheless, ardent and passionate, their energy and enthusiasm can motivate or inspire others, particularly to take action or be more adventurous.

ARCHETYPES FOR ARIES

the Chivalrous Hero

the Warrior

the Daredevil

the Boss

TAURUS
April 21–May 21
Ruling Planet: Venus ♀
Keywords: endurance, persistence, sensuality

Taurus is governed by the element of earth; therefore, Taureans are often practical, steady, and security conscious. Being sensible and quietly determined, once they decide to do something they can be enduring and resolute. At times, however, this can cause them to be very stubborn or fixed. Venus, their ruling planet, usually gives them a pleasant appearance and a calm demeanor, which makes them magnetic and attractive. Their sensual or highly refined senses indicate that they usually appreciate beauty and the luxuries that life can offer. Taureans are not only concerned with their possessions but are keen to get good value for their money. If they are not careful, however, they can become materialistic or self-indulgent. Nevertheless, they are usually highly productive and have artistic or creative talents.

ARCHETYPES FOR TAURUS
>   the Banker
>   the Sensualist
>   the Nature Lover
>   the Steady One
>   the Musician or Singer

GEMINI
May 22–June 21
Ruling Planet: Mercury ☿
Keywords: versatility, ingenuity, talkative

A thirst for knowledge and natural curiosity suggest that Gemini individuals are usually well informed or keep themselves busy learning new things. Although Geminis can be bright, multitalented, and versatile, if they are not careful they can scatter their energies in too many directions. Nevertheless, through mental discipline and education, Geminis can develop a greater depth of thought. Linked to Mercury, people of this sign often can have an androgynous quality and a slim and youthful body. Geminis are also expressive with their hands when conveying their ideas, and with their need to communicate Geminis often can talk for hours. Like their symbol the twins, they are renowned for being able to do at least two things at once, as well as for being flexible and adaptable.

ARCHETYPES FOR GEMINI
>   the Messenger
>   the Salesperson
>   the Communicator
>   the Interpreter
>   the Journalist/Writer
>   the Speaker
>   the Storyteller/Yarn Spinner

CANCER
June 22–July 22
Ruling Planet: Moon ☽
Keywords: sensitive, sympathetic, affectionate

Cancer is governed by the element of water; therefore, Cancerians are ruled by their feelings and are often sensitive. Although their ruler, the Moon, can make them emotionally receptive and intuitive, like the changing tides Cancerians are prone to alternating moods. In order to protect themselves Cancerians can appear shy or reserved, yet this should not be interpreted as a weakness. Masters in the art of passive resistance, they often withdraw to gather strength. Generally domesticated, Cancerians have a strong link to home and family. With their need to nurture, they often take on the role of mother, caregiver, or counselor. Sympathetic and kind, despite their changing moods these individuals are naturally affectionate. They may need, however, to avoid smothering others with their protective love and devotion.

ARCHETYPES FOR CANCER
> the Mother
> the Caregiver
> the Psychic
> the Counselor

LEO
July 23–August 22
Ruling Planet: Sun ☉
Keywords: vitality, confidence, self-expression
Leos want to express themselves and shine just like their ruling star, the Sun. Although they possess a playful side they usually are assertive and see themselves in leading roles rather than in supporting positions. Belonging to a fixed fire sign, Leos can be lively and enthusiastic yet somewhat stubborn. Finding it hard to admit their mistakes, the downside of Leos' strong egos is their tendency to be arrogant or vain. Nevertheless, Leos have big hearts, sunny personalities, and a sense of fun. Generous and friendly, they can be very sociable. Although Leos' regal or commanding manner makes them ideal for leadership, if they take command without being asked they can appear bossy. Leos who do not fulfill their natural potentials may just seek fun and pleasure or fall into idleness. Being image conscious, however, their pride usually will make them work extremely hard and be responsible. Their strength, courage, and integrity can inspire others, and with their sense of drama they often leave a lasting impression.

ARCHETYPES FOR LEO
> the Performer/Player
> the King or Queen
> the Child
> the Lover
> the Actor

VIRGO
August 23–September 22
Ruling Planet: Mercury ☿
Keywords: discriminating, efficient, service
Virgos are governed by the earth element and Mercury is their ruling planet. Generally practical and down-to-earth, Virgos usually love order and pay attention to finer points in order to be more efficient. Articulate and discriminating, Virgos are often excellent organizers. Although they may be economical and prudent with money, Virgos are usually generous with their time and advice should anybody need assistance. Being practical, however, they also expect others to make an effort to help themselves. With their strong work ethic, they constantly are examining and refining everything in order to improve their lives. Unfortunately, this perfectionism may cause them to overanalyze and get lost in small details or be too critical and fault finding. Modest and unassuming, however, Virgos habitually reevaluate their actions and are well aware of their own faults. Virgos can be meticulous and refined, as they usually adopt very high standards.

ARCHETYPES FOR VIRGO
> the Analyst/Researcher
> the Perfectionist
> the Servant
> the Organizer
> the Critic

LIBRA
September 23–October 22
Ruling Planet: Venus ♀
Keywords: balance, diplomacy, relationship
Ruled by Venus, Librans are charming and courteous and have style. Their love of harmony indicates that they usually prefer to keep the peace and use diplomatic means rather

than be confrontational. Although it can be good to be able to compromise, they should, however, avoid sitting on the fence or being indecisive rather than facing issues head-on. Librans' love of beauty usually is reflected in their clothes, homes, and desires for luxury. They also can be artistic or creative, and value their relationships highly. Librans need to be liked and so they are friendly, affectionate, and sociable. Intelligent and usually able to see things from another person's point of view, Librans have a strong sense of justice and fair play.

ARCHETYPES FOR LIBRA
  the Lover
  the Diplomat
  the Partner
  the Socializer
  the Good Host

SCORPIO
October 23–November 21
Ruling Planet: Mars ♂
Keywords: regeneration, secrecy, power

Deeply emotional, people born under the sign of Scorpio can be passionate and strong-willed with a strong sex drive. Tending to have an "all or nothing" attitude, they can be powerful and intense. The extremes of their natures suggest that at times there is a danger of obsessiveness or vengefulness. When positive, however, Scorpios can be extremely focused, strong, and dynamic, with an ability to take on a challenge and totally transform difficult situations. Magnetic but sensitive, they prefer to be in control so they can avoid getting hurt emotionally. Scorpios do not like to show signs of weakness; in fact, they often keep secrets so people do not have an advantage over them. When on your side they can be loyal, loving, and totally supportive. Natural detectives, Scorpios probe for the hidden truth, so they can also be good psychologists.

ARCHETYPES FOR SCORPIO
  the Controller
  the Hypnotist
  the Magician
  the Detective

SAGITTARIUS
November 22–December 21
Ruling Planet: Jupiter ♃
Keywords: honesty, exploration, idealism

Enthusiastic, warm, and generous, Sagittarians are honest individuals with a direct approach. Friendly and optimistic, they look to the future for opportunities to expand and improve their lives. Although they are free spirits with independent styles, their tendency to be outspoken and frank can sometimes make them tactless. Usually, however, their open and idealistic natures or philosophical approach to life saves them from difficulties. As they often love to explore, they value their freedom and dislike being tied down. Travel, sports, higher learning, or just having big plans can be some of the areas that particularly inspire Sagittarians.

ARCHETYPES FOR SAGITTARIUS
  the Traveler
  the Philosopher
  the Optimist
  the Seeker of Truth
  the Foreigner
  the Game Player

CAPRICORN
December 22–January 20
Ruling Planet: Saturn ♄
Keywords: ambitious, conscientious, diligent

Practical, dutiful, and determined, Capricorns are the ultimate realists. As security is important to them, they often take cautious or conservative approaches to life and have slightly reserved personalities. Usually hardworking, Capricorns like precise goals so they can know exactly where they are going—and when.

With a strong awareness of their responsibilities, they can be reliable and solid, executing their work conscientiously. Although usually self-disciplined, Capricorns can also be pessimistic if they doubt themselves, or calculating if they become too selfish. Fortunately, on the other side, they can also have a wonderful dry sense of humor and a tenacity that comes from perseverance and patient resolve.

ARCHETYPES FOR CAPRICORN

    the Father
    the Authority Figure
    the Worker
    the Disciplinarian
    the Traditionalist

AQUARIUS

January 21–February 19
Ruling Planet: Uranus ♅
Keywords: detached, humanitarian,
    independent

Friendly and independent, Aquarians are intelligent individuals with an inventive approach to life. Being interested in people makes them natural psychologists or gives them strong humanitarian streaks. A rebel quality, however, can also cause them to be stubborn or contrary. Aquarians do not usually like to take orders, needing the freedom to think for themselves and do things in their unique ways. With an impersonal approach to life, they often can take a truly objective viewpoint, but they must also be careful not to become too detached or unemotional. Original and unconventional, Aquarians can often be ahead of their time and have strong mental intuition.

ARCHETYPES FOR AQUARIUS

    the Humanitarian
    the Detached Observer
    the Scientist
    the Friend
    the Eccentric
    the Revolutionary

PISCES

February 20–March 20
Ruling Planet: Neptune ♆
Keywords: receptive, visionary, idealistic,
    intuitive

Imaginative and impressionable, Pisceans have wide emotional ranges. The symbol for Pisces is two fish swimming in opposite directions, indicating a dual personality of extremes. They can be sensitive, caring, and hardworking, with an ability to devote themselves to others or a good cause. Alternatively, they can be irritable or moody, stubbornly refusing to listen to anyone. Nevertheless, psychically open to all the more subtle emotions, Pisceans can be very generous and compassionate toward others. If they dissolve themselves in other people's needs, however, there is a danger they may lose their sense of self-worth. It is important that Pisceans continually build up their own confidence. Highly imaginative and acutely aware of their inner feelings, Pisceans have fertile secret dream worlds and strong intuitions.

ARCHETYPES FOR PISCES

    the Visionary
    the Romantic
    the Savior
    the Mystic or Psychic
    the Healer
    the Dreamer

THE SEVEN PLANETS

Mercury ☿

Mercury represents mental ability, the desire to understand, and the need to communicate. Being clever with fast responses, Mercury quickly can get a good grasp of a subject or logically solve problems. Besides being inquisitive and eager to learn, Mercury is articulate and skilled in the expression of ideas, whether through talking or writing. With critical abilities as well as mental agility, this planet can signify discriminative powers and a capacity for being adaptable and versatile. Although there can be a tendency to be nervous or diffused, Mercury is a master of communication. Through this sharing of information, Mercury also is connected to teaching or business and trading. Mercury governs the astrological signs of both Gemini and Virgo.

Venus ♀

Venus relates to values of love and pleasure and therefore harmonizes, bringing warmth, sociability, and a cooperative attitude. Venus would prefer to be easygoing and keep the peace rather than face confrontation and a discordant environment. Venus's function is to bring union, and is therefore connected to intimacy. Being a magnetic planet that draws from the feminine, Venus governs the ability to attract others. Since this attraction can extend to needed resources, Venus can also therefore govern money and possessions. This planet delights in the senses and has a fine appreciation for beauty and sensual indulgence. It is therefore connected to artistic, musical, and creative gifts as well as to sexuality. Bringing good taste, grace, and natural refinement, Venus dislikes coarseness but may be prone to vanity and indolence. In men, Venus represents their feminine side and all the values associated with this, especially relationships, cooperation, and enjoyment in life. Venus governs the astrological signs of Taurus and Libra.

Mars ♂

Action-oriented, Mars is a planet that represents vitality, drive, and motivation. Coura-geous and direct, Mars represents the Warrior archetype. In the male/female polarity Mars governs male energy and sexuality. For a woman, Mars depicts the drive behind her personality and her assertive side. Mars can also represent the type of man she naturally attracts to act out her own male energy. For a man, Mars represents his physical drive and sensuality. Passionate and immediate, Mars stimulates the need to directly gratify desires or use strength and force to defend and protect. Quickly combative or confrontational, Mars can represent anger. If uncontrolled this energy can bring impatience, aggression and destruction. If controlled it can be used constructively to get much accomplished. It also exemplifies the sense of personal power that comes from inner strength and standing up for your needs. Mars governs the astrological signs of Aries and Scorpio.

Jupiter ♃

Jupiter, the largest planet in our solar system, encourages growth and expansion. The spiritual message of Jupiter is to seek development through higher wisdom, philosophy, and truth. The positive aspect of this enlargement is the ability to reach beyond existing limitations and experience the optimism and confidence that come from visualizing something better or greater. Jupiter also enables us to think comprehensively and see the bigger picture. This aptitude can help us perceive large concepts, philosophical ideas, or spiritual and religious values. Although Jupiter usually represents good fortune, some of this planet's less attractive qualities are excess, false optimism, exaggeration, and overexuberance. By nature Jupiter is generous, benevolent, and full of good intentions. On occasions, however, it can inflate the ego, causing individuals to appear opinionated, arrogant, or condescending. Traveling to distant places fits particularly well with Jupiter's desire to expand and gather wisdom through new experiences. The quest for a higher truth suggested by this planet can inspire a pursuit for knowledge, higher learning, and spirituality. Jupiter as the mythological god Zeus is also associated with judgment; therefore, Jupiter represents the judicial system or law and order. Jupiter governs the astrological sign of Sagittarius.

Saturn ♄

Saturn, ruler of the Sun sign Capricorn, is often known as Old Father Time and the taskmaster. Symbolic of "that which we sow we shall also reap," Saturn represents the law of restriction or even of learning through suffering. Saturn relates to discipline, organization, and responsibility. Saturn, being older and wiser, advises that everything can work if we apply methodology to our efforts. It also suggests that the knowledge gained from the restrictive influences associated with obstacles is ultimately worthwhile. In order to balance the expansiveness of Jupiter we have the curtailing influence of Saturn, which can positively restrain overinflation and maintain balance.

The positive qualities of Saturn enable us to create order or work within space and form. It defines boundaries, producing rules and regulations for working systems. This planet requires us to face up to our obligation and duties. Saturn accounts for everything, for the work that has been put in, and for what was not accomplished; everything is repaid exactly. Nevertheless, Saturn's lessons are often uncomfortable, as they can point to what is wrong or missing in our lives. The negative qualities of Saturn can cause pessimism, fear, denial, and even depression. Saturn also repre-

sents anything "hard," such as bones and teeth or when we need to be "hard" on ourselves. The attractive attributes of Saturn are the ability to concentrate and to demonstrate our willpower and self-reliance. This planet will reward individuals for their dedication if they work on their determination and perseverance. With the assistance of Saturn we develop patience, order and authority. Saturn can force us to be realistic and efficient.

Uranus ♅

Uranus rules the sign of Aquarius. This planet governs all types of electric energy: television and radio waves, magnetic fields, lasers, computers, and new technology. Uranus enables us to develop our intuitive skills and ingenuity by being able to think in an objective or abstract way. Uranus brings enlightenment and freedom of spirit by breaking away from old habits or the restrictions of Saturn. This kind of freedom also involves leaving a space for the unexpected. These qualities can encourage individualistic expression and love of independence. Despite the pressures of conformity, Uranus dares us to express our own views or unique style. Uranus's unpredictable element is also associated with sudden happenings, erratic behavior, or eccentricity.

Although Uranus highlights liberty, humanitarian ideology, and a free society, this planet's influence can produce social rebelliousness, anarchy, and revolution. At an individual level it can lead to defiance or obstinate behavior, just for the sake of being different. Nevertheless, Uranus encourages an open-minded attitude and acceptance of new ideas, change, and the latest inventions. Uranus also can widen our points of view to universal concepts such as humanity as a family of brothers and sisters.

Neptune ♆

Neptune governs the sign of Pisces, and as lord of the sea is perceived as enigmatic and mysterious. Unlike Saturn, Neptune knows of no boundaries and can merge with everything. Although this ability to blend can signify integration and unity, it can also slowly and subtly dissolve what we consider permanent or solid, diluting matter and creating ambiguity and confusion. Neptune's influence is more evident on the subconscious level, in dreams, spiritual visions, or supernatural experiences, but some aspects or areas of our lives are not as clear-cut as others due to Neptune's effects. Nevertheless, Neptune can transcend limitations by refining and purifying old or outdated perceptions. The positive qualities of Neptune can lift the spirit with inspiration and let the imagination envisage what is possible. Neptune also can break down the boundaries created by the ego. Since Neptune's receptivity can help us identify with the suffering of others, it can inspire compassion, generosity, and sympathy. Neptune's ambiguity, however, can also mislead and make us gullible. This planet's extreme sensitivity to everything can increase intuition and produce spiritual experiences or metaphysical phenomena. The unattractive qualities of Neptune suggest escapism, deception, or drug and alcohol abuse. Nevertheless, the ability to "lose oneself" in inspired creative endeavors, such as art, music, or drama, indicates that working positively with Neptune's influence can help us to aspire and to dream.

Please note that although like traditional astrology or vedic astrology this system does not intentionally recognize the planet Pluto, the Challenge Card in this system works exactly like Pluto. This influence is intense and can bring out the best or worst of a person or situation, challenging them to transform.

3

Your Personal Card Sequence in the Earthly and Spiritual Spreads

IN ORDER TO understand your card you need to look at the layout of the two Spreads, the Earthly and the Spiritual (Chapter 1, page 000). You will notice that there are planetary lines running horizontally and vertically across the card layout. For example, the 8 of Clubs is positioned horizontally along the Mars line and vertically in the Neptune line. These two planets, Mars and Neptune, play a vital role in influencing the 8 of Clubs's destiny.

YOUR CARD SEQUENCE IN THE EARTHLY SPREAD

In the Earthly Spread you find what influences your daily life. By looking at your own unique pattern of cards you can discover a great deal about your personality traits, talents, and potential as well as your challenges. Each Birth Card has a special seven-card sequence. This sequence is read horizontally from right to left, always starting with the planet Mercury, followed by Venus, then by Mars, Jupiter, Saturn, Uranus, and Neptune. When you get to the end of a row simply move to the row below.

(See diagrams on pages 22–23.) You can find an interpretation of what your individual card sequence means in the pages written about your personal Birth Card (Part II, Description of the Cards).

YOUR CARD SEQUENCE IN THE SPIRITUAL SPREAD

The Spiritual Spread represents life in its ideal state of perfection, or the divine plan, and is therefore orderly and sequential. The first thing you will notice when you look at the Spiritual Spread is that your Personal Card is not in the same position as in the Earthly Spread. (The only exceptions to this are with three cards—the 8 of Clubs, Jack of Hearts, and the King of Spades—where their positions are fixed; see the Fixed and Semi-fixed Cards section following). Due to the change of position you gain another set of planetary influences, which reveal your true hidden inner talents and potential. For example, in the Spiritual Spread the Jack of Diamonds is Venus in the Uranus line. These two plan-

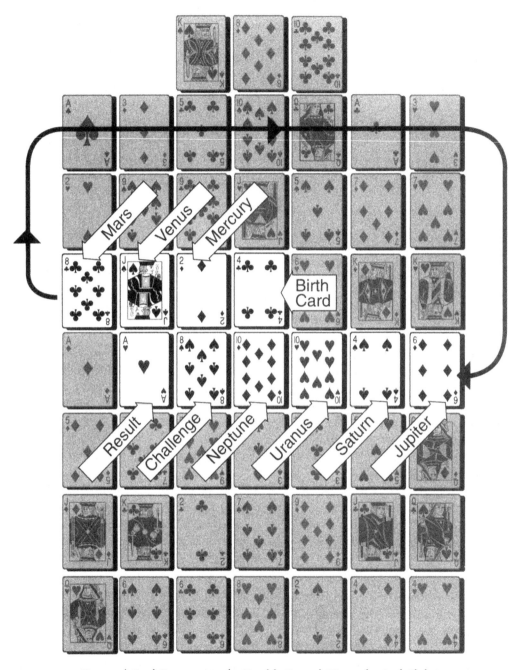

Personal Card Sequence in the Earthly Spread (Example: 4 of Clubs)

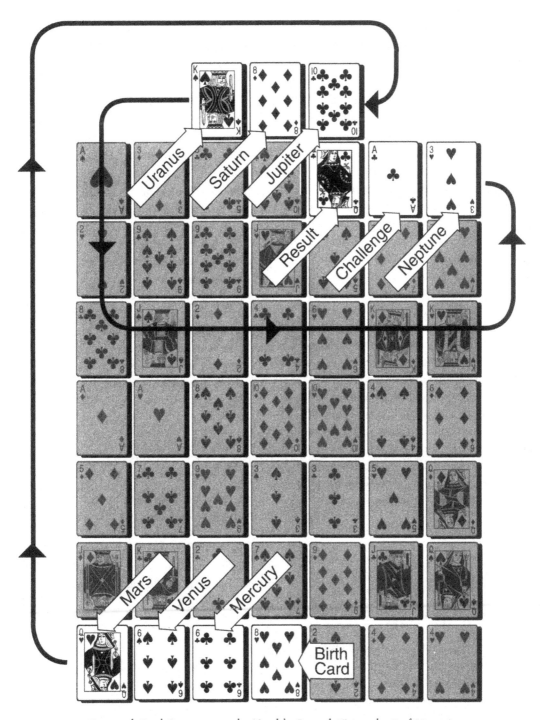

Personal Card Sequence in the Earthly Spread (Example: 8 of Hearts)

ets, Venus and Uranus, become extra important, especially in working with your life purpose.

REPLACEMENT CARDS

To understand the different aspects of your nature, this card system usually incorporates another two cards to represent facets of your personality. The two cards are positioned in the same place as your Birth Card in the Earthly and Spiritual spreads. For example, using the Ace of Hearts, if you look in the two spreads you see that the 3 of Hearts in the Earthly Spread replaces the Ace of Hearts in the Spiritual Spread. In addition, the Ace of Hearts in the Earthly Spread has replaced the Ace of Diamonds in the Spiritual Spread. By examining these other two cards you can reveal your hidden characteristics. Replacement Cards also have a strong influence on your life, on the way you act, and on the people you are attracted to. You can find an interpretation of how your Replacement Cards affect you in the main text for your Personal Card.

Although on the whole these Replacement Cards apply to most cards, exceptions to the rule can be found in the cards mentioned following.

FIXED AND SEMI-FIXED CARDS

Unlike most of the cards, there are seven exceptional cards that are called "fixed" or "semi-fixed" cards. The fixed cards are the 8 of Clubs, the Jack of Hearts, and the King of Spades. These three fixed cards are Master cards. The 8 of Clubs represents mastery through power of the mind; the Jack of Hearts represents mastery through the power of love; and the King of Spades represents mastery through wisdom

or self-mastery. These three fixed cards have the same positions in both spreads.

The semi-fixed cards are the Ace of Clubs and the 2 of Hearts, the 7 of Diamonds and the 9 of Hearts. These two pairs of cards are linked only to each other and reverse positions.

THE JOKER

The Joker represents one exceptional day in the year, December 31. Unlike all the other cards, the Joker does not have planetary influences, a number, a suit, or a seven-card sequence. If you are born on December 31 you have special qualities. You are one of the royal cards and belong to the crown line. You are usually a law unto yourself or gifted with unique talents. One of them is the ability to adapt to any card that you want to in the system. Nevertheless, you may find that either the King of Spades sequence or the Ace of Hearts sequence suit you the best.

THE PLANETS IN YOUR PERSONAL CARD SEQUENCE

Once you have identified your card using the chart on page 3 and read its interpretation in Part II, you can further study the planets in your Personal Card Sequence to obtain more information as to how the seven planets involved can further influence you through different cards.

Mercury

This card represents your thinking habits as well as your childhood years. It describes how you can best express yourself or what you spend much of your time thinking about. Alternatively, this card depicts your intellectual challenges and how well you respond to them.

If, for example, your Mercury Card is the 3 of Diamonds you are likely to be an astute and inventive thinker who can utilize your mental ingenuity and creativity in problem solving. The Diamonds suit emphasizes choices you make about values, work, and finance. Your challenges may be how to overcome indecisiveness and worry about money. If your Mercury Card is the 2 of Hearts, you are mentally receptive and usually keen to collaborate with others. Being concerned with relationships, in your youth you may have developed special bonds or friendships with others or even met your sweetheart. A Hearts Card here suggests your thoughts are usually influenced by the way you feel.

As you see from these two brief examples, we do not all think alike and our views reflect our different aptitudes and needs. If your Mercury Card happens to be a royal card, besides looking at the quality of the card, you can also look out for a person in your youth who could have played a more important role in your early development. A King often represents a strong male figure, while a Queen represents a strong woman. In the case of a Jack it can be either a man or a woman or, say, a brother or sister.

Venus

Your Venus Card can help you discover how you express your feelings and emotional needs. You also can learn your attractive qualities as well as what you most love and desire. Although this card applies to your entire life, it emphasizes especially your early adulthood, when you are freer to follow your aspirations and express your feelings. If, for example, your Venus Card is the 5 of Hearts it often reflects your desire for different emotional experiences or a love of travel. You are likely to make several changes in life or fall in love more than

once. Due to the uncertainty element linked to the number 5 you may need to watch out that your feeling of dissatisfaction does not cause anxiety in your emotional life. If your Venus Card is the 2 of Clubs communicating and sharing your thoughts with others can be what you desire most. This card indicates that you enjoy playing with words, and being witty is one of your innate talents.

As you see from these examples, we all have different desires and emotional needs. Through the symbols of your Venus Card you also can know where your creative talents lie. You can find out whether you are expressing your emotions positively or negatively. If your Venus Card is one of the royal cards, also look out for special talents, especially those developed due to the influence or encouragement of another individual. Kings are usually linked to a strong man, Queens to a strong woman, and Jacks can represent both genders.

Mars

Your Mars Card can help you discover where your strength lies and what motivates your personality. Your Mars Card usually reflects your actions, concentrated effort, and ambition. This card reveals in which area your energies are most assertive. It also represents your aggressive side and where you feel most comfortable competing. For example, if your Mars Card is the 5 of Clubs, you are usually an astute and mentally quick individual with an ability to respond instinctively to situations. Your mental restlessness, however, can also make you impatient or uncertain. Your changing perspectives suggest that you not only want freedom of action but that travel may feature strongly in your life or career. If your Mars Card is the 9 of Hearts you usually project your vitality through your emotions. Your creative urges, idealism, and powerful feelings are the motivating stimulus behind your actions. If you are aware of the power of love, you can be a force for good and bring much joy to others. If you are not in control of these powerful emotions, you can also experience negative feelings such as emotional frustration. If your Mars Card is one of the royal cards, also look out for special talents that you developed due to the encouragement or influence of another individual. Kings are usually linked to a strong man, Queens to a strong woman, and Jacks can represent both genders.

Saturn

Your Saturn Card shows how you deal with discipline, structure, and responsibility. If you avoid opportunities for growth that seem too hard Saturn brings limitations or obstacles until you finally turn around and face your challenges. Sometimes these restrictions can mean illnesses or burdens, but ultimately, if you deal with this planet well you will be more than rewarded. Saturn governs wisdom as well as karma. Eventually, you learn to handle power well by disciplining yourself rather than people or situations doing it for you. The card you have here can give you a clue as to what tests you may have to face and work with. For example, a 2 of Hearts Card suggests your major challenges would be mostly emotional and around the area of relationships. An 8 of Diamonds as your Saturn Card indicates that issues of power, money, and values are associated with responsibility and discipline for you. As Saturn can also govern our careers an 8 card here suggests determination and ambition in achieving success.

Saturn's potential for self-mastery is also important in overcoming self-doubt or building self-esteem. By working with your Saturn Card you can not only empower yourself but develop deep insight in an area that even could

have been problematic for you in the past. Life gets better once you realize that your challenges are your best experiences for gaining wisdom and inner strength if you are willing to work at learning from them. If your Saturn Card is one of the royal cards, not only do you have a special gift in this area, but when it comes to issues of responsibility you may be tested or experience strong influences from outside individuals. This can be a strong woman in the case of a Queen or a powerful man in the case of a King.

Uranus

Your Uranus Card signifies areas where you can expand your life through friendships, working with groups, or progressive ideas. This planet emphasizes the new and different, and is always future-oriented. It shows ways you can expand your life by experimenting and attempting to show your individuality. As it has a group emphasis, it can govern teamwork or humanitarian concerns. If you are acting negatively the more radical innovations of this planet for good can turn and make you rebellious or behave erratically. This is a high-frequency planet on the mental level, so if you have a strong card here it can bestow powerful intuitive insights or an interest in symbolism or metaphysical subjects. It can also indicate that you are ahead of your time. For example, if you have a King of Clubs Card in this position it would show that you could bring excellent mental capabilities to the area of working with progressive and inventive ideas. With a King Card here, you would also display good leadership abilities when dealing with group situations or you could have strong humanitarian influences. It could also show the outside influence of a clever man who at some stage in your life could particularly help you become more objective or stimulate your individuality. Uranian influences can often bring you sudden and unexpected experiences.

Neptune

Your Neptune Card represents an area of your life where you are able to leave behind your usual ego patterning and blend with larger universal forces. This can be in a positive way, such as if you "lose yourself" in creative, artistic, or spiritual experiences or when you experience compassion for others. This card particularly governs healing, dream work, and high-level emotional inspiration. The subtle sensitivity associated with this planet can also work against you, however, if you "lose yourself" in glamour, self-deception, and illusion. False expectations here can bring you disappointment or a tendency for escapism. For example, if you have a 2 of Hearts here, this suggests that you can be sensitive to others and very loving. To avoid deceiving yourself in the area of personal relationships, however, you would have to be extra careful to be objective in this area.

Neptune also represents the ocean, and on a practical level this card can symbolize long journeys over water. This Neptune placement also indicates what type of energy is happening for you at the end of your life. For example, with a 5 Card here, signifying movement and change, you may find yourself doing much traveling in your later years, especially long journeys overseas.

Challenge Card

Although this card system uses only seven planets in your Personal Cards Sequence we have added the interpretation of two further cards, called your "Challenge Card" and "Result of Your Challenge Card." The Challenge Card ties in perfectly with the planet Pluto, as

it denotes the key to your transformation. Pluto is a higher octave of Mars and represents energy that is intense and extreme. If you use this intensity for good then you can really focus on a goal with complete determination and achieve it. You could, for example, turn a barren wasteland into a beautiful garden by the resolute purpose of your intent. This all-or-nothing type of energy does not allow obstacles or defeats to prevent you from achieving your aims. If you are using the negative side of this card, however, it can bring out your worst or destructive qualities. You may become obsessive, try to control others, or want to get even. For example, if you have a 10 of Diamonds Card here, one of your challenges is to be materially successful. If you became too extreme or obsessive you could get too caught up in making money or avoid it altogether, choosing to be really poor. You would have to realize that material achievement is more than just money. Being financially successful needs to be balanced with strong values and a good quality of life. If you respond positively to your Challenge Card you can understand life at a deeper level and act courageously and powerfully. This card can give you a clue as to how you can transform yourself positively.

Result of Your Challenge Card

Through this card you are able to see how well you are responding to your challenges. If you are acting out the negative sides of this card you may well need to review your behavior. Alternatively, if you are responding well to your challenges you should see positive results, especially in the areas represented by this card. For example, if the Result of Your Challenge Card is the 8 of Clubs and you are constantly getting involved in mental power games with others, then you know that this card is reflecting something wrong in your attitude. If, alternatively, you are using the mental power shown by this card to overcome obstacles and achieve success through your knowledge and insight, then this card is working positively.

SUN SIGN RULING CARD

Your Sun sign ruling card provides further information about you and adds to your knowledge of your Personal Card. Since most cards appear a number of times throughout the year, you can differentiate between them by looking at the ruling planet of your Sun sign. You can discover your ruling planet by looking in the table below.

You can then find your ruling planet/ruling card in the text for your Birth Card (Part II). For instance, an Aries 2 of Diamonds shares the same major qualities as a Virgo 2 of Diamonds, but the ruling planet for the Aries would be Mars and the ruling planet for the Virgo would be Mercury. When both these 2s of Diamonds look up their Personal Card Sequence in the text for their Birth Card, the Aries's Mars Card (6 of Diamonds) will be of extra importance and the Virgo's Mercury Card (Jack of Spades) will have the strongest influence. This gives a different and further emphasis as to how they may both express the energy of their cards.

This is relevant to all signs except Leo and Cancer. For Leos, the personal Birth Card and the planetary ruling card are one and the same. For Cancerians there are two options. Some people use the 10 of Clubs for all Cancerians', while others use the first card to the right of your card in the Earthly Spread, taking it as the unconscious.

PERSONALITY CARDS

On the Earthly Plane only, you can also work under your Personality Card, although this card will never be as strong as your Birth Card. We take on Personality Cards when we want to role-play.

A Jack Card usually represents a young person of a particular suit. Often they can represent a person who is playful or immature. High-spirited, creative, and idealistic, musicians and artists, for example, frequently take on the role of a Jack. Kings, on the other hand, usually represent older people of their suit. Alternatively, a person may play a King when they want to represent themselves as a person of authority who is responsible and mature.

Sun Sign	Ruling Planet	Sun Sign	Ruling Planet
Aries	Mars ♂	Libra	Venus ♀
Taurus	Venus ♀	Scorpio	Mars ♂
Gemini	Mercury ☿	Sagittarius	Jupiter ♃
Cancer	Moon ☽	Capricorn	Saturn ♄
Leo	Sun ☉	Aquarius	Uranus ♅
Virgo	Mercury ☿	Pisces	Neptune ♆

A woman can take on a few different Personality Cards, depending on her needs. For example, a 7 of Hearts woman can operate under her card but also under her Personality Card of the Queen of Hearts. She may be in love, and because her Birth Card the 7 of Hearts signifies she can be shy or withdrawn, she role-plays the Queen of Hearts to appear more confident. The Queen of Hearts is a card that is more flamboyant, very feminine, and can represent the "Queen of Love." Underneath, however, she is the same sensitive person her Birth Card represents. Alternatively, at work she may have to manage a team of strong male employees forcefully and may decide to play out the King of Hearts, where she is more forceful and is constantly taking the initiative. A woman can also act out the Jack if she is playing a youthful or creative role, as Jacks have an androgynous quality.

If your Birth Card is already a royal card, say you are a woman who is the King of Clubs, you could also play the Personality Cards of the Queen or Jack of Clubs if appropriate. Gender issues can be different for each individual. You may find that a woman who is a King Card has a lot of male energy, and when operating under her own Birth Card usually does not play the "femme fatale" but prefers to be straightforward and direct. Equally, men who are a Queen Card have strong female energy that they may use, for example, by being creative or nurturing. Individuals who are Jack Cards usually retain a youthful quality well into old age.

4

Your Relationships With Others

BESIDES ENHANCING OUR self-awareness, one of the best features of this card system is that it is excellent for assessing relationships. The system contains planetary connections between your card and other cards. These links represent different types of energy that are generated between you and other people. Some connections are easy, so you find yourself feeling naturally comfortable with a person right from the start. Other links are more challenging, but with the right attitude it is usually possible to get them to work for you so you still get something valuable out of the relationship. For example, Mars links are dynamic, so you may feel active, lively, and enterprising around a person who has a Mars connection to your card.

When you want to find out about relationships there is no simpler or more accurate method than this card system. In the two spreads you will be able to check not only your own card, but also the cards of others, and see how your cards interrelate. According to this system, your strongest relationships are those linked to your card by the planets. You can read these relationship links in a number of ways.

You can read your relationships with other cards horizontally through your seven-card sequence on the Earthly and Spiritual spreads. Moving in the same way that you used to discover your own seven-card sequence, that is, going left from your card, through Mercury, Venus, Mars, Jupiter, Saturn, Uranus, Neptune, and your Challenge Card, you can discover links with other cards.

In this example the main Birth Card belongs to a 4 of Clubs individual. Any Jack of Spades people they meet connect to their Venus Card in their Personal Card Sequence, stimulating Venusian-type energy in the 4 of Clubs. This would be a good link for romance, friendship, creativity, or making money.

When you read the main text of your Birth Card you can find interpretations for each planet in your Personal Card Sequence to see what qualities a person of that card is going to stimulate in you.

You can also find further information about what effect each planet is going to have

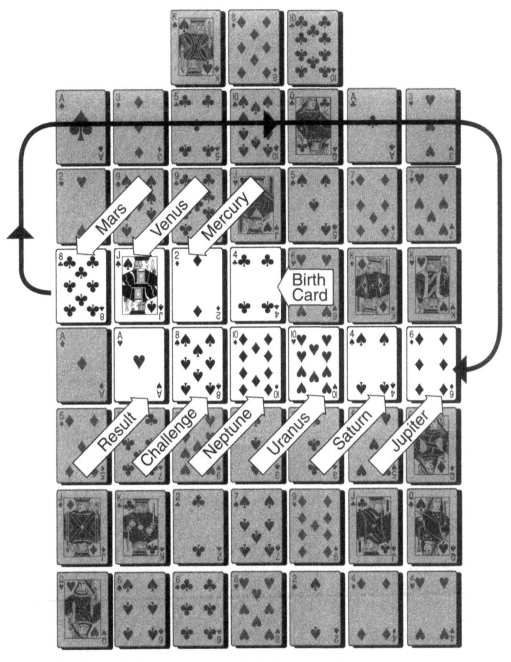

Horizontal Links for Relationships (Example: 4 of Clubs)

upon your relationships later in this chapter. (See Planetary Links in Relationships section.)

If your card appears in the Personal Card Sequence of somebody else, for example, you may be *their* Venus Card, in which case they would be an *unconscious* Venus to you. You would both feel Venusian-type energy between the two of you.

READING THE CARDS VERTICALLY

Reading from your Birth Card and always going upward in the same column, you follow the same planetary sequence, Mercury, Venus, Mars, Jupiter, Saturn, Uranus, and Neptune to find links with other cards.

If the 3 of Clubs in this example meets a 5 of Spades person, this individual will represent Mars to them. A 10 of Clubs individual will be Saturn to the 3 of Clubs person. A 9 of Diamonds individual will be Neptune. When reading vertically, stay in the same column and go up to the top and from the bottom up again in the same column. (See example on page 33.)

READING THE CARDS DIAGONALLY

Reading diagonally from your card in all directions, again you would use the planetary series, Mercury, Venus, Mars, Jupiter, Saturn, Uranus.

Using this example of the 3 of Clubs, the 9 of Spades would be diagonal Mars to the 3 of Clubs and vice versa. The cards would share a diagonal Mars link. In the case of the 3 of Clubs and the Ace of Spades, they would share a diagonal Jupiter link. (See example on page 34.)

REPLACEMENT CARDS IN RELATIONSHIPS

You are likely to feel a particularly strong influence from people who are your Replacement Cards. This can be a very strong link for relationships. Although this link is usually very positive, even if you do not get along with this individual you are likely to have very good insight into how this person operates.

PLANETARY LINKS IN RELATIONSHIPS

Since the planets all represent different types of influence they affect your relationships in different ways.

Mercury in Relationships

This link is often found in partnerships, friendships, and relationships based on mutual understanding and shared interests. If you meet or know someone whose Birth Card is the same as your Mercury Card, you are likely to have good rapport. You may feel that this person is someone you can talk to easily, as they can relate to your way of thinking. It can also be a card of siblings or childhood friends. Although you have a number of optional Mercury Cards, the strongest Mercury Card is often the one from your personal sequence. The best way to enjoy this link is to share some type of interest where you can both learn something beneficial. Every Mercury relationship link is different, depending on the card. For example, if your Mercury Card is the Ace of Diamonds, you like to initiate ideas that are groundbreaking and profitable. With an Ace of Diamonds person you can both become enthusiastic and motivate each other to push ahead. If your Mercury Card is the 9 of Hearts,

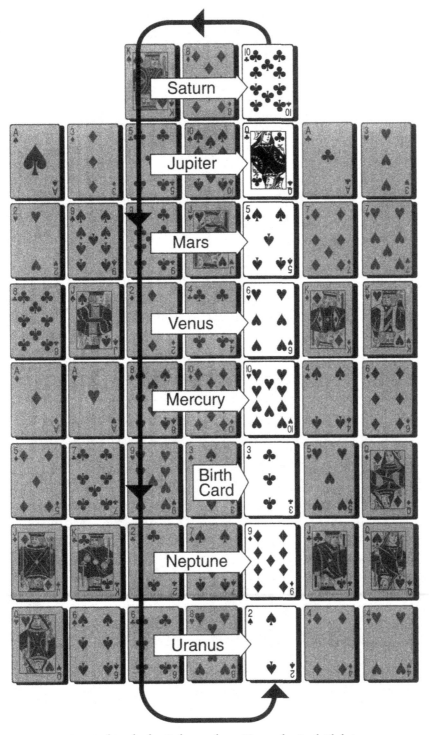

Vertical Links for Relationships (Example: 3 of Clubs)

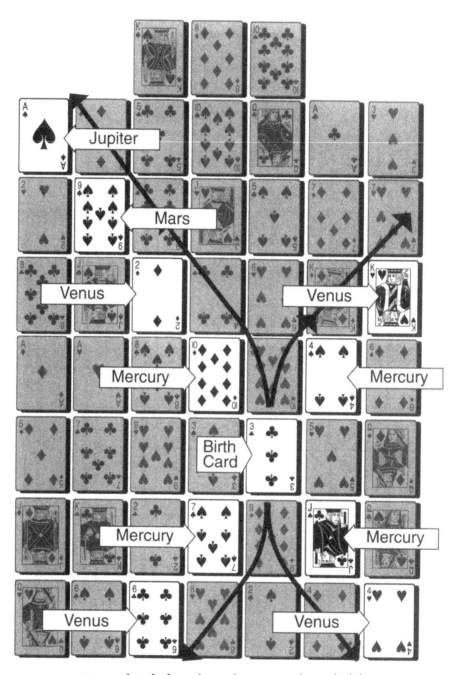

Diagonal Links for Relationships (Example: 3 of Clubs)

your relationship is often based on your ability to feel for each other. These can be feelings of joy or emotional frustration. Sympathetic understanding can help both of you overcome disappointments. If your Mercury Card is the 4 of Diamonds you are likely to work well together and share knowledge useful for your careers. As you both share the same values or business sense you can also establish good working partnerships.

Venus in Relationships

If you know a person who is your Venus Card, you are likely to be attracted to them, as they represent what you most seek in others. You can both have similar interests and succeed by combining your resources in creative enterprises and business. Through sharing the same interests or feelings, you can appreciate the same values or have similar styles or tastes in art and music. Equally, your Venus relationships can make you feel more contented and harmonious. Although you may find your Venus Card link inspiring or entertaining, this person can help you become more aware of your feelings or aspirations, reflecting what you most desire. With your Venus link you can also share special moments of intimacy and affection. By identifying with the emotions of someone other than yourself, you are able to see the world from their point of view. Then you can also understand what kind of effect you have on your lover, partner, or friends. Every Venus link reveals different types of relationships, according to the card. For example, if your Venus Card is the 6 of Clubs you like intelligent individuals who are well informed and mentally stimulating. If your Venus Card is the 8 of Diamonds you like ambitious and determined individuals who are hardworking or career-oriented. Since you both have good business acumen it is probable that you will

want to work together or even will have met through your work.

Mars in Relationships

People who are linked to your Mars Card are likely to stimulate you into action. Usually they project the assertiveness you admire. If you choose to collaborate or work together you will not sit around waiting for things to happen but make exciting plans or embark on new adventures. With people who are your Mars Card link, you need to channel your energies in positive ways. For example, you may share the same interest in sports, go for walks, or work out together. Since these individuals also share some aspect of your fighting spirit, they can become your adversaries. In order to avoid making enemies, resist competing with them or challenging them in negative ways. You can assert yourself in your close Mars relationships, but you may have to learn to deal positively with anger or confrontation. Every Mars Card reveals different types of relationships. For example, if your Mars relationship card is the Ace of Diamonds you are both dynamic and enthusiastic. Nevertheless, you may encounter rivalry or find that you and your partner both want to lead. Though you are both eager to get on with life, resist being bossy. If your relationship Mars Card is the 3 of Clubs you both can collaborate creatively and mentally stimulate each other. If you are prone to indecisiveness you may end up having long yet unproductive discussions or even waste your time arguing.

Jupiter in Relationships

This link suggests a good relationship, as this person is likely to give you positive support or provide opportunities for you in some way. You may share the same values and beliefs or stimulate each other's idealism and future expectations. Together you are likely to feel more optimistic about achieving on a bigger scale. This is a lucky combination, as you will motivate each other to be more honest, direct, and magnanimous. When you are together you can both project high levels of enthusiasm, although you may have to be careful not to get carried away or be excessive. For example, if your Jupiter relationship card is the 2 of Diamonds, you can both especially gain from working partnerships. You can be inspired by the 2 of Diamond's ability to make contacts and work cooperatively with others. You would both feel optimistic and expansive about working together, particularly in work involving sales and negotiation. As it is important for two energies to stay balanced, you would both have to watch out for getting too excited or being excessive. People who are Jupiter relationships can lift your spirits when you are down, often using humor. You may travel together or be attracted to education, religion, or sports. You may, however, have to resist the temptation to take on too much in your desire to expand and prosper. In retrospect, you will usually find that this person has provided you with good fortune in some way or an opportunity to be productive.

Saturn in Relationships

This person can show you the benefits that come from self-control and taking responsibility. Saturn prefers to take things more seriously, so this is often a restraining influence. If you tend to act impulsively this person may help you by bringing a curbing influence to bear on the more impetuous side of your nature, emphasizing self-discipline and helping you become clear about your boundaries. Alternatively, you may feel this person's influence as unwanted criticism, repressing your spontaneity and adding unwanted burdens or responsibilities to your life. When this link is working positively, you respect each other, and this individual is likely to provide you with loyalty, stability, and support. You may have similar goals or work together on self-improvement through listening to each other's suggestions. For example, if your Saturn relationship card is the 8 of Clubs you could both respect each other's knowledge or power of thought. However, if this Saturn influence became negative through one partner acting selfishly, fear could cause either partner to become mentally controlling or manipulative.

If there is an age gap in the relationship you have with someone who is your Saturn Card, one partner may act as a teacher or mentor for the other. Sometimes this can be a karmic relationship from the past, sometimes with one of the partners owing a karmic debt to the other. If a person represents the Saturn Card in your Personal Card Sequence, you are likely to feel the Saturn lesson consciously, while they are receiving it more unconsciously. Either way, even though work is involved, you will usually encounter this relationship as an important learning experience and gain valuable insight into yourself.

Uranus in Relationships

An individual who is linked to you through a Uranus Card can help you be more objective about yourself and your life situations. They can bring you new ideas or experiences that can make you more true to yourself. This relationship can be exciting, unconventional, and future-oriented. As Uranus is a group-oriented planet, the friends or social group you share can be extra important to you both. The main problem with this type of relationship, however, is tension, stubbornness, or a rebellious lack of collaboration if one of you insists on doing thing their way. The relationship usually works best if you respect each other's freedom. For example, if you have a Uranus relationship with the 5 of Clubs you both enjoy exploring new interests to fire your mental enthusiasm. You both need variety to stop you from getting bored. As travel would be an ideal way to stimulate this energy, it would be good, for instance, for a partner who could not travel due to work commitments to allow their 5 of Clubs partner to go for short trips by themselves. Giving their partner freedom acknowledges their own right to freedom and enhances the relationship. Alternatively, in tense situations you can both get restless or impatient. If you are in a Uranus-type relationship, you may share unusual interests, be good with computers, or be attracted to exploring disciplines connected with self-awareness, such as therapy, yoga, healing, astrology, or spirituality. On the other hand, you may become involved in team or collaborative situations. This person can strengthen your individuality or provide you with an alternate view of reality. Moneywise, this relationship can encourage you to be more resourceful and independent or utilize your knowledge of people for profit. In this relationship Uranus can bring the sudden and unexpected. This is a good friendship link.

Neptune in Relationships

You have an emotional link with a person linked to you through Neptune, as you can be receptive to each other's moods and feelings. Because of the sensitivity here, this can be a contact where you have an almost psychic connection. If used positively, this connection can help you both reach deeper levels of awareness. You can link to each other's dreams. This relationship may stimulate your idealism, with the result that you may even feel a spiritual link with this person. If used negatively, however, this individual could sometimes mislead or confuse you. You may have unfulfilled expectations from each other, then be disappointed. Alternatively, you may martyr yourself or become involved in escapist activities together, such as abuse of drugs or alcohol. The subtle sensitivity here can be used constructively, however, such as in music, art, or healing. For example, if your Neptune relationship card is the Jack of Spades, you can be very creative and playful together. As this is a royalty card there can be an emphasis on role-play. If the positive side of the Jack of Spades is being used this is a very productive work influence for you both, and this card can even have strong intuitive or mystical influences. As the negative side of the Jack of Spades can be immaturity or a dubious character, it is best to make sure that you always show honesty and integrity in your dealings with each other. Although having a Neptune relationship can bring excellent emotional receptivity between you, remember to also be practical and down-to-earth.

Challenge Card in Relationships

This relationship can bring strong change or transformation into your life by making you more daring or energized. Being in the company of this person can produce increased awareness of how you react to outside situations and provide you with deeper insight into yourself. They can especially help you to see the light in a dark situation, or you may share the same sense of humor. The relationship is likely to be intense at times, but this can be channeled to produce positive results and may be a vehicle for self-regeneration. For example, if your Challenge relationship is the 8 of Spades, you can both work together on power issues. You can do this in a determined and all-or-nothing way to achieve objectives. Alternatively, you can both generate hidden issues where you both wish to control or dominate.

You will have a deep awareness of how a person in a Challenge relationship responds, if only on a subliminal level, and know how to get a reaction from them. Since they can feel the same way, it is important not to get involved in power struggles unless you both know what you are doing. This link can bring out the best or the worst in you, so avoid becoming overly intense. Through reacting mindfully this influence can bring positive change into your life.

Result of Your Challenge Card in Relationships

The person linked to you through this card can reflect back to you how well you are doing with your Challenge Card. If you are acting out the negative sides of this card you may well need to review your behavior. Alternatively, if you are responding well to your challenges you should especially see positive results in the areas represented by this card. For example, if the Result of Your Challenge is the Ace of Clubs, through your relationship with this person you should see whether you are instigating new ventures or interests that keep you mentally stimulated. You could be learning new things or involved in leadership activities together. Alternatively, if negative you could be bossy or selfish.

Personality Cards in Relationships

On the Earthly Plane only, you can also work under your Personality Card. Although links with Personality Cards are not as strong as links with your Birth Card they can still be significant. You can operate under the King of your suit if you are acting out a strong male or mature and responsible role. You can operate under the Queen if you want to role-play in a strong but female role. Alternatively, you may choose to act as a Jack if you are in a playful or youthful role, such as a musician.

Whatever Personality Card you use this is often most noticeable when you are relating to other cards. For example, a female may look up her relationship with her boyfriend and discover the only link she has with him is when he is playing the Personality Card of the Jack of his suit. This suggests that there is a playful or youthful quality to their relationship. Her boyfriend may be fun and entertaining, but as a Jack he may not want to make a more serious commitment.

A man's Personality Card is usually represented by a King, although all young people's Personality Cards are represented by the Jack of their suit. A woman can also take on the Personality Card of the Queen of her suit. For example, a 6 of Hearts man can operate under the Jack of Hearts or the King of Hearts Personality Cards. When we look for links with other cards we would first look at planetary connections to our personal Birth Card, then Replacement Cards, and lastly see if we have any links with someone through our Personality Cards on the Earthly Spread. For example, a King of Diamonds woman has a relationship link with a male 8 of Clubs. He is the Saturn card in her Personal Card Sequence. This Saturn card is the major link between them. However, when she was operating under her Queen of Diamonds Personality Card and the 8 of Clubs is in a youthful mood playing the Jack of Clubs, he is her Challenge Card. This could be good if he challenges her to react in a playfully creative way but difficult if he continually challenges her due to his immaturity.

Part II

Descriptions of the Cards

♥ ♣ THE ACES ♦ ♠

ACES REPRESENT THE number 1. If you are an Ace then you are a born leader with the need and drive to express your individuality. At your best, you are a confident and self-reliant person who inspires others in a positive way. Ambitious with powerful desires, you may have to learn not to confuse the use of your powerful will with dominance over others. If the number 1 becomes your ego then you can appear selfish or demanding. Others may feel that they are secondary to your personal pursuit for success or recognition. As an Ace you must first learn to stand on your own two feet and express your independence. Once independent, you become aware of your outstanding potential for achievement through the use of your focused willpower. You are then able to create more opportunities to be inventive, daring, and enjoy pioneering new avenues of expression. The focal point of the number 1 then changes from your ego to your spirit and you become capable of exceptional feats. You gain confidence and naturally rise to leading positions through your originality and progressive attitudes. The more positive you become the easier it is for you to develop patience, tolerance, and compassion, taking responsibility for your own actions and developing your remarkable potential.

If you are an Ace Card your strong desires are further modified by your suit as follows:

Ace of Hearts

You are usually motivated by your need for love and your desire to express yourself emotionally. Positively, you can enjoy initiating new ventures or can be a channel of love for others. Negatively, you could be too egotistically involved in your own feelings and become overwhelmed with emotion.

Ace of Clubs

Your desire for knowledge and curiosity about life can lead you to search in many different areas for mental stimulation. Success comes from initiating new ideas and being inventive. This card is very good for education, whether learning or teaching.

Ace of Diamonds

Ambitious and strong-willed, your quest for material satisfaction and status can drive you on to accomplish. You usually succeed best when this is combined with your ideals. Being so determined, you have the power to manifest your desires if you stay positive and focused. Your strong desires for money or material success can be used selfishly or for the good of others.

Ace of Spades

You may be compelled to find your identity through work, productive activities, or spiritual insights. You can have the desire to cut through and get to the heart of things. You may be secretive.

♥ THE ACE OF HEARTS ♥

The dynamic power of the Ace of Hearts suggests that your emotional drive and strong desires are the forces behind your motivation and achievement. When you feel instinctively strong about an issue or a situation you prefer to take the initiative and make things happen. Under the influence of Jupiter and Uranus in the Earthly Spread, you can be idealistic and original. You also possess good organizational skills and farsightedness or strong intuition. Often able to turn situations to your advantage, lucky breaks and fortunate ideas can be the reason why you can turn your life into a success story.

The double influence of Mercury in your Spiritual Spread indicates that you have flashes of inspiration and feel stimulated by exchanges of ideas. Although you possess excellent communication skills, in an attempt to put your plans into action avoid appearing offhanded or impatient to others.

As a card from the Hearts suit, emotional issues, such as a desire for love and personal expression, can play an important part in your life agenda. When new ideas or people inspire you, you can display your spontaneity, but you may need to avoid being impulsive. Aces represent the masculine principle, therefore, you prefer to be straightforward and direct. Although strong-minded and independent, you realize the importance of cooperation and usually seek to create harmonious relationships.

Your Two Replacement Cards Are the 3 of Hearts & the Ace of Diamonds.

As the Ace of Hearts you share the same planetary position as the 3 of Hearts in the Earthly Spread. This signifies that you are sensitive with powerful feelings. Although this provides you with strong creative potential and versatility, it becomes a challenge when you are faced with multiple choices.

You also share the same planetary position as the Ace of Diamonds in the Spiritual Spread. Having two Aces influencing your life suggests that you are strongly motivated and good at manifesting your plans. Keen on taking the lead or initiating new projects, you are best left to your own devices. When you use the qualities of the Ace of Diamonds to your advantage your innate business sense usually guarantees success on a material level. Having the idealism of the Ace of Hearts, self-satisfaction comes from your ability to bring benefits and goodwill to all.

You usually have special or karmic links with people represented by the 3 of Hearts and the Ace of Diamonds, as you share the same planetary positions. You can be soul mates or understand each other very well. Even if you

The Ace of Hearts Planetary Card Sequence

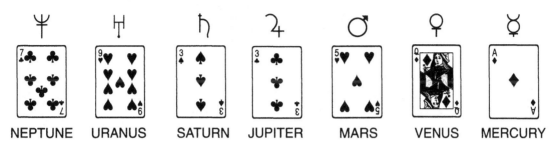

| NEPTUNE | URANUS | SATURN | JUPITER | MARS | VENUS | MERCURY |

do not get along, you can both see clearly how the other person operates.

Your Mercury Card is . . .

The Ace of Diamonds
- Your good money sense and entrepreneurial ideas indicate many opportunities for material success.
- If you stay mentally focused, you can achieve wonders with your willpower.
- To greatly enhance your prospects, avoid being bossy by using your charm, negotiation skills, and innate diplomacy.
- Keen to make money, you probably started work at an early age.
- With your sharp and assertive mind, you enjoy fresh ideas and new beginnings.
- You should have good mental rapport and special communication with people represented by the Ace of Diamonds, as they activate your Mercury card.

Your Venus Card is . . .

The Queen of Diamonds
- In social situations you possess a sense of the dramatic and can combine business with pleasure.
- You are likely to gain support from strong women.

- You usually prefer to be in leadership or authoritative positions.
- An extravagant streak implies that you have to watch your spending.
- Although sometimes stubborn, you can be very generous and loyal with those you love.
- Usually you are attracted to Queens of Diamonds. They are ideal for love and romance as well as close friendships and good business partnerships.

Your Mars Card is . . .

The 5 of Hearts
- You possess quick reactions and an instinctive understanding of people and situations.
- Fluctuating moods or an inclination to be dissatisfied can lead to a change of heart.
- You are likely to lead an active and busy social life.
- You may enjoy flirting or testing your wits against the opposite sex.
- You particularly benefit from adventure, variety, or excitement in your life.
- A 5 of Hearts person can particularly motivate and stimulate you. If you avoid being too competitive with this individual, you can channel the energy productively.

Your Jupiter Card is . . .

The 3 of Clubs

- Although you often appear ambitious and confident, you are prone to suffer from insecurity or stress if you take on too much.
- Usually you are articulate and witty.
- Avoid exaggerating or magnifying things out of proportion.
- Creative and versatile, you enjoy exploring different ways to express yourself.
- You can have a good rapport with 3 of Clubs people as they are often benefactors who can expand and enhance your life. Alternatively, you may have a spiritual link.

Your Saturn Card is . . .

The 3 of Spades

- Your career or work prospects need careful consideration as this is the area where you are likely to be tested most.
- Avoid taking matters too seriously.
- You work better when you solve problems by using your creativity.
- Indecisiveness, particularly over work, can be the cause of your worry or anxiety.
- You often possess many talents and can apply your skills to more than one job.
- 3 of Spades people can be your guides and help you recognize your shortcomings. If you are willing to work on your self-awareness these people can bring valuable lessons.

Your Uranus Card is . . .

The 9 of Hearts

- You possess compassion and humanitarian or selfless qualities that support your liberal views.
- You can avoid emotional disappointment if you develop a detached or philosophical outlook.

- When frustrated you are liable to do something erratic.
- When you express yourself you can be spontaneous and generous.
- If you feel you have been taken advantage of you are more likely to become cold or withdrawn.
- 9 of Hearts people can help you be more objective about yourself. This is also a good friendship link where freedom is valued.

Your Neptune Card is . . .

The 7 of Clubs

- With your ability to probe or analyze you have an aptitude for mysticism, higher wisdom, or philosophy.
- By taking time out to contemplate and reflect, you can restore your mental equilibrium and avoid anxiety or mental stress.
- You have the power to visualize or to communicate imaginative ideas.
- Personal power comes from having faith in your inner vision and intuition.
- 7 of Clubs people have a psychic connection with you. They may link to your visions and ideals or help you to realize your dreams. Nevertheless, stay grounded.

Your Challenge Card is . . .

The 5 of Diamonds

- Strike the right balance between materialism and idealism.
- Benefits come from being flexible and turning your inner vision into action.
- Empowerment or transformation comes from learning to handle fluctuations in your finances or values.
- 5 of Diamonds people can challenge you to express the best or the worst of your personality. Although these people can help you to transform your life, avoid power strug-

gles, acting impulsively, or "get rich quick" schemes.

The Result of Your Challenge Card is . . .

The Queen of Spades
- Naturally shrewd, you usually gain more wisdom from experience than theory.
- Self-discipline is the key to unlocking your outstanding potential.
- You learn to trust your intuition.
- Long-term strategies give you the power to lead and influence others.
- People who are represented by the Queen of Spades can reflect how you are responding to your challenges.

Famous People Who Are the Ace of Hearts

Tiger Woods, Tracey Ullman, Rudyard Kipling, Michael Nesmith, Bo Diddley, Patti Smith, Sandy Koufax

BIRTHDAYS GOVERNED BY THE ACE OF HEARTS

December 30: Capricorn   Ruler: Saturn
Since this is the only day ruled by the Ace of Hearts, it emphasizes the importance of your Saturn Card. Having an immense emotional power under the influence of the 10 of Spades suggests that hard work, ambition, and responsibilities need to be balanced by the desire for creativity and self-expression. When you harness your dynamic feelings there is very little that can stop you from achieving your heart's desires. Self-pity or being overly sensitive can isolate you from others, whereas your charm is often reflected in your good nature and friendly demeanor.

♣ THE ACE OF CLUBS ♣

An inquiring mind and a desire to learn are often the motivating forces behind the discerning power of the Ace of Clubs. This indicates that you have an astute mind, cerebral capabilities, and a capacity to grasp situations quickly that can often take you to leadership positions. Being inquisitive and intelligent, you are usually inspired by knowledge and new ideas.

Under the influence of Mercury and Venus in the Earthly Spread, you enjoy exchanging views and communicating to others. Often articulate, loving, and creative, your friendly disposition and social skills imply that you can captivate others with your clever mentality and engaging personality.

The influences of Venus and Neptune in your Spiritual Spread signify that you are also intuitive, idealistic, and romantic. Loyalty and devotion to the person or project you love is one of your most admirable qualities. Although your idealism can make you generous and hopeful, avoid martyring yourself to unworthy people or unrealistic ideas. As an Ace of Clubs, mental restlessness or strong obsessions can undermine your determination and enthusiasm. While you can be altruistic and spontaneous, you need to be patient and refrain from acting impetuously.

Aces represent the masculine principle; therefore, you are often independent and daring. You may encounter a conflict of interests, however, between pursuing your desire for self-expression and making sacrifices for those you love.

Your Replacement Card Is the 2 of Hearts.

As the Ace of Clubs you share the same planetary position as the 2 of Hearts in the Spiritual Spread. Unlike other cards, the Ace of Clubs has only one Replacement Card. This signifies that underneath your cool-headed exterior you are emotionally very sensitive. It also points out that relationships with others play an extra-important role in your life. Often all or nothing, your feelings can reach both ends of the spectrum. When in love, although you can be demonstrative by showing your love and affection, resist becoming overly dependent on your partner. You can, however, benefit from all types of partnerships, and usually you are trustworthy and honest. Your friends will be able to rely on you if they ever need help.

You usually have a special or karmic link with people represented by the 2 of Hearts, as you share the same planetary positions. You can be soul mates or understand each other very well. Even if you do not get along, you can both see clearly how the other person operates.

Your Mercury Card is . . .

The Queen of Clubs
- Your mind is quick and resolute and your intuition is usually accurate.
- Your mother or a strong woman left a powerful impression on you in your youth.
- If you believe in something you will pursue it with passion and determination.
- Your ability to judge situations instantly gives you the edge.
- Avoid disputes and confrontations with others as it can cause you mental tension and undue stress.

- Rushing into a situation or acting prematurely can be a major stumbling block.
- You can also enjoy communicating with people represented by the Queen of Clubs as they often inspire you with their insight and knowledge.

Your Venus Card is . . .

The 10 of Spades
- You can be especially fortunate through artistic endeavors or working with the public.
- You admire hardworking people who do not shy away from responsibilities.
- If you believe in someone or something your support and effort can help produce excellent results. This is a good card for marriage or working partnerships.
- You usually enjoy working on big projects or in large organizations.
- Your Venus link indicates that you are attracted to people who are the 10 of Spades. Although this card can be a good link for romance and love, it is also ideal for business partnerships.

Your Mars Card is . . .

The 5 of Clubs
- Mentally quick, logical, and practical, you respond well to intellectual debates and discussions.

The Ace of Clubs Planetary Card Sequence

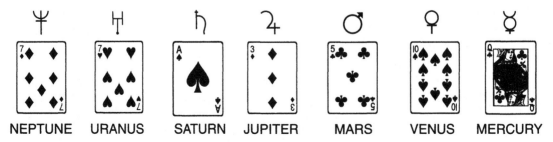

NEPTUNE   URANUS   SATURN   JUPITER   MARS   VENUS   MERCURY

- Being well informed and flexible often gives you the edge when faced with challenges.
- Inventive and versatile, you are a progressive thinker who can embrace new ideas.
- You like to be direct and come straight to the point.
- Mentally restless, you need to overcome a tendency to be impatient or impulsive.
- The relationships you have with 5 of Clubs people are never static or boring; on the contrary, there is often a great deal of activity. Avoid being too argumentative or competitive, however.

Your Jupiter Card is . . .

The 3 of Diamonds
- You have original ideas that can be financially beneficial.
- Learning to budget can minimize your worries about money, so resist spending your hard-earned cash on impulsive buying or luxuries that are not essential.
- Creative and versatile, you enjoy exploring different ways to express yourself.
- Try to avoid scattering your energies on too many projects. Being decisive and sticking to your plans brings rewards.
- Although you may encounter fluctuating circumstances in your finances, you can always count on Jupiter to provide you with the protection you need to feel secure.
- 3 of Diamonds people can expand and enhance your life. If you are in business or partnership with them you can both be successful. Alternatively, these people can inspire you with original and exciting ideas.

Your Saturn Card is . . .

The Ace of Spades
- Although you have a sympathetic and compassionate nature, at times you can appear aloof or indifferent.

- If you trust your intuition you are good at uncovering important information or hidden secrets.
- Your desire to gain knowledge can extend beyond the mundane, so you may feel drawn toward spiritual or metaphysical subjects.
- Your personal interests may turn out to be your vocation or life's work.
- You are often idealistic and willing to be of service to others.
- Although Ace of Spades individuals often play an important role in your life, your relationships with them are not always easy. If you can learn from them, their contributions are often very valuable lessons.

Your Uranus Card is . . .

The 7 of Hearts
- When you express yourself you can be spontaneous and generous; when hurt or frustrated you are liable to do something erratic.
- Although you possess an idealistic or altruistic nature, at times you can lose faith and become cynical. By being more discriminative or detached you can show your emotional power.
- If you feel you have been taken advantage of you are likely to become cold or withdrawn.
- 7 of Hearts people can help you be more objective about yourself due to your Uranus connection. This is also a good friendship link, especially where freedom is valued.

Your Neptune Card is . . .

The 7 of Diamonds
- Even if you experience monetary challenges during your life, rewards can come in later years to compensate for any difficulties you experienced in the past.

- Guard against letting unfounded fears or resentment about your financial matters cloud your judgment.
- If you develop your sensitivity, spontaneity, and intuition through creativity or spiritual activities this can bring you much satisfaction, especially when you are older.
- Partnerships and monetary affairs in later years must be based on honesty and trust.
- 7 of Diamonds people can help you materialize your dreams or ideals, but guard yourself against delusion.

Your Challenge Card is . . .

The 5 of Spades
- Transform yourself through bringing new positive changes into your life.
- Fit into different working environments without becoming anxious or fearful.
- Channel any tendency to be impulsive or restless into new adventures, travel, or a desire to help others.
- Be flexible and accept that things never stay the same, thereby enhancing your understanding or spiritual awareness.
- 5 of Spades people can provoke you to react intensely. This can bring positive change into your life, but avoid power struggles.

The Result of Your Challenge Card is . . .

The Jack of Hearts
- You gain popularity and admiration from others by being generous, warm-hearted, and responsible.
- Naturally idealistic, you can find emotional fulfillment, even if it means making some sacrifices.
- By developing your unique talents, you can express your creativity and feelings.
- Jack of Hearts people can light up your life and be entertaining or cause you to feel sorry

for yourself. Either way they can reflect how you are responding to your challenges.

Famous People Who Are the Ace of Clubs

Meg Ryan, Bruce Springsteen, Gary Busey, Clint Eastwood, Prince Rainier of Monaco, Brooke Shields, Indira Gandhi, Leonard Bernstein, Sean Connery, Martin Amis, Samuel Coleridge, Claudia Schiffer, Frederick Forsyth, Carrie Fisher, John Bonham, Elvis Costello, Ray Charles, John Coltrane, Julio Iglesias, Mickey Rooney, Dizzy Gillespie, Ted Turner, Walt Whitman, Calvin Klein, Jodie Foster

Birthdays Governed by the Ace of Clubs

May 31: Gemini   Ruler: Mercury
Your ruler, Mercury, the planet of reason, intellect, and communication, indicates that you are an intelligent individual with common sense and practical abilities. Your versatility and inquisitive mind suggest that you are usually a creative and progressive thinker who can initiate new ideas. Your interests are often varied and your desire to expand your knowledge is the key to your success and achievements. An ability to articulate your thoughts may also inspire you to write or study your interests in-depth. A certain restlessness or a tendency to act on impulse suggests that you need to persist and be consistent if you want to benefit from your analytical acumen and reach the heights of your potential.

June 29: Cancer   Ruler: Moon
Your ruler the Moon indicates that you are a dynamic individual with emotional sensitivity and exceptional receptivity. Your insecurities or a tendency to fluctuate emotionally suggest that, although you can be warm and loving, erratic behavior or a short temper can undermine your relationships. A mixture of idealism

and pragmatism implies that in order to turn your high aspirations to concrete success you need to overcome self-doubt and skepticism. When you combine your need for creativity with your intuitive thinking you can often excel in all types of intellectual pursuits. Although your need for emotional security or a safe haven is naturally strong, you may have to balance this with your desire for variety and change.

July 27: Leo   Ruler: Sun

Often proud yet reserved, beneath your warm yet tactful manner you are usually a well-informed individual full of initiative and enthusiasm. As a determined person with strong desires and a thirst for knowledge you boost your confidence through intellectual and creative pursuits. Being sensitive yet ambitious indicates that you can achieve more by being open to communication and less critical or bossy. As a good strategist and planner, in most circumstances you are better off thinking independently. In order to exercise your free will you need to learn to trust your own instincts.

August 25: Virgo   Ruler: Mercury

Your ruler, Mercury, the planet of reason and intellect, implies that you are an astute individual with analytical abilities and an eye for detail. Well informed and imaginative, you also want to find creative ways to express yourself. Although a thirst for knowledge and practical competence suggest that you are methodical and thorough, you gain greater understanding and learn more from your personal experiences or past mistakes. If you want to reach the heights of your potential and benefit from your analytical acumen you need to overcome a tendency to be restless or easily bored. Among your many talents, writing, teaching, and academic research can be especially prominent.

September 23: Libra   Ruler: Venus

Your ruler, Venus, the planet of love and beauty, indicates that you are a sociable and friendly individual with an optimistic outlook and kind nature. You are likely to benefit from working with people or enjoy popularity when involved with the public. You can excel especially when promoting new ideas and finding ways to express yourself creatively. An inclination to fluctuate emotionally signifies that you may be prone to changing moods, indecisiveness, or mental restlessness. Nevertheless, your engaging personality and ability to charm others usually compensate for any of your shortcomings.

October 21: Scorpio   Ruler: Mars

Sociable and dynamic, your charisma and friendly personality can often conceal your ambitious and determined nature. As a bright and enthusiastic individual you seek mental stimulation and are keen on initiating new ideas or projects. Although your eagerness to make progress is essential to your success, resist being aggressive or bossy by utilizing your natural diplomacy. If you allow self-doubt and insecurity to undermine your confidence it may influence the balance of power in your relationships or even lead to codependency. Nevertheless, your success in all types of mental pursuits is often assured when you are expanding your knowledge and allowing your creativity to flourish.

November 19: Scorpio   Ruler: Mars

Your ability to communicate your thoughts and ideas quickly and forcefully can make you persuasive and dramatic or give you the edge in debates and discussions. Your ruling planet, Mars, intensifies your feelings and makes you daring or ambitious. Although as an astute and spontaneous individual you can be competitive, your compassionate sensitivity can make you altruistic and generous. Although your enthusiasm implies that you are keen to rise to new challenges, you can quickly lose interest once you have reached your objectives. Nevertheless, your versatility and numerous talents suggest that you are likely to enjoy different experiences and opportunities in your quest for high status and success.

December 17: Sagittarius   Ruler: Jupiter

Innovative and ambitious, your quest for knowledge and enthusiasm can inspire you intellectually and spiritually. Although you may experience inner conflicts or suffer from worry and skepticism, your idealism or desire for greater self-awareness can spark some profound thoughts or deepen your self-awareness. Not easily influenced by others, you usually prefer to develop your innate insight and unique analytical abilities. You often create your own distinctive philosophy and inspire others with your ideas. In order to benefit from your exceptional intellectual abilities and good organizational skills you need to remain positive and less critical. Alternating financial circumstances can be resolved when you use your ingenuity to address them creatively.

◆ THE ACE OF DIAMONDS ◆

Independent and a strong individualist, you are active and enterprising, with a pioneering spirit. Being a strong Diamonds Card suggests that you also possess a sharp sense of values. Proud and determined, you usually prefer to give orders than receive them. This can steer you toward leadership positions or into working for yourself. Under the influence of Jupiter and Neptune in the Earthly Spread, you possess high ideals and a strong desire for material success or status. Trying to reconcile these seemingly opposite forces can sometimes cause

conflict, especially when facing challenges. It is important that you do not go for one at the expense of the other. By keeping your strong vision positive you will be fortunate in overcoming obstacles and enlisting the help of others.

With the influences of Jupiter and Uranus in the Spiritual Spread you are quick to realize opportunities but get the most satisfaction when you are able to share these with others. Original, with a love of freedom, you enjoy finding innovative ways to achieve your goals. Although you can successfully sell your ideals to others, you may become bored easily, so you need variety and a challenge to keep your interest. Your Ace of Diamonds influence suggests that once you are focused on achieving a goal your greatest gift can be your amazing power to realize your will.

Your Two Replacement Cards Are the 2 of Diamonds & the Ace of Hearts.

As the Ace of Diamonds you share the same planetary position as the 2 of Diamonds in the Spiritual Spread. This signifies that you are good at making contacts, which will benefit you financially. In your relationships with others it is important for you to keep a balance between using power tactics and compromise. By using your innate diplomatic skills you gain much from working in collaboration with others. Avoid wasting valuable energies on fears of not having enough money or resources by sharpening, and having faith in, your natural negotiation skills.

You also share the same planetary position as the Ace of Hearts in the Earthly Spread. This suggests that you possess powerful emotions and a strong need for love at a deep level. Your aspirations and your desire for love combine well to ensure that you are often more than willing to give to others from the goodness of your heart. With two Aces here you are especially motivated when inspired or listening to your intuition. You have special or karmic links with people represented by the 2 of Diamonds or the Ace of Hearts. As you share the same planetary positions you can be soul mates or understand each other really well. Even if you do not get along, you can both see clearly how the other person operates.

Your Mercury Card is . . .

The Queen of Diamonds

- Your natural business acumen suggests that you can drive a hard bargain or get value for money.
- A strong female figure, probably your mother, strongly affected your sense of values in your early life.
- With your appreciation of the good things in life you may have to watch an extravagant streak.
- Naturally smart, you fare particularly well when combining organizational and creative skills.
- Avoid a tendency for harsh speech that can spoil your good work.
- Queen of Diamonds people can provide you with ideas for making money or stimulate your leadership ability. This is a good link for communication and mental rapport.

Your Venus Card is . . .

The 5 of Hearts

- You are not afraid to take chances when you are enthusiastic about a relationship or a given situation. You often dive straight in emotionally.
- With loved ones you can be assertive about your needs but often find they do not measure up to your high expectations.
- You can be warm and sociable with a kind and magnanimous heart.
- You need to work at keeping your emotions steady, as you can alternate between being very keen to being not interested, particularly in your love life.
- 5 of Hearts people can stimulate your sense of adventure and enjoyment and restrain your innate restlessness. This is a good card for friendship, business, and love partnerships.

Your Mars Card is . . .

The 3 of Clubs

- Once set on a course of action you will work very hard to achieve your goals, displaying courage and drive.
- If annoyed with others avoid a tendency to be argumentative.
- You can be dynamic and expressive, espe-

The Ace of Diamonds Planetary Card Sequence

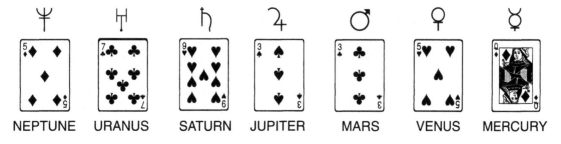

NEPTUNE   URANUS   SATURN   JUPITER   MARS   VENUS   MERCURY

cially with words. This shows strong creative potential.

- Your desire for action can be impaired if you become too indecisive. Better to take positive action that you can change later. Keep it light.
- 3 of Clubs people can stimulate your motivation and creativity. This is a good link for activity and getting things done, although avoid becoming competitive or quarreling.

Your Jupiter Card is . . .

The Three of Spades

- A friendly side to your personality helps you gain through lucky breaks.
- You are capable of thinking on a large scale, especially when sparking with creative ideas.
- Being honest about your feelings can decrease hidden insecurities or jealousies.
- You can be particularly fortunate through writing, publishing, and foreign interests.
- 3 of Spades people can stimulate your honesty or optimism. They can often expand your life and bring opportunities or they may have a spiritual link with you.

Your Saturn Card is . . .

The 9 of Hearts

- One of your main tests is learning to love unconditionally. You may find yourself wanting to be in control or expect more from others than they are capable of giving.
- When you do love unconditionally you love with compassion and great generosity of spirit.
- You have a gift, if used, for teaching others or for healing.
- You may need to keep a balance between love and money, or between being too soft and too hard.

- By letting go of a tendency to hold onto the past you open yourself up for new opportunities.
- 9 of Hearts people can help you realize your own shortcomings and provide valuable lessons. They can be teachers or bring extra responsibilities. This can be a karmic link.

Your Uranus Card is . . .

The 7 of Clubs

- You are an inventive, analytical, and objective thinker who enjoys doing things in your own individual style and is often ahead of your time.
- If you lose faith in yourself or others you can become rebellious, tense, or obstinate.
- You need the freedom to be as spontaneous as possible. This stimulates your natural flow or sharp intelligence.
- Developing your innate humanitarianism suggests you can be at your best when you feel you are being of service to others.
- 7 of Clubs people can bring out your originality, give you an objective picture of yourself, or be a good friend.

Your Neptune Card is . . .

The 5 of Diamonds

- Restlessness and a need for variety will attract you to long distance travel. Your opportunities for this should improve as you get older.
- You have excellent scope to put your strong vision into action as long as your impatience does not cause you to give up.
- You will always be able to come up with some resourceful solutions to life's challenges while you stay positive and do not shirk responsibility.
- 5 of Diamonds people can help you be more adventurous and keep your dreams and vi-

sions alive. This is a psychic link, but stay realistic.

Your Challenge Card is . . .

The Queen of Spades
- Do not operate in circumstances, or be in subordinate positions, well beneath your potential.
- Use your innate wisdom to solve problems rather than relying on sheer struggle and grind.
- Queen of Spades people can challenge you and bring out the best or the worst of your personality. Although these people can help you to transform your life, resist power struggles.

The Result of Your Challenge Card is . . .

The Jack of Clubs
- You enjoy passing on your knowledge and skills to others.
- If you are being stubborn and immature you may need to review your challenges.
- You are positively aware of role-play when it comes to getting your point across.
- People who are the Jack of Clubs can stimulate your creative ideas and reflect how well you are responding to your challenges.

Famous People Who Are the Ace of Diamonds

Daniel Day-Lewis, Guy Ritchie, Tupac Shakur, Ryan Phillipe, Jesse Jackson, Ingmar Bergman, Paul Hogan, Chevy Chase, Sigourney Weaver, Erich Segal, Stan Laurel, Woody Guthrie, Gustav Klimt, Angela Davis, Irving Stone, Mike Nichols, Gerald Ford, Andrew Lloyd Webber, Stephen Sondheim, Wayne Gretzky, Alice Bailey, Pope John Paul II, Marcel Marceau, Paul Newman, Margot Fonteyn, Rainer Maria Rilke, Luther Vandross, Karl Lagerfeld, Arnold Palmer, William Shatner, Cecil B. DeMille, Jessica Lange, Jay-Z, Ellen DeGeneres, Mark Knopfler, Matt Damon

Birthdays Governed by the Ace of Diamonds

January 26: Aquarius   Ruler: Uranus
Friendly and clever, you are a strong and multitalented person with original ideas. With your natural business sense and good insight into human nature, you should have no trouble succeeding, as long as you apply the necessary self-discipline. Keeping yourself busy and enthusiastic with new projects counteracts a tendency to withdraw and appear cold. Usually ahead of your time, you can anticipate trends and capitalize on them. Although you cherish your freedom and work hard to keep it, you may have to balance this out with the high value you also place on home and family.

February 24: Pisces   Ruler: Neptune
Possessing an interesting mixture of keen mentality, strong emotions, determination, and imagination, you usually seek variety in life and new experiences. Since a part of you is home loving and wants routine, yet another part is restless and loves change, it can be especially good for you to travel and still enjoy the comforts of home on your return. Nevertheless, your practicality or good organizational skills can prove to be highly profitable for you in business. Being idealistic, however, you also enjoy using your skills and talents for good causes.

March 22: Aries   Ruler: Mars
Sociable and creative, you constantly need new ideas to keep your restless spirit actively engaged. Enterprising and independent, you usually prefer to work for yourself or in a leadership position. Although your bold impulses

and desire for adventure can sometimes get you into trouble, they can also motivate you into action. You are not afraid to think big but sometimes may not carry your activities through if this involves taking care of the details. A tendency to be stubborn or doubt yourself may stop you from fulfilling your outstanding potential, but when positive you can project confidence and determination to get the support of others.

April 20: Aries/Taurus   Ruler: Mars/Venus
Born on the cusp, you have the assertiveness of Aries and the stubborn determination of Taurus. Although strong-willed and tenacious, you can also be receptive and courteous with a supportive nature. Your strong feelings need a positive channel of expression so that you are able to display your natural creativity and original ideas. With focus and discipline you can be a practical visionary who is able to realize your large plans. Ideally you will get the most satisfaction if these plans help others. You are likely to have good taste or talents in the arts, music, or drama.

May 18: Taurus   Ruler: Venus
Friendly but assertive, you are a warm person who needs creative challenges in life to keep your strong spirit alive. Although you are capable of being generous and big-hearted with those you care for, you also have a desire to keep the reigns of power or be in a leadership position. Naturally practical with a good business sense, you succeed through hard work. Even though you are shrewd when it comes to material things, you can also be idealistic and choose activities that get you enthusiastic and emotionally involved. You have a love of the good life and may have artistic or creative talents.

June 16: Gemini   Ruler: Mercury
Thoughtful, progressive, and mentally sharp, you have a talent for communication and analyzing values. Your critical gifts work best for you when you display them in an open and caring way rather than being domineering or cold. Nevertheless, you can be very generous and supportive of those you love. You want the best that life can provide, both for yourself and your family, and you are usually willing to work hard to achieve it. When confident you will find yourself rising to leadership positions where you are able to spread your knowledge and skills. Although you need material security, you also have a desire to keep updating your learning. You tend to fare particularly well materially when pioneering new ideas.

July 14: Cancer   Ruler: Moon
Intuitive with fast responses, you are quick to support those in your care or causes that are dear to your heart. Strong-willed and pragmatic, you often respond to life with determination and resolve. Nevertheless, your sensitivity suggests that you have a need for security and a more vulnerable side that you may tend to keep hidden. Your home and family therefore play an especially important part in your life script. Nevertheless, you also have natural business acumen, an enterprising spirit, and high ideals. Although you can be hardworking and loyal, avoid being stubborn. The more adaptable and diplomatic you are, the easier it is to get your point across or your desires met.

August 12: Leo   Ruler: Sun
Active and creative, your natural leadership skills often show through from an early age. Proud and dignified, you usually dislike following orders, preferring to take the initiative. You generally appear confident and autonomous, but if you allow yourself to be in de-

pendent situations this can affect your self-esteem. Being friendly as well as assertive, you are usually popular, and have an ability to make things happen. With your regal air you are likely to have talents in drama, writing, music, or the arts.

September 10: Virgo   Ruler: Mercury

Although analytical, meticulous, and down-to-earth, you also possess powerful feelings and high ideals. With your expertise at quickly evaluating situations you possess good critical abilities but avoid using them negatively. Usually your independent nature puts you in leading positions, but you fare better when using your innate diplomatic skills rather than being bossy. Having strong convictions suggests that you can achieve miracles if you keep positively focused on your goals and persevere. You get emotional satisfaction from your desire to be of service.

October 8: Libra   Ruler: Venus

An interesting mixture of charm, assertive drive, and directness, you need projects and interests you can put your heart into. Although you enjoy variety and have an instinctive ability to judge people and situations quickly, you also have to watch an impatient streak that can detract from your charismatic appeal. To avoid restlessness you need work that is not too routine, and travel can prove especially attractive. Strong willpower and an appreciation of beauty and the good things of life ensure that you usually get what you want financially.

November 6: Scorpio   Ruler: Mars

Proud and strong-willed with powerful emotions, you can be forceful and articulate. When positive you are friendly, caring, and broad-minded, so you can be a good adviser for others. If negative, avoid allowing a tendency for worry or insecurity to drain your energies.

Courageous and persuasive, you are particularly good in positions of leadership that utilize your creative ideas. You are also home loving and place a strong emphasis on family. Although sometimes impatient, when your drive is channeled creatively you can perform miracles.

December 4: Sagittarius   Ruler: Jupiter

Friendly yet determined, your strength of mind suggests you possess drive and an adventurous spirit. Mentally sharp and broad-minded, you are usually willing to work hard to achieve your objectives. With your strong convictions, however, be careful how you communicate to others or you may appear stubborn or bossy. A strong creative streak in your character and a gift with words can be developed through writing, drama, or the arts. Alternatively, you may utilize your good ideas and creativity in business. Positively focused, you are enterprising, courageous, and optimistic. Your natural philosophical approach to life usually ensures that when you encounter problems you are not down for long.

♠ THE ACE OF SPADES ♠

Strong-willed and resolute, you can be successful in life through the combination of your determination and ability to work hard. Under the influences of Mercury and Neptune in the Earthly Spread, you possess imagination and a keen and perceptive mind. Although your sharp intelligence allows you to be helpful and insightful, guard against being stubborn.

With the influences of Uranus and Saturn in the Spiritual Spread, you value your independence and do not usually like to take orders, unless it is from someone you really respect. You often do best working for yourself or in a position where you are given the freedom to work in your own way. Although you can be good at realizing your needs, at times frustration can cause you to become overly serious or demanding. By finding ways to lift up the more idealistic and humanitarian side of your nature you can always overcome despondency and be a powerful force for good. Equally, finding a way to delve into the secrets of the universe can answer an unconscious need for something more profound in your life. As a Spade Card your work proves to be an important key in your life purpose. When you combine this with the power of an Ace you have the strength and force to cut through life's obstacles and make things happen. Initiating new projects or pioneering work can be especially beneficial for you.

Your Two Replacement Cards Are the 7 of Hearts & the 2 of Clubs.

As the Ace of Spades you share the same planetary position as the 7 of Hearts in the Spiritual Spread. This signifies that inside you are more sensitive than you appear from your strong personality front. The more you connect emotionally to your inner faith the more you can react to what life puts before you positively and spontaneously.

Your Ace of Spades Card also shares the same planetary position as the 2 of Clubs in the Earthly Spread. This indicates that you

usually fare better when you utilize your natural psychological skills to deal with people diplomatically rather than by being too forceful. Sharing your sharp wit or sense of irony with others can keep you entertained and help you overcome hidden insecurities, but avoid being too provocative. Although independent and strong-willed, you realize the many advantages of collaborative efforts and sharing with others.

You have special or karmic links with people represented by the 7 of Hearts or the 2 of Clubs. As you share the same planetary positions you can be soul mates or understand each other really well. Even if you do not get along, you can both see clearly how the other person operates.

Your Mercury Card is . . .

The 7 of Hearts
- You have the ideal combination of both an analytical yet emotionally sensitive intellect.
- In early life you may have experienced times when you felt really loved then slightly out in the cold.
- Although mentally shrewd, you also possess an idealistic side to your nature that seeks inspiration and knowledge.
- You respond particularly well to creative, imaginative, or positive visions for the future.

The Ace of Spades Planetary Card Sequence

NEPTUNE   URANUS   SATURN   JUPITER   MARS   VENUS   MERCURY

- People who are the 7 of Hearts are likely to stimulate your high ideals or desire to communicate.

Your Venus Card is . . .

The 7 of Diamonds
- Although you can be very giving, in your love life you may alternate between being too hard or too soft.
- When the time is right you can turn on the charm and be sociable and cooperative.
- To avoid feeling isolated in relationships with others, develop your ability to go with the flow and move on rather than dwell on the past.
- Ideally, you need a partner who can match your sharp intelligence.
- 7 of Diamonds people can help you be more loving and spontaneous and are especially good for romance, close friendships, or good business partnerships.

Your Mars Card is . . .

The 5 of Spades
- You possess energy, vitality, and drive that can help your advancement in life.
- Channel any tendency to be impulsive or restless into new adventures, travel, or a desire to help others.
- In your eagerness to bring about improvements remember that learning patience is one of your most powerful lessons.
- You possess fast instincts that can lead you to take charge of situations where others are dithering.
- 5 of Spades people can stimulate your enthusiasm, drive, and productive activity, but avoid being competitive, impatient, or argumentative.

Your Jupiter Card is . . .

The Jack of Hearts
- You possess powerful emotions that can lift you up to the stars or cause you to feel sorry for yourself.
- By being willing to make sacrifices, with the right attitude you can stay open and loving.
- A playful or creative side to your personality can help you to develop artistic, musical, writing, or dramatic gifts; it may also encourage you to inspire others.
- You can be fortunate through opportunities from abroad.
- People who are the Jack of Hearts can expand your horizons and emotionally make you feel more optimistic, though avoid overindulgence. This can be a fortunate or spiritual link.

Your Saturn Card is . . .

The 9 of Clubs
- As you enjoy being up-to-date you especially gain from expanding your knowledge and skills.
- Do not allow frustration or discouragement to undermine your capacity for self-discipline and hard work.
- As a perfectionist you need work that challenges you to activate your outstanding potential.
- When you are enthusiastic about a project or goal you make a good teacher or leader, as you enjoy sharing your knowledge with others.
- 9 of Clubs people can act as teachers or help you realize your own shortcomings. If you are willing to work on your self-awareness these people can bring valuable lessons.

Your Uranus Card is . . .

The 9 of Spades
- If disappointed with others you may become stubborn or rebellious at your own cost.
- Developing your humanitarian tendencies can help you see your personal life from a larger perspective.
- The more detached you become the more you remove an underlying negativity resulting from inner struggles.
- If you work for others in a spirit of true humility you can achieve much happiness.
- You possess the potential for higher wisdom when you persevere with the things you know to be for your own good.
- 9 of Spades people can act to make you see your own situation more objectively or dispassionately; this is also a good link for friendship or stimulating original ideas.

Your Neptune Card is . . .

The 2 of Hearts
- Your emotional receptivity can work for you, making you courteous and affectionate.
- If you become oversensitive you can appear moody or too easily hurt.
- With your longing for the ideal love relationship you must be careful to get the balance right between staying independent and giving to others.
- You possess strong vision and imagination or natural healing ability.
- 2 of Hearts people can connect to your dreams or positively stimulate you to be more loving and compassionate. Alternatively, you may both fall into escapism or develop unrealistically high expectations. There is a psychic link between you.

Your Challenge Card is . . .

The King of Hearts
- Use your natural emotional power and leadership skills in a way that leads through love rather than force.
- Do not allow a busy social life to distract you from the discipline needed to achieve your goals.
- King of Hearts people can challenge you to be more emotionally powerful, but guard against getting locked into ego clashes with them.

The Result of Your Challenge Card is . . .

The King of Diamonds
- Take your position as a leader or an authority figure with a good set of values.
- Help or inspire others with your talents and expertise.
- If you are being too materialistic you may need to review your challenge.
- King of Diamonds people can encourage you to take a creative approach to your life situations and show you how you are responding to your challenges.

Famous People Who Are the Ace of Spades

Jennifer Aniston, Pamela Anderson, Francis Ford Coppola, George Gurdjieff, Karl Marx, Deborah Harry, Tammy Wynette, Burt Reynolds, Sheryl Crow, Josephine Baker, Dan Ackroyd, Bobby Fischer, Soren Kierkegaard, Thomas Edison, Allen Ginsberg, Kelly Rowland, Ornette Coleman, Olivia de Haviland, Billie Holiday, Twyla Tharp, Jackie Chan, William Wordsworth, Curtis Mayfield, Tony Curtis, Liv Tyler, Princess Diana, Russell Crowe

Birthdays Governed by the Ace of Spades

January 13: Capricorn   Ruler: Saturn

Although hard work is associated with your birthday, you can achieve outstanding results through the blend of your determination and strong willpower. A natural creative element can also bring you joy or emotional satisfaction if you can overcome the pessimistic side to your nature. You find it easier to let go of negative thoughts if you develop a positive philosophy on life. Equally, finding work that stretches your sharp intellect particularly aids your rise to success in life. Although practical, you also possess heightened sensitivity that can guide you in your life choices or help others with your special insight.

February 11: Aquarius   Ruler: Uranus

Being friendly yet with a strong sense of individuality, you usually seek people or activities that keep your interest. When positive you are generous and broad-minded in your outlook. By using your natural sense of humor or understanding of human nature to stay detached or let go of the past you are able to overcome many of your difficulties or problems. The study of spiritual or metaphysical subjects can also help you get a larger perspective on life. Being very sociable, your relationships are highly important to you, but avoid being too demanding or dependent on others. Strong-willed and determined, you gain much from the courage to experiment in life.

March 9: Pisces   Ruler: Neptune

Mentally sharp and extra sensitive, you may have to overcome a tendency to go from emotional highs to lows. Being a person of extremes suggests that it is important for you to balance your strong will and independent nature with your natural sympathy and powerful need for relationships. Having imagination and initiative indicates that you can be a practical visionary who enjoys initiating new projects or working to make your dreams come true. Generous and kind, you also possess an idealistic or humanitarian side of your nature. Naturally intuitive, you can particularly profit from channeling your strong emotions into giving to others.

April 7: Aries   Ruler: Mars

Determined yet thoughtful, you are a natural leader who enjoys initiating new ventures or experimenting in untried areas. Often bored with day-to-day routine, you need projects that keep you excited and enthusiastic. If negative, your strong analytical abilities can lead you to become cynical or too self-absorbed, but when you have faith in yourself and your talents, your powerful spirit can encourage others. Behind your confident and assertive exterior you can be sensitive and idealistic, although sometimes people interpret your stubborn resolve as arrogance. Nevertheless, the combination of your drive and perfectionism can work together to bring you greater self-awareness and material achievement.

May 5: Taurus   Ruler: Venus

Practical, analytical, and mentally sharp, yet sociable and affectionate, you need variety to stop you from getting bored or restless. Your strong instincts and desire for different experiences can sometimes be at odds with your need for stability and security. By disciplining your strong will and developing the faith to live spontaneously you can often achieve the freedom you need. Being resourceful and reflective certainly helps you in your quest for success. You usually work best when you channel a tendency to become self-absorbed into inspiring others with your drive and self-awareness.

June 3: Gemini   Ruler: Mercury

Very quick on the uptake, you enjoy learning and expressing yourself. Creative and original in your approach, you need to be working on projects that utilize your sociable nature and many talents. If you ignore your ideals or allow yourself to succumb to worry or indecision, however, you may find yourself becoming cynical or falling short of your outstanding potential. Certainly the use of your excellent communication skills, whether through writing, presentation of your ideas, or being a good conversationalist, greatly aids you in your overall achievement.

July 1: Cancer   Ruler: Moon

Although the combination of your sensitivity, strong will, and natural leadership can sometimes be difficult early in life, as you grow older and start giving more to others your life takes on a deeper and more meaningful purpose. You have much to offer the world with your knowledge and insight if you can overcome a too strong self-interest. Even though you usually like to be in control, your family can be one area where you are willing to make sacrifices to create harmony. Although you may sometimes crave security yourself, if you develop your innate healing powers or desire to serve, you can find great satisfaction as a rock of support for others.

♥ ♣ THE 2 s ♦ ♠

THIS NUMBER BRINGS an emphasis on relationships and cooperation with others. If you are a 2 Card you constantly seek feedback and may sometimes feel incomplete on your own. As well as a flair for people, this number also emphasizes social skills and sharing, so you usually accomplish more by uniting your talents with those of others. Even though you can be considerate and diplomatic, it is important to also keep your independence in order that you achieve a good balance between giving and receiving. If not, people may take advantage of your kind nature or you can weaken yourself by becoming dependent on others. At the other extreme you may need to learn how to be confrontational without being aggressive. Usually friendly and courteous, your card number can stimulate an interest in public relations and negotiation as well as in emphasizing your partnerships and collaborative efforts. Negatively, your strong sensitivity can make you fearful, easily hurt, or lacking in self-confidence unless you can face your fears and overcome them.

2 of Hearts

This card places an emphasis on all love relationships, but especially on romance and friendship. Sensitive to the feelings of others, you may sometimes experience a fear of being alone. You can usually overcome this through giving emotional support to others while still taking care of your own needs.

2 of Clubs

As you often need others for mental stimulation, partnerships can bring enthusiasm and the sharing of ideas. Your ability to understand paradox or irony naturally can activate your sense of humor. Avoid being argumentative.

2 of Diamonds

You have an awareness of relationships or contacts that can produce material rewards. This is good for sales, negotiation, promotion, and public relations. Avoid negative fears about not having enough money.

2 of Spades

This card is good for collaborative work efforts or working partnerships. It is, however, vital for you to get the balance right between being independent or dependent in your close relationships. Usually sociable, sensitive, and considerate, you may have to overcome a contrary streak that can cause a lack of cooperation.

♥ THE 2 OF HEARTS ♥

As a Hearts Card, love and emotional issues play a prominent part in your life agenda. The extra emphasis on relationships suggested by your 2 Card heightens your need for close associations with others. As the Neptune Card in the Venus line of the Earthly Spread, you are sensitive as well as sociable. This enables you to put yourself in other people's shoes, enhancing your natural courtesy and consideration. Highly idealistic, you long for the perfect relationship, but a more practical side to your nature also knows you rarely achieve success without hard work. By developing a practical yet balanced approach to your love life you can avoid hidden fears or compromising too much of yourself for security.

As well as a need to reach out to others, your imaginative nature needs a clear vision or goals to keep you from escaping into fantasies. As the Venus Card in the Mercury line in the Spiritual Spread, communication is also a vital key to success in your life plan. With excellent people skills you have something to say and a friendly and charming way of saying it. You can be diplomatic and enjoy beauty and har-

mony. Your natural flair for public relations helps you in all areas of your life.

Your Replacement Card Is the Ace of Clubs.

As the 2 of Hearts your card belongs to the group of cards called the semi-fixed cards (see page 24). This means that you share the same planetary position as the Ace of Clubs in both the Spiritual Spread and the Earthly Spread. This doubly strong link with the Ace of Clubs signifies that as you are mentally smart, you possess a powerful inner need for knowledge. You enjoy initiating new projects and the discovery of new cutting-edge information. At times, the independent side to your nature can be at odds with your desire for the perfect relationship. This emphasizes the need for you to lead a well-balanced life. This involves keeping your finger on the pulse of what others feel, yet still developing your own mental abilities and latent leadership skills. Nevertheless, some of your happiest times are in relationships or working collaboratively with others.

You have a special or karmic link with people represented by the Ace of Clubs. As you share the same planetary positions you can be soul mates or understand each other very well. Even if you do not get along, you can both see clearly how the other person operates.

Your Mercury Card is . . .

The King of Hearts
- Kindhearted and entertaining, you have a talent for working with the public.
- You can communicate in a daring and dramatic way.
- You must avoid becoming temperamental or self-indulgent.
- If a woman, although feminine, you can think in a straightforward way like a man.

The 2 of Hearts Planetary Card Sequence

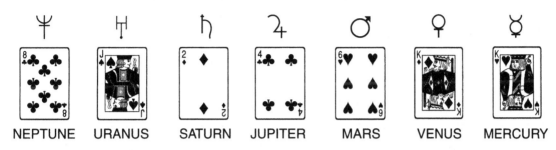

| NEPTUNE | URANUS | SATURN | JUPITER | MARS | VENUS | MERCURY |

- There was likely to be a particularly strong influence in youth from an older man, probably your father.
- King of Hearts people can bring you good ideas and stimulate your communication skills, though you both may want to be the boss.

Your Venus Card is . . .

The King of Diamonds
- You can quickly and astutely evaluate people and situations.
- You are likely to be artistic or creative or enjoy mixing with theatrical people.
- A love of beauty, luxury, and the good life suggests you have a hint of vanity and expensive tastes.
- If a woman, you will be attracted to partners who are materially astute and leaders in their fields.
- People who are Kings of Diamonds can particularly bring love and friendship into your life. This link is good for business as well as romance.

Your Mars Card is . . .

The 6 of Hearts
- Your deep desire for peace indicates you would prefer to avoid direct conflicts.

- Having a safe and secure home and harmonious environment can be especially important to you.
- Lack of positive action or too much action can lead you to suffer from anxiety or feeling overly responsible for others.
- People who are the 6 of Hearts can stimulate you to be more motivated, although avoid becoming competitive or antagonistic.

Your Jupiter Card is . . .

The 4 of Clubs
- Once you have a definite plan for the future this enhances your optimism and confidence.
- You value honesty and people who are straight with you.
- A stubborn or self-satisfied streak can sometimes jeopardize your chances with others.
- When you combine your practicality with enthusiasm you can strike good business deals.
- 4 of Clubs people can stimulate your love of knowledge, provide opportunities, and be good for you financially or spiritually.

Your Saturn Card is . . .

The 2 of Diamonds

- Unfounded fears of not having enough money for your needs can cause you to become overly serious.
- Good negotiation skills and an ability to make contacts can help you achieve your goals.
- It is important for you to have clear aims and objectives, as when you are actively directed toward your goals you can be very determined and tenacious.
- You have to have equal give and take in your relationships with others or you can encounter obstacles and health problems.
- 2 of Diamonds people can show you where you need to work on yourself. This can be challenging or enlightening. Although your relationship with them may not always be easy, their contributions are often very valuable lessons.

Your Uranus Card is . . .

The Jack of Spades

- A youthful and entertaining streak will be part of your nature even until old age.
- You gain from developing your innate humanitarian potential.
- You will work hard when inspired or when you feel you owe it to others.
- You possess natural creativity that can bring you original ideas and make you ahead of your time.
- People who are the Jack of Spades can stimulate your originality and individuality. They can also give you objective feedback and make good friends.

Your Neptune Card is . . .

The 8 of Clubs

- Powerful intuition can help you overcome obstacles or attract you to more spiritual alternatives.
- Image conscious, you have an attractive voice and like to present yourself in an engaging way.
- You are very clever as well as sensitive, but avoid subtle mental power games with others.
- The later years of your life can be most rewarding for the development of your fine intellect.
- You can have a strong psychic link with 8 of Clubs people. They may link to your dreams and ideals. In these relationships, however, you may need to guard against delusion by staying realistic.

Your Challenge Card is . . .

The 6 of Diamonds

- Use your caring or creative nature rather than get stuck in a comfortable rut.
- Create a harmonious environment around you, such as your home, as a haven of peace from the world.
- Stay balanced by giving a little bit of time and energy to everything that needs attention at the time.
- Realize what you put in is what you get back.
- 6 of Diamonds people can challenge you and bring out the best or the worst in you.

The Result of Your Challenge Card is . . .

The 4 of Spades

- You feel optimistic about the future.
- You are working to build solid foundations for what you want to achieve.

- You are being totally honest with others.
- You can see reflected in people who are the 4 of Spades how well you are responding to your challenges.

Famous People Who Are the 2 of Hearts

Ted Danson, Jon Voight, Mary Tyler Moore, Marianne Faithfull, Pablo Casals, Jude Law

Birthdays Governed by the 2 of Hearts

December 29: Capricorn   Ruler: Saturn
Charming, sensitive, and imaginative, yet also mentally sharp, you succeed by combining your excellent communication and people skills. Practical and materially shrewd, you can be diligent in your work or in support of your beliefs. Usually amiable and kindhearted, you are diplomatic and refined with good social graces. If you lose your emotional balance, however, you can become moody or difficult. Nevertheless, usually you are gifted with many creative ideas, a persuasive manner, and a talent for promotion. Even though you are usually concerned with financial security, as an idealist you gain greatly from listening to the guidance of your strong intuitive side.

♣ THE 2 OF CLUBS ♣

As a 2 card of the Clubs suit you are a people person with a sharp and active mind. Keeping a positive mental rapport in your relationships with others is a major key to your happiness and success. Friendly and sociable, you enjoy figuring out what motivates others and are a natural psychologist. As the Saturn Card in the Uranus line of the Earthly Spread you can always come up with unique ways to solve problems or express your original ideas. When disciplined, your outstanding intellect and people skills can take you to positions of power. Your rebel streak, however, may sometimes cause you to sabotage what you have built up or stimulate erratic behavior. Nevertheless, being tenacious and persevering, you often succeed through sheer determination.

As the Mercury Card in the Mars line in the Spiritual Spread your quick thinking can make you witty and smart, with fast responses. With your desire for knowledge and a shrewd intellect you are an assertive communicator and enjoy a good debate, but avoid being argumentative, impatient, or too provocative. An interesting mixture of contrasts, you can appear independent and self-assured, yet deep down you still learn much about yourself from watching your interactions with others. One of your best assets is your wry humor, which often allows you to see the ridiculousness of situations and enables you to stay mentally balanced.

Your Two Replacement Cards Are the Ace of Spades & the King of Hearts.

As the 2 of Clubs, you share the same planetary position as the Ace of Spades in the Spiritual Spread. This signifies that you possess natural leadership ability and will work very hard when focused on a definite goal. You also possess an ability to display moments of insight at extremely fast speed. At times, however, hidden fears may cause you to become overly serious, resulting in your being obstinate or moody. Being highly intuitive, however, the more you learn to trust your instincts the easier it is to access your great store of inner wisdom.

Being a 2 of Clubs, you also share the same planetary position as the King of Hearts in the Earthly Spread. This indicates that you are often a gregarious, kind, and generous individual who enjoys keeping others entertained. Proud and naturally dramatic, you possess strong emotional power, which if you channel constructively can aid your success and help others.

You have special or karmic links with people represented by the Ace of Spades or the King of Hearts. As you share the same planetary positions you can be soul mates or understand each other very well. Even if you do not get along, you can both see clearly how the other person operates.

Your Mercury Card is . . .

The King of Clubs
- You enjoy mentally sparring with others so often say things just to get a reaction.
- Your sharp mind gives you natural leadership ability.
- You can think and communicate in a bold and dramatic way.
- If a woman, although feminine, you can think in a straightforward way like a man.
- There was likely to be a particularly strong influence in youth from an older man, probably your father.
- King of Clubs people can heighten your communication skills, stimulate your ideas, and be good partners for stimulating your wit or fast mental responses.

Your Venus Card is . . .

The Jack of Diamonds
- You possess a playful quality that will stay with you until old age. Although this heightens your social skills, it can also be developed to give you excellent musical, creative, dramatic, or writing skills.
- You are attracted to youthful, stylish, or theatrical people, as well as to those who have a skill in handling money.
- If unrestrained, at times you may display an immature streak that can cause trouble in your relationships.
- Jack of Diamonds people can particularly bring love and friendship into your life. This link is good for business as well as friendship and romance.

Your Mars Card is . . .

The 4 of Hearts
- You possess a generous and warm-hearted side to your nature that enjoys being of practical help to others.
- Once in action you can be fully emotionally involved.
- Although frank and direct guard against an impulsive or stubborn streak in your nature that can cause you trouble.

The 2 of Clubs Planetary Card Sequence

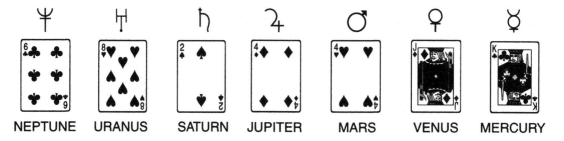

NEPTUNE   URANUS   SATURN   JUPITER   MARS   VENUS   MERCURY

- 4 of Hearts Card people can stimulate you to be more enterprising, dynamic, or daring. Alternatively, you may become competitive or argumentative with them.

Your Jupiter Card is . . .

The 4 of Diamonds
- Once you have a definite plan in life a practical side to your nature will always protect you financially.
- Your work is particularly important to your sense of well-being.
- To make the most of your natural talents you need to build for the future.
- This card in Jupiter provides you with lucky opportunities to achieve success.
- 4 of Diamonds Card people can stimulate your optimism or be fortunate for you in some way. They can provide opportunities or be a spiritual link.

Your Saturn Card is . . .

The 2 of Spades
- Your tests in life can especially center around the area of your partnerships or one-to-one relationships. This can be where you are called upon to be the most responsible.
- When you work cooperatively with others you can achieve good results and enhance your personal power.
- Becoming dependent on others, whether financially or emotionally, causes you to become depressed or frustrated.
- You possess inner strong healing powers you use for yourself or others.
- 2 of Spades people can show you where you need to work on yourself. They can particularly show you where you need to be balanced and independent, as well as to have clear boundaries. This can be testing or instructive.

Your Uranus Card is . . .

The 8 of Hearts
- The emotional power of the 8 of Hearts suggests that the more friendly, objective, and universal you become, the greater your ability to influence others.
- You can be highly inventive and have a knack for combining business and pleasure.
- When you decide to turn on the charm you can be charismatic and dynamic.
- 8 of Hearts people can be good friends or provide you with extra objectivity about yourself or your circumstances.

Your Neptune Card is . . .

The 6 of Clubs
- You have a vivid imagination that can be especially helpful in envisioning your next step in life. Avoid using it in negative thinking, as this can make you anxious.
- You possess strong intuition that can help you greatly if you listen to it.
- Indications are that your later years will be peaceful and home-oriented. Although life can become more relaxed, you are still likely to have many interests to keep your mind active.
- You can have a strong psychic link with people who are the 6 of Clubs Card. You may share the same dreams, but guard against the disappointment that comes from unreasonably high expectations.

Your Challenge Card is . . .

The 6 of Spades
- Create a harmonious or caring atmosphere for yourself and others without being too bossy or interfering.
- Transmute worry or monotony with life into work on realizing your ideals.

- 6 of Spades people usually can dare you to react and bring out the best or the worst aspects of your personality. Your Challenge link also indicates that although these people can help you to transform your life, resist becoming involved in power struggles.

The Result of Your Challenge Card is . . .

The Queen of Hearts

- Being dramatic, you love an audience. Just how others around you respond to your life performance is a good measure of how you are dealing with your challenges.
- People who are the Queen of Hearts can resonate with you emotionally and reflect how you are responding to your tests.

Famous People Who Are the 2 of Clubs

Mick Jagger, Carl Jung, Wynonna Judd, Benny Goodman, A. S. Byatt, Jean Jacques Rousseau, Snoop Dogg, Mel Brooks, Peter Paul Rubens, John Cusack, Kathy Bates, Aldous Huxley, Stanley Kubrick, Blake Edwards, Philip K. Dick, Joan Jett, George Bernard Shaw, Jane Austen, Michael Faraday, Fay Weldon, Margaret Mead, Ludwig van Beethoven, Tom Petty, Sandra Bullock, Noel Coward, Arthur C. Clarke, Kevin Spacey

Birthdays Governed by the 2 of Clubs

May 30: Gemini   Ruler: Mercury

Possessing very fast mental responses and a friendly personality, you are a quick learner with good social skills. Having a gift for words, whether written or spoken, you can be an excellent communicator, as long as you don't become too confrontational. Your talent for synthesizing information and your natural creativity can combine to help you in your rise to the top. You may have to overcome worry or feelings of insecurity, however. Working in partnerships that stimulate your mental ingenuity and resourcefulness can be particularly positive for you.

June 28: Cancer   Ruler: Moon

Sympathetic and caring yet strong-willed and proud, you have your finger on the pulse of public opinion. With leadership potential you may decide to use your good psychological skills to help others. Equally, you are a good organizer and can succeed in enterprising ventures. Since you are so sensitive it is essential to keep your emotions channeled into positive areas, where they can bring many rewards. Although you are ambitious, your home and family play an especially important part in your life agenda, so it is essential to balance work and family time.

July 26: Leo   Ruler: Sun

Being proud and determined, and with a strong sense of the dramatic, you enjoy your independence. You equally realize the importance of working as part of a team with so many advantages to be gained from partnerships or cooperative ventures. A quick and creative thinker with the ability to make fast decisions, you can be witty and entertaining and enjoy an intellectual challenge. Although usually fortunate, you may have to watch a tendency to push your luck or go too far. Nevertheless, you can be very supportive of others in their times of need.

August 24: Virgo   Ruler: Mercury

Intelligent and precise, your astute and discerning intellect can prove to be one of your greatest assets. Self-assurance comes from being diligent and hardworking with an ability to pay attention to the detail. Although usually quiet and dignified, you can sometimes be provocative and surprising. Equally, an inner dramatic sense can emerge to place you in leading positions. Responsible and home loving, you gain much from your gift for clear communication and an ability to be of practical service to others.

September 22: Virgo   Ruler: Mercury

Born on the cusp, you have the friendly people skills of Libra and the shrewd intellect of Virgo. With your keen mentality you are a natural communicator, and have progressive ideas and intuitive insight into human nature. Being sensitive as well as analytical, avoid going over anxieties in your mind and making yourself nervous. Although practical with a perfectionist streak, you particularly value your emotional relationships and can be highly intuitive. Although you have a talent for criticism, be careful to use it positively rather than to start arguments.

October 20: Libra   Ruler: Venus

Persuasive with good social skills and artistic potential, you can achieve much if you develop and discipline your natural talents. As relationships are a major emphasis in your life, you are interested in understanding others, but be careful of dependent situations. It is important to balance the two sides of your personality, as you can be both sensitive, tactful, and considerate and outspoken, moody, or sarcastic. Nevertheless, your excellent brain power and desire for justice can contribute much to your success. Being impressionable, you also need a harmonious working environment.

November 18: Scorpio   Ruler: Mars

Strong-willed with definite opinions, you can be a law unto yourself. You are mentally quick and humorous with insight into the personalities of others, but your provocative side can also get you into trouble. Once set on a course of action, you are pointed and relentless in pursuit of your goals. This definitely works in your favor when you are doing the right thing. With your strong "death and rebirth" Scorpio energy you may find yourself going through a few total transformations in the course of your life. Although very proud and independent, you still gain much from joint ventures with others.

December 16: Sagittarius   Ruler: Jupiter

Friendly and mentally sharp, you usually succeed through the use of your superior intellect and fast responses. Although you can display a proud and confident persona to the world, you can also be thoughtful. Nevertheless, guard against being impatient or too opinionated. Optimistic and enterprising, you usually seek inspiration, particularly through travel, law, religion, spirituality, education, or the arts. Equally, you may prefer experimenting with bold ventures. Analytical as well as intuitive, you have good insight into people.

♦THE 2 OF DIAMONDS♦

Although you are often ambitious and single-minded, the key to your accomplishment is usually linked to your people skills and cooperative efforts. You particularly gain from partnerships and have an ability to make helpful contacts. As you are likely to possess two different sides to your personality, one tough and focused and the other soft and idealistic, it is important for you to avoid going to extremes by developing equilibrium. Being a Diamond Card implies that you can increase your prospects for success by establishing a clear set of values and getting your priorities right. In order to maintain stability in your life you also need to feel financially secure. Paradoxically, this is often achieved when you minimize your worries about money. Fortunately, your card suggests that you will have many opportunities to display your natural business acumen so your fears over money issues are often more habit than rational.

The planetary influences of Saturn and Mars in your Earthly Spread indicate that you need to combine your willpower and desire for action with patience and perseverance. When you couple your determination and resolve with your networking skills you can be highly persuasive. This indicates that you are very good at selling or promoting an ideal, concept or product as long as you really believe in it. Although at times you need to overcome inner doubts or frustration, you can also be an excellent strategist. When focused on a definite goal and acting decisively, you can be very hard-working and achieve remarkable results.

The influences of Neptune and Jupiter in your Spiritual Spread suggests that you also have strong imagination, profound insights, and an attraction toward the arts or healing. When expressing your natural sensitivity you can be sympathetic and generous. You often obtain the most satisfaction when you combine your desire to help others with your enterprising spirit and focused determination.

Your Two Replacement Cards Are the 6 of Clubs & the Ace of Diamonds.

As the 2 of Diamonds you share the same planetary position as the Ace of Diamonds in the Earthly Spread. This signifies that you are a dynamic individual with strong desires, especially for power or material success. Although this Ace provides you with leadership qualities and strong ambition, it becomes a challenge if you act too independently or with no regard for others. Nevertheless, as an intuitive and idealistic individual with natural business sense and good negotiating skills, you can mo-

tivate others and initiate new and profitable projects that benefit all.

You also share the same planetary position as the 6 of Clubs in the Spiritual Spread. Since this card is often associated with the dissemination of knowledge and ideas, it is your positive outlook, original ideas, and creative thinking that lead you to accomplishment and monetary gains. This card also indicates that you possess an inner pride and strong need for recognition that can drive you to accomplish. At times this may conflict with your need for a peace and harmony that emphasizes the importance of a secure and congenial home environment.

Usually you have special or karmic links with people represented by the 6 of Clubs and the Ace of Diamonds. You can be soul mates or understand each other very well since you share the same planetary positions. Even if you do not get along, you can both share similar characteristics.

Your Mercury Card is . . .

The Jack of Spades
- This royal card emphasizes your shrewd insightfulness and sharp intelligence.
- A rebellious streak from youth may have influenced you.
- Your intuition or an interest in metaphysical subjects can widen your horizons and shed light on many profound issues that may concern you.
- Your quick perception and flair for the dramatic can spark your creativity and special talents, especially writing, art, music, dancing, or acting.
- You should have good mental rapport and special communication with people represented by the Jack of Spades, as they activate your Mercury Card.

The 2 of Diamonds Planetary Card Sequence

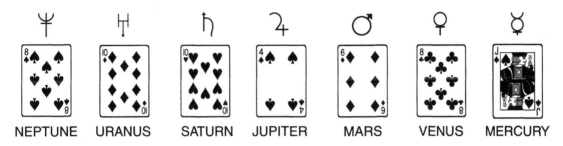

| NEPTUNE | URANUS | SATURN | JUPITER | MARS | VENUS | MERCURY |

Your Venus Card is . . .

The 8 of Clubs

- With your good sense of structure you can visualize your actions and turn your ideas into tangible results.
- Usually you are attracted to clever and powerful individuals with strong convictions.
- You can use your charm and people skills in business.
- Although you can be fixed in your views, avoid being stubborn or getting hooked into power and control struggles with close loved ones.
- Debates, discussions, and intellectual or creative activities stimulate your imagination and benefit your relationships.
- Usually you are attracted to 8 of Clubs people, as they are ideal for love and romance as well as close friendships and good business partnerships.

Your Mars Card is . . .

The 6 of Diamonds

- Adopting a good sense of values and developing a pragmatic approach to money can stop you from acting in haste or getting into debt.
- Financial gains can motivate you into action and help you overcome an inherent ten-

dency to procrastinate or fall into the monotony of the tried and tested.
- The law of values suggested by this card indicates that when you put a great deal of effort into a project, you get your just rewards.
- The relationships you have with 6 of Diamonds people can be special if you both share the same aspirations. Resist being competitive with these people, however, or they can drain your resources.

Your Jupiter Card is . . .

The 4 of Spades

- This card suggests that you are fortunate when it comes to work opportunities.
- You prefer to be direct and honest in your dealings with others.
- You benefit from establishing steadfastness or a firm foundation at work and in your private life.
- A philanthropic streak stimulates your generosity.
- 4 of Spades people can be of help to you or be linked with work opportunities. If you are in business or partnership with them you can both be successful.

Your Saturn Card is . . .

The 10 of Hearts

- If you adopt a selfish attitude it will usually backfire on you.
- Your caring and friendly manner can enhance your success in people-related activities.
- Although at times you can be too emotionally sensitive and your major tests in life usually revolve around love, you also have the inner power to heal yourself.
- Your social activities and being popular are important to your overall well-being.
- You will always find a helping hand when you need it most.
- While you can attract many people, avoid becoming involved in emotionally demanding situations.
- 10 of Hearts people can play an important role in your life if you are able to learn from them about loyalty and dependability. Although your relationship with them may not always be easy, their contributions are often very valuable lessons.

Your Uranus Card is . . .

The 10 of Diamonds

- You possess excellent organizational skills and your ideas can be modern, effective, and profitable.
- You can gain materially through friendships.
- Opportunities for material success can appear out of the blue.
- You may be engaged in promoting innovative ideas, especially in careers relating to the public.
- Success and achievement often occur in middle age.
- Your altruistic interests may lead you to humanitarian or public work.

- 10 of Diamonds people can offer you valuable insights into what is truly valuable in life or new financial opportunities. This is also a good card for friendship.

Your Neptune Card is . . .

The 8 of Spades

- Your self-confidence in taking charge, or opportunities to demonstrate your capabilities, will increase with time.
- When working constructively you can be a powerful visionary for yourself or others.
- Your steady progress is rewarded in the second part of life.
- Your endurance and stamina will not diminish with the passing years, so you are likely to be very active even in old age.
- 8 of Spades people can help you to empower yourself or they can connect to your dreams. They may inspire you spiritually, although you have to be clear in your dealings, as there could be issues of control or power games.

Your Challenge Card is . . .

The Ace of Hearts

- If you act impulsively your strong desires may become a challenge to you.
- You empower yourself when you fully understand what motivates you emotionally.
- Resist letting your ego get the better of you, as this can make you bossy, too demanding, or undermine your popularity.
- You have the potential to lead others by projecting love or loving what you do.
- Ace of Hearts people can force you to face some of your emotional issues. They may reflect aspects of your behavior you do not like. Nevertheless, they can also help you transform yourself for the better.

The Result of Your Challenge Card is . . .

The Ace of Diamonds
- Being highly motivated is often one of the keys to your success.
- Initiating new projects can be enjoyable and highly profitable.
- When you heed your inner voice, money, power, and success usually follow.
- Ace of Diamonds people can motivate you or help you to realize some of your ambitious plans. Your reaction to them often reflects how you are responding to your challenges.

Famous People Who Are the 2 of Diamonds

Hugh Grant, Ozzy Osbourne, Virginia Woolf, Harrison Ford, J. S. Bach, Robert Burns, Jacqueline du Pre, Johnny Winter, Gram Parsons, Dennis Hopper, Ryan Adams, Peter Fonda, Leo Tolstoy, Timothy Dalton, Arthur Rackham, Dudley Moore, Yo-Yo Ma, R. D. Laing, Otis Redding, Sam Shepard, Julie Walters, Waylon Jennings, M. A. Rothchild, Jayne Mansfield, Paloma Picasso, Enya, Adam Sandler, Thom Yorke, Kate Hudson, Alicia Keyes, Courteney Cox Arquette

Birthdays Governed by the 2 of Diamonds

January 25: Capricorn   Ruler: Uranus
Your ruler, Uranus, adds stamina and determination to your ambitious nature. Its influence also allows you to judge people or situations quickly. Not afraid to think big, your analytical skills and innate business sense provide you with the opportunity to play a pivotal role in any successful enterprise. Since your success often depends on your good understanding of values, resist allowing inner fears or insecurity to undermine your confidence and sense of self-worth. By creating the balance of give and take in your cooperative efforts your relationships usually flourish. Intuitive and mentally creative, your original ideas can often bring large financial gains.

February 23: Pisces   Ruler: Neptune
As an intuitive and receptive individual your ability to relate to others suggests that partnerships or relationships are key to your happiness. Neptune, your ruler, can stimulate your imagination and vision. As an idealist, however, unless you feel truly inspired by an idea or project your resolve may not be so obvious. You may sometimes alternate between being very motivated and inert. Nevertheless, the incentive to make money and the determination to empower yourself often motivates you to do something worthwhile. Your idealistic notions or motives can encourage you to be philanthropic and help others.

March 21: Aries   Ruler: Mars
Your enthusiasm, drive, and gregariousness indicate that you are a highly motivated individual who enjoys interacting with others. Although you see the benefits that come from being cooperative, Mars, your ruler, often urges you to take a leading role. You can succeed when you find ways to express yourself and be of use to others. If you fail to establish a good balance in your relationships you can alternate from being moody or insecure to becoming overly confident, argumentative, or bossy. Nevertheless, when you instill a good sense of values into your financial affairs and your partnerships, the rule of cause and effect will truly work in your favor.

April 19: Aries   Ruler: Mars
Although your confidence and desire for action is accentuated by Mars, your ruler, your

success is often found in your cooperative efforts. Your natural leadership abilities and independent spirit suggest that you are bold enough to take the initiative. By establishing a good sense of values and learning to handle your financial responsibilities there is little that you cannot do. Your adventurous nature often brings you into contact with all types of people, and in order to avoid troublesome relationships you need to use your discriminative powers. Devoting time in equal measure to yourself and others can also help you to focus on what is important and create balance in your life.

May 17: Taurus   Ruler: Venus
According to Venus, your ruler, being productive, finding inner peace, and creating harmony are usually your main goals. Thoughtful and refined, your strength often lies in your strong convictions and ability to inspire others. Your intuition and analytical powers indicate that you gain your self-esteem and understanding from your emotional experiences. Therefore, the more you invest in your creative talents and education the more confident you become. Your sensitivity and subjective viewpoint imply that, although you are usually agreeable, when you feel insecure you often respond by being stubborn or uncooperative. Developing a more detached or objective philosophy can help you create better relationships with others.

June 15: Gemini   Ruler: Mercury
Young at heart and restless, Mercury, your ruler, indicates that you are a bright and dynamic individual with exceptional creative talents. Being astute and quick to grasp new ideas, in debates and discussions you are often a persuasive communicator. Although your easygoing manner can conceal the fact that you are ambitious and enterprising, when you feel inspired you can be hardworking and very determined. An innate stubborn streak, however, suggests that rather than listen to advice you often learn in retrospect from your past mistakes. Issues concerning maturity also imply that becoming responsible and self-disciplined is essential if you want to achieve success.

July 13: Cancer   Ruler: Moon
Sensitive, intuitive, and security conscious, your ruler, the Moon, signifies that by showing your friendly and caring nature you can often find emotional fulfillment. A tendency to become easily irritable warns against indulging in obstinate behavior based on fears and insecurities. When you can create and maintain emotional balance and inner harmony your success is often assured. If you indulge in negative feelings they can undermine your confidence and threaten your relationships. Nevertheless, as a talented, practical, and enterprising individual you usually have a developed sixth sense about people that can help you gauge their moods.

August 11: Leo   Ruler: Sun
Inspired, idealistic, and determined, your ruler, the Sun, suggests that you are often a dynamic individual with quick responses and an optimistic outlook. Although you are usually practical and full of energy, a tendency to fluctuate between great highs and equal lows warns that you need to be self-disciplined and to maintain a steady pace in order to succeed. Since you have natural leadership qualities and a compelling desire to be with others, you need to find the balance between your personal desires and the needs of people around you. Although you can be stubbornly proud or egocentric, with a touch of modesty you can usually restore your dignity and self-esteem.

September 9: Virgo   Ruler: Mercury

Intuitive and receptive, you can tap into deep emotional or mental levels. The double impact of the number 9 associated with your birth date also implies that spiritual awareness or an interest in metaphysical subjects can help you to discover unique talents and lead to personal fulfillment. Although usually generous and mentally sharp with good critical abilities, you may at times be too hard on yourself or others. The influence of your ruler, Mercury, suggests that through learning from disappointments you can overcome many of your personal challenges. Key ingredients to your success are often your self-discipline, creative mental expression, and ability to stay lighthearted when faced with responsibilities. You may also have a special talent for writing or presenting your ideas.

October 7: Libra   Ruler: Venus

The creative and mental power indicated by your birthday implies that you are a sensitive and unique individual. Your ruler, Venus, signifies that along with your refined taste and innate charm you also need to express yourself creatively. Usually your desire for knowledge can inspire you to delve into spiritual realms and transcend the ordinary. At times you may have to balance your need for your own space with your need for relationships with others. Much depends on your openness and ability to communicate your thoughts and feelings. Your engaging personality, creative talents, and excellent people skills imply that careers involving the public can lead to success and personal fulfillment.

November 5: Scorpio   Ruler: Mars

Although usually pleasant and composed, underneath your reserved manner you are a determined and mentally sharp individual. Your corulers, Mars and Pluto, reveal that the strength of your critical mind is usually well hidden and your biting cynicism can hit hard when you feel irritated or threatened. Nevertheless, your prosperity often lies in your ability to work successfully with others. Usually you minimize your inner restlessness or reluctance to compromise when you learn to discipline and restrain your intense emotions.

December 3: Sagittarius   Ruler: Jupiter

Adaptable and optimistic, Jupiter, your ruler, indicates that usually you are a clever and multitalented individual. Having many interests suggests that if you can overcome your tendency to scatter your energies in too many directions you are likely to succeed. By focusing on fewer goals you can also enjoy the good opportunities that pave your path. Although as a sociable and generous individual you possess a talent for mixing business and pleasure, avoid excessive indulgence in the good life, as it can weaken your determination. Nevertheless, much of the help and assistance you receive is through your contacts and friendships.

♠ THE 2 OF SPADES ♠

The number 2 usually symbolizes cooperation and partnerships. This signifies that you benefit greatly from working or interacting with others, so even if you are a self-reliant individual your potential for success is enhanced by your collaborative efforts.

The spiritual power of the Spades suit hints that there are mystical influences associated with your card. Your ability to create and maintain balance and equality is a major key to your success. Power games, anxieties, or fearfulness, on the other hand, can undermine your tremendous potential. The planetary influence of Mars and Neptune in your Earthly Spread signifies that you can accomplish a great deal if you combine your imaginative ideas and foresight with decisive action. You can also overcome many of your personal challenges by having faith in your capabilities and showing your determination.

The double influence of Uranus in your Spiritual Spread signifies that you are usually strong-willed, freedom loving, or unconventional. Although you value your independence, obstinacy, impulsiveness, or eccentric behavior can work against you. Developing your detached and objective viewpoint can enhance your personal development and increase your prosperity. Uranus can also provide flashes of inspiration that stimulate your bright ideas and highly inventive mind.

Your Two Replacement Cards Are the King of Clubs & the Six of Spades.

As the 2 of Spades you share the same planetary position as the King of Clubs in the Earthly Spread. This royal card gives you cerebral power and an ability to take the lead by using your mental acumen and determination. Although this card can provide you with strong analytical abilities and leadership qualities, it can become a hindrance if you try to force your opinions on others. Nevertheless,

you can obtain much satisfaction from sharing your special insight and knowledge.

Your card occupies the same planetary position as the 6 of Spades in the Spiritual Spread. This conveys the idea of idealism and the laws of cause and effect. In order to achieve your goals you may need to be responsible and put in a great deal of effort, but in return you will get your just rewards. The key here is often motivation and your ability to endure without feeling trapped in monotony. Your strong inner need for harmony may attract you to music, healing, or the arts.

You usually have special or karmic links with people represented by the King of Clubs and the 6 of Spades, as you share the same planetary positions. You can be soul mates or understand each other very well. Even if you do not get along, you can both see clearly how the other person operates.

Your Mercury Card is . . .

The 8 of Hearts
- Your warm approach suggests that you have the power to charm others.
- To greatly enhance your prospects use diplomacy and tact in your communications.
- Although you can be popular, avoid becoming involved in power games, as they can lead to emotional stress.

The 2 of Spades Planetary Card Sequence

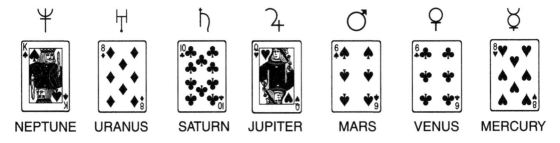

NEPTUNE   URANUS   SATURN   JUPITER   MARS   VENUS   MERCURY

- You can express your feelings through your creative intellectual activities.
- If you focus too much on yourself you may inadvertently come across as moody or selfish.
- You should have good mental rapport and special communication with people who represent the 8 of Hearts, as they can share your interests or be on your wavelength.

Your Venus Card is . . .

The 6 of Clubs

- You enjoy stimulating exchanges of ideas.
- Although security and harmony are important to you, especially in your home, avoid falling into a comfortable rut.
- Good communication is essential in your close relationships.
- You can express yourself well when you think creatively.
- You admire motivated people who are knowledgeable or well informed.
- Your Venus link implies that you are attracted to people who are the 6 of Clubs. This card can also represent business partnerships, close friendships, and romance.

Your Mars Card is . . .

The 6 of Spades

- You succeed when you persevere and turn your inspired ideals into actions.
- Although you are often a hard worker, resist letting fixed ideas, dissatisfaction, or stubbornness cause inertia or block your progress.
- Until you find the right vocation or career you may find it hard to be truly motivated.
- Your idealism and willingness to serve can aid your success.
- The relationships you have with 6 of Spades people can be good if you both share the same aspirations or stimulate each other into activity. Avoid being aggressive or competitive with these people.

Your Jupiter Card is . . .

The Queen of Hearts

- The emotional power of this royal card suggests that you are a creative, sensitive, and dramatic individual.
- You can benefit from the help of influential women.
- Your generosity and compassion can help you gain success and popularity.
- Working with people or being involved with humanitarian projects can be highly rewarding.
- Avoid being indulgent and acting on emotional impulses to relieve your boredom.
- Queen of Hearts people can be instrumental to your success or enhance your life. These people can expand your opportunities, inspire you creatively, or be the source of exciting ideas.

Your Saturn Card is . . .

The 10 of Clubs

- Your personal success often comes from using your natural leadership skills or persevering with intellectual accomplishments.
- Being smart, good education can further enhance your analytical abilities.
- Combining your insight and intuition with higher knowledge is a key to your success.
- You have the power to influence or heal others with your positive thoughts.
- 10 of Clubs people can play an important role in your life if you are able to learn from them. Although these relationships may not be easy, their contributions are often very valuable lessons.

Your Uranus Card is . . .

The 8 of Diamonds
- Safeguarded financially, you have a fortunate influence that can protect you from experiencing material hardship.
- When you correctly read current trends your original and innovative ideas can be very profitable.
- Although you may focus on monetary gains, do not overlook the spiritual advantages of this card.
- Financial rewards can come unexpectedly.
- 8 of Diamonds people can offer you valuable insight about business or people due to your Uranus connection. This is also a good card for friendship.

Your Neptune Card is . . .

The King of Spades
- The special power hidden in this royal card bestows great potential for achievement in the latter part of your life.
- By applying the power of this card to yourself you can display leadership qualities through hard work and the use of your vision and idealism.
- If you are interested in gaining insight into the profound complexities of life you can benefit from studying philosophy and spirituality, especially in your later years.
- You may wish to develop your sensitivity and imagination through photography, art, music, or healing.
- King of Spades people can help you realize your dreams. If they are wise and knowledgeable they can become your inspiration. They can also encourage you to follow a spiritual path. In these relationships, however, you may need to keep your feet firmly on the ground and guard against self-delusion.

Your Challenge Card is . . .

The 3 of Hearts
- Be clear and decisive about your feelings.
- Express your emotional needs.
- Be lighthearted or bring hope and harmony to your life and to others.
- Don't let negative emotions about love or friendship be the source of your discontent and disappointment.
- You may find it hard to express your creative talents if you are constantly changing your objectives.
- 3 of Hearts people can fascinate you but also provoke you. Although they may force you to express yourself, they can also touch upon your emotional insecurities or the worst aspects of your personality. Although these people can help you to transform your life, resist power conflicts with them.

The Result of Your Challenge Card is . . .

The Ace of Clubs
- You feel inspired when you increase your knowledge.
- You gain insight and learn about your personal relationships.
- New ideas can flow freely when you feel emotionally secure and hopeful.
- You can kick-start your career by being decisive about your future objectives.
- When you feel confident you can initiate and promote new products or concepts.
- Ace of Clubs people can help you understand your emotions, and your reaction to them often reflects how you are responding to your challenges.

Famous People Who Are the 2 of Spades

Howard Stern, Harry Houdini, John Singer Sargent, Jimmy Durante, Thomas Hardy,

Boris Pasternak, Jack London, Roberta Flack, Bertolt Brecht, Lance Bass, Micky Dolenz, Randy Travis, Robert Wagner, Lynn Redgrave, Andre Previn, Laura Dern, Freddie Prinze, Jr., Audrey Hepburn

Birthdays Governed by the 2 of Spades

January 12: Capricorn   Ruler: Saturn

According to Saturn, your ruler, underneath your courteous and charming appearance you are a determined and strong-willed individual. When you fully concentrate and persevere you can apply your rational pragmatism and achieve your goals. Generally you prefer long-term security with a slow but sure method of advancement. In order to benefit from Saturn's influence you need to be self-disciplined and positive when faced with challenges. Since the key to your success depends on your cooperative efforts, you need to apply your innate diplomacy and inspired leadership rather than your unyielding willpower.

February 10: Aquarius   Ruler: Uranus

Action-oriented and strong-willed, according to Uranus, your ruler, you are usually a self-reliant individual who values freedom and resents restrictions. Progressive and original, your enthusiasm for new ideas or ventures also indicates that you can be courageous and daring. If you choose to rebel and go it alone you may find the road ahead more unpredictable or challenging. Your powers of perception and objective judgment can often advance your career or lead to positions of responsibility. You often achieve success when you balance your unique leadership qualities with the more humanitarian side of your nature and show your willingness to compromise.

March 8: Pisces   Ruler: Neptune

Although according to your ruler, Neptune, you are usually receptive, agreeable, and gentle

in appearance, the influence of your number 8 birthday signifies that you can be an ambitious and determined individual with powerful perception and unique insight. In order to accomplish your goals you need to develop your endurance and self-discipline. Usually you begin your projects with great enthusiasm, yet maintaining this momentum is hard. The key to your success is to complete projects you have already started. When you take on the responsibilities of leadership there is very little that you cannot do or achieve.

April 6: Aries   Ruler: Mars

Charismatic and friendly, your engaging manner often conceals the dynamic power of your ruling planet, Mars. Your refined taste and love of ease also suggests that you dislike unpleasantness. Although your greatest enemy is often inertia, Mars urges you to follow your ideals or take action to create something worthwhile. When you feel inspired you can be a hardworking and dedicated individual. You may settle for less than you deserve, however, if you always choose the easier route or fail to acknowledge your responsibilities. Nevertheless, due to your diplomacy and networking skills you can make an excellent negotiator and counselor.

May 4: Taurus   Ruler: Venus

Although you often appear to be a pragmatic and hardworking individual, Venus, your ruler, reveals that you are more romantic, sensitive, and affectionate than you care to admit. A compelling need to be involved with others through relationships or partnerships indicates that you enjoy and benefit from working with others. A tendency to be inflexible, however, can undermine these cooperative endeavors and lead to power struggles. By using your charm and diplomacy, rather than controlling tactics, you can usually get what you want. As you can also be prone to fluctuating moods it is important to live in a congenial atmosphere of sharing and equality.

June 2: Gemini   Ruler: Mercury

Mentally sharp, versatile, and communicative, Mercury, your ruler, indicates that you are able to enchant others with your conversational skills and sympathetic attitude. The double emphasis of the number 2 in your card and day reinforces the influence that people and close relationships have on your life. The key to your success, therefore, often lies in maintaining balance and equality in cooperative efforts and partnerships. Being receptive to others can be a blessing as well as a curse; if you want good rapport and harmony in your life surround yourself with positive people who like to communicate and share ideas.

♥ ♣ THE 3 s ♦ ♠

THE NUMBER 3 emphasizes the joy of life and a desire for creative self-expression. If you are a 3 card you are usually friendly, with a need for freedom and social interaction with others. Possessing good communication skills, you are likely to have a talent with words, whether through speaking, writing, or singing. You could also be good at synthesizing information. Being multitalented, some of your greater challenges center on making decisions and not scattering your energies in too many directions. If you become indecisive you can be prone to worry or feeling unprepared, so it is important to stay focused on achieving your goals. Learning to express your feelings as well as your thoughts directly can help you overcome any feelings of insecurity you may experience. You usually prefer life to be bright and optimistic, and have a definite need for fun or artistic expression.

3 of Hearts

Emotionally creative or uncertain about love, you may have to decide whether to concen-trate on positivity or waste your time in worry. Although making choices may be a major issue for you, you are usually at your best when utilizing your natural ability to be light, sociable, and kindhearted. Avoid an indulgent streak. Your card can be very creative or musical.

3 of Clubs

Being charming and intellectually bright, you often have many choices as to which way to go. Although you can be enthusiastic about numerous projects, avoid allowing indecision to undermine your great potential. At your best you can be cheerful and productive, with many creative ideas.

3 of Diamonds

Bright and personable, many of your life choices are likely to center around money and values. Just be careful that your desire for material security or worry and indecision do not undermine your outstanding creative potential or spiritual sensitivity.

3 of Spades

Much of your life work can revolve around your desire for self-expression and creativity rather than succumbing to worry or scattering your forces. The decisions you have to make may often involve your work situations. This can be a highly productive card if you are willing to discipline yourself and be responsible.

♥ THE 3 OF HEARTS ♥

Although clever and seldom at a loss for words, your 3 of Hearts Card suggests that love and emotional issues play a strong part in your life. As a 3 Card you like to take a creative approach to your problems, whether purely practical or personal. When positive you are able to lift up people with your cheerful attitude and friendly demeanor, or to inspire them with your many talents. When down you are prone to worry and indecision, particularly about expressing your feelings. With the double influence of Mercury in the Earthly Spread, you enjoy communicating your ideas. Equally, you should find it easy to socialize and attract others with your natural charm. As you also are the Mars Card in the Mercury line of the Spiritual Spread you can be quick-witted, with fast responses and a love for action. Multifaceted

and versatile, you are usually eager to learn, but you may have to watch a tendency to be restless or nervous or to outsmart yourself. Being adaptable, with good presentation or writing skills, you can easily fit into any social or work environment. As you are also emotionally sensitive you need to have avenues of self-expression that can bring out the best of your natural gifts.

Your Two Replacement Cards Are the Ace of Hearts & the Queen of Clubs.

As the 3 of Hearts, you share the same planetary position as the Ace of Hearts in the Spiritual Spread. This signifies that underneath your sharp intelligence is a powerful desire for love and a need to radiate that force out to others. If you doubt yourself or become insecure, however, you may close off this love, becoming too self-conscious or inconstant in your close personal relationships.

You also share the same planetary position as the Queen of Clubs in the Earthly Spread. This signifies that your natural dramatic sense can place you in leading positions, especially where you can help others with your knowledge. You possess an ability to share information and be a networker, connecting people from all different social groups.

You usually have special or karmic links

The 3 of Hearts Planetary Card Sequence

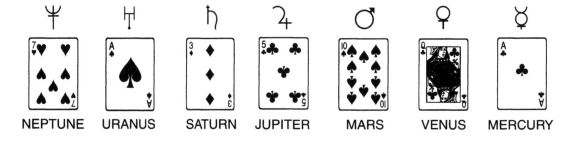

NEPTUNE   URANUS   SATURN   JUPITER   MARS   VENUS   MERCURY

with people who are represented by the Ace of Hearts and Queen of Clubs, as you share the same planetary positions. You can be soul mates or understand each other very well. Even if you do not get along, you can both see clearly how the other person operates.

Your Mercury Card is . . .

The Ace of Clubs
- You will be interested in learning new things throughout life. You also have a gift for teaching others what you know.
- Mentally strong-willed, be careful not to dominate others with your opinions.
- Your many ideas and intelligent approach can place you in leadership positions or those where you have an opportunity to express your strong individuality.
- You can have a particularly good mental rapport with people who are the Ace of Clubs Card. This can be good for stimulating your communication and also for ideas. You may wish to initiate something together.

Your Venus Card is . . .

The Queen of Clubs
- Your good social skills ensure that you enjoy entertaining, particularly those of intelligence and influence.
- You are likely to have encountered a particularly strong female influence growing up, probably your mother.
- Relationships work better when you find a partner who can keep up with your fast mind.
- Queen of Clubs people can be highly attractive to you or stimulate your natural friendliness. This is a good card for love, friendship, or making money together.

Your Mars Card is . . .

The 10 of Spades
- When you believe you will be successful you can actively project strong confidence, attracting the interest of others.
- You have a lot of energy and drive when you have a definite goal in mind.
- You can be pointed and courageous in achieving your objectives, but avoid impatience.
- 10 of Spades people can stimulate your ambitions and enthusiasm and spur you into action. Avoid becoming argumentative or competitive with these people.

Your Jupiter Card is . . .

The 5 of Clubs
- You should have many fine opportunities for travel in your life. Alternatively, foreign interests can bring you good fortune.
- Being mentally quick, with a thirst for knowledge, you can become bored easily when you feel you are no longer learning from a situation. Nevertheless, you have a gift for earning while you learn.
- You are often willing to speculate or take risks to improve your situation and expand your horizons.
- 5 of Clubs people can have an expansive or beneficial effect on you. This link can bring opportunities and make you feel more optimistic. You may develop big plans together.

Your Saturn Card is . . .

The 3 of Diamonds
- Your challenges often revolve around decision making. Usually it is best to remember life is short rather than to worry too much about money or material situations.

- You enjoy learning a skill and take pride in your work.
- Responsibility and self-discipline ultimately bring you joy.
- 3 of Diamonds people help you to see your weaknesses and can act as either a burden or a teacher. You may be working out karmic lessons with this person.

Your Uranus Card is . . .

The Ace of Spades
- You need to have working projects that utilize your original and inventive ideas.
- If you become egotistical it can make you stubborn, overly serious, or rebellious.
- When detached and objective you possess a strong natural wisdom that can take you to progressive or leading positions.
- Ace of Spades people can inspire you to start new projects, see your situation more clearly, or be a good friend.

Your Neptune Card is . . .

The 7 of Hearts
- Although part of you seeks the idealistically perfect love, this can often be found in the simple and subtle joys of life.
- If you allow yourself to become disillusioned with life you may experience feeling cynical or isolated.
- Your sensitivity and intuition work well for you when you have faith in your own vision.
- You have a subtle emotional or psychic link with people who are the 7 of Hearts Card. They can stimulate your imagination or your dreams. Stay realistic, however.

Your Challenge Card is . . .

The 7 of Diamonds
- Get the balance right between work and play as well as control and trust.

- Allow your life to flow spontaneously.
- 7 of Diamonds people can challenge you to transform yourself.

The Result of Your Challenge Card is . . .

The 5 of Spades
- You will always be working dynamically on creating more opportunities for positive change in your life.
- You will be channeling restlessness or impatience into exciting new projects.
- You can see in 5 of Spades people how you are reacting to your challenges.

Famous People Who Are the 3 of Hearts

Denzel Washington, Maggie Smith, Nigel Kennedy, Woodrow Wilson, Billy Idol, David Mamet, Abbie Hoffman, Winston Churchill, Jonathan Swift, Mark Twain

Birthdays Governed by the 3 of Hearts

November 30: Sagittarius   Ruler: Jupiter
Inventive, with a gift for words, you are articulate and outgoing, with a sociable nature. Usually optimistic, with the ability to think big, you can be courageous and broad-minded, but guard against impatience or being hotheaded. With a need for freedom, you usually enjoy travel and all forms of self-expression. With your finger on the pulse of public opinion, you also have a talent for dealing with people. You learn fast, so you need projects that keep your interest. As you tend to be offered many opportunities at once you need to avoid worry and be decisive.

December 28: Capricorn   Ruler: Saturn
Ambitious and creative, you are amiable yet quick-witted. Your fast intelligence blends well

with your capacity for hard work, though guard against a tendency to worry or scatter your energies. Being sociable, you enjoy opportunities to express your keen mentality, talents, and good communication skills. Under your friendly personality you can be resolute in achieving your goals. When you utilize your strong will positively this builds your confidence and stimulates your drive to achieve. Your strong heart energy responds well to creative and joyful enterprises, whether for work or for pleasure.

♣ THE 3 OF CLUBS ♣

The quick intelligence of the 3 of Clubs suggests that you are a natural communicator and usually seek to express yourself in some creative way. A need for variety and mental stimulation also implies that you enjoy mixing with people from different walks of life. Often active and enterprising, you do not let life become dull or boring. Putting your thoughts to paper or clearing misunderstandings can often uncover the sources of your worries or concerns.

Although you are versatile, if you allow mental restlessness to dictate your course of action it can undermine your great potential. Whereas belonging to the Clubs suit implies that you feel energized by learning from new experiences, under the influence of Mars and Saturn in the Earthly Spread, you need to clearly define your long-term goals. When positive you can be a good strategist and remain focused and persistent despite dealing with restrictions. This can build your endurance and determination. Able to synthesize thoughts and generate life into old ideas, you can often create something original or introduce a unique concept. If you do not occupy yourself with positive thoughts, however, jeal-

ousy, worry, or insecurity can cause you to become overly serious.

The double influence of Venus and Mars in your Spiritual Spread emphasizes your passionate nature, artistic capabilities, and natural flair for creative self-expression. In order to maintain your interest in people or your work you usually need to stay animated and enthusiastic. Although you can become exuberant, resist fluctuating from being too excited to becoming disinterested.

Your Two Replacement Cards Are the King of Diamonds & the 5 of Diamonds.

As the 3 of Clubs you also share the same position as the King of Diamonds in the Earthly Spread. The force behind this royal card gives you business acumen and the impetus to attain your goals and achieve prosperity. This card often motivates you to take leadership positions or be enterprising. Although this card aids your executive abilities and potential for success, being bossy or controlling can undermine your authority.

You also share the same planetary position as the 5 of Diamonds in the Spiritual Spread. This influence implies that you value your freedom and dislike being restricted or told what to do. Although you have many opportunities to advance and succeed, you may experience fluctuations in your income due to changes in work or circumstance. This can cause concern if you do not budget, save, or look after your finances. Nevertheless, the 5 influence here also brings an adventurous spirit and a love of variety.

You usually have special or karmic links with people represented by the 5 of Diamonds or the King of Diamonds, as you share the same planetary positions. You can be soul mates or business partners, as you understand each other very well. Even if you do not get

The 3 of Clubs Planetary Card Sequence

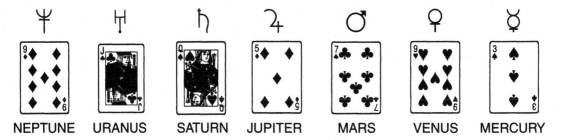

| NEPTUNE | URANUS | SATURN | JUPITER | MARS | VENUS | MERCURY |

along, you can both see clearly how the other person operates.

Your Mercury Card is . . .

The 3 of Spades

- This card implies that you are versatile and talented in more than one field.
- Acting on impulse can leave you with misgivings later.
- Your spontaneity and intuitive abilities are part of your persuasive charm.
- The 3 of Spades here cautions against indecisiveness or self-doubt.
- You find contentment when you have a clear goal in sight.
- You should have good mental rapport and special communication with people represented by the 3 of Spades, especially if you share the same interests.

Your Venus Card is . . .

The 9 of Hearts

- Often charismatic, generous, and sociable, you have no problems attracting friends and admirers.
- You can make great sacrifices for the people you love.
- If your expectations are too high or you hang onto the past, you may experience emotional disappointment in your relationships.

- Being patient, cautious, and sure of what you feel can eliminate these obstacles.
- Usually you are attracted to 9 of Hearts people, as they are ideal for love and romance, as well as for close friendships and good business partnerships.

Your Mars Card is . . .

The 7 of Clubs

- A positive mental attitude and faith in yourself can be the fuel to your ambition and achievements.
- If you become cynical, insecure, or pay too much attention to others you risk losing your confidence.
- You can profit from friendly competition.
- Avoid being too argumentative or critical.
- Discipline your fine mental energies through training or education.
- The relationships you have with 7 of Clubs people can be good if you both share the same aims and objectives. You could encourage each other to be active and motivated, but avoid quarreling.

Your Jupiter Card is . . .

The 5 of Diamonds

- Lucky breaks indicate that you benefit from making changes or taking advantage of new opportunities, especially if they involve travel.

- This card can minimize the danger of falling into a rut.
- Being too extravagant can cause you to overspend or get into debt.
- You could be fortunate with work away from your place of birth.
- Budgeting is essential if you want to avoid financial fluctuations.
- 5 of Diamonds people can be linked with good opportunities. If you are in association with them you can both be successful, but watch out that they do not encourage you to overspend.

Your Saturn Card is . . .

The Queen of Spades

- The influence of this royal card indicates that women play an important role in your development and maturity.
- Women can also symbolize responsibilities or a burden.
- When you work hard you will eventually reap your rewards.
- This royal card can heighten your intuition or direct you toward a spiritual path.
- Although women can act out the role of a teacher or a demanding boss in the workplace, if you can learn from your relationships with them you can gain invaluable insight. The motto "no pain no gain" is doubly emphasized here due to the spiritual nature of the Spades suit.
- Queen of Spades people can show you where you need discipline or work on yourself. They may teach you about boundaries. This positively can be a relationship of respect and loyalty, or alternatively this person can be hard work. Either way, it is an enlightening experience.

Your Uranus Card is . . .

The Jack of Clubs

- In adulthood you prefer to adopt a more progressive view, even though it may differ from others.
- Your independent outlook, knowledge, or skills can lead you to executive positions or encourage you to strike out on your own.
- You can particularly benefit from writing, taking up a course of study, or pursuing new interests in your middle years.
- You may also find metaphysical subjects a great source of inspiration.
- People represented by the Jack of Clubs can offer you valuable insights into new financial opportunities. This is also a good card for friendship, especially if you share intellectual pursuits.

Your Neptune Card is . . .

The 9 of Diamonds

- Your contentment in later years is often found in the more meaningful quest for what is truly valuable.
- If you have done good deeds in the past these will be returned to you in legacies or unexpected rewards.
- This card warns against overindulgence, escapism, or taking unnecessary financial risks.
- 9 of Diamonds people can stimulate your visions, dreams, and imagination. They may be connected to you through a more psychic or spiritual connection, but guard against delusion and keep your finances secure.

Your Challenge Card is . . .

The 7 of Spades

- Inspiration can be achieved and maintained when you hold onto your faith and overcome doubt.

- Selflessness and service can be a great tool for personal empowerment.
- Avoid working in employment that is well below your capabilities.
- Spiritual awareness can bring powerful illuminations or realizations.
- 7 of Spades people can fascinate you but also challenge you. Although these people can help you to transform your life, resist power struggles.

The Result of Your Challenge Card is . . .

The 2 of Clubs
- Issues of trust and loyalty are often played out in partnerships.
- You get the balance right between give and take, helping to establish rewarding alliances.
- Your cooperative efforts prove vital to your success.
- You have a good sense of humor.
- 2 of Clubs people can collaborate with you on work projects or help you understand your partnerships better. Your reactions to them often reflect how you are responding to your challenges.

Famous People Who Are the 3 of Clubs

John F. Kennedy, Matt LeBlanc, Bob Hope, Don Johnson, Gene Kelly, Helen Keller, Danny DeVito, H. G. Wells, Gustav Holtz, Rock Hudson, J. Paul Getty, Leonard Cohen, Noel Gallagher, Stephen King, John le Carré, Ricki Lake, Bill Murray, Larry Hagman, Martin Scorsese, River Phoenix, Tobey Maguire

Birthdays Governed by the 3 of Clubs

May 29: Gemini   Ruler: Mercury
Mercury, your ruler, indicates that you are a courteous and sociable individual with strong instincts and good perception. Charismatic, mentally quick, and idealistic, there is usually more to you than meets the eye. Sometimes secretive, you may hide behind a cheerful smile and reveal as little of yourself as possible. As a sensitive and versatile individual, you are usually seeking new ways to express yourself. Although you have many opportunities to do so, insecurities, indecisiveness, or a lack of consistency may undermine your efforts to fulfill your high potential. When inspired, however, you can rise to the challenge and surprise others with your unique talents.

June 27: Cancer   Ruler: Moon
Armed with initiative and inexhaustible energy, you usually have the strength to face up to your challenges and persevere. The Moon, your ruler, endows you with emotional strength and common sense based on good intuition. Although you are security conscious and family-oriented, your unique views suggest that you like to think independently and freely. As a versatile person with the ability to pay attention to detail, you have exceptional organizational skills and the mental creativity to achieve success. When you harness the emotional restlessness that resides within you and focus on your goal, there is very little that you cannot accomplish.

July 25: Leo   Ruler: Sun
Proud, dramatic, and gregarious, you are a versatile individual with many talents and quick perception. Being mentally fast yet also thoughtful, you benefit from exploring intellectual or philosophical subjects. Your ruler, the Sun, indicates that you are idealistic, imaginative, and creative. Although you are often enterprising and daring, fluctuating moods and self-criticism can cause inner restlessness and self-doubts. When you accept the responsibilities of leadership, however, your people

skills and enthusiasm can inspire others. You often prefer to develop your own methods of work, and the knowledge that you gain is based on personal experiences and re-evaluating past mistakes.

August 23: Virgo   Ruler: Mercury
Intelligent, hardworking, and well informed, your ruler, Mercury, suggests that you possess a thirst for knowledge and good analytical skills. Although your dynamic nature can make you popular, the key to your success often lies in your ability to organize yourself and be self-disciplined. If you try to accomplish too many things you may be in danger of scattering your energies. A tendency to be at times overly confident warns against acting on impulse or throwing caution to the wind. Your fulfillment is often found through creative self-expression and finding an inspiring occupation that keeps you interested.

September 21: Virgo   Ruler: Mercury
Charming and sociable, you enjoy mixing with people and stimulating conversation. Mercury, your ruler, indicates that you are versatile, intelligent, witty, and highly intuitive. Although you often appear confident and cheerful, your mental sensitivity and need for reassurance indicates that you are clever at disguising your worries. Prone to indecisiveness, however, you need to guard against self-condemning criticism as it can undermine your self-esteem. Nevertheless, your charismatic and alluring manner often compensate for your moods or changing attitudes. Naturally creative, you gain from developing your innate talents, especially writing.

October 19: Libra   Ruler: Venus
Your powerful emotions and idealistic nature imply that you are a dynamic and sensitive individual. Although you have a strong need to be involved with people, you also highly value your independence or individuality. Your ability to inspire others with your enthusiasm and ideas also points to your innate leadership qualities. Venus, your ruler, indicates that you can be passionate, creative, and versatile. Your charismatic charm and sympathetic nature usually attracts many admirers, yet without using your discretion you may end up wasting much of your energy on pleasing others. Nevertheless, you can find success in all types of people-related occupations.

November 17: Scorpio   Ruler: Mars
Your survival instincts and willpower indicate that you can overcome obstacles and succeed when you are self-assured and focused. Mars, your ruler, gives you courage and urges you to use your practical skills in a creative way. A tendency to feel disheartened through worry and indecision warns that without inner faith and a positive mental outlook you can feel restless or waste your mental energies. Although you are able to conceal your thoughts and feelings by being charming, entertaining, and witty, when you feel undermined or threatened your sarcasm can quickly rise to the surface. Nevertheless, you can keep secrets and be a loyal friend.

December 15: Sagittarius   Ruler: Jupiter
Motivated and restless, your optimistic attitude and natural charm indicates that you are likely to enjoy a life of excitement and variety. Although you project a confident front, your changing moods indicate that you can be prone to anxieties and insecurities. A tendency to change your views or values also warns that you can fluctuate emotionally or drift in different directions. Nevertheless, practical skills, natural creativity, and a sixth sense about monetary matters suggest that you can make your own luck where material issues are concerned.

Worldly and enthusiastic, travel can broaden your horizons and be an important component of your success.

◆ THE 3 OF DIAMONDS ◆

Creative, sociable, and quick-witted, you are a communicator with something to say and many talents. Under the influence of Uranus and Mercury in the Earthly Spread, your sharp intellect brings you original ideas and good insight into people's characters. With a strong need for self-expression, you value the freedom to be yourself yet still have a natural understanding of how the system works. At times you may experience doubt or uncertainty that can cause indecision or worry, especially about money matters. It is always best for you to take the lighter approach rather than get bogged down, as you usually get your best ideas when you feel inspired. If you develop your innate humanitarian streak you can introduce new ideas to help others.

As your card is Mercury in the Saturn line in the Spiritual Spread this indicates that you have the potential to be a deep thinker with an ability to go directly to the heart of a matter. Mentally tenacious, you also have a natural gift for writing or presenting your views. Although usually truthful, you should avoid a tendency to become obstinate or uncommunicative if you become distrusting of others. Nevertheless, being innovative, resourceful, and inventive, your natural creativity will always prove to be the vital key to your achievement and success.

Your Two Replacement Cards Are the 6 of Hearts & the Queen of Diamonds.

As the 3 of Diamonds you share the same planetary position as the 6 of Hearts in the Spiritual Spread. This signifies that your inner sensitivity can endow you with compassion and powerful intuition if you are willing to listen to it. Despite your ambitious quest for material achievements in the world, inner peace and love is your interior goal. If unaware of this you may sacrifice your spirit in the rat race, becoming anxious without really knowing why. It is important, therefore, to keep a sense of balance and harmony in your life. This can be particularly reflected through music and the arts or your love of home, nature, and pleasing surroundings.

Your card also shares the same planetary position as the Queen of Diamonds in the Earthly Spread. This signifies that you are naturally dramatic and have good leadership or evaluation skills. Although you possess shrewd business acumen, you can be very generous to those you love.

You usually have special or karmic links with people represented by the 6 of Hearts or the Queen of Diamonds, as you share the same planetary positions. You can be soul mates or business partners, as you understand each other very well. Even if you do not get along, you can both see clearly how the other person operates.

Your Mercury Card is . . .

The Ace of Spades
- By exercising your full concentration, you avoid scattering your energies.
- A desire to understand at a deeper level may lead you to study metaphysics or spirituality, where you can excel as a teacher.
- Although you appear very confident, self-doubt, secrecy, or worry can undermine your outstanding potential.
- You particularly succeed when initiating new projects or pioneering new concepts.
- People who are the Ace of Spades can stimulate your leadership skills and encourage you to think and exchange ideas.

The 3 of Diamonds Planetary Card Sequence

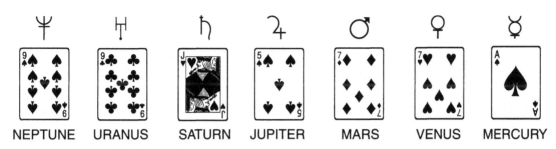

| NEPTUNE | URANUS | SATURN | JUPITER | MARS | VENUS | MERCURY |

Your Venus Card is . . .

The 7 of Hearts
- You gain from learning to deal with people and partners by trusting your judgment spontaneously in the moment.
- Craving an idealistic form of love, it can sometimes be hard for partners to meet your high expectations. This may sometimes cause you to alternate between being loving and affectionate and withdrawing or appearing cold.
- Developing your spirituality brings more love into your life.
- If you find yourself in unsuitable relationships avoid sacrificing yourself for security.
- 7 of Hearts people can prove to be a good link for romance and friendship. This card may also be good for business.

Your Mars Card is . . .

The 7 of Diamonds
- Being mentally sharp, you usually enjoy friendly rivalries.
- Once you are in action you can be very focused and driven, although you may swing from being very hardworking to total inactivity.
- You prefer to analyze all sides of a situation before you take action, especially as you have a strong perfectionist streak.
- People who are the 7 of Diamonds can stimulate you to become more active, enterprising, and dynamic. Alternatively, you may argue with this person.

Your Jupiter Card is . . .

The 5 of Spades
- You need variety to keep you optimistic and stop you from being bored. This card is excellent for travel or constantly updating your approach.
- An inner restlessness and impatience may cause you to overindulge or overspend. Keeping a regular physical exercise program or having positive plans can help you overcome this tendency.
- When in organizational mode you like to work fast and will take risks. But avoid being too impulsive, especially if you are overconfident.
- People who are the 5 of Spades can stimulate your self-belief or provide you with lucky opportunities. Sometimes this can be a spiritual link.

Your Saturn Card is . . .

The Jack of Hearts
- Your major life tests usually involve affairs of the heart.

- You gain from taking a youthful or playful approach to your work.
- Although you can be self-sacrificing, especially for those you love, be careful not to go too far and play the martyr.
- You have an ability to make money or a career from a creative pastime.
- People who are the Jack of Hearts Card can have a karmic link with you. This person can show you where you need to work on yourself. This can be testing or enlightening.

Your Uranus Card is . . .

The 9 of Clubs
- When you are able to look at life in an objective or dispassionate way you display a strong universal side to your character that you can use to help others.
- If you hang onto disappointments or frustrations you are likely to become tense, rebellious, or obstinate.
- Education or developing a positive philosophy in life is vital to making the most of your outstanding potential.
- People who are the 9 of Clubs can make you more objective about your life or could be good friends.

Your Neptune Card is . . .

The 9 of Spades
- At times, your emotional sensitivity can cause you difficulty in dealing with the harsh, cruel world. You may have to work at keeping your serious side in check and travel light.
- On occasion you can have profound insights into more mystical realms. Through self-discipline you may wish to develop these special gifts.
- If you utilize your innate humanitarianism you will find much fulfillment in the later years of your life.

- You can have a psychic link with 9 of Spades people. They can connect to your dreams, ideals, and positive visions or alternatively link to your escapist tendencies. It is important to stay grounded in this relationship.

Your Challenge Card is . . .

The 2 of Hearts
- Stay independent but work collaboratively with others.
- Create healthy relationships where you can give and receive love.
- Stay emotionally balanced.
- 2 of Hearts people can dare you to react emotionally. They will generally make you very aware of how you are handling your relationships or can help you transform your life.

The Result of Your Challenge Card is . . .

The King of Hearts
- You naturally rise to leading positions or are not afraid to take the initiative in situations that need to be resolved.
- You take responsibility for using your emotional power and dramatic gifts.
- You are in a position to help others.
- King of Hearts people can reflect how well you are responding to your challenge. If you are being bossy and autocratic you may need to review your Challenge Card.

Famous People Who Are the 3 of Diamonds

George Lucas, Janet Jackson, Bill Cosby, Gianni Versace, Neil Diamond, Boy George, Donald Trump, Steffi Graf, Gabriela Sabatini, Harriet Beecher Stowe, Modigliani, Georges Seurat, Edith Wharton, Drew Barrymore, Frederic Chopin, John Belushi, Peter Sellers, Nastassja Kinski, Christian Lacroix, Walter

Cronkite, Maria Callas, Monica Seles, Henrik Ibsen, William Hurt, Michael Redgrave, Holly Hunter, Che Guevara, Antonio Banderas, Sean "P. Diddy" Combs, Spike Lee

Birthdays Governed by the 3 of Diamonds

January 24: Aquarius   Ruler: Uranus

Friendly and direct, you have a shrewd understanding of human nature and many creative ideas. You like to be honest and give a broad and objective viewpoint on life. Even though your independence is very important to you, the comforts and security of home can also play a strong part in your life. You value loyalty but may have to be careful of a stubborn streak that can sometimes spoil your associations. A natural humanitarian side to your nature can be developed further to aid others and for your own personal satisfaction.

February 22: Pisces   Ruler: Neptune

Although you are emotionally sensitive, intuitive, and imaginative, you also have a sharp, keen, objective mentality. Your need for creative expression is complemented by a natural practicality that can help you manifest your dreams. Being idealistic and impressionable suggests that you work well when having a clear vision of what you want to achieve and even better if your vision includes helping others. As your birthday is a master number it reinforces the necessity for self-discipline to achieve your outstanding potential, otherwise, you may be prone to moods or escapism.

March 20: Pisces   Ruler: Neptune

Being born on the cusp of Pisces and Aries suggests that you are in a position to add the action and drive of Aries to your Piscean feeling and intuition. As you have original ideas and are often ahead of your time you may be drawn to enterprising ventures or ideas of reform.

Working partnerships or cooperative activities can often play a key part in your life plan. Being so receptive and impressionable, whether at work or at home, you need a congenial atmosphere around you to be happy.

April 18: Aries   Ruler: Mars

Determined and strong-willed and common-sensical, yet also imaginative and original, you enjoy actively utilizing your many creative ideas. Being assertive with a sharp mind, you like to be direct with others, but be careful of uncontrolled emotions. With your dynamism and energy you can achieve much when enthusiastic about a project. You are helped by the combination of your good communication skills, natural leadership, and organizational abilities, although guard against being reckless or bossy.

May 16: Taurus   Ruler: Venus

Although friendly, intelligent, and sociable, you still have a more thoughtful side to your nature. As you enjoy beauty and the finer things of life you are usually willing to work hard to achieve the opulence you desire. Blessed with creative talent, a shrewd business sense, and a humanitarian interest in people, you can succeed in just about anything, as long as you stay decisive and choose inspiration and faith over just plain material security. The mixture of your keen intellect, ambition, and sensitivity can prove rewarding for you both spiritually and materially.

June 14: Gemini   Ruler: Mercury

A sharp communicator with quick responses, your original views and psychological insight can make you attractive to others. Being so quick also suggests that you need variety and new learning experiences to stop you from being bored, but avoid scattering your energies. With a natural dramatic sense and so many progressive and creative ideas, you can particularly excel in writing, communications, or working with people. Although you can be direct, clever, and articulate, be careful that instability does not bring you problems. A deeper side to your personality may be interested in philosophy or spirituality.

July 12: Cancer   Ruler: Moon

You are fortunate enough to have a quick and keen intellect combined with a strong imagination. Sensitive and aware of others, the security of home and family plays a major part in your life script. Although you may be prone to worry, when positive the humanitarian side of your nature wants to make a difference in improving the lives of others. Your special communication skills indicate a flair for writing or presentation of your ideas. Self-discipline and finding ways to express yourself ensures that you avoid emotional ups and downs and utilize your exceptional talents.

August 10: Leo   Ruler: Sun

The combination of your natural leadership skills, ambition, and inventive ideas can be a winning combination. Being dramatic, you enjoy fun and self-expression but also have a more serious side that thinks more deeply. Being creative, you can excel in anything needing good ideas, but particularly with writing, projects that need a progressive approach, or working for yourself. Although proud and strong-willed, guard against a tendency to be overbearing or self-centered. Nevertheless, you are usually, kind, warmhearted, and interested in others.

September 8: Virgo   Ruler: Mercury

Practical, effective, yet creative, you usually display a blend of determination and sharp intelligence. Hardworking and thorough, you possess a natural business sense and organizational abilities. You may, however, have to avoid anxiety or uncertainty, particularly regarding financial affairs. Analytical and critical, you have a strong need for material security and usually prefer to be in control. Your psychological insight or original approach can be a special advantage in all your dealings.

October 6: Libra   Ruler: Venus

Friendly and sociable, you are smart and creative and have a broad-minded approach. A natural adviser with a strong love of home, you care about others but you should avoid a tendency to be bossy or indecisive. Talented, with an additional gift for socializing or entertaining, you may wish to further develop your abilities, especially in writing, art, music, and drama. If your need for self-expression is not met you may end up feeling anxious or cynical. Being idealistic as well as materially shrewd, you also enjoy having positive outlets for the more compassionate side of your nature.

November 4: Scorpio   Ruler: Mars

Emotionally strong-willed with a love of knowledge, you can be analytical, practical, and hardworking, with inventive and original ideas. You may hide your sensitivity behind your keen intellect and objective viewpoint. Determined and judicious, you can be loyal and self-disciplined, but you should avoid being bossy. When it comes to expressing your ideas the use of your good communication skills greatly aids your success. You may not be quite so forthcoming, however, about your more hidden emotions.

December 2: Sagittarius   Ruler: Jupiter

Sensitive and creative, your ability to come up with successful ideas can often place you in the limelight. Although you are ambitious and possess sharp insight into people, you fare best when following your high ideals. Travel, education, religion, and law are all areas that may inspire you or in which you can be especially successful. Writing is also another area where you can do well. Usually optimistic and humanitarian, the combination of your keen mentality and adventurous and daring nature can help you achieve anything you desire. Just try to avoid becoming hot-tempered or overly sensitive. You place a high value on your relationships.

♠ THE 3 OF SPADES ♠

The creative power of the 3 of Spades implies that you want to express yourself through your high aspirations and unique skills. Having varied interests and being talented on more than one front suggests that you can work in different jobs or try your luck in a number of careers. If you are not sure of your goals employment can become a dilemma, and even a real source of worry. By recognizing your special talents and developing your perseverance, you can rise above your inner doubts and succeed.

Under the influences of Jupiter and Saturn in the Earthly Spread, you need to be patient and persist if you want to achieve success. Adopting the slow but sure approach will inevitably bring good rewards. Discontent, on the other hand, can cause you to feel frustrated, and as a result you may experience self-doubt and a lack of self-confidence.

The influences of Uranus and Neptune in your Spiritual Spread indicates that your idealism, inner vision, and intuition are the keys to your success. When these attributes are developed they can be the source of inspiration, creativity, and uniqueness. These qualities may even draw you to metaphysical subjects or spiritual enlightenment.

Your Two Replacement Cards Are the Jack of Diamonds & the 6 of Diamonds

As the 3 of Spades you share the same planetary position as the Jack of Diamonds in the Earthly Spread. This royal card signifies that you possess business acumen, executive skills, and leadership qualities. Although this provides you with strong earning potential and youthful energies, it highlights your need to be responsible and mature in financial matters.

You also share the same planetary position as the 6 of Diamonds in the Spiritual Spread. The karmic influences of this card implies that money can become a bone of contention in partnerships if you ignore your financial responsibilities. It may also indicate being involved in lawsuits. Your success depends on honest conduct and being honorable in your dealings with others.

You usually have special or karmic links with people represented by the 6 of Diamonds and the Jack of Diamonds as you share the same planetary positions. You can be soul mates or understand each other very well. Even if you do not get along, you can both see clearly how the other person operates.

Your Mercury Card is . . .

The 9 of Hearts
- Your generous and charming manner can win you many friends and admirers.
- High expectations can be the cause of your emotional frustrations.
- An inability to communicate your true feelings can create difficulties in close relationships.
- Your highest creative expression can be reached through emotional maturity.
- You should have good mental rapport and special communication with people repre-

The 3 of Spades Planetary Card Sequence

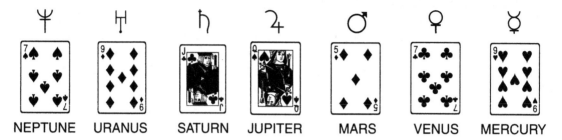

NEPTUNE   URANUS   SATURN   JUPITER   MARS   VENUS   MERCURY

sented by the 9 of Hearts, as they activate your Mercury card.

Your Venus Card is . . .

The 7 of Clubs
- In matters of love you need to balance your emotions with rational thinking.
- By being selective in your choice of friends and lovers you can eliminate anxiety and worry.
- Although you can be very loving and enthusiastic in partnerships, if negative avoid withdrawing or being critical.
- Sharing your knowledge and skills with others can bring emotional fulfillment and success.
- If your close relationships are to last, honesty and total trust are a prerequisite.
- Usually you are attracted to people who are represented by 7 of Clubs, and especially if they share your creative interests. They are ideal for love and romance as well as for close friendships and good business partnerships.

Your Mars Card is . . .

The 5 of Diamonds
- Travel and continual change in circumstances can play a crucial role in your career or financial activities.

- The restlessness indicated by this card suggests that you need to avoid acting impulsively by being self-disciplined and patient.
- With your need for freedom and movement, avoid getting into monotonous, inactive, or restrictive situations.
- Overcoming a reluctance to take counsel from others can minimize your stress in uncertain situations.
- The relationships you have with 5 of Diamonds people can be good if you both motivate or energize each other, but resist being competitive or arguing.

Your Jupiter Card is . . .

The Queen of Spades
- Women usually play an important role in the advancement of your career.
- An interest in self-awareness or metaphysical subjects can add to your strength and spiritual empowerment.
- Astute and intuitive, you can tap into your storehouse of knowledge to find the right solution to your problems.
- You can put a lot of effort and hard work into things you truly believe in.
- Queen of Spades people and hardworking women can be linked with good opportunities. If you are in partnership with them you can both be successful, especially if you share the same spiritual values.

Your Saturn Card is . . .

The Jack of Clubs

- Even though it may involve making sacrifices and hard work, you benefit from developing your fine intellect.
- Take your time to discipline your creative thoughts and persevere with your ideas.
- If you want to accomplish your goals and achieve in your career avoid rebelling against your responsibilities.
- You may have to look out for or care for a male relative or someone younger who will need your help.
- Jack of Clubs people can play an important role in your life if you are able to learn from them about your responsibilities. Although your relationship with them may not always be easy, their contributions are often very valuable lessons.

Your Uranus Card is . . .

The 9 of Diamonds

- You can reinforce your security by planning ahead and making long-term investments.
- Although you can make generous gestures, you benefit from developing a pragmatic approach to financial matters.
- Under the right circumstances you can be very lucky with money.
- Guard against acting on impulse when dealing with important financial issues.
- Being too extravagant or engaging in speculative ventures can prove costly.
- 9 of Diamonds people can often bring new opportunities, but resist making financial commitments too quickly. This is also a good card for friendship, especially if you share the same interests.

Your Neptune Card is . . .

The 7 of Spades

- The influence of your Neptune Card suggests that in later years you benefit from developing your intuition or psychic awareness.
- Studying spiritual subjects or writing can be very fulfilling activities in the second half of your life.
- Whether through diet or exercise you benefit from looking after your health, especially later in life.
- 7 of Spades people may link to your visions, dreams, and ideals. Although you may have a psychic connection with them, guard against delusion by staying pragmatic.

Your Challenge Card is . . .

The 2 of Clubs

- Being cooperative and learning to see the advantages in joint ventures can lead you to good partnerships and successful endeavors.
- You can create harmony and balance in your life by minimizing your tendency to fluctuate from highs to lows.
- Keep your sense of humor despite outside obstacles.
- Being a good leader does not mean taking control or acting in a domineering fashion.
- 2 of Clubs people can cause you to react or challenge your authority. Although these people can help you to transform your life, resist power conflicts with them.

The Result of Your Challenge Card is . . .

The King of Clubs

- When you learn to work with the powers of the 2 of Clubs you can utilize your leadership qualities to rise to positions of influence.

- The knowledge that you gain throughout your life is often linked to self-mastery.
- You stay well informed and mentally alert in order to take advantage of your great gifts.
- If you wish you can also empower yourself and gain insight into life mysteries through reading and exploring philosophy or mysticism.
- King of Clubs people stimulate you mentally. They may influence you as positive authority figures. Your reactions to them often reflect how you are responding to your personal challenges.

Famous People Who Are the 3 of Spades

Morgan Freeman, Mary J. Blige, Marilyn Monroe, James Whistler, Frank Sinatra, Craig David, Doris Day, Golda Meir, Piet Mondrian, Tammy Faye Bakker, Carole King, Sugar Ray Robinson, Alice Walker, Mena Suvari, Spencer Tracy, Colin Powell, Mia Farrow, Bette Davis, James Brown, Alanis Morissette

Birthdays Governed by the 3 of Spades

January 11: Capricorn   Ruler: Saturn
A strong desire to find expression for your inspired ideas suggests that you're a dynamic individual who requires the freedom to explore different possibilities. Although your ruler, Saturn, indicates that you can be realistic, you are also capable of embracing profound or lofty ideas. When you synthesize this idealism with your innate practical skills your versatility and creativity can lead you to important accomplishments or success. In order to achieve your ambitious goals you may need to exercise self-discipline and develop your sense of responsibility. Nevertheless, your subtle charm and youthful demeanor indicates that you can have many friends and admirers.

February 9: Aquarius   Ruler: Uranus
You are a sensitive and unique individual with intuitive understanding and inspired vision. Uranus, your ruler, indicates that your ideals can lead you to great achievements as well as disappointments. Although your insight and good knowledge of human nature usually works to your benefit, self-doubt and insecurities can undermine your confidence. Learning to let go and move on at the right time can also enhance your prospects for success. Your financial investments usually materialize due to altruistic motives or long-term planning rather than through taking chances and throwing caution to the wind.

March 7: Pisces   Ruler: Neptune
The number 7 of your birthday suggests that you can be thoughtful and benefit from gaining greater knowledge and awareness or exploring metaphysical subjects. Your ruler, Neptune, indicates that you are a sensitive and receptive individual with special talents and a need to find creative or emotional self-expression. Due to your unique qualities, perhaps one of your greatest challenges is to find your individuality through your work and original ideas. This can be achieved easily if you blend your need to be of service with a need to be independent.

April 5: Aries   Ruler: Mars
Your dynamic drive and daring nature suggests that you are an ambitious, independent, and versatile individual with numerous talents. Often hardworking and practical, your ruler, Mars, usually urges you to move on and do something different. On many occasions travel away from your home will play an important role in transforming your life. Inner restlessness or an inclination to be impatient warns, however, that you need to establish clear objec-

tives before you embark on new projects or adventures. Although your security is undermined at times by financial fluctuations and changing circumstances, guard against falling into monotonous or mundane jobs that lack challenge, excitement, and change.

May 3: Taurus   Ruler: Venus

The double impact of the number 3 on your birthday suggests that you are a friendly and entertaining individual with special talents and inspired ideas. Your ruler, Venus, grants you quiet charm, a love of nature, and innate artistic talents you may wish to develop. When you realize that your unique gifts lie in intellectual realms or creative abilities you will be able to find original ways to express yourself. Unfortunately, indecisiveness and inner doubts imply that if you are not careful you can waste your talents on emotional quandaries and worry. By developing your inner faith and trust you can project a confident and positive personality.

June 1: Gemini   Ruler: Mercury

The dynamic influence of the number 1 in your birth date indicates that you are a direct and idealistic individual who can be charming and ambitious. Your acts of selfless kindness are often rewarded by new opportunities. According to Mercury, your ruler, your reasoning is often based on your innate intuition and emotional needs. If you are not careful, however, at times your idealistic notions can suffer setbacks, and your high expectations will turn to disappointments. Nevertheless, you possess a sharp mind and are quite capable of turning situations to your advantage. In order to succeed you need to stay focused on just a few objectives at a time and develop your self-discipline.

♥ ♣ THE 4 s ♦ ♠

THE NUMBER 4 conveys a pragmatic approach to life and an ability to achieve through hard work. The orderly power of the number 4 indicates stability, practical systems, and a need for a strong foundation. If you are a number 4 Card you can be honest, frank, and straightforward with a down-to-earth approach to life. Your ability to be methodical and orderly suggests you can also be persistent and self-disciplined. You are likely to possess either organizational skills, a good sense of form, mechanical skills, or a hands-on approach to getting things done. Although you can be very determined, the fixed quality of the number 4 indicates that you can also be stubborn and inflexible or may be inhibited in expressing your emotions. Solid and exact, your ability to plan and structure can identify you with the builder archetype. Being security conscious suggests that you value loyalty and like to be well organized. Be careful, however, of a strict side to your personality, which can sometimes emerge and cause you to be bossy or resentful. Nevertheless, you can be a solid rock of support for others, and when you work you like to do a job properly.

4 of Hearts

As your card is identified with the Heart suit it is important for you to build your foundation in life on love. For this reason your card is often identified as the marriage card, a time when one wants to build something solid emotionally. Avoid becoming stubborn or too excessive.

4 of Clubs

Enthusiasm combined with practical planning can prove to be your forte. A positive thinker, when you share your knowledge with others you can achieve emotional satisfaction and remarkable results. Although you are honest and straightforward, you should avoid being inflexible.

4 of Diamonds

A good worker, you enjoy being productive, methodical, and well organized. Even though you can be practical, your sensitivity implies you have strong spiritual potential, but should avoid being obstinate. You prefer to be honest and straightforward in your dealings with others.

4 of Spades

A practical realist and good organizer, you are likely to have a natural business sense. Although aware of financial security, you still value wisdom and realize that effort needs to be put in to accomplish goals and objectives. Your card has good work influences, but you may have to avoid being too bossy or stubborn by concentrating on your positive plans.

♥ THE 4 OF HEARTS ♥

As a 4 of Hearts you are a charismatic individual with a friendly nature. Usually you want to put your talents, imagination, and emotions into something substantial and useful. With a need for self-expression high on your agenda, you can articulate your feelings, creative visions, and idealistic ideas. Belonging to the Hearts suit indicates that you need human contact to express yourself emotionally and close relationships are very important to you. Being a highly receptive individual implies that you are also attuned to the subtlest nuances and feelings of other people. You may, however, need to resist a tendency to be self-centered, and instead of displaying vanity or smugness choose a warm heart.

Under the planetary influences of Mercury and Neptune in the Earthly Spread, you possess a sympathetic nature and the power to create a congenial atmosphere. A talent for writing can also help you to explore your creativity, especially through mental imagery or fantasy. Since the influences of these two planets can also cause confusion, they warn against self-deception or escapism.

Luckily, the influences of Mercury and Jupiter in your Spiritual Spread implies that you possess an optimistic outlook and sound common sense. Although they can lead to positive thoughts and fortunate decisions, make sure that you do not overstretch your confidence and keep your feet firmly on the ground. The double influence of Mercury in your planetary spread also implies that your sharp intellect is usually stimulated by a wealth of ideas and a natural business sense.

Your Two Replacement Cards Are the 4 of Spades & the 10 of Spades.

As the 4 of Hearts you share the same planetary position as the 10 of Spades in the Earthly Spread. This powerful card signifies that you are not afraid to take on large projects and challenges. In order to reach the great heights of success, however, you need to establish self-discipline and accept hard work willingly. In fact, your success often comes as a result of your concentrated efforts and dedication.

As the 4 of Hearts you also share the same planetary position as the 4 of Spades in the Spiritual Spread. Since this card is also associated with the Spades suit it doubly emphasizes the importance of your work or career. This card, being part of the Spiritual Spread, indicates that your fulfillment comes from finding a vocation that can include your idealistic views.

You usually have special or karmic links with people represented by the 4 of Spades and the 10 of Spades, as you share the same planetary positions. You can be soul mates or understand each other very well. Even if you do not get along, you can both see clearly how the other person operates.

Your Mercury Card is . . .

The 4 of Diamonds
- You have an innate sense of values and a talent for commerce.
- Your pragmatic outlook is ideal for putting theories into practice.
- You need to resist acting on impulse when making important decisions about money or being overly indulgent.
- As long as you do not abandon your plans too quickly you can turn your ideas into profitable ventures.
- You should have good mental rapport and special communication with 4 of Diamonds people, as they activate your Mercury Card. These people can also be good business partners or coworkers.

Your Venus Card is . . .

The 2 of Spades
- You benefit from partnerships and generally prefer to work with others rather than alone.
- Your sensitivity and receptivity to beauty, art, and music indicate creative talents and good taste.
- Idealistic about love, you need to maintain the balance of power in relationships if you do not want to become too dependent on others.
- You can have a special rapport and feel attracted to people represented by the 2 of Spades. These people are also ideal for love and romance. If they are close friendships you may end up working together.

Your Mars Card is . . .

The 8 of Hearts
- Your charismatic personality can attract success, as people warm to your magnetic charm.
- You thrive on expressing your powerful emotions through some type of productive or creative outlet.
- You can succeed in all types of public-oriented careers, especially in the field of entertainment.
- Although your charismatic allure can make you very persuasive, guard against misusing your emotional power.
- 8 of Hearts people can particularly motivate and stimulate you. If you avoid being too competitive with this person you can both channel your emotional energies constructively and get a great deal done.

Your Jupiter Card is . . .

The 6 of Clubs
- You benefit from all types of intellectual activities or involvement in education or teaching.

The 4 of Hearts Planetary Card Sequence

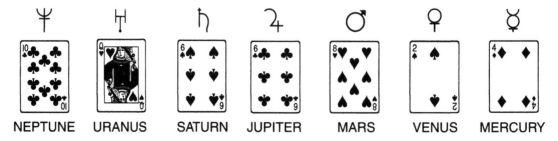

NEPTUNE   URANUS   SATURN   JUPITER   MARS   VENUS   MERCURY

- Your success is often based on your intuitive understanding and sensitivity to people and situations.
- Although you can be worldly aware, you also have a strong love for the peace and comforts of home and family.
- Learning to staying mentally positive can eliminate most of your insecurities.
- A desire for harmony can be reflected through appreciation of or talent in music and the arts.
- 6 of Clubs people can be benefactors who expand and enhance your life, especially if you share the same interests. Alternatively, these people can have a spiritual link with you.

Your Saturn Card is . . .

The 6 of Spades

- Your ambitious plans usually come to fruition only through persevering and staying motivated.
- You may have some karmic responsibilities concerning someone close to you.
- You have innate healing powers to regenerate yourself and other people.
- Resist falling into a comfortable rut, as inertia and laziness are your biggest challenges. They may undermine your spirit of adventure or minimize your determination to succeed.
- It is important for you to work at keeping a sense of balance in your life, especially between work and play; otherwise, you can suffer from worry or anxiety.
- 6 of Spades people can be your teachers or guides and help you realize your shortcomings. Although these people may sometimes bring burdens, if you are willing to work on your self-awareness they can also offer you valuable lessons.

Your Uranus Card is . . .

The Queen of Hearts

- Your charming and unique personality is one of your greatest assets.
- You have creative talents that can be original and progressive.
- Usually you are attracted to independent people or strong individualists.
- You can benefit from working in groups or exploring unusual or metaphysical subjects.
- Queen of Hearts people can help you be more objective about yourself due to your Uranus connection. This is also a good relationship or friendship link where freedom is important.

Your Neptune Card is . . .

The 10 of Clubs

- You can gain recognition and success in the second part of life, particularly through writing, intellectual pursuits, or projects that fire your enthusiasm.
- You can also benefit from learning new subjects, especially philosophy and spirituality.
- Traveling and expanding your horizons can bring unexpected rewards.
- 10 of Clubs people can have a psychic connection with you. You may share the same ideals; they may inspire you or help you to realize your dreams. In these relationships, however, you may need to be practical and guard against self-delusion.

Your Challenge Card is . . .

The 8 of Diamonds

- By establishing the right set of values you can focus on the things that really matter.
- You can overcome many of your obstacles by balancing your spiritual and material needs.

- Resist letting your strong desire for material success undermine your integrity.
- 8 of Diamonds people can usually stimulate you to react. Therefore, they can bring out the best or the worst aspects of your personality. Although these people can help you to transform your life, avoid power struggles.

The Result of Your Challenge Card is . . .

The King of Spades
- When you believe in your own skills and capabilities, you can rise to leadership positions and succeed.
- You can achieve a great deal through self-discipline and hard work.
- You have access to a storehouse of knowledge and wisdom when you feel motivated and inspired.
- King of Spades people can encourage you to be disciplined and often reflect how you are responding to your challenges.

Famous People Who Are the 4 of Hearts

Gérard Depardieu, Marlene Dietrich, Johannes Kepler, Louisa May Alcott, Louis Pasteur, Jan Vermeer, John Keats, Heather O'Rourke, Michael Landon, Jane Pauley, C. S. Lewis

Birthdays Governed by the 4 of Hearts

October 31: Scorpio   Ruler: Mars
Charismatic and dynamic, your personal power and determination are often concealed by your charm and calm manner. Mars, your ruler, provides you with the willpower and vitality necessary to achieve your objectives or go after the things you want. Although you may not appear ambitious, your inner confidence and positive outlook suggest that you possess the vital ingredients to achieve success. Since your resolve can make you quite persuasive, guard against letting stubbornness or an inflexible attitude undermine your great efforts. Your inner peace and emotional stability, nevertheless, are the necessary qualities that will allow you to find material fulfillment and happiness.

November 29: Sagittarius   Ruler: Jupiter
As a sensitive and receptive individual, your success is often based on your intellectual capabilities and ability to establish a good philosophy in life. A desire for knowledge suggests that when you are well informed or feel inspired your self-confidence increases. Jupiter, your ruler, also indicates that you can expand your horizons and gain greater success, as long as you stay optimistic and open to new ideas. Emotional fluctuations or a tendency to worry should be resisted, as they can sap your energies. When you channel your emotional power positively, however, you can be effective and influential.

December 27: Capricorn   Ruler: Saturn
Cautious and intuitive, your constructive attitude and resolve signifies that you are a determined individual who is responsible and hardworking. Your unique intellect and creative qualities can help you achieve success, especially if found through pursuits such as research and analysis. Although you can at times overindulge or be excessive, your ruler, Saturn, implies that you are usually a diligent and resourceful individual. Methodical and practical, the harder you work the more successful you become. Even though you are often reserved or skeptical, you can achieve greater success by learning to trust your intuition.

♣ THE 4 OF CLUBS ♣

Friendly yet direct, your 4 of Clubs Card suggests that you are an interesting mixture of keen intelligence, enthusiasm, and practical common sense. A keen learner, you seek inspiration and are attracted to those who can teach you how to expand your opportunities. Under the influences of Jupiter and Mars in the Earthly Spread, you are not afraid to think big and possess a spirit of enterprise. Straightforward and down-to-earth but with a persuasive manner, you can influence others, especially when you have a positive plan in mind. You do, however, need a definite set of beliefs from which to guide your life. This helps keep you constructively occupied rather than caught up in self-indulgent activities or acting too impulsively. Success comes from realizing that nothing comes for free.

As your card is also Mars in the Mars line of the Spiritual Spread you possess quick instincts, can make fast decisions, and do not suffer fools gladly. Usually outspoken, you have a desire for action and change, but you should guard against impatience or being too competitive. With such a strong Mars influence, women of this birthday often have masculine attitudes, valuing their independence rather than being domesticated. You do especially well when you combine your positive, forthright approach with your ability to plan and take action.

Your Two Replacement Cards Are the 5 of Clubs & The 6 of Hearts.

As the 4 of Clubs you share the same planetary position as the 5 of Clubs in the Spiritual Spread. This signifies that although sometimes restless you have an adventurous or bold side to your character. This trait can often take you into uncharted territory, whether through travel, expanding your knowledge, or improving your opportunities. With your fast intelligence you need to always be learning new things; otherwise, you can become bored.

Your card also shares the same planetary position as the 6 of Hearts in the Earthly Spread. This implies that your inner sensitivity and vulnerability may not be obvious from the outer personality you show the world. This more compassionate side to your character seeks peace and is willing to make sacrifices. Often feeling your responsibilities keenly, you may need to learn to care for others without becoming interfering or bossy. Realizing that it takes courage to explore your inner depths and be honest with yourself can be a key to obtaining the ultimate peace you are seeking.

You usually have special or karmic links with people represented by the 5 of Clubs or the 6 of Hearts, as you share the same planetary positions. You can be soul mates or business partners, as you understand each other very well. Even if you do not get along, you can both see clearly how the other person operates.

Your Mercury Card is . . .

The 2 of Diamonds

- Your natural business acumen indicates that you are good at negotiation. This skill may have been taught to you from a young age.
- It is good to have a balance between the two different ways you mentally approach life. One is businesslike and focused and the other is imaginative and idealistic.
- You may have an ungrounded fear of not having enough money or resources that can influence your thinking or come out in your communication with others.
- You have good ideas and a gift for making contacts, especially financially.

The 4 of Clubs Planetary Card Sequence

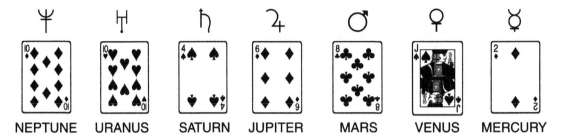

NEPTUNE URANUS SATURN JUPITER MARS VENUS MERCURY

- You can sell anything, whether a concept, product, or project, if you really believe in it.
- People represented by the 2 of Diamonds can act as a stimulus to your entrepreneurial spirit. You can also talk to them and develop many good ideas together.

Your Venus Card is . . .

The Jack of Spades

- You will always have a youthful or playful side to your personality.
- Although attracted by clever and confident individuals, be careful of an attraction to those of slightly dubious character.
- Your social life can often be connected to your work.
- Being independent and smart you need a partner who will keep up with your quick mind and give you freedom and space.
- Be careful of a tendency to be overcritical of those you love.
- Your brother or father may have played an especially strong part in your early life.
- You are more likely to overcome your reluctance to show your emotional vulnerability with a partner you respect and admire.
- Jack of Spades people can stimulate you socially or romantically or be helpful in business. Positively, they can stimulate your desire for wisdom.

Your Mars Card is . . .

The 8 of Clubs

- Determination coupled with imagination suggests you are best taking action when you have a clear vision of what it is you want to accomplish.
- Avoid using too much mental force or manipulation in arguments to get your own way. A love of debate, however, can work well for you in law or politics.
- Your unusual combination of assertive mental power and sensitive intuition can be combined to advance you both materially and spiritually.
- 8 of Clubs people can make you feel more dynamic, courageous, or ambitious. Alternatively, they may bring out a fear of domination and make you argumentative.

Your Jupiter Card is . . .

The 6 of Diamonds

- Your home is highly important in your life plan. It is a place to find the peace and security you seek, and it also can be lucky for you financially.
- Although usually active, a part of you craves routine and can get stuck in a comfortable rut.
- Your love of truth and a philosophical outlook can help you to see the good sides of

difficult situations. It can also attract you to religious or spiritual affairs, although you are not likely to take an orthodox approach.

- If you become anxious you may overindulge as a form of escapism.
- 6 of Diamonds people can bring you harmony and make you aware of your responsibilities. This can be a beneficial link that brings fortunate opportunities or is often a spiritual link.

Your Saturn Card is . . .

The 4 of Spades

- You are protected by your practical common sense and desire for constructive work.
- Some of your major tests in life revolve around slowly building up your patience, perseverance, and discipline.
- You can overcome most difficulties through having a clear-cut plan and sticking to it. You can be good with long-term planning.
- You may have to overcome emotional tensions and inhibitions that block your success.
- People represented by the 4 of Spades can often be teachers or testers. They can show you were where you need to work on yourself. You could both be stubborn.

Your Uranus Card is . . .

The 10 of Hearts

- The more you develop your innate humanitarianism the happier you will be.
- If you allow your ego to get emotionally carried away you can lose your objectivity and become rebellious or obstinate.
- A very loving part of you ensures that you can turn on the charm when in social situations or show compassion for people in real need.

- 10 of Hearts people can stimulate your objectivity and detachment. They can also make good friends.

Your Neptune Card is . . .

The 10 of Diamonds

- You can make money through the use of your image awareness, intuition, or vision.
- Do not let desires for material achievement divert you from your high ideals.
- Finances and opportunities to travel or foreign investments improve later in life.
- You can have an emotionally subtle or almost psychic link with people who are the 10 of Diamonds. You can encourage each other to have big dreams, but remember to stay practical.

Your Challenge Card is . . .

The 8 of Spades

- Avoid getting locked into power challenges with others.
- Clearly define your needs and challenges.
- Avoid extremism in your behavior, such as the workaholic/doing nothing polarity, or feeling very powerful and then feeling totally powerless.
- Think things through and be well structured.
- Use your drive, determination, and experience for achieving wisdom rather than just material success.
- People who are the 8 of Spades Card can dare you to be stronger and more forceful, bringing out the best or the worst of your personality. This can be a transformative influence.

The Result of Your Challenge Card is . . .

The Ace of Hearts

- You will always be starting new endeavors that you can put your heart into.
- Love, affection, and high principles become your major goals in life.
- If you are too selfish or bossy you may not be rising to your challenge and using your natural power and love to guide others.
- People who are the Ace of Hearts can have a strong emotional link with you. They can often show you how well you are responding to your challenges.

Famous People Who Are the 4 of Clubs

Jennifer Lopez, Kirsten Dunst, Bo Derek, Stan Smith, Martina Navratilova, Kylie Minogue, Gladys Knight, Willie Nelson, Pearl S. Buck, Colin Wilson, George C. Scott, Chuck Berry, John Lee Hooker, General N. Schwartzkopf, Ray Bradbury, Dorothy Parker, Jean-Claude Van Damme, Burgess Meredith, Tori Amos, Claude Debussy, Sophia Loren

Birthdays Governed by the 4 of Clubs

April 30: Taurus   Ruler: Venus

Friendly and creative with common sense, you like to be honest and direct. With a gift for words and latent artistic talent, you may wish to develop your need for self-expression through writing, music, art, or drama. When you have a goal in mind you can be very focused and driven, but you should avoid an inclination to scatter your forces. Although inspired by mentally sharp people with a sense of fun or drama, make sure they also have integrity.

May 28: Gemini   Ruler: Mercury

Articulate and direct, your quest for knowledge often takes you on many adventures. Although you will never lose the desire to learn, you eventually temper your restlessness or impatience with the quest for inner peace. Having a sensitive nervous system, it is important for you to develop tolerance and equanimity. You are helped by your innate idealism, which wants you to share your knowledge with others. Even though you are independent and enterprising, you can gain financially from working partnerships.

June 26: Cancer   Ruler: Moon

Proud and determined yet imaginative and caring, you have an honest and down-to-earth approach to life. Generally cheerful, you have a great love of family, but you also possess a need for adventure and mental challenge. You appreciate beauty and have innate creative talents, but you should pay attention to a stubborn streak that can spoil your appeal. With innate business acumen you work well when you have a positive plan of action or are discovering new areas of interest.

July 24: Leo   Ruler: Sun

Dramatic and idealistic but also practical and straight-talking, you are a positive planner with strong opinions. Being proud and enterprising with a dislike of taking orders suggests that you enjoy being in a leading position or working for yourself. Although you must guard against a stubborn streak, usually you are honest and fair with a need to constantly update your knowledge and skills. Being creative with good organizational skills, you may decide to use your leadership abilities and many talents for the good of the community.

August 22: Leo/Virgo   Ruler: Sun/Mercury

Born on the cusp, you have both the creativity of Leo and the practicality of Virgo. With an inner sense of nobility, you enjoy being active, often seeing life as a drama. With an ability to confront situations directly and good organizational skills you often enjoy creative problem-solving. The more you trust your natural intuition the stronger it gets, providing you with inner guidance either for yourself or others. Although pragmatic, you also have a very sensitive side that you may wish to develop further through the arts, spirituality, or healing.

September 20: Virgo   Ruler: Mercury
You can succeed in life through your ability to be persuasive and articulate, especially when combined with your sociability and charm. Practical and quick thinking, you take pleasure in improving your opportunities and knowledge. Fortunately, you have a flair for public relations, business negotiation, or dealing with people. Your relationships play an especially valuable part in your life, particularly your working and business partnerships. Being enterprising, you are always looking for new ideas. If you can find projects that combine your idealism with your shrewd business awareness then so much the better.

October 18: Libra   Ruler: Venus
Being verbally expressive, determined, and able to display good people skills can make you popular. Progressive and innovative, you need stimulating mental pursuits to keep your interest; otherwise, you can quickly become bored. To overcome a possible selfish or intolerant streak you need to utilize your sharp mind and many talents for the good of others. Generally, you are able to lift people up with your practical advice and innate healing ability. You may wish to develop your inborn artistic or creative gifts through music, art, writing, or drama.

November 16: Scorpio   Ruler: Mars
As a person you possess a wide range of talents, being both sensitive and intuitive yet practical and mentally keen. Although usually thoughtful, you are intense with a capacity to express yourself dramatically. Being ambitious and wanting to advance in life, you can be assertive and respond quickly. You may, however, experience a pull between your self-expression and a love of home and family. You possess a strong desire to be open and honest yet also can keep secrets back that sometimes makes you seem aloof. Nevertheless, you are usually responsible and caring, and have natural psychic abilities.

December 14: Sagittarius   Ruler: Jupiter
Adventurous and cheerful, you seek information and new experiences that stop you from getting bored. Philosophical in outlook, you can bounce back from difficulties, but you may need to guard against being stubborn or thoughtless. With a love of the good life, you enjoy little luxuries and indulgences, but you are usually willing to work hard to make things happen. At times you may have to balance your desire for stability with your need for variety and change. Fortunately, your good-humored attitude and shrewd common sense usually come to your aid. Being idealistic, you are often inspired by wisdom and opportunities to expand your horizons, particularly through education and travel.

◆ THE 4 OF DIAMONDS ◆

The pragmatic attitude associated with the number 4 indicates that by nature you are a self-reliant individual with good strategies and a constructive approach. Belonging to the Diamonds suit suggests that you have a good sixth sense when it comes to evaluating people or situations. Although you can pay attention to small details and persist until you get your own way, in your attempts to achieve your objectives you should resist being stubborn or too critical.

Your willingness to put a great deal of effort and hard work into what you believe in implies that you have the determination to reach your aims. Usually you take pride in your work, so finding work opportunities is rarely a serious problem for you, as you frequently prove yourself to be a competent organizer or valuable employee.

Although as a 4 of Diamonds you have excellent opportunities to achieve success materially, the planetary influences of Neptune and Venus in the Earthly Spread suggests that your sensitive awareness and sociability also play an important role in your personal development. To help you to find the contentment you seek, you often need to blend your imaginative ideas or aspirations with your practical plans or financial objectives.

The planetary influences of Venus and Saturn in your Spiritual Spread indicates that while your responsible attitude and realistic views can give you the edge, at times you can appear uncooperative or unsympathetic. Nevertheless, meticulous, loyal, and sincere, your direct approach can help you to achieve harmonious conditions at home as well as at work.

Your Two Replacement Cards Are the 5 of Spades & the 5 of Hearts.

As the 4 of Diamonds you share the same planetary position as the 5 of Hearts in the Earthly Spread. This card signifies a strong desire for freedom of movement and a resistance to being restrained either by people or circumstance. At times these feelings may conflict with your need for stability, security, and hard work and cause you fluctuating moods. You possess a warm heart, however, that enjoys reaching out to help others.

As the 4 of Diamonds you also share the same planetary position as the 5 of Spades in the Spiritual Spread. This indicates that while you can be pragmatic and instinctive, restlessness and impatience can sometimes undermine your great efforts. The karmic influence of this card implies that fated changes or alternating circumstances concerning work will bring a constant flow of new people or situations in your life. It also suggests that you may prefer a career that involves action, a fast pace, or travel.

You usually have special or karmic links with people represented by the 5 of Spades and the 5 of Hearts, as you share the same planetary positions. You can be soul mates or understand each other very well. Even if you do not get along, you can both see clearly how the other person operates.

Your Mercury Card is . . .

The 2 of Spades

- Usually encouraged or vitalized by collaborative efforts, you benefit from partnerships and all type of work associations.
- Your friendly approach and ability to assist others benefits your relationships.
- Help from others can come suddenly or when you least expect it.
- You have a natural talent for quickly assessing people intuitively.
- You should have good mental rapport and special communication with people who represent the 2 of Spades, as they activate your Mercury Card. These people can also be lifelong friends or business partners.

Your Venus Card is . . .

The 8 of Hearts

- With your strong feelings and charismatic charm, you can captivate others.
- You can succeed through activities relating to the public or be highly creative.

The 4 of Diamonds Planetary Card Sequence

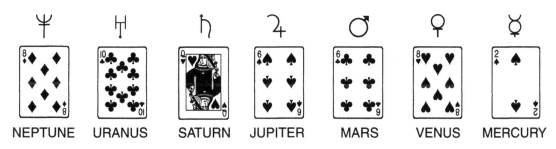

| NEPTUNE | URANUS | SATURN | JUPITER | MARS | VENUS | MERCURY |

- You can empower yourself when you realize how much you can achieve with the power of love.
- Guard against being too demanding or emotionally controlling. Alternatively, you may attract dominating partners who may cause you to sulk or become involved in power struggles.
- Romantic and attractive, you can be a passionate lover.
- Usually you are drawn to people who are represented by 8 of Hearts, especially if they share your creative interests. They are ideal for love and romance as well as for close friendships and good business partnerships.

Your Mars Card is . . .

The 6 of Clubs
- Curious and astute, you often rely on your intuition to make judgments.
- Worry and stress can deplete your drive and vitality.
- You benefit from having a challenging interest that keeps you mentally stimulated.
- To gain the most out of this card you need to be continually acquiring skills and knowledge.
- Avoid getting into monotonous, inactive, or restrictive situations, as this can make you impatient or restless.
- The relationships you have with 6 of Clubs

people can be good if they stimulate your drive or you both share the same aspirations. Resist being competitive with these people, as this can drain your energy.

Your Jupiter Card is . . .

The 6 of Spades
- Being responsible, your efforts are usually rewarded justly.
- As an idealist you can put a lot of effort and hard work into things you truly believe in.
- Interest in metaphysical subjects can add to your strength and spiritual empowerment.
- Astute and intuitive, you can tap into your storehouse of knowledge to find the right solution to your problem.
- Although you are security conscious, inactivity can lead to inertia.
- 6 of Spades people can bring positive opportunities. If you are in business or partnership with them you can both be successful, particularly if you share the same values.

Your Saturn Card is . . .

The Queen of Hearts
- Even though it may involve self-sacrifice and hard work, you benefit from disciplining your sensitive feelings or creative thoughts.
- If you want to accomplish your goals put your powerful emotions into something

worthwhile and accept the responsibilities that come with your leadership card.

- Some of your life lessons may involve having to look out for or care for someone who will need your help, especially a woman.
- People who are the Queen of Hearts can play an important role in your life if you are able to learn from them about responsibilities. Although your relationship with them may not be always easy, their contributions are often very valuable lessons.

Your Uranus Card is . . .

The 10 of Clubs

- Benefits come from developing your fine mind, especially in your middle years.
- Your foresight and probing mind can get to the heart of the matter or come up with original thoughts and ideas.
- You can achieve higher rates of success when your interests involve philosophical concepts, new technological breakthroughs, or projects that fire your enthusiasm.
- Your inventive approach and determination to succeed are often a winning combination.
- You can get much satisfaction from working in humanitarian activities.
- 10 of Clubs people can stimulate your mind and offer you valuable insight into new philosophies or opportunities to explore new ideas. This is also a good card for friendship.

Your Neptune Card is . . .

The 8 of Diamonds

- In latter years you are likely to benefit from material stability and see the rewards of all your past efforts.
- A practical visionary, if you combine your imaginative ideas with determination or business sense this can help you to realize your dreams and achieve success.

- The spiritual influences of your Neptune Card suggest that you gain from developing your universal awareness.
- Your foresight can help you make good long-term investments.
- 8 of Diamonds people can stimulate your imagination, dreams, and visions for the future. You can both be emotionally sensitive to each other, but guard against delusion by staying realistic.

Your Challenge Card is . . .

The King of Spades

- You can create harmony and balance in your life if you minimize your tendency to fluctuate from highs to lows.
- Being cooperative and learning to see the advantages in compromise can lead you to good partnerships and successful ventures.
- A tendency to be bossy or wanting to be in control can undermine your leadership qualities.
- King of Spades people can captivate you but also challenge your authority. Although these people can help you to transform your life, resist becoming involved in ego battles.

The Result of Your Challenge Card is . . .

The 3 of Hearts

- Your natural charm and friendly approach can be your biggest assets.
- By recognizing and expressing your emotional needs you can overcome indecisiveness or feelings of insecurity.
- You are able to utilize your innate leadership qualities for finding creative and productive ways to show your love and emotional sensitivity.
- 3 of Hearts people can encourage you to express yourself emotionally and creatively. They can also inspire you to be more loving.

Your reactions to them often reflect how you are responding to your personal challenges.

Famous People Who Are the 4 of Diamonds

Humphrey Bogart, Sir Bob Geldof, Edouard Manet, Nina Simone, Hubert de Givenchy, Philip Roth, J. P. Morgan, Victoria Beckham, Pierce Brosnan, Pierre Curie, W. B. Yeats, Malcolm McDowell, Yul Brynner, Giorgio Armani, Whitney Houston, Buddy Holly, Queen Elizabeth I, Elia Kazan, Chrissie Hynde, Bette Midler, Bruce Willis, Charles Bronson, Richard Pryor, Roseanne, Glenn Close, Michael Andretti, Woody Allen, Mary-Kate and Ashley Olsen, Melanie Griffith

Birthdays Governed by the 4 of Diamonds

January 23: Aquarius   Ruler: Uranus
The constructive influence of your card implies that you are usually an independent individual with good practical skills. Often resourceful and a quick learner, at times you may have to overcome a tendency to be restless or impatient. According to your ruler, Uranus, you are an inventive and progressive individual with a desire to transcend the mundane or find something truly inspiring that can motivate you or keep you absorbed. Your knowledge of human nature and flair for dealing with people is one area you can excel in and not get bored.

February 21: Pisces   Ruler: Neptune
Receptive and sociable, you are a sensitive and romantic individual with restless emotions. Although according to your ruler, Neptune, you are often an imaginative dreamer, the pragmatic influence of the number 4 suggests that you also have a good head for business and the organizational skills to make your dreams come true. Your unique perspective and indi-vidual style implies that you can express yourself in original ways. Although you may be protected materially, in order to succeed you will have to work hard and show your dedication.

March 19: Pisces   Ruler: Neptune
The dynamic influence of the number 1 associated with your birth date indicates that you are an idealist with leadership qualities. Your innate sixth sense and need for recognition or acceptance also implies that you are highly receptive to people and your environment. According to your ruler, Neptune, you are an insightful visionary with vivid imagination and creative talents. When you feel inspired your youthful enthusiasm can captivate others. In order to make your dreams come true, however, you need to develop self-discipline and show your maturity by accepting responsibilities such as learning to complete what you have started.

April 17: Aries   Ruler: Mars
According to your ruler, Mars, you possess the vitality and determination to move forward and succeed. Armed with practical skills, intuitive insight, and a head for business, you like to make up your own mind and think independently. Your success may be linked to your unique understanding and talents. Although you often prefer to be self-reliant, resist a tendency to be too fixed in your opinions. The mental sensitivity linked to your day also suggests that your accomplishments are often greater when you develop your analytical skills and feel emotionally inspired or motivated.

May 15: Taurus   Ruler: Venus
Intelligent, instinctive, and engaging, your charismatic appeal indicates that you are a friendly and gregarious individual who can impress people and be popular. Venus, your ruler, endows you with poise, sensuality, and creative

talents. Your desire for material comforts and a love of luxury imply that you are often willing to work for the good things in life. However, a preoccupation with material possessions and overindulgence can minimize your resolve and undermine your sense of moderation. Even though you are not the most ambitious individual, your practical skills and a head for business suggest that you are likely to have many opportunities to accomplish success.

June 13: Gemini   Ruler: Mercury

Courteous and progressive, your ability to quickly grasp situations indicates that you are a pragmatic and highly intuitive individual. Although you are an independent thinker with good organizational skills and a unique style of doing things, your success usually depends on how cooperative you are. Even though your enthusiasm can motivate other people, guard against being too bossy or too argumentative. An ability to understand market forces and a good head for business also imply that you can initiate new projects or ideas that appeal to the public at large.

July 11: Cancer   Ruler: Moon

Idealistic and motivated, your sincerity, enthusiasm, and drive can encourage you to achieve and accomplish in a big way. Your ruler, the Moon, indicates that you are an intuitive, caring, and sensitive individual with strong family ties. Security conscious and receptive, although you usually want to create a congenial atmosphere, a tendency to manipulate people or situations can disturb the harmonious conditions around you. Nevertheless, being idealistic and pragmatic indicates that when you feel inspired you are a hard worker who is likely to succeed.

August 9: Leo   Ruler: Sun

Your idealism and enthusiasm indicate that although you are a determined and ambitious individual, you can be thoughtful and generous. The Sun, your ruler, makes you dramatic and dynamic. When inspired by an idea or a project your resolve and persistence can make you a prolific worker. Yet the sensitivity implied by your number 9 birthday suggests that you can at times be vulnerable to temperamental behavior as a result of frustration or disappointments. Nevertheless, your intuitive understanding of market trends and a head for business also signifies that you usually achieve prosperity and success.

September 7: Virgo   Ruler: Mercury

Mentally quick and well informed, your ruler, Mercury, grants you good analytical and administrative skills. Your methodical approach and ability to pay attention to details suggest that you can refine and improve existing methods of work. Although your skeptical viewpoint suggests that you prefer to think independently, with trust and flexibility you can increase your chances for success. By being supportive, patient, and less critical you can also win others to your way of thinking. Nevertheless, helpful and thoughtful, you are a good listener and your advice is usually objective.

October 5: Libra   Ruler: Venus

Instinctive and charismatic, your ruler, Venus, empowers you with natural charm and a flair for dealing with people. Success-oriented, self-reliant, and entertaining, you can gain many admirers and be popular. A mixture of inner restlessness and ambition suggests, however, that although you can be pragmatic and pay particular attention to practical considerations you can also be impulsive. Since you are likely to find greater satisfaction through creative means or public-related occupations, mundane jobs are likely to make you bored or discontented. A desire to transform your circumstances or make vital changes signifies that throughout your life you are likely to change direction several times.

November 3: Scorpio   Ruler: Mars

Ambitious and idealistic, your ability to focus on your objectives suggests that success is within reach when you are calm and confident in your opinions. Although your ruler, Mars, gives you vitality, strong willpower, and the determination to accomplish much in life, resist pursuing these goals with ruthless zeal. As you like to be well informed, gaining knowledge is likely to be one of your main priorities. Alternatively, your creativity, versatility, and mental sensitivity indicate that you are a highly receptive and imaginative individual who seeks ways to express your unique intellectual abilities.

December 1: Sagittarius   Ruler: Jupiter

Independent, confident, and idealistic, your optimistic outlook and practical skills imply that you can take the lead in all types of enterprises. Your ruler, Jupiter, suggests that although you can be hardworking and down-to-earth, you need the freedom to be constantly expanding your horizons and enjoying different experiences. Despite materialistic inclinations, your innate creativity, quest for truth, and strong sixth sense also imply that you realize money alone will not be the answer to your inner needs and personal fulfillment. Nevertheless, when your enthusiasm and strong aspirations are combined with practical considerations, you can achieve the success you want.

♠ THE 4 OF SPADES ♠

Straightforward and down-to-earth, yet friendly and confident, you are an attractive individual with a determined mind. Being strong-willed with an ability to turn on the charm, you can be very entertaining. Nevertheless, you may need to learn that being too direct can also cause antagonism. Under the influences of Venus and Jupiter in the Earthly Spread, you are both ambitious and sociable, often combining business with pleasure. Achievement-oriented, you have good organizational abilities and can particularly attain success through your work. With a taste for the good life, you enjoy beauty and luxury, but may have to watch a tendency for overindulgence. Although you usually keep your feet on the ground, you often have many big plans to improve your situation and can be quite determined in realizing them. Your card is particularly fortunate when it comes to financial security.

As your card is also Mercury in the Neptune line of the Spiritual Spread, you are blessed with a strong imagination and an intuitive mind that can pick up on situations very quickly. If developed and not wasted on escapism this strong vision is a powerful tool to help you achieve your many ideals.

Your Two Replacement Cards Are the 10 of Clubs & the 4 of Hearts.

As the 4 of Spades you share the same planetary position as the 10 of Clubs in the Spiritual Spread. This signifies that when genuinely enthused about a project you can radiate success, confidence, and positive zeal. This in turn attracts others to believe in you. An independent thinker, you like to be well informed and admire those who have knowledge or expertise.

As your card also shares the same planetary position as the 4 of Hearts in the Earthly Spread you highly value emotional honesty, preferring to tell people what you really feel. Although not everybody can handle your frankness, you are loyal and others know exactly where they stand. Equally, you like to build a strong foundation to whatever you achieve. Although usually warm and friendly, at times you can become too rigid and project a hard side to your character. Nevertheless, you are usually kind and generous, often giving others practical and emotional support.

You usually have special or karmic links with people represented by the 10 of Clubs or the 4 of Hearts, as you share the same planetary positions. You can be soul mates or business partners as you understand each other very well. Even if you do not get along, you can both see clearly how the other person operates.

Your Mercury Card is . . .

The 10 of Hearts
- Your excellent communication skills signify that you can particularly make progress in people-related activities.
- Your intuitive intellect suggests you fare better when linked to projects with which you have an emotional connection.
- Your natural talents may lead you to develop skills such as writing, music, art, or drama.
- In early life you were likely to have been surrounded by a loving or strongly emotional family.

- 10 of Hearts people can stimulate your thoughts for success and may encourage you to discuss your many ideas. This is a good communication link.

Your Venus Card is . . .

The 10 of Diamonds
- You have a knack for attracting opportunities for money and success or turning difficulties to your advantage.
- As financial issues often play a strong part in your personal relationships, be careful not to become too materialistic at the expense of your happiness.
- Your ability to make good social contacts helps you gain money and status. You like to mix with people of intelligence, means, and influence.
- People who are the 10 of Diamonds can prove to be a good social, romantic, or friendship link with you. This can also be a valuable link for money or business.

Your Mars Card is . . .

The 8 of Spades
- You enjoy the dynamics of power and are usually fortunate to have drive and motivation.

The 4 of Spades Planetary Card Sequence

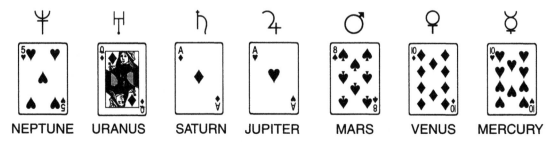

NEPTUNE   URANUS   SATURN   JUPITER   MARS   VENUS   MERCURY

- Your spirit of enterprise combined with hard work can help you make remarkable achievements.
- When actively involved you possess determination, courage, and authority, but you should guard against becoming overbearing or domineering.
- 8 of Spades people can stimulate your willpower, love of action, and resolve, although they may also cause you to be competitive or get locked in power conflicts with them.

Your Jupiter Card is . . .

The Ace of Hearts
- With a love of new and exciting activities, you usually enjoy large-scale planning or expansive opportunities. Initiating projects, especially those that involve foreign interests, can be especially beneficial.
- Although your pride usually serves you well, avoid allowing it to spill over into arrogance by practicing humility.
- You do not like to take orders from others and are best working for yourself or in management positions.
- People who are the Ace of Hearts can have an expansive or beneficial effect on you and bring opportunities. Even though this can often be a good spiritual link, it may also stimulate overindulgence.

Your Saturn Card is . . .

The Ace of Diamonds
- When focused and working hard you have an amazing ability to manifest your goals.
- Even though your strong will and desires imply that you often get what you want, be careful of selfishness.
- Being independent, with an original approach, you are usually best when left to do things your own way.

- Ace of Diamonds people can stimulate your leadership and discipline. Alternatively, they could prove to be restrictive or testing. There are valuable lessons to be learned either way.

Your Uranus Card is . . .

The Queen of Diamonds
- This royal card suggests that women can be good friends or bring you fortunate material help.
- Your good evaluation skills and inventive approach can be further developed through metaphysical and spiritual studies, experimenting in new areas, or humanitarian work.
- If you become stubborn or tense, be careful of a tendency for harsh speech.
- You can be a loyal friend to others, but be careful of attracting those who want to take advantage of your generosity.
- Queen of Diamonds people can make you more objective about your "act." They can often stimulate your dramatic and inventive qualities or be good friends.

Your Neptune Card is . . .

The 5 of Hearts
- Quick to pick up on others' feelings, dreams, and aspirations, you can respond in a warm and dynamic manner.
- If you become overemotional or confused you are likely to become impatient or restless. This can lead you to escapist activities or cause you to do something impulsive.
- Ingenious and resourceful, you usually enjoy new experiences.
- Travel is highlighted for you, especially in your later years. This is likely to include long journeys over water.
- 5 of Hearts people can stimulate your sense of adventure or desire for change. You can

have a psychic link with this person. They can share your dreams or ideals but also stay down-to-earth.

Your Challenge Card is . . .

The 3 of Clubs

- Put your many creative ideas into action rather than just talk about them.
- Enthusiastically express the joy of life.
- People who are the 3 of Clubs can challenge you to bring out the best or the worst of your personality.

The Result of Your Challenge Card is . . .

The 3 of Spades

- If you respond positively to your challenge you will not suffer from insecurity, jealousy, or worry as you find positive channels for your strong self-expression and practical wisdom.
- You will make your decisions based on the principles of truth and choose your beliefs to support you positively.
- People who are the 3 of Spades can be a mirror for you as to how you are facing your challenges.

Famous People Who Are the 4 of Spades

James Dean, Jack Lemmon, Robert Downey, Jr., Emanuel Swedenborg, Lana Turner, Michelangelo, James McNeill Whistler, Dick Fosbury, Rod Stewart, Bing Crosby, Satyajit Ray, Elizabeth Barrett Browning, Muddy Waters, Jules Verne, Gabriel Garcia Marquez, King Vidor, David Beckham, Evangeline Adams, Kiri Te Kanawa, Mary Wilson, Elmer Bernstein, Anthony Perkins, Tom Arnold, Nick Nolte, Shaquille O'Neal, Maya Angelou

Birthdays Governed by the 4 of Spades

January 10: Capricorn   Ruler: Saturn

Determination and a direct manner are matched by your friendly personality. Although independent, when you learn not to lean on others your natural leadership skills come to the fore. Being ambitious, material success and prestige are important, so you are usually willing to work hard to achieve them. Fortunately, you have the gift of charm or warm sociability to help you in your climb to the top. Intelligent and innovative, you have a strong presence and powerful convictions, so to avoid becoming overbearing you may need to develop patience and the ability to compromise.

February 8: Aquarius   Ruler: Uranus

Friendly and generous, your strong will and drive is matched by your individuality. Although open minded to ncw and progressive ideas, you still like to do things your way. This is fine as long as you do not become stubborn or too rebellious. Being very sociable, you value friendship and will often go out of your way to help others. This natural humanitarian side of your nature can be further developed, and if you combine it with your natural business sense you are able to achieve outstanding results. With all your knowledge and strong intuition you succeed particularly well when creatively inspired.

March 6: Pisces   Ruler: Neptune

Imaginative with strong feelings, you need large projects that you can throw yourself into with enthusiasm and drive. Although you can be worldly aware, you also have a strong love for the peace and comforts of home and family. Idealistic and determined, you can especially succeed in the arts, whether writing, music, drama, or dancing. In the caring/healing professions you also get a chance to utilize your sensitivity and powerful intuition. Being friendly, sympathetic, and practical, you may find yourself an adviser to others.

April 4: Aries Ruler: Mars
Your drive and determination are matched by your direct and down-to-earth approach to life. Generally optimistic, with the ability to think big, you can be very enterprising. Although usually kind, magnanimous, and popular, guard against a tendency to be stubborn or bossy, as this may spoil some of your many charms. Ambitious, with the ability to work hard, you prefer to keep busy. Pioneering new ventures, particularly those that involve busi-

ness, the arts, executive skills, or dealing with people, are where you can especially shine.

May 2: Taurus Ruler: Venus
With your magnetic charm and warm personality, people may not see your steely determination underneath. Practical and ambitious as well as kind and considerate, you have a knack for dealing with people and making good social contacts. Although you value status, you also enjoy helping those less fortunate than yourself. Proud and dignified, you are usually willing to work hard to support your expensive tastes and favorite causes. With your natural diplomacy and gift for precise speech, you can be a representative of goodwill for others.

♥ ♣ THE 5 s ♦ ♠

THE NUMBER 5 influence suggests the ability to be quick and instinctive as well as a gift for fast learning. If you are a number 5 card you need freedom and are likely to enjoy variety, change, and an active life or you may start to feel trapped. Usually you are progressive, with fast reactions and an ability to adjust yourself to new situations. It may be necessary, however, for you to channel some of your restlessness or impatience into enterprising projects or developing your sense of adventure. Opportunities for travel or exciting ventures can also stir your enthusiasm and desire for action. By developing your perseverance and sense of purpose you can avoid drifting through life never quite finding your true vocation. Although you usually enjoy meeting new people and seeing different places, guard against boredom or doing things on the spur of the moment that might be regretted later. Nonetheless, it does usually help you to change your regular routine to keep fresh and vital or to put some of your excess adrenaline into physical activities such as walking or sports. At your best you can be self-disciplined and focused, with a sharp mind and swift responses.

The following suits further modify the effect of your number:

5 of Hearts

Your card indicates that you are liable to have fast emotional changes or reactions. You may be prone to feeling one way one day and then differently another. Highly instinctive, you pick up on situations around you very quickly. Although kind and warmhearted, you may have to overcome reacting too impulsively.

5 of Clubs

With your strong desire for mental stimulation you need to be constantly learning new things or finding new adventures. If not, you can become bored and mentally restless. Clever and adaptable, you respond well to travel and are creative at problem solving. Although daring and freedom loving, be careful of being reckless.

5 of Diamonds

Your card is one of changing material circumstances. On a positive level this suggests much variety or movement, bringing new experiences or people into your life. You may enjoy being on the move, traveling, or just going to the gym. If your dynamic energy isn't channeled productively, however, it can produce impatience and restlessness. As your monetary situation can also be prone to change it is good to save for the long term.

5 of Spades

Many of your changes in life revolve around your work. If you are bored and restless you may need to make an effort to bring new energy into your life and revive your sense of adventure and excitement. Freedom loving and progressive, you particularly gain from travel and activities that keep your interest.

♥ THE 5 OF HEARTS ♥

As a number 5 in the Hearts suit you are a person of fast instincts and powerful yet changeable emotions. Your strong 5 influence signifies that you love adventure and variety, yet the double influence of Saturn in your life cards also suggests that your need for security may be at odds with your free spirit. Under the influences of Venus and Saturn in the Earthly Spread you fare well if using the sociability and charm of Venus to help you achieve your goals. Under the influence of Saturn, however, you really do not start achieving in life until you develop your self-discipline and perseverance. Often able to combine business with pleasure, you can benefit from activities that involve the public and are away from routine.

Equally, Venus and Saturn can give you the ability to put artistic or creative gifts into some form of solid structure. With a strong love of freedom and a tendency for restlessness, however, you may need to avoid focusing on dissatisfaction with your current situation, whether in your work or your relationships. Concentration or techniques such as meditation are good for stilling your emotions and bringing you peace and acceptance. As your card is also Saturn in the Mercury line of the Spiritual Spread, working with communication in all forms, whether writing, speaking, or presenting your ideas to others can be a major part of your life plan.

Your Two Replacement Cards Are the 4 of Diamonds & the 5 of Clubs.

As the 5 of Hearts you share the same planetary position as the 4 of Diamonds in the Spiritual Spread. This signifies that developing a foundation for your achievements and your work in general can be very important to you. Inside you have a need for order, practicality, and accomplishment that can be achieved by constant and consistent progress. Equally, honesty and loyalty are expressions of your inner spirit that need to be lived out in your daily life. Guard against stubbornness, however, which may deny you opportunities for expansion.

You also share the same planetary position as the 5 of Clubs in the Earthly Spread. This card suggests that, being dynamic and mentally quick, you enjoy learning and can be good at encouraging others to improve their situations. With a spirit of enterprise, you enjoy exciting activities or journeys of exploration and earning while you learn.

You usually have special or karmic links with people who are represented by the 4 of Diamonds and the 5 of Clubs, as you share the same planetary positions. You can be soul mates or understand each other very well. Even if you do not get along, you can both see clearly how the other person operates.

Your Mercury Card is . . .

The 3 of Clubs
- You are full of creative ideas and often choose to explore many avenues of interest, although avoid scattering your forces.
- The more decisive you are, the more your life falls into place. It is better not to labor and worry about your choices. Keep things light, make one choice, and if that doesn't work make another.
- You enjoy social situations where you are able to communicate and collect knowledge.
- People represented by the 3 of Clubs are usually those you can talk to. This link is good for communication in general, expressing your views, creative ideas, and making contacts.

Your Venus Card is . . .

The 3 of Spades
- The love and relationships area of your life is one where you may need to work at developing wisdom.
- When positive and enjoying what you are doing you can be expressive and highly creative.
- Insecurity, jealousy, or indecisiveness can cause you problems with your love life if you don't work at overcoming these obstacles.
- You are very sociable and gain much gratification from seeing people happy.
- People who are the 3 of Spades can stimulate your sociability and desire for pleasure. This can be a good link for romance, friendship, or business.

Your Mars Card is . . .

The 9 of Hearts
- Usually, your natural reaction is to reach out with warm compassion for others.
- The more you hold onto emotional disappointments from the past the harder it is for you to take definite action.
- You may need to get the balance right between caring too much or totally withdrawing.
- People who are the 9 of Hearts can encourage you to be more dynamic and courageous, but avoid being impulsive or argumentative with these individuals.

Your Jupiter Card is . . .

The 7 of Clubs
- When you have faith in yourself you can be very enthusiastic and daring, even enjoying friendly rivalry or competition.
- With your sensitive intellect, you may be drawn to things of a spiritual or mystical nature.
- Although you can be analytical, when you trust yourself to be spontaneous or go with the flow you discover new confidence.
- Feeling that you are constantly obtaining new information or expanding your horizons stops you from becoming cynical or self-indulgent.
- People who are the 7 of Clubs can have a beneficial influence on your life. They can provide fortunate or expansive opportunities or be a spiritual influence.

Your Saturn Card is . . .

The 5 of Diamonds
- It will aid you greatly to go for long-term goals rather than taking the quick fix.

The 5 of Hearts Planetary Card Sequence

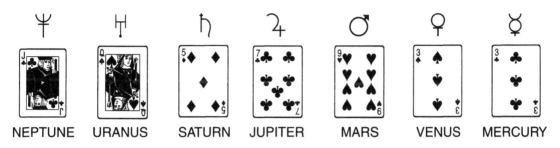

| NEPTUNE | URANUS | SATURN | JUPITER | MARS | VENUS | MERCURY |

- Your tests particularly revolve around taking responsibility rather than letting restlessness or impatience stop you from facing issues.
- You can be very resourceful and focused when you are either challenged or have a definite strategy in place.
- Your love of travel and new experiences imply that short breaks away from your responsibilities can help you overcome any possible feelings of restriction.
- People who are the 5 of Diamonds can be either teachers or liabilities. Either way they can make you more aware of boundaries and responsibilities and often help you see the areas where you need to work on yourself.

Your Uranus Card is . . .

The Queen of Spades

- You possess a shrewd and astute insight into people, particularly in group situations or when dealing with friends.
- A strong female influence suggests that hardworking women can stimulate your originality, leadership skills, and individuality.
- A humanitarian side to your nature can be further developed to bring you wisdom and satisfaction.
- People represented by the Queen of Spades can make you more objective about yourself

and help you value your unique approach to life, or could be a good friend.

Your Neptune Card is . . .

The Jack of Clubs

- Highly imaginative and sensitive, you possess not only strong visionary abilities but also the potential to write or express them to others.
- If you allow the Jack influence here to tempt you to be irresponsible rather than playful and creative you may never unlock your outstanding potential for self-expression or education.
- You can be inspired and enthusiastic when you have a clear vision of what you want.
- Jack of Clubs people can connect to your sensitivity, making an almost psychic link between you. Although this can stimulate your dreams and imagination, be careful to stay realistic and keep your feet on the ground.

Your Challenge Card is . . .

The 9 of Diamonds

- Let go of your attachments to old situations.
- Use humor to let you see the irony of life.
- Transmute any frustrations with your material situation into developing your business acumen in an unemotional way.

- 9 of Diamonds people provoke you to intense reactions. This can be good if it produces positive change and you rise to the challenge, but resist power struggles.

The Result of Your Challenge Card is . . .

The 7 of Spades

- If you respond to your challenges positively you will be actively building your faith, both in yourself and in what you are doing.
- You will not be in work that is well below your capabilities.
- You will have opportunities to use your natural wisdom rather than be cynical.
- People represented by the 7 of Spades card can stimulate your faith or show you how well you are responding to your challenges.

Famous People Who Are the 5 of Hearts

Grace Slick, Randy Newman, William Blake, Nancy Mitford, Henry Miller, Rita Mae Brown, Friedrich Engels, Louis Malle, Phil Spector, Berry Gordy, Jr., Chairman Mao, Ed Harris, Steve Allen, Ezra Pound, Henry Winkler

Birthdays Governed by the 5 of Hearts

October 30: Scorpio   Ruler: Mars

With your powerful emotions and desire for self-expression you can present a strong image to the world. Fortunately, you also have a quick and creative mind and a way with words either in conversation, through writing, or in presenting your ideas. This doesn't stop you from making sharp comments, however, that can also show a talent for debating or criticism. Due to your personal desire for happiness and unconditional love you are often willing to show compassion for others. You particularly gain from developing emotional detachment and letting go of the past.

November 28: Sagittarius   Ruler: Jupiter

Friendly and strong-willed with an idealistic nature, you seek change and adventure to stop you from becoming bored. Although you enjoy expanding your horizons, whether through travel, education, or enterprising ventures, you may have to guard against a restless or intolerant side to your personality. When positively motivated you can be creative, ambitious, and daring. Your quest for truth and honesty may lead you to philosophical, metaphysical, or spiritual interests.

December 26: Capricorn   Ruler: Saturn

Your strong emotions and drive enable you to work dynamically toward your aims and objectives. Often a tower of strength for others, you place great value on having a secure home environment from which to operate. Bored by routine, however, you may have to overcome a restless streak that could cause you to avoid the discipline needed to manifest your ideals. Nevertheless, proud and determined, you possess a heightened inner sensitivity that can be constructively channeled, either creatively or for the good of others.

♣ THE 5 OF CLUBS ♣

As the 5 of Clubs, you are often versatile, action-oriented, and keen on a fast pace. Being mentally agile and adaptable, you enjoy exploring new ideas or trying out different lifestyles. As a fast learner you gain a great deal of insight from your mistakes as well as your successes. Although you usually benefit from your sharp responses, you need to resist letting boredom or restlessness cause you to be discontented or scatter your energies in too many directions. In order to avoid uncertainty in life you need to apply structure, continuity, and self-discipline to your wonderful talents. Nevertheless, your need for mental stimuli suggests that you are better off in careers that involve variety, movement, and a great deal of mental activity.

Under the planetary influences of Saturn and Mercury in the Earthly Spread, you can be pragmatic and methodical, with good organizational skills. Although you often react instinctively, when you feel inspired by an idea you can also be patient and focused, taking time to develop your talents and skills. The key to your success is therefore often founded on discipline, good training, or education. Although you can achieve a great deal in a short period of time you usually benefit most from taking a steady but sure route that can guarantee success.

The planetary influences of Jupiter and Mars in your Spiritual Spread indicate that your ability to assess situations and make decisions quickly gives you the edge. Equally, your natural enthusiasm, optimistic outlook, and love of enterprise urge you to be independent and daring. It warns, however, that your love of freedom may lead you to rebel against restrictions or feel frustrated by limitations.

Your Two Replacement Cards Are the 4 of Clubs & the 5 of Hearts.

As the 5 of Clubs you share the same planetary position as the 4 of Clubs in the Earthly Spread. This card signifies that you possess common sense and are usually well informed. When necessary you can discipline yourself and show your willingness to work hard. Your usual positive outlook also suggests that you like challenges and are good at problem solv-

ing. As the 5 of Clubs you also share the same planetary position as the 5 of Hearts in the Spiritual Spread. The double influence of the number 5 indicates that although your fluctuating emotions can inspire great creativity and enthusiasm, your mood swings can destabilize your personal relationships.

You usually have special or karmic links with people who are represented by the 4 of Clubs and the 5 of Hearts, as you share the same planetary positions. You can be soul mates or understand each other very well. Even if you do not get along, you can both see clearly how the other person operates.

Your Mercury Card is . . .

The 3 of Diamonds

- You have a talent for communicating your ideas and turning them into wonderful financial opportunities.
- You also possess a natural talent for problem solving, new innovations, or technical skills.
- To succeed use your originality, intuition, and shrewd business sense.
- By attempting to do too much you can become indecisive and worried about your career or money matters.
- You should have good mental rapport and special communication with people represented by the 3 of Diamonds, as they can share your interests or enterprising ideas.

Your Venus Card is . . .

The Ace of Spades

- You like to take the lead in creative ventures and enjoy initiating new projects that allow you to express your imaginative ideas.
- Although you are idealistic and sensitive, you can also be elusive or secretive about your feelings.

The 5 of Clubs Planetary Card Sequence

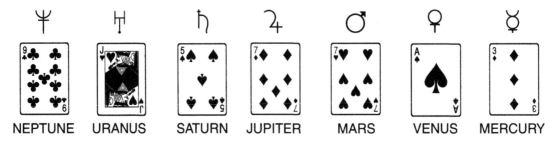

NEPTUNE   URANUS   SATURN   JUPITER   MARS   VENUS   MERCURY

- Your high expectations of others can sometimes lead to disappointment.
- Your important relationships often have clandestine undertones or strong spiritual links.
- Your feelings run deep, giving you an intuitive understanding of people.
- Your Venus link indicates that you are attracted to people who are the Ace of Spades. This card can also represent business partnerships, close friendships, and special loved ones.

Your Mars Card is . . .

The 7 of Hearts
- You are more likely to be interested in work that involves people or the public.
- You possess great emotional vitality, and your enthusiasm can be a positive influence on other people.
- Your intense emotions can be a force for good, so resist unnecessary confrontations and willful behavior.
- It is important that you believe heartily in the work you do.
- The relationships you have with 7 of Hearts people can be special or good if you both share the same ideals. This person can stimulate your faith and drive, but avoid being competitive with this person.

Your Jupiter Card is . . .

The 7 of Diamonds
- Under the influence of Jupiter, this card suggests luck with financial endeavors and money matters in general.
- It is wiser if you develop your analytical and practical sense and resist acting on impulse.
- Although you can worry about your material situation, when your financial resources are good you can be generous and spontaneous.
- 7 of Diamonds people can be instrumental to your success or enhance your life. If you are in business or partnership with them you can both be successful. Alternatively, these people can inspire you creatively and be the source of exciting ideas.

Your Saturn Card is . . .

The 5 of Spades
- The unsettled influence of this card indicates that you are likely to change your career or interests on more than one occasion.
- You are also likely to move or travel in connection with work.
- Stay focused on your goals and guard against letting dissatisfaction and restlessness undermine your determination.

- 5 of Spades people can have a strong karmic link with you or play an important role in teaching you about discipline and limitation. These relationships can sometimes be short-lived yet powerful. Although these relationships are not always easy, their contributions are often very valuable lessons.

Your Uranus Card is . . .

The Jack of Hearts
- Friendly and beguiling, you enjoy social gatherings and being with others.
- You can express yourself in a dramatic way.
- Although you are romantic by nature, your independence is important to you.
- Acting on your strong emotional impulses may lead to immature behavior.
- Jack of Hearts people can stimulate your social life or be good friends. Although they can make you more objective about your life, avoid becoming stubborn.

Your Neptune Card is . . .

The 9 of Clubs
- This card emphasizes a need for a positive attitude, mental clarity, and intellectual self-expression in later years.
- Resist letting self-defeating attitudes cloud your thoughts and cause you to worry or get confused.
- Your imaginative ideas can come to fruition, particularly in the latter part of life.
- Fulfillment comes through sharing your knowledge and spiritual insight with others.
- Avoid being skeptical or cynical, as it may undermine your great possibilities.
- 9 of Clubs people can help you materialize your dreams. If they are wise and knowledgeable they can inspire you spiritually. In these relationships, however, you may need to guard against delusion.

Your Challenge Card is . . .

The 9 of Spades
- In order to achieve your objectives you will have to develop your inner faith and show your dedication through hard work.
- Adopting an approach that "everything happens for a reason" will help you to steady the pace of your life and also aid you in developing a philosophical attitude.
- Being of service to others can bring you great spiritual rewards.
- Staying positively focused in the face of adversity and learning to let go when necessary can help you to progress and prosper.
- 9 of Spades people can fascinate but also challenge you. Although they may force you to express yourself, they can also touch upon your insecurities or the worst aspects of your personality. Nevertheless, these people can help you to transform your life if you can avoid power struggles.

The Result of Your Challenge Card is . . .

The 2 of Hearts
- Issues of trust and creating harmonious relationships are of vital importance to your well-being.
- Able to create a congenial atmosphere, you enjoy sharing and being in the company of others.
- As a result of overcoming your challenges you will be able to establish close or intimate relationships with those you love.
- People who are represented by the 2 of Hearts can help you understand your emotions and your reaction to them often reflects how you are responding to your challenges.

Famous People Who Are 5 of Clubs

Eminem, René Descartes, Joseph Haydn, George Orwell, Mary Todd Lincoln, Montgomery Clift, Rita Hayworth, Evel Knievel, Dick Van Dyke, Christopher Plummer, Daniel Day-Lewis, Michelle Pfeiffer, André Agassi, Georgia O'Keeffe, Carly Simon, Henry Kissinger, Isadora Duncan, Colin Farrell, Christopher Lee, Al Gore, William Randolph Hearst, Princess Margaret, Raymond Chandler, Count Basie, Kenny Rogers, Christopher Walken, George Michael, Jerry Seinfeld

Birthdays Governed by the 5 of Clubs

March 31: Aries   Ruler: Mars

Mentally quick, action-oriented, and restless, your ruler, Mars, indicates that you are an idealistic and ambitious individual. Your innate charm and gentle manner must not be taken for granted, however, as you also possess intense feelings and strong willpower. Your resolute or independent streak can at times come into conflict with your heart's desires. As a versatile and talented individual you need to find constructive ways to express your intense yet sensitive emotions. Failure to do so can create emotional fluctuations and uncertainty. By being patient and emotionally disciplined you can empower your sensitive nature and achieve spiritual victory.

April 29: Taurus   Ruler: Venus

Along with your quick perception, your deep-seated feelings and personal power indicate that you are a highly intuitive individual with powerful emotions. Although you can be warmhearted and loving, your thoughts and desires are often concealed. A need for greater emotional or spiritual awareness indicates that you seek to transform your life or find ways to gain recognition for your talents. When you

feel inspired your enthusiasm and practical skills imply that you can achieve success and be highly productive. Not afraid to take on or start large projects, your leadership qualities also suggest that you can inspire others.

May 27: Gemini   Ruler: Mercury

Your inquiring mind, originality, and versatility suggest that you have many interests and a natural flair for dealing with people. The intellectual power supplied by your ruler, Mercury, indicates that you enjoy variety and change and can adapt quickly to new situations. Articulate and sociable, your independent view, sound judgment, and direct approach can also help you to assess people and situations quickly. Although you may thrive on change or feel restless, your business sense and desire for material security suggest that you are apt to take financial matters very seriously. Luckily you are not a quitter, and with your tenacity and determination you can accomplish a great deal.

June 25: Cancer   Ruler: The Moon

Receptive and curious, your ability to assess intuitively all types of experiences signify that your sixth sense is highly developed. Although your mental capabilities are strong, your emotional worries or critical attitude can incite fluctuating moods or impulsiveness. Nevertheless, your caring nature, according to your ruler, the Moon, implies that you can be sympathetic and supportive, especially when others turn to you for moral support. Your success often comes when you develop your analytical skills and the self-discipline needed to achieve your great ambitions.

July 23: Cancer/Leo   Ruler: Moon/Sun

Born on the cusp of Cancer and Leo implies that you are usually bright, dramatic, and sensitive. The double emphasis of the number 5 reinforces the changeable qualities associated with your card and birth date. These indicate that you are an action-oriented and restless individual with powerful yet sensitive emotions. Although you are quite adventurous and ambitious, an inclination to be impulsive or impatient suggests that at times you need to curb your enthusiasm and resist taking unnecessary risks. By adopting a more diligent attitude, however, you can combine your originality with self-discipline and channel your enthusiasm into productive mental creativity.

August 21: Leo   Ruler: Sun

Your wealth of ideas and numerous talents imply that you are usually a witty, creative, and versatile individual. The dramatic flair and enthusiasm suggested by your ruler, the Sun, usually invigorate your gregarious nature. Although your strong urge to achieve something special can be the motivating force that leads you to success, changing objectives and uncertainty can cause inner restlessness and undermine your efforts. When you combine your quick perceptions with self-discipline, however, your executive and practical skills can impress others and lead you to positions of leadership. As a sociable individual with an engaging personality, you can accomplish much through careers related to the public.

September 19: Virgo   Ruler: Mercury

A strong desire to find creative expression for your intellectual attributes and versatility indicates that you are a determined individual with cerebral power. According to the number 1 influence on your birth date, you are also independent and charismatic. Before you embark on the road to success, however, you need to decide where you want to invest your time and money. Indecision or lack of clear objectives caution that you can be too susceptible to other people's influence. Nevertheless, your

ruler, Mercury, implies that your adaptability and unique ideas can help you solve your problems in original ways.

October 17: Libra   Ruler: Venus

Wanting to make your distinctive mark in life suggests that you are an independent thinker with quick comprehension and analytical skills. Although your ruler, Venus, indicates that you can be sociable and charming, the emotional sensitivity associated with the Ace of Spades implies that you can be secretive and vulnerable to criticism. Venus can nevertheless grant you an engaging personality and unique creative talents that can help you achieve outstanding success. Usually by being patient and learning to be more flexible or less critical you can clear misunderstandings and achieve harmony in your personal relationships.

November 15: Scorpio   Ruler: Mars

Idealistic and emotionally intense, your determination and quick comprehension indicate that you are a sensitive individual with creative talents and resolute nature. As you are likely to spend a great deal of your time in the pursuit of your goals or on the move, it is vital that you develop the emotional independence needed to stay focused on your objectives. Although you are able to make great sacrifices for your inspired ideas or those you love, resist allowing your willful nature or negative feelings to undermine your efforts. In your relationships, honesty and tact can also help you to overcome resentment and achieve spiritual victory.

December 13: Sagittarius   Ruler: Jupiter

Your ability to overcome obstacles with courage and resolve indicate that you are a dynamic and practical individual. Your ruler, Jupiter, usually supplies you with enthusiasm and optimism to pursue your dreams and desires for success. This is often helped by the fact that when you develop your inner faith, you feel inspired. Although you can be freedom loving and adventurous, your innate talents and business sense imply that you can also be highly ambitious and hardworking, especially when there are financial incentives. Even if you have humble beginnings, when you achieve material success you can inspire others with your lofty ideas and generosity.

◆ THE 5 OF DIAMONDS ◆

Born under the influence of the 5 of Diamonds, you are a clever yet impressionable individual with a need for action. You possess the fast instincts of a number 5, so you can usually trust your first impressions. As you dislike routine you need change or variety to keep your interest. You may need to develop patience and perseverance, however, in order to overcome restlessness. Being from the Diamond suit, you also have a shrewd ability to evaluate material situations. This particularly can help bring you success if you look to long-term plans rather than taking instant rewards.

Under the influences of Neptune and Saturn in the Earthly Spread, you are a practical idealist with strong visionary abilities. Although you may have to work hard, you will reap big rewards as you make your dreams come true. You are helped by the combination of your innate business sense, intuition, and imagination. Surprisingly, although usually considerate, on occasion you may have to watch a tendency to dominate. Nevertheless, you can be idealistic and unselfish when you care about others. With the influence of Mars in the Saturn line of the Spiritual Spread there is no getting away from your responsibilities. If you try to do so you will only suffer from frustration. If Mars and Saturn's energies are used

positively, however, you can be very focused and driven when set on a definite course of action. Your determination and ability to make things happen at these times can be very impressive.

Your Two Replacement Cards Are the 9 of Diamonds & the 3 of Clubs.

As the 5 of Diamonds you share the same planetary position as the 9 of Diamonds in the Spiritual Spread. This signifies that you can be generous and resourceful. Your broad-minded attitude can also lead to a humanitarian outlook on life. A tendency to be extravagant suggests, however, that you may need to budget to minimize financial worries.

Your card also shares the same planetary position as the 3 of Clubs in the Earthly Spread. This indicates that at times you can be highly creative and inspired. If you waste your energy on negativity, however, you can suffer from insecurity or become intolerant. Through self-expression and constantly updating your knowledge you are able to build your confidence and self-esteem. Good with words, you can have a gift for writing, singing, acting, or presenting your ideas.

You usually have special or karmic links with people who are represented by the 9 of Diamonds and the 3 of Clubs, as you share the same planetary positions. You can be soul mates or understand each other very well. Even if you do not get along, you can both see clearly how the other person operates.

Your Mercury Card is . . .

The Queen of Spades
- The leadership card here indicates superior mental ability and suggests that you do not like to take orders from others.
- There was likely to be a strong female influ-

The 5 of Diamonds Planetary Card Sequence

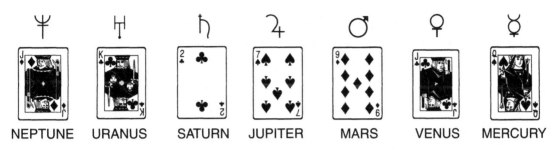

| NEPTUNE | URANUS | SATURN | JUPITER | MARS | VENUS | MERCURY |

ence, probably your mother, representing strong principles in your youth.

- Education or self-knowledge is important to bringing out your outstanding mental potential and latent wisdom.
- Queen of Spade individuals can stimulate your communication skills and sense of drama. You could have a good mental rapport with this person.

Your Venus Card is . . .

The Jack of Clubs

- Sociable and entertaining, you are likely to seek the company of mentally stimulating people.
- As the Jack is a youthful card you can also enjoy a playful side to your relationships with others.
- Avoid mixing with people who waste their lives in trivia.
- You are attracted to independent individuals who can share your interests and give you intelligent feedback.
- Jack of Clubs people can act as catalysts for your pleasure and enjoyment. This is mainly through romance or friendship, but as Venus can also represent money, this can also be a good link for business partners.

Your Mars Card is . . .

The 9 of Diamonds

- By having the courage to face, accept, and deal with your personal frustrations you can avoid becoming overly serious or holding onto resentments and disappointments.
- There is the likelihood of your living or working far from your birthplace or in a foreign country.
- The process of removing clutter from your life makes you feel more dynamic.
- You can gain much from physical exercise such as sports, swimming, walking, yoga, etc., or taking an active part in humanitarian projects.
- The more you pull back and try to take a detached view about what action you are going to take rather than just acting impulsively, the better your life works.
- 9 of Diamonds people can stimulate your dynamism and desire for action positively. Avoid being competitive or arguing with these people, as Mars is also the god of war.

Your Jupiter Card is . . .

The 7 of Spades

- By having faith in yourself and your abilities you radiate success and draw it toward you as well as attracting the help of others.
- As you have a tendency for fluctuating

finances or uncertainty, it is generally good for you to put some money by for the long term that you can't access immediately.

- You have the potential to develop a latent spirituality that can radically improve your life and bring you many lucky opportunities.

- People who are the 7 of Spades can have a beneficial effect on you, stimulating your optimism, confidence, and ability to think big. Sometimes this can be a spiritual link, although avoid overindulgence or overspending with this person.

Your Saturn Card is . . .

The 2 of Clubs

- By working on your self-development you can overcome hidden fears.

- You possess a sharp and unusual sense of humor. This can help you to see the positive side of difficult situations and make it easier to stay mentally balanced.

- You are a good psychologist and enjoy sharing your knowledge with others.

- Most of your major tests involve your relationships. If you get frustrated or disappointed avoid becoming argumentative. Work on creating harmony and cooperation.

- People who are the 2 of Clubs can have a karmic link with you. They can show you where you need to work on yourself, particularly your discipline and sense of responsibility. This can be testing or enlightening.

Your Uranus Card is . . .

The King of Clubs

- You possess original ideas that are often ahead of their time.

- Freedom is an important issue for you. If you feel someone is curtailing your liberty

you are likely to become rebellious or do something erratic.

- You can be a leader, especially in teamwork, groups, or humanitarian work.

- People represented by the King of Clubs can stimulate your inventive ideas and help you to see your life role more objectively. Equally, they can encourage your individuality or be a good friend.

Your Neptune Card is . . .

The Jack of Diamonds

- Opportunities to use your natural creativity and imagination get stronger as you get older.

- In business you have an ability to sell others a dream. You can also create wonderful images, whether through film, art, music, drama, or writing.

- This second Jack influence indicates that if you do not face your responsibilities you will always have a somewhat immature attitude, even into old age.

- You can have a sensitive or psychic link with people who are the Jack of Diamonds. This can be creative or you can share the same dreams. Alternatively, to avoid false expectations you have to stay very practical and grounded.

Your Challenge Card is . . .

The 4 of Hearts

- Be emotionally honest with others.

- Build a strong foundation for what you want to achieve and feel that you are slowly but surely moving forward in life.

- People who are the 4 of Hearts can dare you to bring out the best or the worst in your personality. This can be a transformative influence.

The Result of Your Challenge Card is . . .

The 4 of Diamonds

- You will be loyal and solid as a rock for others.
- You will have your money and material side organized.
- Your work will prove to be extra important as a way of expressing your optimism for the future.
- People who are the 4 of Diamonds can reflect how well you are responding to your challenges.

Famous People Who Are the 5 of Diamonds

Kelsey Grammer, Kurt Cobain, John Hurt, Kingsley Amis, Lord Byron, Edgar Cayce, Charlie Chaplin, Kareem Abdul-Jabbar, David Byrne, David Rockefeller, Michael Hutchence, Robert Altman, George Lucas, D. W. Griffith, Buster Keaton, George H. W. Bush, Marcel Proust, Anne Frank, Arthur Ashe, St. Francis of Assisi, Peter Ustinov, Nelly, Susan Sarandon, Cate Blanchett, Dustin Hoffman

Birthdays Governed by the 5 of Diamonds

January 22: Aquarius   Ruler: Uranus

Friendly, original, and inventive, with a good understanding of others, you need people and diversity to keep your interest. The experimental side to your nature works well when you are building positively for the future. If you are restless, however, you may be prone to do something impetuous or erratic. Fortunately, a charismatic personality and universal viewpoint can make you a practical idealist who can work hard to achieve your dreams. You can find many writers, poets, actors, and musicians born on your birthday as, like yourself, they often have sometime unique to express.

February 20: Pisces   Ruler: Neptune

Emotionally intuitive yet mentally quick, your good people skills enable you to mix in any social circle. Disliking routine, you need variety and change to keep your enthusiasm alive. Be careful, however, of a restless streak that may make you react impulsively or cause you to give up too easily. Although sensitive, once set on a course of action you can be determined, pointed, and enterprising. You usually fare best when you are able to combine your high ideals with practical monetary rewards. When you trust your strong intuition and develop patience you gain much, especially if you find outlets for your creative expression. Your relationships figure high on your priority list, and you can often profit from working in collaboration with others.

March 18: Pisces   Ruler: Neptune

Intelligent with psychic or intuitive abilities, you can be progressive and resourceful. Although very sensitive, at times you need a challenge to really get you going. Broad-minded and ambitious, you can be determined when you get down to work, but guard against a stubborn or immature streak that might spoil your chances. As you like power you may want to develop your administrative and management skills. By developing your detachment and innate humanitarian qualities, you can build up your confidence and get emotional satisfaction.

April 16: Aries   Ruler: Mars

Your exceptionally quick responses and sharp intelligence suggest that you need new projects, fresh information, and a challenge to keep your interest. If patient enough you can have a talent for writing or may use your leadership skills to direct others. Thoughtful yet ambitious and daring, you are usually friendly and active, though you need regular time alone for self-reflection and to replenish your energies. Although confident with a sharp wit, you still need to develop your perseverance in order to stop experiencing inner tensions or becoming too cynical.

May 14: Taurus   Ruler: Venus

Practical and down-to-earth yet also quick and instinctive, you need mental stimulation to create success, especially in your work. Being independent, it is usually better if you are in the driver's seat, as you do not like to take orders. Guard against being stubborn, however. Although pragmatic you are also imaginative and sensitive and may wish to use this creatively. Since you have a desire for adventure and a need for material security, you may have to find projects that keep your attention yet still give financial rewards.

June 12: Gemini   Ruler: Mercury

Mentally versatile and expressive, with a sense of drama, you have excellent communication skills. Friendly and popular, you can be psychologically sharp and creative. With your talent for words, you have an innate gift for debating, writing, or presenting your ideas. Although resourceful, at times you may experience a pull between your ideals and financial interests. As you enjoy talking and tend to move fast you gain much guidance and assistance when you learn to slow down and listen to others, as well as to your own strong intuition.

July 10: Cancer   Ruler: Moon

Possessing emotional sensitivity and quick mental responses, you can be progressive with strong convictions. Although interested in new experiences, you still place great value on the security of home and family. Proud and ambitious, you often display determination and drive in achieving your goals, but you may

have to watch a tendency to be impatient or overbearing. When positively dynamic your pioneering spirit can have you exploring new areas of opportunity or leading others.

August 8: Leo   Ruler: Sun

With your leadership skills and need to shine, you may find yourself at the front of your activities or being pulled toward show business. Determined and versatile with sharp perception, you can react quickly to any situation and also be entertaining. Optimistic and imaginative, with a desire for wide horizons, you need plenty of variety in life. As you enjoy power you may choose to develop your organizational and executive skills. These all help you overcome a tendency to become restless or discouraged.

September 6: Virgo   Ruler: Mercury

Although sensible and down-to-earth, you can still be imaginative and caring. With your keen intellect you like to see practical results and are good at mental explorations, such as research or psychology. Equally, you enjoy being of help to others, but you may need to watch a tendency to care too much and become bossy. Being impressionable and sensitive to atmosphere, you need harmonious surroundings to be happy. As your home and family are especially important you usually make an effort to be a responsible and caring parent.

October 4: Libra   Ruler: Venus

Honest and creative, with warm social skills, you are an original thinker with many interests. Although you can be diplomatic, you like to be straightforward and value loyalty. Usually you are willing to work hard to achieve the luxuries or beautiful and harmonious surroundings that you enjoy. With a strong visual sense and heightened imagination, you may wish to use this creativity in the arts, through healing, or in exploring spirituality. You never lose your practicality, however, so you realize that to achieve results you need to develop your patience and self-discipline.

November 2: Scorpio   Ruler: Mars
With strong emotions and inner sensitivity you are dynamic yet considerate and friendly. You enjoy power and can be very determined and confident once set on a course of action. Equally, if you become oversensitive you can be prone to moods, frustration, or begin to lack confidence. Nevertheless, your ability to deal with people, good concentration, and strong intuition can all help you to achieve outstanding results in life. The more detached you are, the easier your financial affairs fall into place.

♠ THE 5 OF SPADES ♠

Under the changing influence of the number 5 your life path is not likely to be static or uneventful. Usually the signs are that you will find the urge for freedom and new experiences irresistible. Alternatively, dissatisfaction with restrictive situations may cause you to seek your fortunes somewhere else. Belonging to the Spades suit implies that travel and relocation may be closely related to health and career opportunities or important new interests.

Under the influences of Mars and Venus in the Earthly Spread you are usually a passionate individual with creative talents and a charismatic nature. Although you can show your pragmatism and sensitive awareness, at times your excitability can lend itself to an overzealous attitude. Nevertheless, sensual and instinctive, with your engaging personality you can charm those you come in contact with.

The influences of Neptune and Venus in your Spiritual Spread suggest that you are an imaginative, romantic, and idealistic individual. Your willpower and motivation usually increase when you feel truly inspired by an ideal or a concept. This visionary aspect of your nature also indicates that interest in mysticism or the arts and music can be highly rewarding. Although you may experience delays or obstacles in your path, your ability to visualize your goals and dreams suggest that in order to succeed you need to develop your perseverance and determination.

Your Two Replacement Cards Are the 10 of Hearts & the 4 of Diamonds.

As the 5 of Spades you share the same planetary position as the 4 of Diamonds in the Earthly Spread. This card indicates that you like to pay close attention to practical considerations when making a move or changing your direction. It also signifies that when you stay focused and grounded your business acumen usually protects you financially. Since this card has a stabilizing effect on the changeable influences of your own card, it suggests that wherever you go you usually can find new opportunities or employment.

Your card also shares the same planetary position as the 10 of Hearts in the Spiritual Spread. This implies that you possess powerful feelings, charm, and a touch of glamour. If you choose to work in the public eye or in entertainment you can achieve popularity and success. Alternatively, you can inspire others with your passionate nature, beliefs, and ideals.

You usually have special or karmic links with people who are represented by the 4 of Diamonds or the 10 of Hearts, as you share the same planetary positions. You can be soul mates or understand each other very well. Even if you do not get along, you can both see clearly how the other person operates.

Your Mercury Card is . . .

The Jack of Hearts
- When you channel your emotions positively you can generate warmth and express yourself creatively.
- You are often an idealist with lofty ideas.
- Charming and friendly, you can be generous and caring toward other people.
- Since your emotional awareness is high, your powerful feelings can have a definite positive or negative effect on the way you think and act.
- You should have good mental rapport and special communication with Jack of Hearts people, as they activate your Mercury card and understand your feelings easily.

Your Venus Card is . . .

The 9 of Clubs
- You enjoy sharing your knowledge and communicating with others.
- You are drawn to, or inspired by, optimistic, positive, and intelligent people.
- If your personal relationships are causing you a great deal of frustration it may be that you are expecting too much from others.
- Since your intellectual potential is high, you benefit from developing your mental capabilities.

- Usually you are attracted to 9 of Clubs people, as they are ideal for love and romance as well as close friendships and good business partnerships.

Your Mars Card is . . .

The 9 of Spades
- With a positive mental approach, you have the power to endure and work hard for what you believe in. If you want to succeed in life, therefore, you need to adopt a steady and determined attitude.
- Resist pushing yourself beyond your limits, as it can have an ill effect on your health and vitality.
- Tendencies to overreact or become disappointed and frustrated with delays and obstacles can increase your irritability and undermine your idealism.
- The relationships you have with 9 of Spades people can be good if you stimulate each other's courage and dynamism. Resist being competitive with these people, however.

Your Jupiter Card is . . .

The 2 of Hearts
- Your greatest asset is your people skills, and you can usually benefit from all types of partnerships and unions.

The 5 of Spades Planetary Card Sequence

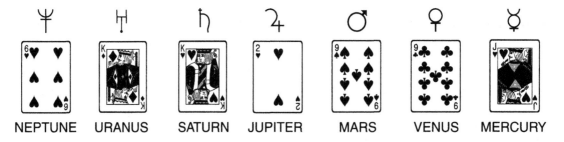

NEPTUNE   URANUS   SATURN   JUPITER   MARS   VENUS   MERCURY

- Able to put people at ease, you can use your charm and diplomacy to avoid tension and confrontations.
- You can also succeed in work that involves the community or the public at large.
- Your partner can be very fortunate for you and prospects for love and marriage can also appear in middle years.
- People who are represented by the 2 of Hearts can be of help to you or linked with beneficial partnerships or personal relationships. This link is good for opportunities.

Your Saturn Card is . . .

The King of Hearts
- You are a strong individual with powers to heal or influence people emotionally.
- A responsible attitude to loved ones can help you overcome problems.
- You need to address emotional issues with maturity and compassion.
- King of Hearts people can play an important role in your life, especially in middle years. Alternatively, a karmic link with an older male may have played a significant role in shaping your destiny. Although your relationship with them may not be always easy, they can be valuable learning experiences.

Your Uranus Card is . . .

The King of Diamonds
- Your original and creative ideas can be highly profitable financially.
- Your organizational or executive skills and business acumen can bring new opportunities or unexpected benefits in middle years.
- Although this card is a beneficial sign for material success, resist turning money into your central focal point.
- King of Diamonds people can offer you a valuable insight into new financial or career

opportunities. This is also a good card for friendship.

Your Neptune Card is . . .

The 6 of Hearts
- Family and friends play a pivotal role in securing your happiness, especially in old age.
- After a life of much activity and change, your later years are blessed with the freedom to do more of what your heart desires.
- By exploring creative avenues or socializing, you may find the contentment you seek.
- 6 of Hearts people can inspire you to be creative, more spiritually aware, or empower you emotionally. Be realistic when dealing with them, however.

Your Challenge Card is . . .

The 4 of Clubs
- A major quest in life may center on achieving peace of mind through finding a philosophy or something worthwhile to believe in.
- You can also accomplish much when you think positively, plan for the future, and occupy your mind with gaining knowledge.
- You need to adopt a practical attitude and be methodical and well organized if you want to achieve success.
- 4 of Clubs people can force you to re-evaluate some of your opinions, beliefs, and ideas. Your reactions to them can be intense and bring out the best or worst of your personality. These people can have a transformative affect on you.

The Result of Your Challenge Card is . . .

The 2 of Diamonds
- Maintaining equality of power in relationships is vital to your success.

- Good partnerships and cooperative efforts, especially in business, can be a key to your accomplishments.
- Considering others often yields unexpected rewards.
- You gain from blending spiritual needs with your material requirements.
- You find peace of mind by overcoming fear about money issues.
- 2 of Diamonds people can inspire you or offer you new financial opportunities. Your dealings with them often reflect how you are responding to your challenges.

Famous People Who Are the 5 of Spades

Marlon Brando, Chris Rock, Charles Dickens, Simone de Beauvoir, Sinclair Lewis, George Herbert, Crystal Gayle, Ashton Kutcher, Tim McGraw, Gypsy Rose Lee, Jimmy Page, Joan Baez, Dave Matthews, A. J. McLean, Bob Denver, Scott Carpenter, Richard Nixon, Alec Baldwin, David Hyde Pierce, Eddie Murphy, Garth Brooks

Birthdays Governed by the 5 of Spades

January 9: Capricorn   Ruler: Saturn
Although you are probably hardworking, tough, and tenacious under the influence of your ruler, Saturn, your deep-seated feelings and innate charm signify that you are a highly sensitive individual with inspired motives. If your dramatic sense is not disciplined or channeled, however, it can cause you to vacillate between elevated moods and low depressions. Intuitive and restless, your quick comprehension and cerebral power implies that you need to find some type of creative or intellectual expression. Alternatively, when your feelings are aroused they can inspire you to speak out or take leadership positions.

February 7: Aquarius   Ruler: Uranus
According to Uranus, your ruler, you are an independent and free-thinking individual with good analytical skills. Insightful and authoritative, your strong sense of values can give you the edge in the business world. Although you are often pragmatic and pay attention to practical considerations, your unsettled nature and lack of persistence can undermine your great potential. When you develop your inner faith and become less preoccupied with small details your confidence and certainty increases. Since monotonous occupations are not ideally suited to your restless nature, you are better off working independently or in a free and changing environment.

March 5: Pisces   Ruler: Neptune
Receptive and insightful, according to Neptune, your ruler, you are an imaginative and hopeful individual with an adventurous nature. Being highly instinctive and adaptable, you are often keen to bring about drastic changes that can transform your life or make your dreams come true. On your road to success, do not underestimate the power of your sympathetic approach and natural charm, as it gives you the edge in all types of people-related activities. Alternately, your idealism and compassion may inspire you to work for humanitarian causes. Nevertheless, you may need to learn to differentiate between noble causes and martyring yourself on hopeless objectives.

April 3: Aries   Ruler: Mars
Although Mars, your ruler, usually endows you with bold courage, it is your determination and ability to persevere regardless of frustrations and setbacks that can lead you to accomplishment and success. As a versatile and independent person you like to take the initiative or plan ahead. Careerwise, you prefer to

be your own boss or tackle large projects where you can express your ingenuity and creativity. Your dynamic drive warns, however, that if you let restlessness or impulsive actions dictate your pace you may scatter your energies in too many directions.

May 1: Taurus   Ruler: Venus
Your number 1 birthday suggests that you are an instinctive and independent individual with quick perception and a resolute nature. Creative and security conscious, yet impatient, watch out that your impulsive actions do not undermine your efforts. Luckily, since you probably want a great deal from life, your ruler, Venus, grants an engaging personality and charm as well as innate talents. If you are willing to invest the time and patience to develop these fine attributes you will discover that you possess a refined intellect and the creativity to produce something original. Although you can be idealistic and caring, a self-seeking attitude can also reveal your insecurities.

♥ ♣ THE 6 s ◆ ♠

THE NUMBER 6 indicates a desire for harmony and balance, a strong sense of responsibility, and an awareness that "what we sow we reap." If you are a number 6 card you are likely to be worldly yet also emotionally sensitive. Although you can be caring, in attempting to help others there is a danger that you may also become interfering and dominating. In your quest for peace your greatest challenge may be to start with yourself. This can be difficult, however, if you become stuck in a monotonous routine. Nevertheless, you can be compassionate and humanitarian, with high ideals. Having strong family ties suggests that you can be a good parent or a supportive influence for others. With your good taste and natural artistic sense, you may especially enjoy beautifying your home. As a number 6 individual, however, avoid anxiety or being too critical and judgmental. You can nonetheless be a trustworthy and good-hearted individual who is often a natural adviser for others.

The following suits further modify the effect of your number:

6 of Hearts

Emotionally sensitive, you are working under the principle that whatever love you put out you also receive back. With a strong need for peace and harmony in your surroundings, as well as a safe home environment, you usually find it easier to take a passive, easygoing approach to life. This may not always help you in your dealings with others or in the drive to achieve your goals. Yours can be a very caring card.

6 of Clubs

You are working with knowledge and the principle that whatever information you share with others will also come back to you. A mixture of ambition and inertia, your Clubs suit suggests an enthusiastic desire for cognition, but your number 6 influence just wants an easy and relaxed life. Intuitive and mentally fast, you can be a "messenger" of ideas for others.

6 of Diamonds

It is very important for you to create harmony in your outer environment. You therefore possess a strong love of or interest in your home. Awareness of karma or an understanding that "what you put out, you get back" can make you aware of your debts or obligations. Equally, by being responsible you can reap material rewards for your past efforts.

6 of Spades

You may have to work at creating peace by balancing difficult situations or keeping your family together. Your card can be especially good for the caring professions or work in music, art, interior design, healing, or activities that bring harmony into life. You are best to avoid situations that are too routine.

♥ THE 6 OF HEARTS ♥

An inner need to express yourself emotionally and creatively is strongly emphasized by the 6 of Hearts. Although as a positive 6 of Hearts you can be fair and a peacemaker, an inner desire to excel indicates that once challenged you can also be highly competitive. Socially aware, your charismatic personality can engage others and make them feel at ease. When you incorporate your sensitivity and include the emotional factor into your everyday life you can touch people's hearts in subtle yet powerful ways. If you are inclined to escape from your emotional responsibility toward others you may miss the wonderful opportunities available to you.

Belonging to the Hearts suit implies that you are idealistic, sensual, and receptive. Often talented, you have innate gifts that can help

you to excel and succeed. The double planetary influence of Mars in your Earthly Spread signifies that, although you can go through periods of inactivity, once you set your goals you become highly motivated and determined. Your willpower and idealistic convictions indicate that you are also able to transcend the mundane. In your search for emotional fulfillment, however, guard against wasting your energy on too much pleasure and enjoyment. This Mars influence also warns against being impulsive, aggressive, or one-sided.

The planetary influences of Uranus and Mercury in your Spiritual Spread indicate that you are intuitive, inventive, and often ahead of your time. Your sudden realizations or ideas suggest that you can also act with lightning speed. Usually you can contribute to your field of interest by offering something new and unique. If you can resist scattering your energies by having too many interests or objectives you can rise above the ordinary by being original, creative, and productive.

Your Two Replacement Cards Are the 4 of Clubs & the 3 of Diamonds.

As the 6 of Hearts you share the same planetary position as the 3 of Diamonds in the Earthly Spread. Versatile and astute, you usually seek to have more than one way to earn your living. This also signifies that if you approach financial challenges creatively you can overcome money worries or vacillating material circumstances. Although you have wonderful potential, you can deplete your energy or resources through indecisiveness, especially if you have too many agendas on the go at once. Luckily, as the 6 of Hearts you also share the same planetary position as the 4 of Clubs in the Spiritual Spread. The straightforward mental approach of this card suggests that once you focus on a solid plan of action you are able to solve your problems and succeed. Although you can excel in intellectual discussions, resist being stubborn or dogmatic in your thinking.

You usually have special or karmic links with people who are represented by the 3 of Diamonds or 4 of Clubs, as you share the same planetary positions. You can be soul mates or understand each other very well. Even if you do not get along, you can both see clearly how the other person operates.

Your Mercury Card is . . .

The 4 of Clubs

- Usually you are mentally quick and keen on communicating or learning.
- You have a practical approach and are good at problem solving.
- To avoid mental restlessness or boredom you need an intellectual challenge.
- You possess a cerebral talent to articulate your thoughts through speaking or writing.
- You should have good mental rapport and special communication with 4 of Clubs people, as they activate your Mercury Card. This is especially evident if you are learning together or engaged in intellectual pursuits.

Your Venus Card is . . .

The 2 of Diamonds

- You prefer to work in partnerships or with others and usually your joint ventures are profitable.
- With your excellent people skills, you can often mix business with pleasure and attract luck as well as good contacts.
- A need for balance of power in relationships suggests that you need to avoid dependency situations.

- Do not let worries over money undermine your relationships.
- Your Venus link indicates that you are attracted to 2 of Diamonds people. This card is ideal for love and romance, close friendships, and good business partnerships.

Your Mars Card is . . .

The Jack of Spades

- Honesty is the best policy when dealing with others.
- Once you become energized and determined you can also be playful.
- Although other people, especially males, can stimulate you to take action, avoid irresponsible or risk-taking individuals.
- Your desire to transcend the mundane may inspire you to travel or explore metaphysical subjects.
- Jack of Spades people can particularly motivate and stimulate you. If they are on your side their business acumen can benefit you. Avoid being too competitive with this person by channeling the energy constructively.

Your Jupiter Card is . . .

The 8 of Clubs

- In order to manifest your imaginative concepts, you need to develop your powerful intellect.
- When you rely on your personal expertise and business acumen you can succeed admirably; therefore, the more knowledge you gain the more successful you become.
- You can also profit from combining your people skills with your creative mental abilities.
- Usually you have a good rapport with 8 of Clubs people, as often they are benefactors who can expand and enhance your life or have a spiritual link with you.

The 6 of Hearts Planetary Card Sequence

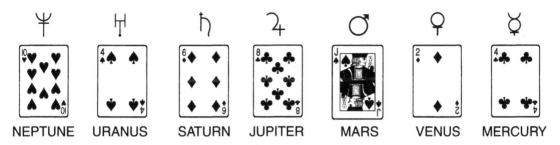

| NEPTUNE | URANUS | SATURN | JUPITER | MARS | VENUS | MERCURY |

Your Saturn Card is . . .

The 6 of Diamonds

- A responsible attitude and hard work are often the keys to your achievements.
- If you choose to ignore financial commitments this can cause you anxiety and uncertainty.
- Developing a good sense of values is essential to your success.
- 6 of Diamonds people can be your guides and help you realize your shortcomings. You may have to look after or help someone financially. If you are willing to work on your self-awareness these people can bring valuable lessons.

Your Uranus Card is . . .

The 4 of Spades

- The stabilizing influence of this card indicates that with patience you can find good conditions that will guarantee security and work.
- New opportunities can come from unexpected sources.
- If you encounter health problems your recovery is often quick.
- If you work diligently at your job you can expect recognition and rewards for your efforts.
- 4 of Spades people can help you be more objective about yourself or be good friends or helpful business partners.

Your Neptune Card is . . .

The 10 of Hearts

- Your idealism, charm, and grace can be put to good use in all types of people-related activities.
- Your later years are blessed with good and loving relationships.
- Your creative output can increase with time, and artistic talents can also reach a high point in later life.
- Emotional excesses can lead to escapism.
- You have the power to heal through your deep emotions.
- 10 of Hearts people have a psychic connection with you. They may link to your visions and ideals or help you to materialize your dreams. In these relationships you need to also be practical.

Your Challenge Card is . . .

The 10 of Diamonds

- Developing a true understanding of the power of money can help you overcome your worries and insecurities.
- You fare better when you learn to handle your financial affairs. Resist overspending, as it can become a source of worry.

- Realizing your true worth can transform the way you value yourself and add to your success.
- 10 of Diamonds people can challenge you to bring out the best or the worst of your personality. Although these people can help you to transform your life, resist becoming involved in disputes over money or power struggles.

The Result of your Challenge Card is . . .

The 8 of Spades
- Disciplined and self-reliant, you empower yourself when you take charge of your own destiny.
- With your determination and hard work, you can focus on the things that matter most.
- By using your foresight and spiritual awareness you can overcome many of your obstacles.
- 8 of Spades people can mirror how you are reacting to your challenges, especially regarding your personal power.

Famous People Who Are the 6 of Hearts

Humphrey Bogart, Winona Ryder, Isaac Newton, Richard Dreyfuss, Rod Serling, Barbara Mandrell, John Keats, Bruce Lee, Sissy Spacek, Annie Lennox, Caroline Kennedy, Jimi Hendrix

Birthdays Governed by the 6 of Hearts

October 29: Scorpio   Ruler: Mars
Capable of intense emotions, you have the idealism and determination to rise to the heights of self-expression. Yet without the necessary self-discipline and dedication, you may scatter your talents away on dubious activities. Although lofty ideas rather than ambition often inspire you, when you feel motivated you can be a prolific worker with a touch of genius. Mars, your ruler, indicates that your steely grace can be both polite and assertive. As a perfectionist with intuitive powers and a discerning mind, you have the ability to evaluate people or situations with cunning precision.

November 27: Sagittarius   Ruler: Jupiter
Although you are a sensitive and thoughtful individual, your vision and insight suggest that you possess excellent intellectual abilities and innate talents. Your charismatic charm and good people skills indicate that you can also be a people magnet. Even so, in order to overcome your challenges and achieve your goals you need time away on your own to regenerate your energies. If you take the time to seek spiritual enlightenment you will find that metaphysical subjects will fulfill your desire for knowledge and higher wisdom. Your independent nature or unique talents signify that your original, imaginative, and creative output can get you the recognition you deserve.

December 25: Capricorn   Ruler: Saturn
Receptive and sensitive, your intuition and sympathetic nature indicate that you possess unique insight into people and their characters. If you feel emotionally insecure, however, you can become restless or withdrawn. The influence of Saturn, your ruler, signifies that if you take your financial responsibilities seriously and combine your creativity with your business acumen you can succeed admirably. By adopting the view that you reap what you sow, you will work hard to receive your just rewards. Alternatively, you may use your knowledge in the world of finances to help others.

♣ THE 6 OF CLUBS ♣

As a 6 of the Clubs suit your love of peace and harmony combined with your fiery enthusiasm can give you an almost dual nature. Under the influences of Saturn and Neptune in the Earthly Spread, half of you wants to stay home, relax, and do nothing whereas the other half is almost ruthlessly determined and industrious. The key to getting you off the couch is having a clear vision of what you want to achieve and a need for recognition. When confusion enters the picture you are liable to avoid confronting your responsibilities or fears until anxiety finally causes you to move into action. Fortunately, you possess excellent strategic skills due to the influences of Saturn and Mars in your Spiritual Spread. When you have visible goals and a plan of attack you are like an army general, creating marvelous achievements through action, perseverance, and focused attention. The influences of both the number 6 and the planet Neptune also suggest you have great sensitivity. If used positively this can give you foresight, a readiness to sacrifice, or a desire to take care of others. Although your interesting mixture of ambitious realist and dreamer may pull you between materialism and your ideals, usually the more energy you exert the more your life falls into place.

Your Two Replacement Cards Are the 8 of Spades & the 2 of Diamonds.

As the 6 of Clubs you share the same planetary position as the 8 of Spades in the Spiritual Spread.

This signifies that you enjoy power and possess an inner tenacity and resolve. This is aided by an innate business sense that ensures you can commercialize your many talents and skills once you put in the necessary self-discipline.

As you also share the same planetary position as the 2 of Diamonds in the Earthly Spread you have a wonderful knack for making contacts that can always hold you in good stead. The 2 influence indicates that you fare well when working in partnerships or in cooperation with others. The Diamond influence adds skill in negotiation and bargaining. Just watch that a groundless fear of not having enough material resources causes you unnecessary anxiety.

You usually have special or karmic links with people who are represented by the 8 of Spades and the 2 of Diamonds, as you share the same planetary positions. You can be soul mates or understand each other very well. Even if you do not get along, you can both see clearly how the other person operates.

Your Mercury Card is . . .

The 6 of Spades
- Being intelligent with a perceptive mind implies that you can solve problems for yourself or others. This makes you a natural adviser.
- You may have experienced a fairly stable but predictable upbringing.
- A strong mental awareness of your responsibilities can emphasize your desire for fair play, or if overaccentuated can cause you worry.
- You should have good mental rapport and special communication with 6 of Spades people, as they activate your Mercury Card.

Your Venus Card is . . .

The Queen of Hearts
- This royalty card indicates a love of the dramatic. If a man, you may be attracted to women who have strong feelings and can project confidence.

The 6 of Clubs Planetary Card Sequence

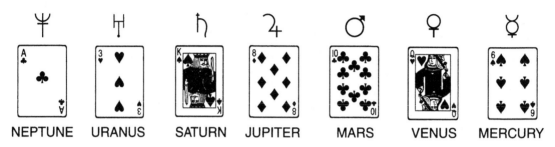

NEPTUNE   URANUS   SATURN   JUPITER   MARS   VENUS   MERCURY

- This signifies a strong female influence in your life, especially growing up.
- You have a wide emotional range and can be a warm and affectionate lover.
- Avoid being a drama queen.
- This is a powerful card for creative self-expression, particularly through music, art, photography, drama, or writing.
- You can turn on your strong emotional power and charm to win others over.
- People who are represented by the Queen of Hearts Card can be a good link for romance or friendship or make valuable business partners.

Your Mars Card is . . .

The 10 of Clubs
- Physical exercise such as sports, swimming, walking, yoga, etc., are especially good for activating your feelings of success.
- You usually need to be passionate about something to become motivated.
- When enthusiastic about an enterprise you can really project confidence and win people to your side.
- People who are the 10 of Clubs can stimulate your drive, courage, and enthusiasm. Alternatively, you may feel competitive and argue with this person.

Your Jupiter Card is . . .

The 8 of Diamonds
- You have good financial opportunities through foreign interests.
- If you become entangled in power struggles with others first check if you have become arrogant or overconfident before confronting the people involved.
- You have excellent executive abilities and usually enjoy planning on a large scale.
- 8 of Diamonds people can bring you beneficial opportunities or increase your optimism and determination. This can sometimes be a spiritual link, although avoid excesses.

Your Saturn Card is . . .

The King of Spades
- Although willing to work very hard when you have a set goal in mind, you need to be disciplined without being ruthless on yourself or others.
- When being responsible and helpful you will find yourself naturally drawn to positions of leadership or authority.
- Your life lessons involve self-mastery. Positively, this can bring great wisdom, or negatively you could be too controlling in order to evade facing your fears or doing the work necessary to master yourself.
- King of Spades people can stimulate you to

achieve or show you where you need to have clear boundaries. Although sometimes testing, if you are willing to discipline yourself these people can bring valuable lessons. This can be a karmic link.

Your Uranus Card is . . .

The 3 of Hearts
- You find it easier to be happy when you have ways to express your natural originality and inventiveness. This gives you a feeling of freedom and makes it easier for you to connect to the joy of life.
- Being sociable and responsive, you often have good and supportive friends.
- Insecurity and indecision brings you tension or makes you stubborn or rebellious.
- You may often find that two opportunities come up at once. Don't allow this to cause you worry. Stay light, and circumstances usually become clearer.
- 3 of Hearts people can help you be more creative and objective about yourself. This is often a good friendship link.

Your Neptune Card is . . .

The Ace of Clubs
- Your ambitious and informed side is good at selling others your personal vision of the way things could be.
- If you become too self-oriented or fearful you are prone to escapism and hiding your head in the sand. This becomes a self-defeating habit blocking your natural creativity.
- This card suggests that a search for knowledge, self-awareness, and wisdom can bring you much satisfaction, especially in your later years.
- When working positively you can often become a teacher or adviser for others, passing on the information you enjoy accumulating.

- People who are the Ace of Clubs can often have a psychic link with you. They can stimulate your leadership abilities, dreams, or imagination. Be careful to stay realistic, however.

Your Challenge Card is . . .

The Queen of Clubs
- Use your innate leadership skills, especially if this involves organization and spreading knowledge.
- Recognize your keen mental sensitivity and dedicate it to the service of others.
- People represented by the Queen of Clubs can usually stimulate you to react in an extreme or intense way for good or bad. Although these people can have a positive transformational effect on you, resist power conflicts.

The Result of Your Challenge Card is . . .

The 10 of Spades
- If you feel some success or sense of achievement in your work then you are responding well to your Challenge Card.
- Any efforts you put in will not be lost, as in the long run it will all work together for your overall success.
- People who are represented by the 10 of Spades can stimulate your feelings of accomplishment. They often reflect how you are responding to your challenges.

Famous People Who Are the 6 of Clubs

Claude Monet, Fred Durst, Prince Charles, Warren Beatty, Vincent Van Gogh, Melanie Klein, Eric Clapton, Angela Lansbury, Günter Grass, Harper Lee, John Wayne, Stevie Nicks, Tracy Chapman, Eugene O'Neill, Amelia Earhart, Bob Dole, Robert Plant, Isaac Hayes,

Oscar de la Renta, Terence Stamp, Oscar Wilde, Danny Glover, Greta Garbo, Aaron Copland, Dionne Warwick, Lenny Kravitz, Jennifer Connolly, Jessica Alba, Celine Dion, Yanni, Jada Pinkett Smith, Frank Sinatra

Birthdays Governed by the 6 of Clubs

March 30: Aries   Ruler: Mars

Dynamic and expressive, with a fast mind, you need to keep active and progressive. Life often works best when you are pioneering new ventures, although your good social skills ensure that you are popular and can be successful in all people-related activities. Although impatient, you may wish to expand your creative potential and gift with words through writing, drama, art, interior design, or music. To counteract selfishness or insecurity you need projects that get you enthusiastic and really fired up. At these times you project success and confidence and want to share your happiness with others.

April 28: Taurus   Ruler: Venus

Proud, practical, and determined, yet affectionate and loving, you can be a person of extremes. Although you can be competitive, ambitious, and daring, you can also experience a lack of motivation and listlessness. Nevertheless, you have good concentration and strong will when focused on a goal, though avoid using excessive force to achieve your ends. Your natural dramatic sense may stimulate you to develop your innate creativity through singing, acting, landscape gardening, or music, where you can excel. Even though you are talented with inspired ideas, you gain much from working steadily and evenly and confronting difficulties head-on.

May 26: Gemini   Ruler: Mercury

Practical and caring, with strong ambitions, you have a need for recognition and prestige. Your desire to learn combines well with your need to communicate and flair for the dramatic. Acquiring a harmonious home environment can also play a particularly important part in your plans. When positive you can be responsible, clear thinking, and supportive, especially of family members. If negative you may become anxious or controlling. Persevering and focusing on one goal at a time can help unlock your exceptional potential and increase your opportunities for success and happiness.

June 24: Cancer   Ruler: Moon

Even though you can be businesslike you feel a strong connection with home and family. Kind, sympathetic, and supportive, you can make an excellent parent, although you may have to watch interfering in your desire to help. Although sensitive, you are also proud, with a touch of the dramatic. Security, and therefore hard work is important to you, but you may have to overcome moods when you just don't feel like doing anything. You have natural advisory skills that you may wish to develop, whether through counseling, financial affairs, or in social reform.

July 22: Cancer   Ruler: Moon

Born on the cusp of Cancer and Leo, you have both the emotional intuition and impressionability of Cancer and the pride and confidence of Leo. Although practical and down-to-earth, you still possess a delicate nervous system, so it is important to work at keeping balanced. Born with a fighting spirit and a protective concern for others, you will loyally defend your home and family. Although imaginative, you can be a good organizer and have innate business acumen that works well when you are disciplined and focused.

August 20: Leo   Ruler: Sun

Dramatic and strong-willed but considerate and diplomatic, you can express a wide range of emotions. Possessing warm people skills, a keen intellect, and ambition to succeed you can do very well in all areas of life as long as you conquer inertia, anxiety, or oversensitivity. Fortunately, you have drive and enthusiasm, and do particularly well in partnerships or group ventures. With a caring personality and many creative ideas, you can also excel in the arts or in philanthropic ventures.

September 18: Virgo Ruler: Mercury
Being intelligent with keen perception and a perfectionist streak suggests that you analyze everything in order to understand it. At times this may make you critical or affect your delicate nervous system. Nevertheless, you need to be learning constantly; otherwise, your desire for peace and security may lead you into a comfortable rut. Efficient and resolute when working on a set project, you can be a good strategist and enjoy power. If too rational or too emotional you may end up feeling misunderstood, so it is important to trust your natural intuition and use it to guide your practical and perceptive intellect.

October 16: Libra Ruler: Venus
The combination of your sharp intelligence and excellent social skills can win you success and admirers. Being proud and stylish, you are aware of image and usually enjoy making your home attractive and comfortable. With your tendency to swing between hardworking ambition and idleness it is important to lead a well-balanced life. Avoid self-indulgence or escapism. Loving and affectionate, you will often make compromises to keep the peace. Although faithful, caring, and supportive you also need feedback and appreciation from others. Even though your relationships are of vital importance in your life, being thoughtful you also need time alone for self-reflection.

November 14: Scorpio Ruler: Mars
Your strong will and intense emotions blend well with your amiable personality. Although at times you can be too fixed or speak out of turn, your ambition and desire for status usually gives you the ability to rise to positions of power and achievement. You are likely to place your work as high importance in your life and need projects that you feel passionate about. Even though you can be dramatic, you can also be sensitive and refined. Your natural idealism and intelligence works best when you are in action rather than just theorizing.

December 12: Sagittarius Ruler: Jupiter
Behind your friendly persona you possess determination, a natural business sense, and a strong desire for self-expression. Preferring to be up front with people, you can be an honest idealist who needs to be constantly expanding your opportunities. You may, however, have to get the balance right between your desire for relationships and your need to express your individuality. Nevertheless, you can display an innovative and progressive personality as long as you resist allowing doubt or an overpreoccupation with material concerns to drain your energies. You have all the potential to achieve in a big way if you do not scatter your energies.

♦THE 6 OF DIAMONDS♦

Belonging to the Diamonds suit indicates that you need to be aware of the law of values. Under this law, 6 of Diamonds usually discover that without effort there is no real reward. By knowing your self-worth through personal experiences you also learn that settling your debts or being economical and responsible can free you from worry and obstacles. If you apply this premise to your everyday life you can overcome periods of inertia or material challenge.

The influence of the number 6 implies that in your desire for fairness and balance you usually want to stay impartial. Sociable, friendly, and security conscious, you usually care a great deal about your home and family. The planetary influences of Mercury and Jupiter in your Earthly Spread also signify that you perform well when you combine your optimistic outlook with common sense. Full of ideas, your agile mind seeks activities that are mentally stimulating and profitable. Being honest and direct, you like to speak your mind, and with your strong convictions will often stand up for your ideals or support the underdog.

The planetary influences of Jupiter and Saturn in your Spiritual Spread indicate that patience and perseverance or carrying through with your plans are the keys to your success. Discontent and lack of self-confidence on the other hand can cause frustration or deplete your energies. Your sense of responsibility and mature approach is usually developed through overcoming, or by learning from past difficulties.

Your Two Replacement Cards Are the 9 of Clubs & the 3 of Spades.

As the 6 of Diamonds you also share the same planetary position as the 3 of Spades in the Earthly Spread. This card indicates that you are talented, inventive, and sensitive. Associated with creative inspiration and versatility, this card's influence suggests that you can find satisfaction and success through personal self-expression, whether through your work or other interests. If you find it difficult to define your objectives or life purpose, however, you may experience self-doubt or find it hard to live up to your inspired ideas. Nevertheless,

gregarious and friendly, you are often lucky with money and with your strong sense of justice, you are fair and loyal.

As the 6 of Diamonds you share the same planetary position as the 9 of Clubs in the Spiritual Spread. This card signifies that you possess an agile and intuitive mind that can embrace all types of ideas. You can turn your imaginative thoughts into profitable ventures by staying detached and developing patience. Resist letting irritability or frustration cloud your judgment. In order to utilize your powerful intellect you need to stay realistic and adopt the right values.

You usually have special or karmic links with people who are represented by the 9 of Clubs or the 3 of Spades, as you share the same planetary positions. You can be soul mates or understand each other very well. Even if you do not get along, you can both see clearly how the other person operates.

Your Mercury Card is . . .

The 4 of Spades
- Your open and agreeable manner can help you influence people.
- Practical, honest, and direct, you have a straightforward mental approach.
- Although you have strong determination, guard against being fixed or stubborn.
- You understand form and are often skilled with your hands.
- Security is brought to your attention from an early age.
- New opportunities can come through friends and family members.
- You should have good mental rapport and special communication with people who represent the 4 of Spades, as they activate your Mercury Card.

The 6 of Diamonds Planetary Card Sequence

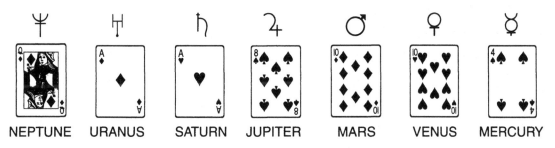

| NEPTUNE | URANUS | SATURN | JUPITER | MARS | VENUS | MERCURY |

Your Venus Card is . . .

The 10 of Hearts

- Your emotional power can inspire others.
- Friendly and charismatic, although you can attract many admirers you need to be discriminating in your choice of friends and partners.
- You can find success in careers related to the public.
- Avoid letting your strong desires lead you to overindulge in the good life.
- Usually you are attracted to people represented by the 10 of Hearts Card, especially if they share your creative interests. They are ideal for love and romance, friendship, and good business partnerships.

Your Mars Card is . . .

The 10 of Diamonds

- Your efforts and perseverance are often rewarded with material good fortune.
- Attainment comes from a wise use of financial resources, so invest your money sensibly.
- Avoid get-rich-quick schemes or high-risk speculations.
- 10 of Diamonds people can particularly motivate and stimulate you. There is often a great deal of energy in this type of relationship you can channel constructively, but resist being too competitive.

Your Jupiter Card is . . .

The 8 of Spades

- This can be an excellent influence for work, success, and prosperity if you add willingness and determination to the wonderful opportunities you are given.
- Although you can accomplish much by being productive and ambitious, time invested in gaining higher wisdom will not be wasted.
- With your insight and vitality, you have the power to overcome challenges and heal yourself and others.
- 8 of Spades people are often benefactors who can expand and enhance your life. Usually you have a good rapport with them or these people can have a spiritual link with you.

Your Saturn Card is . . .

The Ace of Hearts

- Without self-love you may sacrifice too much of yourself to others. Therefore, recognizing and fulfilling your own needs is essential to your well-being.
- Your creative self-expression can become a vocation or a labor of love.
- Too much self-condemnation can cause inertia and emotional blockages.
- Your intuitive understanding of people and

their needs suggests that you can find happiness by helping those who are less fortunate than yourself.

- Ace of Hearts people can play an important role in your life if you are able to learn from them about responsibilities. Although your relationships with them may not always be easy, their contributions are often very valuable lessons.

Your Uranus Card is . . .

The Ace of Diamonds

- This powerful card suggests that underneath a laid-back attitude, you can be ambitious.
- Inventive and progressive, your individual approach makes you unique and original.
- You particularly succeed when you balance your desire for material abundance with your awareness of social and spiritual issues.
- Working with or for the public can be especially profitable and rewarding.
- Ace of Diamonds people can offer you valuable insights and new financial opportunities or motivate you with their determination. This is also a good card for friendship.

Your Neptune Card is . . .

The Queen of Diamonds

- Your receptivity to market forces and a flair for promotion and merchandizing can help your success in business.
- To avoid worry over money you need to learn from early on how to manage your finances sensibly.
- A woman of influence may play an important role in your career.
- You have a natural gift for working with image, whether you use this in your home, for creative projects, or in business.
- Queen of Diamonds people may link to your visions, dreams, and ideals or have

a psychic connection with you, but stay grounded.

Your Challenge Card is . . .

The 5 of Hearts

- Do not let your changing emotions negatively influence your long-term relationships.
- Break from your comfortable routine by being more emotionally adventurous.
- Transmute your irritability with others into tolerance, patience, and a generous heart.
- You trust your fast instinctive responses about people or situations.
- Recognize your emotional need for variety and new experiences in order to change your life.
- 5 of Hearts people can captivate you but also challenge you emotionally. Although these people can help you to transform your life, resist ego conflicts.

The Result of Your Challenge Card is . . .

The 3 of Clubs

- You can creatively express yourself and discover your own unique talents.
- You are able to clearly articulate your thoughts and ideas.
- You can accomplish more by focusing on fewer objectives rather than scattering your energies.
- You can openly express your needs and overcome your insecurities.
- 3 of Clubs people can inspire you or help you to develop and refine your ideas. Your reactions to them often reflect how you are responding to your personal challenges.

Famous People Who Are the 6 of Diamonds

Tom Hanks, Gene Wilder, Cindy Crawford, Nicolaus Copernicus, Gore Vidal, Jesse James,

Christian Dior, Nat King Cole, Richard Strauss, Placido Domingo, Lee Marvin, Raquel Welch, Nikola Tesla, Emma Thompson, Courtney Love, Leonardo da Vinci, Smokey Robinson, Freddie Mercury, Rudolph Nureyev, David Hockney, Geena Davis, Jacques Cousteau, Prince Andrew, Rob Lowe, Stevie Wonder, India.Arie, David Duchovny, Charlize Theron, Kurt Russell

Birthdays Governed by the 6 of Diamonds

January 21: Capricorn/Aquarius
Rulers: Saturn/Uranus
Charming and gregarious, your sociable nature needs to be involved with other people. A mixture of conservatism and a love for freedom indicate that, although you usually take your responsibilities seriously, you are also an idealistic and forward-thinking individual. Usually you are more enthusiastic when initiating new projects. You can be highly motivated when you feel inspired, but a lack of self-esteem or periods of inertia may hamper your plans. By realizing your true worth, however, you can balance your desires and ideals with practical considerations and achieve both success and emotional fulfillment.

February 19: Aquarius/Pisces
Ruler: Uranus/Neptune
Dramatic and intuitive, your innovative and imaginative mind suggests that you are usually an enthusiastic individual with inspired ideas. Although your ruler, Uranus or Neptune, indicates that you have a compelling need to be part of a larger group, a desire to establish your own identity signifies that a prerequisite to your well-being is confirming your worth. Nevertheless, your head for business and practical understanding implies that if you take responsibility for your finances you can achieve material success. A strong sense of fairness also

suggests that you can be compassionate and sympathetic to the needs of others.

March 17: Pisces   Ruler: Neptune
Insightful and receptive, your ruler, Neptune, indicates that you are a gifted and imaginative individual with good analytical and organizational skills. Although you may give the impression that you are amiable and easygoing, your profound thoughts and understanding usually gives you the edge or the opportunities to take charge and lead others. If you want to find emotional fulfillment resist letting financial consideration take precedence over your idealism and spiritual needs. Nevertheless, your ability to achieve success and security through your innate foresight implies that you can be altruistic as well as materially comfortable.

April 15: Aries   Ruler: Mars
Intelligent and witty, with a generous and compassionate nature, you are a friendly and sociable individual with the ability to generate success. Usually, your big plans and thoughts for success are likely to be the motivating forces that stop you from sinking into a comfortable rut. Although material security and financial issues can be vital to your peace of mind, your ruler, Mars, urges you to get ahead and do something spectacular. Your quick instincts and dynamic drive can add to your business acumen, but impulsive action or carelessness can undermine your efforts. Nevertheless, learning to manage financial affairs can help you to achieve the success you desire.

May 13: Taurus   Ruler: Venus
Your charismatic charm and determination indicate that you can be warm and engaging yet resolute. Although your main concerns are often security and prosperity, your idealistic and creative attributes imply that you want to find different ways to express your talents. Your in-

nate sense of values and business acumen also suggest that you can be responsible with your finances, so resist being extravagant. The key to your success is having the incentive to be a prolific worker and not rely on luck to provide you with the luxuries of life.

June 11: Gemini   Ruler: Mercury

Having Mercury as your ruler signifies that underneath your inspired ideas or altruistic motives you are a practical and mentally quick individual who is goal-oriented and highly capable. If you include motivation and perseverance in all your bright ideas or plans there is very little that you cannot achieve. In fact, you can be a prolific worker if you find a vocation or a meaningful cause. Sociable and a good conversationalist, your likeable yet persuasive manner can sway people to your way of thinking. Innately intuitive, although your nervous system is sensitive, your excellent sixth sense is generally highly accurate.

July 9: Cancer   Ruler: Moon

As an intuitive individual with a sympathetic nature, you are usually protective toward those you love and care for. Your ruler, the Moon, also gives you an ability to quickly evaluate people or situations. Although you are usually mentally quick, impulsive behavior born out of frustration can undermine your efforts and cause worry. Your strong sense of values suggests that, although you may be preoccupied with material issues, especially your home, your altruistic nature can motivate you to spend your time, knowledge, or money on helping other people. When you rise above your financial challenges you can be both successful and thoughtful.

August 7: Leo   Ruler: Sun

Being practical and determined indicates that you possess the willpower and determination to make headway and succeed. Often proud and dignified, your ruler, the Sun, signifies that you have a great deal of vitality and creativity at your disposal. As an independent individual you prefer to trust your own judgment, and usually you learn quickly from your past experiences and mistakes. A need to develop your analytical skills and positive outlook suggests that when you blend your intellectual sensitivity with your business acumen you can be original and highly successful.

September 5: Virgo   Ruler: Mercury

Being practical and intuitive implies that Mercury, your ruler, endows you with quick perception and strong instincts. Although you are concerned with finding material security, your desire to transform your life can give you the incentive to get ahead or be adventurous. A tendency to let your strong instincts guide you also signifies that you need to develop your methodology if want to execute your grand ideas. In order to empower yourself you may need to blend your visionary thoughts with practical skills and concrete plans. Investing in self-education is also advantageous to your curious mind.

October 3: Libra   Ruler: Venus

Gifted and charismatic, your powerful emotions and strong desires indicate that you are a passionate individual with deep feelings. Usually Venus, your ruler, grants you refined taste, creative talents, engaging mannerisms, and a flair for dealing with others. Your desire for self-expression or a prosperous life-style may be just the right incentive to get you motivated. Although you have good organizational skills and business acumen, resist being extravagant or wasteful. By overcoming and letting go of the past and staying focused on your present goals you will be able to find more of the happiness and joy you want out of life.

November 1: Scorpio   Ruler: Mars
Your dynamic drive and urge to take action indicate that you have big plans and leadership qualities. Mars, your ruler, under the auspicious influence of the 10 of Diamonds signifies the potential for substantial success in the world of commerce. Since the concepts of freedom, idealism, and generosity often play an important role in your success story, you may want to share your success with others. Although you want to make sure that you are well-provided-for materially, do not ignore the spiritual message of your card in matters concerning fair play, humanitarian work, and the rights of workers.

♠ THE 6 OF SPADES ♠

As a 6 of Spades Card you are a person who often has a sense of mission about your life. If you rise to the outstanding potential of your card you can be someone who taps into the unconscious desires of your generation and can somehow manifest them to others. A sensitive and refined personality, with strong image awareness, you respond well to inspiration and positive ideals. Under the influences of Uranus and Neptune in the Earthly Spread, you possess strong individuality and a love of freedom that suggest you like to do things your way.

Working on getting the balance right can be part of your life plan. It is usually better for you to give a little bit of time and energy to everything that needs attention at the time rather than leaving things incomplete. Being caring, you want to give to others, yet if you give too much you can take on other people's responsibilities and become anxious or interfering. Equally, if you go the other way you may not take responsibility for the work needed to fulfill your outstanding potential. An innate desire for harmony can translate as people skills, compassion for others, or talent in the arts. Equally, it emphasizes the importance of your home, where you can create your own hideaway from the world. Be careful, however, that your desire for peace does not turn into inertia or getting stuck in a rut. When you combine your interest in worldly affairs with a positive attitude, you possess strong insight and may become an adviser for others. Your life is usually helped by an ability to project a charismatic quality that influences others.

Your Two Replacement Cards Are the 9 of Spades & the 2 of Spades.

As the 6 of Spades you share the same planetary position as the 9 of Spades in the Spiritual Spread. This signifies that you are working on an inner level to develop detachment and a universal approach, although you may not fully understand this until later in life. You may experience tests in which you have to cut loose or leave people and situations behind. By being generous and dispassionate you can work on a more humanitarian or charitable level.

You also share the same planetary position as the 2 of Spades in the Earthly Spread. This suggests that your work is especially important to you. You generally work well in partnerships or in cooperation with others, although sometimes hidden fears can influence your relationships. Fortunately, you are usually responsible and hardworking, and are well able to hold your own in social situations.

You usually have special or karmic links with people who are represented by the 9 of Spades and the 2 of Spades, as you share the same planetary positions. You can be soul mates, working partners, or understand each other very well. Serious, hardworking, or career-oriented, even if you do not get along, you can both see clearly how the other person operates.

Your Mercury Card is . . .

The Queen of Hearts
- You have a strong sense of drama and can communicate in either a warm, loving, and sociable way or, if negative, be self-indulgent and temperamental.
- Articulate, with quick responses, you can get your ideas across in a powerful manner.
- Mentally receptive and multifaceted, you enjoy improving your knowledge and skills.
- A strong female influence in your youth, probably your mother, was likely to have been emotionally strong and kind.
- Queen of Hearts people can stimulate you mentally and creatively. You should always be able to talk to this person and discuss your many ideas.

Your Venus Card is . . .

The 10 of Clubs
- Success comes through doing things in your life that you love and that make you truly enthusiastic. This has to be genuine; you can't pretend.
- In relationships you are attracted to those who are knowledgeable and informed or radiate an aura of confidence.
- You can do particularly well in people-related activities.
- People represented by the 10 of Clubs card

are a good link for pleasure, romance, friendship, and business relationships.

Your Mars Card is . . .

The 8 of Diamonds
- The thought of material success usually motivates you to achieve.
- Avoid power struggles with others, particularly when you are angry.
- You can be very determined and businesslike when set on a course of action.
- 8 of Diamonds people can make you more active, dynamic, and forceful. Avoid arguments or control issues with these people.

Your Jupiter Card is . . .

The King of Spades
- The outstanding potential of this Master Card suggests that you can make remarkable achievements in life, whether materially or spiritually, through discipline and faith.
- You respect and admire those who have achieved self-mastery and power.
- You possess natural organizational or leadership skills that when developed can ensure that you attract good opportunities.
- Although you can be caring, avoid being bossy or too tough.
- Wise or hardworking men can be especially fortunate for you.

The 6 of Spades Planetary Card Sequence

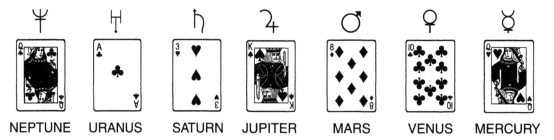

NEPTUNE   URANUS   SATURN   JUPITER   MARS   VENUS   MERCURY

- King of Spades people can expand your horizons and bring you beneficial chances to improve your situation in life. Although they can have an expansive influence, avoid overindulgence.

Your Saturn Card is . . .

The 3 of Hearts

- Your tests are most likely to concern your relationships or the emotional choices you have to make.
- Avoid worry or indecision, as this can block your natural creativity.
- By putting your need for self-expression into a definite structure, such as singing, writing, drama, etc., you can often find satisfaction, overcome insecurity, or make light of any problems you may have.
- 3 of Hearts people can be your guides and help you realize your shortcomings. If you are willing to work on your self-awareness these people can bring valuable lessons. This can often be a karmic link.

Your Uranus Card is . . .

The Ace of Clubs

- If you develop the strong intuitive insight shown by this Ace Card you can have flashes of inspiration and be a good, detached observer.
- You enjoy starting new projects that involve updating your skills, learning fresh information, or passing your knowledge on to others.
- Mentally willful, your strong desires can either make you rebellious and stubborn or lead you to take a powerful and original approach to life that others will follow.
- People who are the Ace of Clubs can stimulate you to initiate activities and make you

more objective or humanitarian. This is a good link for friendship.

Your Neptune Card is . . .

The Queen of Clubs

- An idealistic side to your nature and a quest for truth can attract you to philosophical, religious, or mystical subjects.
- You possess a keen mental understanding of how to present images to others.
- In later years you are likely to be connected to intelligent and interesting people. You may act as a link-up person between different social groups.
- Queen of Clubs people can link to your dreams and ideals or have a psychic connection with you, but guard against delusion.

Your Challenge Card is . . .

The 10 of Spades

- Think and radiate a success that comes through knowing that you have worked hard and put the time in, and now you deserve to reap the benefits.
- Transmute personal ego into inspired and progressive ideas or leadership.
- People who are the 10 of Spades can dare you to bring out your best or your worst qualities and can be a transformative influence of you. Avoid power games.

The Result of Your Challenge Card is . . .

The 5 of Clubs

- If you are actively seeking knowledge, adventure, or new experiences in your life, then you are responding well to your challenge.
- If you are in a rut and feeling restless and impatient you may need to review your Challenge Card again.

- People represented by the 5 of Clubs can stimulate you to expand your knowledge and skills and reflect how you are responding to your challenges.

Famous People Who Are the 6 of Spades

Elvis Presley, Stephen Hawking, Ronald Reagan, Bob Marley, Hans Christian Andersen, Axl Rose, Antonio Vivaldi, Emile Zola, R. Kelly, Babe Ruth, Rip Torn, Emmylou Harris, Marvin Gaye, François Truffaut, Dana Carvey, Natalie Cole, Alec Guinness, David Bowie

Birthdays Governed by the 6 of Spades

January 8: Capricorn   Ruler: Saturn
Being ambitious with an enjoyment of power, you can be very determined once directed toward your goals. Practical and down-to-earth, yet very imaginative, you have a need for self-expression. Preferring to be in a position of influence, if not fulfilled you may be prone to insecurity, indecision, or frustration. Overcoming obstacles works to help you build up your strength and perseverance. By utilizing your natural leadership abilities, business acumen, and warm social skills you have the potential for remarkable success.

February 6: Aquarius   Ruler: Uranus
Friendly and progressive, with good communication skills, you have an ability to teach or inspire others. When positive you can be persuasive, hardworking, and responsible, with an understanding of universal brotherhood. Although you value freedom, you also possess a strong love of home and family. Just be careful not to be so concerned that you become bossy or intrusive. An interest in worldly affairs or a desire to make changes in society may take you into politics or social reform.

March 4: Pisces   Ruler: Neptune
Impressionable and receptive, you have strong intuition and high ideals. Although your love of harmony and a touch of inertia could happily keep you lounging around at home, you are often hardworking, businesslike, and worldly wise. Even though you are usually loyal and generous, guard against your love of the good life turning into self-indulgence or escapism. Highly imaginative and refined, with a quest for truth, you possess innate creative talents and spiritual gifts.

April 2: Aries   Ruler: Mars
Pioneering and dynamic yet sensitive and considerate, you like to keep active. With a fast and resolute mind you can impress others with your strong will, enterprising spirit and considerate nature. Although there are times when you may have to avoid sarcasm or impulsive behavior, you usually succeed when you have the discipline to just quietly getting on with things. Proud of home and family, you are usually responsible but avoid dependent situations.

♥ ♣ THE 7 S ♦ ♠

ON A SPIRITUAL LEVEL the number 7 is often associated with insight, intuition, and mystical experiences. Although it emphasizes the ability to intellectualize, rationalize, and reflect, in metaphysical sciences the number 7 is categorized under the wisdom that is gained through observation and receptivity. Although uncertainty and skepticism may at times hold you back, you prefer to feel, act, or think independently. Being well informed and meticulous implies that you enjoy gathering information and have an excellent memory. Analytical and thoughtful, you enjoy debating and winning arguments. If you feel insecure, however, you may create misunderstandings by contradicting others. Introspective and reflective, you seek greater self-awareness, and quality time alone is often important for your well-being. You often learn through personal experiences rather than advice from others. Depending on the type of suit you belong to, your number 7 Card has unique powers and gifts that will allow you to discover the real you.

The following suits further modify the effect of your number:

7 of Hearts

Your emotional sensitivity and powerful feelings often instigate personal experiences that can test your faith. By rising above petty squabbles or negative emotional expressions, you can show your inner strength. By being spontaneous and developing emotional detachment, you become more independent and carefree.

7 of Clubs

Receptive and intuitive, you are inspired by knowledge, which you like to share with others. Your ability to reflect, analyze, and reason suggests that if you can overcome a tendency to indulge in worry and self-doubt you can surpass your own expectations. When you employ your sensitive intellect creatively you can achieve your inspired goals.

7 of Diamonds

Your objectivity and sensitive awareness about business can help you to assess monetary issues accurately. Thoughtful and insightful, you can achieve prosperity when you combine your intuition and foresight with your practical affairs. Having enough faith in yourself and being spontaneous can also attract success. With resolve and a positive outlook, you can free yourself from financial worries.

7 of Spades

Although you can sometimes be bogged down by responsibilities, your self-discipline and inner faith can generate a great deal of positive energy to free you from mundane existence. Learn to trust your inner voice and allow your intuition to guide you. An interest in metaphysical subjects can elevate you to a higher spiritual realm.

♥ THE 7 OF HEARTS ♥

As a number 7 of the Hearts suit you are emotionally sensitive yet can also be analytical, rational, and perfectionist. These extremes of your nature work well when you have faith in yourself and your abilities. This helps you to be spontaneous by living in the moment and believing all will work out as it is supposed to. The major problems arise when you lose faith and suddenly come to a stop, feeling that life has passed you by and you somehow missed out. This can lead to feelings of isolation, so it is important to make sure that you go with the flow of life. Under the influences of Mercury and Venus in the Earthly Spread, you possess good intellectual abilities and creative ideas with a talent for clearly analyzing situations.

Although you possess innate charm and magnetism, do not allow a tendency to become cynical and withdrawn block your amazing potential. By developing your communication skills and natural gifts you can achieve remarkable results.

Influenced by Neptune and Mercury in the Spiritual Spread, your mental receptivity is increased, bringing you strong visionary abilities. You may wish to develop this more imaginative side of yourself through the arts, or combine it with your critical skills in technology, business, or science. Your mental sensitivity also endows you with strong intuition if you can trust your inner guidance. If you build on the idealistic or more spiritual side of your nature you can achieve much emotional contentment.

Your Two Replacement Cards Are the 8 of Hearts & Ace of Spades.

As the 7 of Hearts you share the same planetary position as the 8 of Hearts in the Spiritual Spread. This signifies that you possess much inner power, determination, and resolve that can sometimes come out and surprise others. With your charismatic charm and innate money sense, you can sometimes be in the lucky position of being able to mix business with pleasure. If your powerful emotions become blocked, however, your ability to inspire others can turn to moods or power struggles.

As your card also shares the same planetary position as the Ace of Spades in the Earthly Spread, your work is extra important to you. You need new ventures to work on and projects that challenge you. Be careful, however, that the Ace, or number 1, influence here is not your ego rather than you being an initiator and selfless guide for others. The strong desires of the Ace of Spades can lead you to either self-will or suspicion, or to meaningful work. In order to explore life's deeper mysteries and wisdom you need some time for reflection and self-analysis.

You have special or karmic links with people who are represented by the 8 of Hearts or Ace of Spades. As you share the same planetary positions you can be soul mates or understand each other very well. Even if you do not get along, you can both see clearly how the other person operates.

Your Mercury Card is . . .

The 7 of Diamonds
- Thoughtful and analytical, your sharp intellect can make you reflective and a perfectionist.
- Although usually warm, considerate, caring, and loving, at times your mental processes can make you seem cold, secretive, or aloof.
- You have good critical abilities and a strong understanding of structure.
- Being too self-absorbed can bring on feelings of loneliness, jealousy, or being misunderstood.
- You are likely to have an attractive voice, refined thinking, and an appreciation of beauty, form, and design that is excellent for writing or artistic pursuits.
- People who are the 7 of Diamonds can stimulate your spontaneity and communication

skills. You should be able to talk and exchange ideas with this person.

Your Venus Card is . . .

The 5 of Spades
- A love of variety and change may manifest as a desire for adventure, excitement, or travel.
- You need a partner who will keep up with your fast responses and changing emotions. If you become bored you can get impatient or restless.
- Being idealistic and sensitive, the demonstration of love and affection can be especially meaningful to you.
- 5 of Spades people can stimulate your Venus card and be a good link for love, romance, friendship, and business. You could have much pleasure or travel or have adventures with this person.

Your Mars Card is . . .

The Jack of Hearts
- Linked to your drive and need for action is a playful or childlike quality. This can be highly creative or alternatively suggests immaturity and a desire to avoid responsibility.
- Helping or making sacrifices for others can prove to be very rewarding as long as you

The 7 of Hearts Planetary Card Sequence

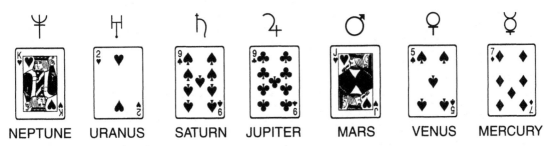

| NEPTUNE | URANUS | SATURN | JUPITER | MARS | VENUS | MERCURY |

don't play the martyr or feel sorry for yourself in the process.

- Your dramatic side often swings into action when you are either angry or entertaining others with your warm and affectionate sociability.
- Jack of Hearts people can stimulate your ambition, courage, and get-up-and-go. Alternatively, they may cause arguments or be competitive with you.

Your Jupiter Card is . . .

The 9 of Clubs

- Being clever, with a natural philosophical turn to your thinking, you do best when you have a definite belief system and are constantly updating your knowledge and awareness.
- Holding onto frustration or disappointments can block your faith and opportunities for expansion.
- When enthusiastic you can impress others with your knowledge and may enjoy an informed debate or discussion.
- You may have a strong interest or especially gain from foreign people and places, a quest for truth, or humanitarian interests.
- People who are the 9 of Clubs can open up your opportunities and make you feel more confident and expansive. Sometimes this can be a spiritual link.

Your Saturn Card is . . .

The 9 of Spades

- Your tests often involve being able to let go of the past and move on.
- When positive you can be noble, generous, and benevolent.
- You may become disillusioned if you, or life, does not measure up to your high expecta-

tions. This can cause fluctuating moods or a tendency for escapism.

- By developing your impersonal detachment you are able to put your experiences into a universal or larger perspective. This heightens your intuitive awareness and helps you overcome all obstacles.
- Although at times you are capable of a profound level of awareness, you may also have times when you are capable of indulging in self-destructive negativity.
- By developing your self-discipline you enhance your innate spirituality and connect to your natural wisdom.
- 9 of Spades people can be your guides and help you recognize your shortcomings. If you are willing to work on your self-awareness these people can bring valuable lessons.

Your Uranus Card is . . .

The 2 of Hearts

- Cooperative ventures such as partnerships or group activities can be especially fortunate for you.
- Getting yourself into dependent situations can cause you to be rebellious or behave erratically.
- Although you tend to enjoy your own company, emotional partnerships stimulate your natural creativity, inventiveness, and sense of individuality.
- 2 of Hearts people can bring love into your life and show you how to be more objective about yourself. This is a good friendship link.

Your Neptune Card is . . .

The King of Hearts

- You possess natural dramatic or acting skills and a warm, loving nature.

- Later in your life you may find yourself in the forefront of your social group.
- It is vital that you show integrity with the truth; if you deceive yourself you can be prone to inner confusion, nervous sensitiveness, or faulty judgment.
- Being idealistic and aware of subtle emotions, you possess sympathetic and compassionate understanding for others.
- Your imaginative or visionary skills are of a very high caliber and can be used to bring you emotional satisfaction as well as material success.
- Kings of Hearts people can connect to your emotional sensitivity and vision. This can be a psychic link, although avoid getting into escapism or illusion with this person.

Your Challenge Card is . . .

The King of Diamonds

- Use your innate business sense or good evaluation skills for the good of humankind.
- Dare to take a leading position whether with family, your peer group, or in social and work situations. This can be through responding positively to competition.
- Constantly reassess your values so that you do not place too much emphasis on materialism.
- King of Diamonds individuals can confront you to transform old patterns if you rise to the challenge, but it might be intense.

The Result of Your Challenge Card is . . .

The 6 of Hearts

- You will be enjoying a reasonable amount of peace within yourself and be caring enough to try and bring it into the lives of others.
- You will value calm, tranquility, and harmony.

- If you are stuck in a rut and suffering from anxiety you need to respond more positively to your challenges.
- 6 of Hearts people can help stimulate the caring or responsible part of your nature. Your reactions to them often reflect how you are responding to your personal challenges.

Famous People Who Are the 7 of Hearts

Bill Gates, Julia Roberts, Jonas Salk, Ava Gardner, Francis Bacon, Desiderius Erasmus, Charles Schulz, Johnny Mathis, Tyco Brahe, Robert Joffrey, Ricky Martin, Mary Higgins Clark, Jenna Elfman, Tina Turner, Joaquin Phoenix, Truman Capote, Howard Hughes, Kieran Culkin

Birthdays Governed by the 7 of Hearts

September 30: Libra   Ruler: Venus

You are a person with many facets to your personality. At one extreme you are friendly, refined, gracious, and creative, yet at the other extreme you can be mentally analytical or technical, with a desire to withdraw and be alone. Being very sensitive, you need positive outlets for your powerful emotions or you may suffer from doubt, worry, and insecurity. If you develop your creativity you can particularly excel in the arts, music, writing, or drama. Nevertheless, learning about how to deal with relationships can be an especially important part of your life. Developing faith in your talents and your ability to handle life spontaneously is a major key to your happiness.

October 28: Scorpio   Ruler: Mars

A need to succeed is matched by your independence and strong will. Although you can be sensitive, you can also be daring and ambitious. If, however, you become too dependent on others you may lose some of your drive and resort to cynicism or bossiness. Underneath your strong convictions, competitive spirit, and leadership potential is an idealist with creative ideas and a strong psychic sixth sense. With your penetrating intellect and analytical skills you gain much when you pool your resources in cooperative ventures.

November 26: Sagittarius   Ruler: Jupiter
You are an interesting blend of opposites. At times you can be proud, optimistic, and enthusiastic and at others skeptical and withdrawn. Equally, you can be idealistic and caring, but also pragmatic or bossy. With your fine mind and need for inspiration, you can often balance the extremes of your nature and prosper when you persistently work toward your goals with faith and trust. Outspoken and often worldly wise, you have natural executive ability and innate business sense.

December 24: Capricorn   Ruler: Saturn
Practical, clever, and ambitious, with keen emotional perceptions, you are a realist with strong ideals. When positive you can combine your sensitivity, determination, and ability to turn on the charm to motivate others. Although proud, a tendency to be stubborn or uncommunicative, however, may cause destructive behavior or undermine your appeal. Nevertheless, with your perfectionist streak you like to analyze situations in order to improve them. You can be responsible and open-minded, with the resolve and abilities to rise to high positions in life.

As your home and family are likely to be an especially strong focus in your life it is important for you to build a safe and secure haven of peace from the world.

♣ THE 7 OF CLUBS ♣

The intellectual expression of the number 7 implies that you possess a sensitive yet powerful mind. With a positive attitude and inner faith, you can overcome mental tensions and life's stresses. Your analytical abilities and powers of observation suggest that you learn quickly and are happiest when gaining new knowledge or information. Since your opinions are usually based on independent evaluations, you can also at times be cynical and skeptical. A desire to transcend the mundane side of the material world indicates that you can also be intuitive, receptive, and introspective.

The Clubs suit also emphasizes the intellectual potential and mental acumen of your number 7 Card. Under the influences of Saturn and Uranus in the Earthly Spread, you are likely to experience unusual emotional tensions and strains. The urge for freedom may also come into conflict with your need for stability and security. Nevertheless, you can bring new and inventive ideas to old systems, and being willful and determined you can persevere and endure even in difficult circumstances.

The planetary influences of Uranus and Mars in your Spiritual Spread imply that you value your freedom and independence and are reluctant to yield to pressure from others. This self-determined power gives you courage and stamina. It also suggests that you can achieve extraordinary results when you feel inspired and combine your intuition with your special talents.

Your Two Replacement Cards Are the Jack of Spades & the 8 of Diamonds.

As the 7 of Clubs you also share the same planetary position as the Jack of Spades in the Earthly Spread. This royal card gives you special creative power, idealism, and the ambition to accomplish your heart's desires. This card represents an important spiritual challenge, however, concerning choices. Although this card offers an initiation into a life of spiritual insight and integrity, it warns against immature behavior and mixing with dubious characters.

As the 7 of Clubs you also share the same planetary position as the 8 of Diamonds in the Spiritual Spread. This card suggests that you can rise to powerful positions in your profession. Usually you have innate business acumen and the potential to make money. In order to achieve your goal, however, you need to be hardworking, determined, and confident enough to express your inner power. Acquiring the right set of values can ensure your success and accomplishment.

You usually have special or karmic links with people who are represented by the Jack of Spades and the 8 of Diamonds, as you share the same planetary positions. You can be soul mates or understand each other very well. Even if you do not get along, you can both see clearly how the other person operates.

Your Mercury Card is . . .

The 5 of Diamonds

- Mentally you pick up on situations very quickly.
- A need for adventure or uncertainty about money suggests that you may seek to venture out on your own at an early age.
- A need to be learning new things implies that you enjoy a challenge and do not like being stuck in a predictable situation.
- Travel can be particularly good for stimulating your mind and inspiring you.
- Sudden changes in circumstances can add to your sense of uncertainty, so it is good to have overall long-term plans.
- You should have good mental rapport and

special communication with people who represent the 5 of Diamonds, as they activate your Mercury card.

Your Venus Card is . . .

The Queen of Spades

- Women can have a beneficial influence on you, especially in matters concerning your relationships and career.
- Loyal and practical, you admire hardworking, insightful, and ambitious individuals.
- Trust your intuition and listen to your inner voice.
- Self-discipline is also the key to your success and accomplishments.
- This card suggests that you can attract success through being of service to others.
- Your Venus link indicates that you are attracted to Queen of Spades people, as they are ideal for love and romance, close friendships, and good business partnerships.

Your Mars Card is . . .

The Jack of Clubs

- Astute and young at heart, you benefit from all types of intellectual pursuits.
- Investing time and effort in learning new information or skills can reap great rewards.
- You admire people who are spirited, witty, or mentally quick.
- Sharp and intellectually creative, you like a challenge to test your wits.
- Jack of Clubs people can particularly motivate, stimulate, and energize you, but channel the energy constructively.

Your Jupiter Card is . . .

The 9 of Diamonds

- Generous and considerate, you are often willing to assist others, and those you help usually reward you with kindness.

The 7 of Clubs Planetary Card Sequence

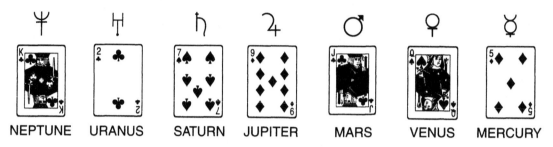

NEPTUNE   URANUS   SATURN   JUPITER   MARS   VENUS   MERCURY

- The beneficial influence of Jupiter indicates that you can be lucky with money and legacies.
- Even if you acquire large amounts of money, an extravagant streak suggests that managing it can still remain a challenge.
- Preoccupation with possessions can block your potential or path to self-awareness.
- 9 of Diamonds people are often benefactors who can expand and enhance your life. Usually you have a good rapport with them. They can also be good partners if you both resist overspending.

Your Saturn Card is . . .

The 7 of Spades

- Getting the recognition you deserve requires effort and hard work.
- You may work in seclusion or behind the scenes.
- Underneath your bright and easygoing personality you are a sensitive, thoughtful, and analytical individual.
- Although you have a good health, worry or mental anxiety can cause all types of health complaints.
- 7 of Spades people can be your guides and help you recognize your shortcomings. If you are willing to work on your self-awareness these people can bring valuable lessons.

Your Uranus Card is . . .

The 2 of Clubs

- A willingness to share your knowledge implies that you benefit from cooperative alliances, group activities, or shared common goals.
- A need for sincerity and openness indicates that partnerships based on secrecy can lead to arguments and anxiety.
- You can establish good friendships through your quest for knowledge.
- Although you can hold your own in debates, resist using sarcasm as a weapon when you feel insecure.
- 2 of Clubs people can help you be more objective about yourself. You can both be freedom loving and share a zany sense of humor or some unusual interest. This is also a good friendship link.

Your Neptune Card is . . .

The King of Clubs

- This royal card suggests that you can achieve your dreams in the latter part of your life.
- If you are willing to take the responsibilities that come with an executive position your leadership qualities develop as you get older.
- The more you invest in developing your intellect and skills or perfecting your area of

expertise, the more confident and successful you become.

- King of Clubs people can have a psychic connection with you; they may link to your visions, ideals, or dreams. Although these individuals can inspire you, guard against delusion or escapism.

Your Challenge Card is . . .

The Jack of Diamonds
- Handling financial matters may be one of your challenges, so a disciplined and responsible attitude is called for in all matters of business and finance.
- When you realize your self-worth you can successfully promote yourself and be enterprising.
- Through self-evaluation you can learn what is most important to you in life.
- People represented by the Jack of Diamonds can challenge or provoke you. Although these people can help you to transform your life, resist power struggles with them.

The Result of Your Challenge Card is . . .

The 4 of Hearts
- Emotional stability and security are high on your list of priorities.
- You want to be surrounded by peace and harmony.
- Self-expression needs to be linked to something tangible.
- Self-contentment and satisfaction can come from being creative and productive.
- People represented by the 4 of Hearts can reflect how you are responding to your challenges.

Famous People Who Are the 7 of Clubs

Robin Williams, Bill Clinton, Ernest Hemingway, Lil' Romeo, Ralph Waldo Emerson, Miles Davis, Isaac Stern, Eric Idle, Sheena Easton, Coco Chanel, Malcolm Forbes, Friedrich Nietzche, P. G. Wodehouse, Sarah Ferguson, Whoopi Goldberg, Robert Louis Stevenson, Christina Onassis, Josh Hartnett, Mike Meyers, Matthew Perry, Lauryn Hill

Birthdays Governed by the 7 of Clubs

March 29: Aries   Ruler: Mars

Gifted with intellectual attributes and quick perception, your ingenious mind, inspired ideas and spirit of enterprise can accomplish a great deal. Usually your ruler, Mars, gives a real boost to your mental vitality and indicates that you can comprehend much in a short space of time. Although your cerebral power can make you forceful and persuasive, resist being sarcastic or verbally aggressive. A tendency to worry or be secretive also warns that lack of inner faith may lead to stress or nervous anxiety. Nevertheless, when you put your fine mind to work you can be a good communicator with leadership qualities. Alternatively, you can develop your creative mind, especially through literature, science, or jobs that require technical skills.

April 27: Taurus   Ruler: Venus

Along with practical skills and a fine intellect, Venus, your ruler, grants you charm, good taste, and emotional sensitivity. As a hardworking and productive individual you like to keep a high standard when it comes to work and responsibilities. Although you are often receptive to others, at times you can appear reserved or aloof. Nevertheless, your dedication, personality and creative output signifies that when you believe in yourself and take charge you can achieve a great deal. Alternatively, even in a supportive role your quick comprehension and organizational skills suggest that you are usually indispensable.

May 25: Gemini   Ruler: Mercury

Your ruler, Mercury, suggests that your quick and shrewd perception usually gives you the edge when assessing situations or picking up new ideas. Friendly and engaging by nature, you are an imaginative and thoughtful individual. Being versatile and mentally restless implies, however, that you can be distracted from your path if you do not truly believe in your goals. Learning how to manage your financial affairs by planning ahead can still leave you free to take advantage of new opportunities. Although an inclination to be spontaneous or impulsive may bring changes and new beginnings, you benefit from developing your long-term strategies and patience.

June 23: Cancer   Ruler: Moon

Highly intuitive and mentally quick, your ruler, the Moon, indicates that you are sensitive, with a strong connection to your family. Your inquisitive mind and strong feelings urge you to express yourself creatively and intellectually. Possessing powerful feelings also suggests that you benefit from developing your sixth sense and letting your inner voice guide you. Once equipped with this foresight you can also overcome tendencies such as worry and emotional uncertainty, as these often cause mental stress or anxiety. Nevertheless, through developing and tuning your fine mind you can accomplish much both in the material and spiritual worlds.

July 21: Cancer   Ruler: Moon

Idealistic and creative, your inspired ideas and curious mind indicate that you are an astute individual with intellectual gifts. When you combine your caring approach with inner strength and vision you can succeed admirably. Although your ruler, the Moon, usually adds imagination and intuition to your acute awareness, fluctuating moods or impatient restlessness can stir up your sensitive emotions. When you become decisive and patient you usually prosper and advance toward your inspired goals. Sociable and determined, you enjoy mixing with other people and want to live life to the full.

August 19: Leo   Ruler: Leo

Dramatic with sharpened awareness and inspired thoughts, you usually appear confident and proud. Yet underneath your bold front you are often a sensitive individual with a tendency to fluctuate emotionally. Fortunately, your ruler, the Sun, grants you vitality, leadership qualities, and an engaging personality. Since you can easily impress others, resist being too eager or aggressive in your approach. Your strong desire to find your own creative outlets indicates that you can express yourself in unique ways. When you develop these talents and combine your bright personality with your mental acumen you can captivate an audience or stand out in the crowd.

September 17: Virgo   Ruler: Mercury

Clever and inquisitive, your ruler, Mercury, grants you good analytical skills and an eye for detail. With your quick perception and unique talents, you can be blessed by a touch of genius. Yet without channeling these powerful mental energies into something constructive you are also in danger of wasting your time on worry and inner doubts. The key to your success is often found when you add time and effort to your inherent insight and inspired ideas. Developing your inner faith rather than skepticism can also benefit your wonderful potential.

October 15: Libra   Ruler: Venus

Although your sociable nature is often inclined to seek comfort and ease, you can be a prolific worker when you have a clear goal in mind. Mentally quick and highly intuitive, your ideas or inspired thoughts can direct you to great achievement especially through intellectual pursuits. Your ruler, Venus, grants you charm, creative talents, and a flair for dealing with people. Although your zest for life can inspire your humanitarian views, at times you can be very direct. Hastiness or an inclination to scatter your energies suggests that, in order to recognize the possibilities of your brilliant mind, you need to invest your special attributes into something worthwhile.

November 13: Scorpio   Ruler: Mars
High-spirited and tenacious, your dynamic drive gives you the incentive to get ahead or find ways to express yourself creatively or intellectually. Although your curiosity or inquisitive mind can delve deep in order to find the truth, guard against letting a tendency to be critical turn you into a sarcastic or argumentative individual. Able to access information quickly, you can put your knowledge and shrewd perception to good practical use. Once you make up your mind to do something, your vitality and innate faith can help you achieve your goals.

December 11: Sagittarius   Ruler: Jupiter
Your mental power comes into its own when you use the necessary self-discipline to master your skills and manifest your unique talents or ideas. Jupiter, your ruler, and your optimistic outlook usually guarantee good fortune. As a spontaneous and fun-loving individual you want the material freedom to enjoy life. Luckily your good sense of values and business know-how indicates that you possess business acumen and an aptitude to achieve success. Being keen and young at heart also implies that your spirit of adventure can urge you to follow your inspired dreams.

♦ THE 7 OF DIAMONDS ♦

As a number 7 of the Diamonds suit you can combine a sharp analytical intellect with a shrewd sense of values. Although practical, you can also display the spiritual qualities of the 7 by overcoming inhibitions and restrictions to act spontaneously in the moment. By having the courage to be yourself you can be someone for others to follow. Under the double influence of Venus in the Earthly Spread you possess excellent social awareness and have a natural love of beauty and luxury. You can be very charming and are likely to have developed your people skills and natural diplomacy to deal with problems.

Although Venus indicates a soft, affectionate, and friendly side to your nature, the double influence of Saturn in the Spiritual Spread shows that you can also be hard, disciplined, and inflexible. When these contrary influences are balanced, however, you can be loving, caring, and appreciative of the pleasures of life, yet still be powerful with clear boundaries. Equally, you can combine social skills with business or put artistic and creative ideas into some form or structure. Although money can be an important issue, you are usually willing to work hard to achieve financial benefits. Be careful not to compromise your principles for material security, however, as this ultimately can block your enjoyment of life.

Your Replacement Card Is the 9 of Hearts.

Your card is one of the more unusual ones in the deck in that it is only displaced by one card, the 9 of Hearts (see Semi-fixed Cards, page 24). This shows that your inner learning is inextricably linked to the love, compassion, and universal quality of this Hearts Card. By being able to develop and show unconditional love for others, you become generous enough

to give with no expectation of anything in return. Ironically, this draws everything you
need toward you. By perseverance and learning to let go and trust, you increase your self-
esteem and overcome a need for control based
on fear. Equally, money flows into your life
when you feel open enough to use your natural
creativity rather than worry.

You have a special or karmic link with people who are represented by the 9 of Hearts. As
you share the same planetary positions you can
be soul mates or understand each other very
well. Even if you do not get along, you can
both see clearly how the other person operates.

Your Mercury Card is . . .

The 5 of Spades
- Mentally quick, you have good first instincts
  and fast responses.
- You are likely to have experienced restrictive
  influences in your home growing up that
  may have influenced you later.
- You need variety or to be continually learning new things; otherwise, you can become
  mentally restless.
- Travel can be particularly good for stimulating your mind and inspiring you.
- People who are the 5 of Spades encourage
  your communication skills and can bring
  some excitement into your life. This is a
  good link for exchange of ideas.

Your Venus Card is . . .

The Jack of Hearts
- Sensitive and loving, you are often willing to
  make big sacrifices for those you love.
- Being sociable and affectionate, you highly
  value your relationships. A youthful and
  playful side to your nature will stay with you
  until old age. This is excellent for creative
  ideas or developing skills in art, music, film,
  writing, or drama.
- Avoid self-pity or playing the martyr, especially in romantic situations.
- You may be involved in relationships with
  people of a different age group.
- Your Venus link indicates that you are attracted to people who are loving, creative,
  and entertaining. Jack of Hearts people are
  ideal for love and romance, close friendships, and good business partnerships.

Your Mars Card is . . .

The 9 of Clubs
- You are likely to have a sharp edge in the
  brain department, but avoid being curt or
  impatient.
- You usually enjoy actively discussing your
  opinions or an informed debate.
- You can be generous with your time and energy and like to be of practical help.
- Avoid allowing frustration or disappoint-

The 7 of Diamonds Planetary Card Sequence

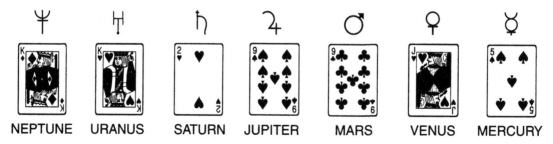

| NEPTUNE | URANUS | SATURN | JUPITER | MARS | VENUS | MERCURY |

ment with others to cause you to do something impulsive.

- 9 of Clubs people can particularly motivate and stimulate you. If you share the same goals you can both be enthusiastic in achieving your desires, but avoid arguing.

Your Jupiter Card is . . .

The 9 of Spades
- Although usually industrious, remember to get the balance right between work and play.
- Idealistic and impressionable, you possess strong foresight and compassion.
- Transmute a tendency to be self-absorbed or overly serious into a desire to encourage and lift up others.
- With your universal receptivity, if you develop the humanitarian side to your nature this can bring you much satisfaction.
- Usually you have a good rapport with 9 of Spades people, as they are often benefactors who can improve your opportunities and make you feel better about life. Alternatively, these people can have a spiritual link with you.

Your Saturn Card is . . .

The 2 of Hearts
- You often work well in partnerships, but make sure that neither you or your partner is dependent on each other.
- You also work well in team situations.
- Your major tests often come in the form of restrictions, responsibilities, or obstacles in your emotional relationships.
- You have a strong sense of duty, are loyal, and have endurance.
- You may find yourself having the responsibility of helping or looking after others, such as a relative, or this could be on a professional basis.

- 2 of Hearts people can be your guides and help you recognize your shortcomings. If you are willing to work on your self-awareness you can learn valuable lessons from your experiences with these people.

Your Uranus Card is . . .

The King of Hearts
- Your life improves as you get older and are more able to express yourself emotionally.
- You have an innate ability to guide and direct others.
- The more you express your individuality and originality the more dramatic or theatrical you become.
- You can be good at entertaining company, which makes you popular with friends.
- You have a strong desire for freedom, both for yourself and others.
- People who are represented by the King of Hearts can help you be more objective about yourself. They may support your unique process of growth or be a good friend.

Your Neptune Card is . . .

The King of Diamonds
- The combination of your good evaluation skills, sensitivity, and vision can bring you success or place you in advisory positions.
- You should be in a good material situation in your later years. This should enable you to travel.
- You possess natural intuitive talents that can attract you to mystical or religious subjects.
- You enjoy artistic and creative endeavors where you are able to lose your ego in the greater whole.
- King of Diamonds people can have a psychic connection with you. You may share the same ideals or dreams, but remember to also stay realistic.

Your Challenge Card is . . .

The 6 of Hearts

- Lead an emotionally well-balanced life and not allow yourself to get into a comfortable rut.
- Although you care, don't allow this to turn into anxiety or misplaced sympathy.
- Connect to your ideals, compassion, and creativity, yet still be responsible.
- Avoid being too critical or judgmental.
- 6 of Hearts people can usually dare you to react. They can provide opportunities for you to transform your life for the better even if the situation with them is confrontational.

The Result of Your Challenge Card is . . .

The 4 of Clubs

- You have trained yourself to think positively and be honest with others.
- You have definite plans for the future.
- You have overcome a stubborn streak and always display integrity in your dealings with others.
- 4 of Clubs people can stimulate you to learn and build strong foundations to your projects. They often reflect how you are responding to your challenges.

Famous People Who Are the 7 of Diamonds

Sting, Judy Garland, David Lynch, Cybill Shepherd, Robert Mitchum, Yoko Ono, Federico Fellini, Marianne Williamson, Loretta Lynn, Lord Tennyson, Katharine Hepburn, Yogi Berra, Dante Gabriel Rossetti, Richard Wright, John D. Rockefeller, Nelson Rockefeller, Andy Warhol, Donna Karan, Lucille Ball, Bernardo Bertolucci, John Gielgud, Rod Steiger, Ramakrishna, M. Night Shyamalan, Groucho Marx, Helen Gurley Brown, John Travolta, Dr. Dre, Ving Rhames, Toni Morrison, Sarah Michelle Gellar, Mahatma Gandhi, Béyoncé Knowles

Birthdays Governed by the 7 of Diamonds

January 20: Capricorn   Ruler: Saturn

An interesting mixture of opposites, you can be considerate, caring, and lovingly affectionate while also capable of being tough, disciplined, and reserved. If you listen and trust your natural intuition rather than being too pragmatic you can find projects that inspire you, allowing you to let go of your need to control. Gracious and often charming, you particularly gain from cooperative ventures or working partnerships. Although dutiful, you also need spontaneity in your life, so you may need to push yourself to be more experimental or daring.

February 18: Aquarius   Ruler: Uranus

Ambitious and assertive, you are a strong individualist with a fine brain and strong convictions. Although usually friendly, there are times when you can withdraw and appear cold. You may need to develop ways to just go with the flow or balance responsibilities with fun. Strong-willed and dramatic, you also have an appreciation of art and beauty that you may wish to develop. Equally, your natural business sense can help you achieve in life. Although you can rise to positions of authority, you also have a humanitarian streak that wishes to help others.

March 16: Pisces   Ruler: Neptune

Intelligent and quick thinking, you are a friendly Piscean with strong feelings. The combination of your good judgment and imaginative vision can aid your success. You may, however, have to adjust your need for freedom and self-expression with your responsibilities to others. Although thoughtful and security conscious, avoid overanalyzing financial affairs. If you do your best and trust your strong intuition you will receive the guidance you need at the right time.

April 14: Aries   Ruler: Mars

Practical, straightforward, and assertive, you can be direct and outspoken. Although sometimes restless or impulsive, you realize that nothing is achieved without hard work. Clever and analytical, you are also broad-minded, determined, and resourceful. Your work is particularly important to you as it can combine your need to expand your opportunities with your need for something solid and secure. Although you can be sensitive, guard against a stubborn or impatient streak. Sociable with leadership skills, you can be generous and supportive of those you care about.

May 12: Taurus   Ruler: Venus

Friendly and affectionate, you are a person who appreciates beauty and the good things of life. Equally, you are usually responsible and willing to work hard to bring about the results you want. When you combine your discipline with your playful quality you can particularly excel in creative endeavors, such as singing, music, drama, writing, interior design, or landscape gardening. People-oriented, a desire to help others practically can also draw you to work with a service element.

June 10: Gemini   Ruler: Mercury

Mentally sharp, you are an individual with leadership potential, a sociable approach, and strong convictions. You learn quickly but also have a delicate nervous system you need to protect. Independent, with a natural flair for the dramatic, you are a good conversationalist who has a talent for dealing with people. Nevertheless, at times you may need to guard against being selfish or overbearing. Being proud and keen to master your favorite sub-

jects suggests that success and accomplishment are extra-important to you.

July 8: Cancer   Ruler: Moon

Determined and optimistic, you are a person who can combine businesslike drive with emotional sensitivity. Security conscious and family oriented, you can be very protective of those in your care. You may also wish to develop your natural organization or leadership skills to bring you prosperity as well as help others. Although you enjoy power, guard against becoming too materialistic. Nonetheless, you are caring and sympathetic, with creative gifts. You can also be fortunate to find help from people in influential positions.

August 6: Leo   Ruler: Sun

With your ambition, sharp mental responses, and warm social skills you are an individual who can achieve much in life. Although interested in world affairs, your home and family play an especially important part in your life agenda. Be careful, however, that in your desire to care for others your strong disciplinarian qualities do not become bossiness. With the ability to think on a large scale, you can be enterprising yet still retain a playful side. Life works better for you when you include others in your big plans.

September 4: Virgo   Ruler: Mercury

Charming but somewhat reserved, you are an intelligent and hardworking individual with a serious nature. Sociable, with an interest in others, you like to be honest, loyal, and down-to-earth. When positive your sharp critical or analytical skills usually work to ensure your success. Practical and thorough, you can gain particularly from research, technical matters, or writing. Although you enjoy being of service to others, you may also have to guard against being stubborn. Among your many good qualities you possess an appreciation for beauty as well as business acumen.

October 2: Libra   Ruler Venus

Creative, courteous, and diplomatic, you possess a strong sense of fair play and excellent social skills. Although you have a gift with people, you still need time alone to recharge your batteries and for self-analysis. Your relationships are of vital significance to you, but it is important that you also keep your independence. You may wish to develop your natural artistic and creative gifts, or you can be successful in law and occupations dealing with the public. A person of extremes, your strict self-discipline may lead you to self-mastery and the search for spiritual wisdom.

♠ THE 7 OF SPADES ♠

Under the influence of the number 7 you are likely to be sensitive to the mystical influences of life. Paying attention to your innate intuition, therefore, is highly beneficial to your well-being. Usually introspective, you prefer to evaluate situations and people on your own terms. As an independent thinker you can also communicate your visions and ideals.

The planetary influences of Uranus and Jupiter in your Earthly Spread signify that you have the ability to grasp situations quickly and recognize their advantages. Valuing knowledge, freedom, and independence, you may not like to feel restricted but resist taking risks or acting in an obstinate manner. On occasion your sensitivity can cause you to withdraw and appear cold; being thoughtful, however, you do also need time alone for reflection and self-analysis. Often your aim is to find something inspiring that will elevate you above the demands of everyday life. When you can act

spontaneously by trusting your strong inner perceptions you can make fortunate decisions and achieve remarkable success.

The planetary influences of Jupiter and Neptune in your Spiritual Spread indicate that developing your inner faith and idealism can further your prospects. With your powerful imagination and an ability to express your emotions creatively, you can rise above your challenges. At times, however, you may experience conflict between your high ideals and the very different reality. A positive use of your talents is best found in creative endeavors, helping others, or in spiritual and humanitarian interests.

Your Two Replacement Cards Are the 8 of Hearts & the King of Diamonds.

As the 7 of Spades you share the same planetary position as the 8 of Hearts in the Earthly Spread. This signifies that you can be compassionate and charming. This card also suggests that by developing your innate determination and resolve you are able to produce prolific amounts of work. When positive you can particularly attract others with your charismatic personality and desire to emotionally lift up others. If you do not consciously recognize your inner power, however, you may experience moods or become involved in power struggles with others. Nevertheless, you do possess the emotional power to heal others.

As the 7 of Spades you also share the same planetary position as the King of Diamonds in the Spiritual Spread. This royal card grants you protection on the material level as well as inner strength, leadership skills, and psychological insight. Your astute understanding of values can assist you in the material world, where business acumen is crucial. Although you have good evaluating skills, learning to listen to the advice of others can make you less single-minded or bossy.

You usually have special or karmic links with people who are represented by the 8 of Hearts and King of Diamonds, as you share the same planetary positions. You can be soul mates or understand each other very well. Even if you do not get along, you can both see clearly how the other person operates.

Your Mercury Card is . . .

The 2 of Clubs

- Being witty and wanting to share your knowledge suggests that you enjoy communicating or collaborating with others.
- When you feel insecure you need to resist expressing your fears by being sarcastic or argumentative.
- Your sharp perception about people usually helps you to understand their strengths and weaknesses.
- You should have good mental rapport and special communication with 2 of Clubs people, as they activate your Mercury Card.

Your Venus Card is . . .

The King of Clubs

- You enjoy being in charge or taking a leading role.

- Your special analytical skills can prompt you to become your own boss or help you to rise to executive positions.
- Your potential to excel in all types of study implies that you enjoy keeping yourself intellectually active and greatly benefit from acquiring knowledge.
- You usually prefer maturity and experience to youth, and admire intelligent or authoritative figures who show leadership qualities.
- Your Venus link indicates you are attracted to people represented by the King of Clubs as they can be ideal mates, close friends, or good business partners.

Your Mars Card is . . .

The Jack of Diamonds

- Your youthful enthusiasm and talent for commerce suggests that you are enterprising and clever at doing business.
- Versatile and charming, you have good social skills and many creative talents.
- A responsible attitude toward finances and a resolute mind can motivate you to put enough effort and hard work into your projects.
- Jack of Diamonds people can particularly arouse you into action or stimulate your creativity, but avoid being competitive.

The 7 of Spades Planetary Card Sequence

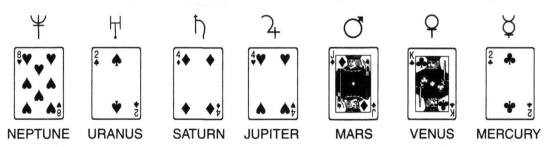

NEPTUNE   URANUS   SATURN   JUPITER   MARS   VENUS   MERCURY

Your Jupiter Card is . . .

The 4 of Hearts

- You particularly seek emotional stability and security within close relationships.
- Your ability to attract others indicates that you enjoy popularity and succeed in all type of people-related careers or work with the public.
- You can also benefit financially from your personal relationships or get help and assistance to advance in life.
- 4 of Hearts people can bring your fortunate opportunities so you usually have a good rapport or spiritual link with them.

Your Saturn Card is . . .

The 4 of Diamonds

- The protection of this card indicates that you can enjoy financial security and prosperity, especially if you are willing to work hard to achieve it.
- Although you are also protected in matters concerning health, resist overindulging or jeopardizing your well-being.
- Your practical skills or your understanding of business and market forces can help you turn your theories into financial rewards.
- If you become too stubborn this works against you.
- 4 of Diamonds people can be your guides and help you recognize your shortcomings. If you are willing to work on your self-awareness these people can bring valuable lessons.

Your Uranus Card is . . .

The 2 of Spades

- Although you often prefer to act independently, you need to recognize the importance of partnerships.

- In middle years a business or personal partnership plays a vital role in your personal development.
- Staying objective and practicing detachment and equality can assist you in establishing good and profitable partnerships.
- 2 of Spades people can help you be more objective about yourself. This is also a good friendship link where fairness and freedom is important.

Your Neptune Card is . . .

The 8 of Hearts

- The emotional power of this card appears twice in your card sequence, as your Replacement Card and Neptune Card. Its positive influence suggests that you will enjoy a good social life and friendships throughout your life.
- Your sensitivity and strong intuition can really help you achieve in life, but if you become oversensitive you may be prone to escapism or moods.
- You may find the most rewarding or the most challenging relationships later on in life.
- 8 of Hearts people can have a psychic connection with you. They may link to your visions and ideals or help you to materialize your dreams, but avoid delusion.

Your Challenge Card is . . .

The 6 of Clubs

- Create inner peace and overcome your mental frustrations or worry.
- Occupy your mind with creative or intellectual pursuits and do not alternate between overworking and inertia.
- Share and inspire others with your knowledge and insight.

- You take responsibility for the work needed to fulfill your outstanding potential.
- 6 of Clubs people can provoke you to react. Although these people can help you to transform your life, avoid power struggles.

The Result of Your Challenge Card is . . .

The 6 of Spades

- You are responsible and caring, but not at your own expense.
- Developing your inner vision and an interest in metaphysical subjects can be very rewarding.
- A labor of love can be the motive for genuine ambition and productivity.
- Inspiration can come through altruism or service to others.
- People who are represented by the 6 of Spades can reflect how you are responding to your challenges.

Famous People Who Are the 7 of Spades

Nicholas Cage, Katie Couric, Jean Harlow, Sergei Rachmaninoff, St. Bernadette of Lourdes, Bobby Brown, Abraham Maslow, Henry "Hank" Aaron, Debbie Reynolds, Ali MacGraw, Christopher Guest, William Burroughs

Birthdays Governed by the 7 of Spades

January 7: Capricorn   Ruler: Saturn

Determined and contemplative, your ruler, Saturn, usually provides you with the ambitious drive to achieve your goals. The double influence of the number 7 signifies that although you are highly intuitive, you prefer to think independently and therefore also learn by trial and error. The desire to be self-reliant or free from restrictions can lead you to unusual occupations or vocations that are

founded on your unique skills and practical abilities. Your common sense and earning opportunities also suggest that your business acumen and shrewd intuition can lead to material success.

February 5: Aquarius   Ruler: Uranus

Your restless nature or a desire to transform your status indicates that you value your freedom a great deal. Your ruler, Uranus, empowers you to quickly grasp situations and with your organizational skills and creative thoughts, you often have a number of plans. Although being independent allows you to become involved in many social activities, a need to collaborate or create an emotional balance in your personal life implies that your close relationships play a pivotal role in your spiritual development. For deeper awareness you may need to apply your objectivity constantly and learn to trust your instincts.

March 3: Pisces   Ruler: Neptune

The double influence of the number 3 in your birth date suggests that you usually possess deep and powerful emotions as well as personal magnetism. Versatile, imaginative, and creative, your emotional fulfillment is often found through personal self-expression. Although you may enjoy a good social life and fun friendships, your close relationships are likely to be more testing. When you feel positive your enthusiasm and imaginative thoughts can be very inspiring; just guard against overfantasizing. In order to achieve your dreams in life you need to stay focused on your goals and back them up with inner faith.

April 1: Aries   Ruler: Mars

The dynamic drive of your ruler, Mars, urges you to be daring and enterprising. When you adopt a serious attitude to your responsibilities you can find that you have the resolve and determination to make your mark in leadership positions. A good sense of values and an aptitude for business and finance indicates that when you gain the necessary experience you can be a practical and clever negotiator. Although you may have to fend for yourself from time to time, these experiences will add to your spiritual growth and self-empowerment. When you combine your vision and inner faith you are able to gain greater spiritual awareness.

♥ ♣ THE 8 s ♦ ♠

THE SYMBOLISM OF the number 8 comes under the influence of mastery, controlled power, hard work, and foresight. Known as the "architect," a number 8 individual is often endowed with good conceptual and planning skills. These strategic skills signify that as a number 8 person you usually prefer long-term projects that will secure your position. Generally, you have the common sense, pragmatic attributes, and business acumen necessary to utilize your administrative and organizational skills. Concerned with accomplishment, material success, and self-empowerment, you usually are promoted to positions of responsibility because of your dedication and perseverance. Your preference for executive positions indicates that you usually have the courage and strong convictions to take the lead. You may, however, need to watch how you use your position and influence. You may face tough opposition if you abuse the powers at your disposal. By being patience and tolerant, however, you show your true power.

The following suits further modify the effect of your number:

8 of Hearts

Your allure and personal magnetism indicate that you possess the persuasive charm to attract those you come in contact with. Your healing powers can inspire others when you use your sensitive feelings, creativity, or idealism for selfless reasons. The influence of the 8 of Hearts is also excellent for working with the public.

8 of Clubs

Your foresight and intuitive understanding are the keys to your success, especially if you have invested time in developing your cerebral power. In your intellectual pursuits and quest for wisdom, a rigid attitude can minimize your success, so stay objective and open-minded.

8 of Diamonds

Your strong sense of values, pragmatic approach, and practical abilities enable you to achieve success in the material world. If you become too preoccupied with material and financial matters, however, you may lose sight of the important things in life that money cannot buy.

8 of Spades

Your organizational skills, determination, and hard work empower you to be influential and productive. Your ability to heal others through your wisdom is where your true power lies. In your quest for success and achievement resist becoming involved in challenging power struggles in order to reach your objectives.

♥ THE 8 OF HEARTS ♥

The positive attributes of the number 8 signify that usually you have a strong presence and the determination to endure and overcome obstacles. Belonging to the Hearts suit indicates that you possess warmth and idealistic beliefs. Usually, you have at your disposal the charm and charisma to attract or impress others. Since these attributes can be used negatively for selfish reasons, your dilemma is often how to utilize the power of love constructively and express your feelings.

Although the influence of the number 8 signifies that you can be ambitious and hardworking, having Neptune and Jupiter in your Earthly Spread suggest that you have an innate sensitivity toward music, art, and, in particular, people. Unfortunately, if not careful this influence can also turn you into a pleasure seeker or an idle dreamer. Nevertheless, when you combine your receptivity with your powerful feelings you can express yourself cre-

atively. The influences of these two planets can also lead you to work for humanitarian causes or altruistic projects.

The influences of Venus and Mercury in your Spiritual Spread suggest that your appreciation of art and beauty and the ability to communicate your feelings can make you graceful and witty. With your charm, people skills, and creative thoughts you can entertain others or be successful in work with the public.

Your Two Replacement Cards Are the 7 of Hearts & the 7 of Spades.

As the 8 of Hearts you share the same planetary position as the 7 of Hearts in the Earthly Spread. This signifies that you are highly sensitive and idealistic. While you can show your strong moral sense and desire for perfection, you can also become intolerant, cold, or irritable through petty emotional issues. It's your trust, selflessness, and honesty that really impress others and not your moods or distant manner.

As the 8 of Hearts you also share the same planetary position as the 7 of Spades in the Spiritual Spread. The mystical influences of this card signify a need to find inspiration. If you are able to rise above the mundane in matters concerning work and health, you can also channel the knowledge of a higher power. The double influence of the number 7 in both your Replacement Cards emphasizes your need to develop your intuition and inner faith.

You usually have special or karmic links with people who are represented by the 7 of Spades and the 7 of Hearts, as you share the same planetary positions. You can be soul mates or understand each other very well. Even if you do not get along, you can both see clearly how the other person operates.

Your Mercury Card is . . .

The 6 of Clubs

- Inspired by knowledge and new ideas, you benefit from mentally stimulating activities.
- As a perfectionist with a tendency to worry, you may be overly critical, so be careful of what you say to others.
- You can be very enthusiastic about your favorite subjects.
- Imaginative and intuitive, it is better to be productive than waste time daydreaming.
- You should have good mental rapport and special communication with people who represent the 6 of Clubs, as they activate your Mercury Card.

Your Venus Card is . . .

The 6 of Spades

- In your relationships loyalty and security are very important to you.
- Do not let inertia or lack of motivation become a stumbling block in your determination to achieve your heart's desires.
- The karmic influence of this card suggests that you may have to care for someone close to you.
- When inspired you can be highly productive or act in a selfless manner.

- Usually you are attracted to people represented by the 6 of Spades, as they are ideal for love and romance as well as for close friendships and good business partnerships.

Your Mars Card is . . .

The Queen of Hearts

- Charming, creative, and sensual, when you channel your powerful emotions positively you can succeed in achieving your objectives.
- Usually you are able to mix your social and professional activities.
- Although you have an appetite for an active social life, you occasionally may need to resist being too aggressive, especially in your pursuit of pleasure.
- Through creative pursuits you can express your powerful feelings and strong desires.
- Queen of Hearts individuals can spur you into action, but avoid being competitive with these people. If you both share the same creative or social aspirations, when you join forces your dynamic power can generate a great deal of success.

Your Jupiter Card is . . .

The 10 of Clubs

- Usually you have a discriminative mind and quick perceptions.

The 8 of Hearts Planetary Card Sequence

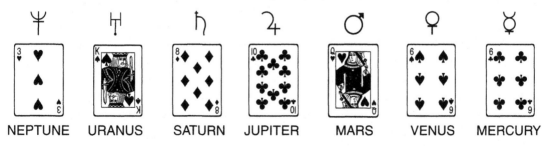

| NEPTUNE | URANUS | SATURN | JUPITER | MARS | VENUS | MERCURY |

- You benefit greatly from gaining knowledge and developing your analytical capabilities.
- You can project success when you are really enthusiastic about a project.
- Developing your self-awareness can heal your inner conflicts and emotional dilemmas.
- Opportunities for expansion and success in business are often linked to your intellectual competence or strong spirit.
- 10 of Clubs people can be very beneficial for you, stimulating your optimism, confidence, or ability to think big. Sometimes this can be a spiritual link.

Your Saturn Card is . . .

The 8 of Diamonds
- Your willingness to persevere and your determination to overcome challenges can help you to achieve your goals.
- Financial issues may burden you or you may have to work especially hard when in positions of authority.
- Money and material benefits can come through inheritance.
- 8 of Diamonds individuals can play an important role in your life. If you are able to learn from them about values, business, and responsibilities they can be highly beneficial. Although your relationship with them may not always be easy, their contributions are often very valuable lessons.

Your Uranus Card is . . .

The King of Spades
- You value your freedom and usually want a great deal of independence.
- You have an excellent memory or a unique ability to access knowledge.
- Your strong and determined presence implies that you are more comfortable in leadership positions or working for yourself.

- This card suggests that you want to rise above the mundane and empower yourself through knowledge and wisdom.
- You are drawn toward people who have a strong individual presence.
- People, and especially men, who are represented by the King of Spades can offer you good advice or valuable insight. This can be a good card for friendship.

Your Neptune Card is . . .

The 3 of Hearts
- Although you are idealistic and romantic, you need to be honest about your feelings if you want to avoid disappointments in your personal relationships.
- In order to fulfill your emotional needs you enjoy meeting different people or experiencing different types of relationships.
- Emotionally sensitive and versatile, you can express your imaginative ideas in numerous ways.
- You have a subtle emotional or psychic link with people who are represented by the 3 of Hearts Card. They can stimulate your imagination or your dreams. Stay realistic or guard against self-delusion, however.

Your Challenge Card is . . .

The Ace of Clubs
- Find new ideas and projects that keep your interest.
- Adopt new ways of thinking in order to overcome your obstacles.
- Although you are curious about life and people, your challenges are often related to how motivated you are.
- Ace of Clubs people can stimulate you intellectually or provoke you to change.
- Even though these people can help you to transform your life, resist power conflicts.

The Result of Your Challenge Card is . . .

The Queen of Clubs

- You are able to succeed by combining your knowledge and skills with your desire to help or inspire others.
- You can overcome self-doubt by learning to trust your inner voice and letting your intuition guide you.
- You can express yourself creatively, particularly through writing or other forms of communication.
- The more objective you are, the better you become at utilizing your discerning abilities and foresight.
- People, who are represented by the Queen of Clubs, and especially women of the Clubs suit, can help you better understand yourself. Your reaction to them often reflects how you are responding to your challenges.

Famous People Who Are the 8 of Hearts

Richard Gere, Lord Nelson, Roy Lichtenstein, Theodore Roosevelt, Andrew Carnegie, Dylan Thomas, Itzhak Perlman, Christina Applegate, James Coburn, Joe DiMaggio, John F. Kennedy, Jr., Kelly Osbourne, Van Morrison, Jerry Lee Lewis, Jane Pauley, John Cleese, Eddie Vedder, Susan Lucci

Birthdays Governed by the 8 of Hearts

August 31: Virgo   Ruler: Mercury

Your engaging personality and powerful emotions indicate that you possess alluring qualities that often attract others. Usually your ruler, Mercury, endows you with good analytical and practical skills. You also possess a discerning mind and a thirst for knowledge. Security conscious and caring, when you combine your unyielding determination with the power of love, there is very little that you cannot achieve. Nevertheless, to avoid obstacles on your way to success, be open to advice and guard against letting selfishness or obstinacy undermine your efforts.

September 29: Libra   Ruler: Venus

The emotional vitality at your disposal usually only works effectively when you apply it in an affectionate way. According to Venus, your ruler, you are loyal and loving, so your partnerships are really important to your well-being. Venus also grants you charm, idealism, and intuitive pragmatism that can help you rise to influential positions. Although you can be a hardworking individual when inspired, inertia may tame your ambitious plans. Fortunately, your need for material security and intense emotions can urge you to make progress. Your more idealistic beliefs may inspire you to find a vocation rather than a career. Whatever you choose to do, you will succeed more when you seek emotional fulfillment rather than just financial rewards.

October 27: Scorpio   Ruler: Mars

Your magnetic charm and resolute nature make a dynamic combination when it comes to impressing others and gathering support for your grand plans. Your ruler, Mars, suggests that you can be unyielding and daring. Although your aloof manner and intense feelings can emphasize your leadership qualities, resist a tendency to be overbearing or too radical. Fortunately, your intuitive sensitivity and social awareness implies that you can assess situations accurately and quickly channel your powerful emotions positively. Your emotional fulfillment often comes through your own creative pursuits or working with the public.

November 25: Sagittarius   Ruler: Jupiter

Your mental acumen and passionate nature indicate that you are an idealistic individual with integrity and excellent analytical ability. The influence of your ruler, Jupiter, usually grants you optimism and the ability to grasp spiritual or abstract ideas. Usually in the pursuit of knowledge you have the opportunities to live out your high aspirations. With your inquisitive mind, you can gain a great deal of insight from probing into philosophy, mysticism, and metaphysics. When inspired you can elevate yourself to great heights and motivate others with your thoughts and ideas.

December 23: Capricorn   Ruler: Saturn

Although due to your restless emotions you may want to go in different directions, it is your perseverance and determination to overcome your challenges that ultimately leads you to your success. Your ruler, Saturn, suggests that underneath your charm and people skills you can be a versatile and dynamic individual with imaginative ideas and ambitious plans. Although your innate business sense and organizational skills aid to your progress, it is often your imaginative and creative thoughts that elevate you to accomplish. When you develop the necessary patience and channel your emotions into constructive thoughts and actions you can also find emotional fulfillment.

♣ THE 8 OF CLUBS ♣

The outstanding mental power of the 8 of Clubs suggests that you have remarkable potential if you can add self-discipline to the drive and vision revealed by your card. An interesting mixture of emotional sensitivity and focused determination, you possess a friendly amiability and good organizational abilities. Under the influences of Neptune and Mars in both the Earthly and Spiritual Spread, you have the added advantage in life of a strong

psychic or insightful awareness about people and situations. Highly imaginative, once you have a clear vision of your objectives there is no stopping you. On occasion, however, confusion can crop up to block your way forward. If you connect to your higher mental intuition, however, you can avoid a tendency for escapism. Once you bring your full concentration to bear on a project you can impress others with your focused attention, dedication, and strong convictions.

Realizing knowledge is power, you like to find people and situations you can learn from. The more you are inspired the greater your enthusiasm. When challenged you get motivated and come up with solutions, often being blessed with help just at the right time. An in-built emotional subtlety ensures that when you want to you can enchant others, or at least temper your assertiveness, with a certain charm. Although your quick intelligence puts you in the lead, avoid getting involved in mental power games. Being idealistic with strong emotions, however, once you swing into action you have the ability to inspire others. A natural business sense also helps you in your climb to the top.

As your card keeps the same planetary position of Neptune in the Mars line in both the Earthly and Spiritual spreads, it is one of the only three cards in the deck that does not have a Replacement Card but is fixed in the same position (see Fixed Cards, page 24).

Your Mercury Card is . . .

The 6 of Diamonds

- You have an eye for beauty, style, and form or value justice and fair play.
- The easygoing influence here suggests that you can get by fairly well without trying too hard, so you may have to fight a tendency for inertia.

The 8 of Clubs Planetary Card Sequence

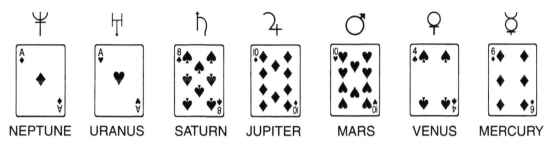

| NEPTUNE | URANUS | SATURN | JUPITER | MARS | VENUS | MERCURY |

- Sensitive to your environment, you need harmonious surroundings or enjoy making your home attractive.
- You are likely to have had a fairly stable upbringing.
- You should have good mental rapport and special communication with people represented by the 6 of Diamonds, as they activate your Mercury Card. These people can stimulate an exchange of ideas.

Your Venus Card is . . .

The 4 of Spades

- In your relationships you are drawn toward those who are hardworking and down-to-earth as well as to those who share your values or beliefs.
- Being sensitive and affectionate, you can be seductive and a tender and caring lover.
- You appreciate loyalty, preferring to be honest and direct with others, though at times you can be stubborn.
- Usually you are drawn to people who are represented by 4 of Spades, especially if they share your material aspirations or creative interests. This link is ideal for love and romance as well as for close friendships and good business partnerships.

Your Mars Card is . . .

The 10 of Hearts

- Friendly and success-oriented, you can combine charm with a shrewd business sense to enhance your people skills.
- Although you can be affectionate, sociable, and engaging, be careful of getting carried away and becoming emotionally self-indulgent.
- The emotional power here signifies that if you love what you are doing you can project dynamic drive and purpose, influencing others and bringing you real mastery over circumstance.
- 10 of Hearts people can particularly motivate and stimulate you into action. Avoid disputes or being competitive with these individuals by channeling your emotional energies constructively.

Your Jupiter Card is . . .

The 10 of Diamonds

- Your expansive viewpoint suggests you usually think big and often enjoy taking a risk.
- Ambitious and progressive, you are constantly looking for good opportunities, though be careful this doesn't lead to becoming too materialistic.
- If developed you can show a benevolent and

philanthropic side to your nature by sharing your good fortune with others.

- Usually you have a good relationship with 10 of Diamonds people. You may enjoy socializing, share the same interests, or expand each other's opportunities, but avoid overindulgence. This can sometimes be a spiritual link.

Your Saturn Card is . . .

The 8 of Spades

- With a power card in this area of discipline and structure, if you put the work in you have the potential for remarkable achievement through strength of will and mental focus.
- As you want to be in control, some of your tests can come from a fear of being dominated by others. This fear could result in power battles in your relationships or you may try to assert power covertly through manipulation.
- Natural organizational skills and a dislike of taking orders suggest that you do better when working for yourself or in management positions.
- 8 of Spades people can be your teachers or guides and help you realize your shortcomings. Although these people may sometimes bring burdens or responsibilities, if you are willing to work on your self-awareness they can also offer you valuable lessons.

Your Uranus Card is . . .

The Ace of Hearts

- You learn quickly and like to be always updating your knowledge.
- Being in groups or with friends can bring out your independent nature, original approach, and natural leadership skills.

- If you are being selfish this especially brings out a rebellious or obstinate side to your nature.
- When positive the combination of your strong emotions, mental power, and intuitive awareness suggest that you can be a progressive force for good in the lives of others.
- You can gain especially from further developing your sensitivity through spiritual or metaphysical studies. If so, you can become a teacher in your own right.
- People who are represented by the Ace of Hearts Card can inspire you or provide you with valuable insight. They can also help you be more detached about yourself. This is a good friendship link.

Your Neptune Card is . . .

The Ace of Diamonds

- As you are extrasensitive with a strong desire nature, you have to be particularly careful of escapism through fantasy, drugs, or alcohol.
- You are likely to be in a strong financial position later in life.
- You have the magical power to manifest your needs through clarity of purpose and directed will toward your goals. It is important to keep a clear and definite focus, however.
- When working unselfishly you possess compassion for others that you can channel practically through philanthropic ventures or healing activities.
- Your strong imagination gives you powerful vision that you can use either in business or creatively.
- Ace of Diamonds people can have a psychic connection with you. You may share the same dreams and ideals or they may inspire you to start new projects, but stay realistic.

Your Challenge Card is . . .

The Queen of Diamonds

- Avoid going for material security at the cost of being more daring.
- Combine your natural dramatic or creative gifts with your astute business ability.
- Employ your shrewd evaluation skills or natural leadership constructively for the good of others.
- Queen of Diamond individuals can confront you to bring out the best or the worst of your personality. This person could help you to transform old habit patterns if you rise to the challenge.

The Result of Your Challenge Card is . . .

The 5 of Hearts

- You will always be finding new and interesting experiences and projects in your life.
- If you are constantly restless and impatient you may not be responding well to your challenge.
- Your heart will go out to people before your mind has had a chance to register what's happening.
- People represented by the 5 of Hearts can help mirror back to you how you are dealing with your emotions and your challenges.

Famous People Who Are the 8 of Clubs

Bob Dylan, Meryl Streep, Priscilla Presley, Neil Young, Carlos Santana, Kris Kristofferson, B. B. King, David Copperfield, Eugene Delacroix, Dwight Eisenhower, Tonya Harding, Ralph Lauren, Robert Redford, Roman Polanski, Roger Moore, Ludwig Wittgenstein, Julia Stiles, Kenneth Branagh, St. Theresa of Avila, Reba McEntire, Billy Wilder, Lauren Bacall, Peter Falk, Christian Slater, Edward Norton

Birthdays Governed by the 8 of Clubs

March 28: Aries   Ruler: Mars

With your strong drive and convictions you can achieve a great deal, especially if you utilize your natural business acumen. Although you are better in a leadership position, you also realize the benefits of working as a team. Being idealistic and smart, you usually work best when putting your many creative ideas into action. Pioneering in new areas stimulates your sense of daring and is more exciting for you. Even though assertive, you can also be sensitive when needed, so by developing patience and diplomacy you avoid upsetting others or acting too impulsively.

April 26: Taurus   Ruler: Venus

Smart and pragmatic, your natural mental power can help you achieve success. Your drive can also put you in leading positions, but you never lose sight of the importance of your home and family. Although you can be strong for others, avoid being controlling. You value honesty and fare best when your practical side has a definite and clear-cut plan for the future. With your flair for financial affairs, education, or artistic and creative pursuits, you have plenty to keep you busy; you just need to keep focused and be disciplined.

May 24: Gemini   Ruler: Mercury

Mentally quick and perceptive with strong determination, you are an individual with something to say. Being sensitive and somewhat of a visionary makes you stand by your ideals, although this does not mean that you cannot be businesslike. With your keen intellect and good communication skills you can excel at writing or presenting ideas. Guard against mental power games with others, however. Honest and direct, you benefit from continually learning, especially when this includes your self-development. If disciplined you can reach exceptional heights materially or spiritually.

June 22: Gemini/Cancer
Rulers: Mercury/Venus

Born on the cusp of Gemini and Cancer you have the advantages of both the quick intelligence of Gemini and the sensitivity of Cancer. Caring yet down-to-earth, you need work or active goals on which to focus your imagination or you may become oversensitive and lazy. Highly intuitive, you really succeed when you practically apply your inner guidance. Although proud and seemingly independent, you need others and can be supportive of family members. Even though you have a fragile nervous system you need to protect, you can be determined and resolute when set on a course of action.

July 20: Cancer   Ruler: Moon

Gracious and receptive, underneath your friendly charm is strong mental power and determination. Although your emotional impressionability implies you may have had to overcome shyness or oversensitivity, once ready to act you can impress others with the combination of your drive, vision, and social skills. Your relationships tend to play an extra important place in your life plan, and you often succeed in working partnerships or through team efforts. You may wish to channel your powerful imagination into creative projects.

August 18: Leo   Ruler: Sun

Courageous and enterprising, you are action-oriented with a need to be the boss. You also possess natural people skills, ensuring your popularity. Being mentally quick, business-minded, and having a strong visionary sense can help you in your climb to success, but re-

sist becoming too materialistic. It is important for you to have clear aims and objectives to avoid escapism or overindulgence. Although you enjoy power and are strongly aware of financial considerations, you can also be idealistic and humanitarian with a love of knowledge.

September 16: Virgo   Ruler: Mercury

Analytical yet imaginative, you possess the unusual combination of being gifted with practical technique and sensitive intuition. These opposing qualities work well when you utilize your vision or strong feelings to guide your decisions and then realistically structure how to put these decisions into action. You may, however, sometimes encounter a pull between your need for personal self-expression and your sense of responsibility toward others. By finding time for self-reflection you can work toward greater insight and be of practical help to others.

October 14: Libra   Ruler: Venus

Friendly and amiable, your natural people skills help you achieve in life. Being intelligent, you need mental stimulation, particularly the kind that you get from your relationships with others. Work or positive action helps you to avoid a tendency for escapism or indecision. If you become restless then you may need to examine your long-term planning. When you have clear structured goals you can utilize your vision, knowledge, and sensitivity for your own achievement and to help others. You may wish to develop your natural creative sense through the arts, music, writing, or drama.

November 12: Scorpio   Ruler: Mars

With your powerful emotions and keen intelligence, you have the potential to make great achievements in life, especially when you are decisive and love what you are doing. When positive you can be dynamic and radiate success, but if you become overemotional there is a danger you may get carried away or react too extremely. Although you have a need to express yourself, you may also encounter a pull between going it alone, your own creativity, and your relationships. Even though mentally sharp, you are also naturally psychic, connecting to the subliminal signals of others and making you a good psychologist.

December 10: Sagittarius   Ruler: Jupiter
With your keen intelligence, natural creativity, and vivid imagination, you need projects that keep your interest. You do particularly well when inspired and passing your ideas on to others. Being independent and strong-willed, you are better when in charge or working for yourself. Although usually honest and direct with a kind heart, try to avoid being tactless or manipulative. As you are not afraid to think big, and have a natural business sense and a lucky streak, it is extra important for you to apply self-discipline in making the most of your remarkable potential. With your delicate nervous system and emotional sensitivity, you also need harmonious surroundings.

◆ THE 8 OF DIAMONDS ◆

The influence of the number 8 indicates that you are a spirited, instinctive, and determined individual. Associated with strength and accomplishment, the number 8 is also a symbol for action and triumph over challenges. Ambitious and willing to work hard, you are likely to rise to executive or leadership positions by using your foresight and strategic skills.

Belonging to the Diamonds suit signifies that your lessons are usually based on issues concerning values. Although you can achieve material success, be careful not to let a preoc-

cupation with money or possessions undermine the wonderful power available to you. If this influence is expressed negatively you may be prone to self-indulgence. The planetary influences of Jupiter and the Sun (Crown Line) in your Earthly Spread indicate that you usually present a proud and confident front to the world. Your willpower, vitality, and capability to attain outstanding achievements suggest that you can also be creative and dynamic. With these great attributes, however, also come responsibilities. Even though you can be very generous with those you love, guard against letting your need to be in control turn you into a dominating individual. The planetary influences of Uranus and Saturn in your Spiritual Spread suggest that you have the ability to persevere and endure with tenacity and toughness. This influence, however, also insinuates that you can experience strong emotional tensions if you become obstinate or too self-willed. Nevertheless, you succeed through your determination, resolve, and strong convictions.

Your Two Replacement Cards Are the Queen of Spades & the 7 of Clubs.

As the 8 of Diamonds you share the same planetary position as the 7 of Clubs in the Earthly Spread. This signifies that you are an independent thinker who is insightful, intuitive, and mentally quick. Avoid a tendency to worry, however, as it can deplete your energies. Establishing a solid foundation through some form of education can equip you with confidence and help you to develop your innate perceptions. Keen on self-improvement, you have the potential to turn your knowledge and skills into moneymaking opportunities.

As the 8 of Diamond you also share the same planetary position as the Queen of Spades in the Spiritual Spread. This royal card indicates that you are likely to work very hard. If you develop the necessary self-discipline you can be sure to reach your rightful place and gain the respect you deserve. The Queen of Spades is also associated with spiritual wisdom and your soul purpose is often associated with self-knowledge or self-mastery. If you recognize the spiritual value of this card you will be able to overcome any preoccupation with material difficulties.

You usually have special or karmic links with people who are represented by the Queen of Spades and 7 of Clubs, as you share the same planetary positions. You can be soul mates or understand each other very well. Even if you do not get along, you can both see clearly how the other person operates.

Your Mercury Card is . . .

The King of Spades
- You are usually a pragmatic realist with a serious outlook.
- This royal card suggests that your early years left a strong impression on you.
- Your father or an authoritative male figure played an important role in your upbringing.
- If a woman, you prefer to think independently and be in charge.
- Your intuition is based on a storehouse of knowledge.

- Avoid entertaining repressive or negative thoughts that can cause anxiety.
- You should have good mental rapport and special communication with people who represent the King of Spades, as they activate your Mercury Card.

Your Venus Card is . . .

The 3 of Hearts
- You are a sociable individual with an engaging personality.
- If you work hard you also want to play hard and indulge in the good things in life.
- You can be passionate about drama, art, or music. Alternatively, you can have creative or artistic skills.
- Emotional indecisiveness suggests that you may encounter doubts about your close relationships.
- Usually you are attracted to 3 of Hearts people, as they are usually sociable, sensitive, or creative. They are also ideal for love, romance, close friendships, and good business partners.

Your Mars Card is . . .

The Ace of Clubs
- Mentally quick, you are usually action-oriented and persuasive.

The 8 of Diamonds Planetary Card Sequence

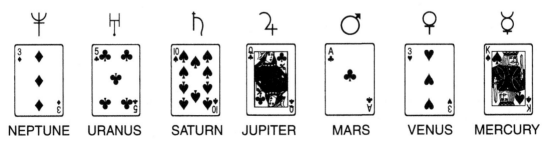

NEPTUNE   URANUS   SATURN   JUPITER   MARS   VENUS   MERCURY

- Resist being argumentative or aggressive in your communication or manner.
- Curiosity and a desire for information can often inspire you into action.
- Sharing intellectual pursuits with others can be rewarding and socially beneficial.
- The relationships you have with Aces of Clubs can be good if you both share the same desires. These people can motivate you or encourage you to be more dynamic. Resist being competitive, however.

Your Jupiter Card is . . .

The Queen of Clubs
- You have a strong dramatic sense, enjoy entertaining others, and can gain from your ability to mix with people from all different social groups.
- This royal card indicates that women can be highly beneficial to you, especially in business or when you share the same interests.
- You benefit from all type of mentally stimulating activities, as they broaden your horizons.
- Developing your innate intuition and learning to trust your own wisdom can help you overcome doubts and insecurities.
- Queen of Clubs people can help you to expand your opportunities or learning. This is usually a fortunate or spiritual link.

Your Saturn Card is . . .

The 10 of Spades
- Although you may need to put a great deal of effort into your work, Saturn usually rewards you for all your hard labor.
- This card also suggests that you have special powers to heal and the ability to undertake large tasks.

- When you recognize your spiritual responsibilities you can accomplish success or self-mastery.
- 10 of Spades people can play an important role in your life, if you are able to learn from them about loyalty and dependability. Although your relationship with them may not be always easy, their contributions are often very valuable lessons.

Your Uranus Card is . . .

The 5 of Clubs
- Your quick and instinctive responses to changing circumstances can give you the edge in all your dealings.
- Sparks of inspiration can suddenly alter your views and understanding.
- Your restlessness can stem from a tendency to change your mind or feel uncertain.
- An ability to accept new ideas can help you to change and grow.
- You have a rebellious streak that can come out if you become bored or impatient.
- 5 of Clubs people can help you be more objective about yourself. This is a good friendship link especially where freedom is valued.

Your Neptune Card is . . .

The 3 of Diamonds
- New opportunities or choices can present themselves in old age or you may adopt a completely different life-style.
- Indecisiveness, doubts, and confusion about which avenue to take can undermine your security and become an obstacle to success.
- Your ingenuity and creative problem-solving can further your earning power.
- 3 of Diamonds people can inspire you or help you realize your dreams and ideals, but stay grounded.

Your Challenge Card is . . .

The Ace of Spades

- Fear of the unknown or not being in control can be one of your greatest challenges.
- Learning to let go of the past and finding the courage to make drastic changes and new beginnings can help you to transform inwardly and outwardly.
- Exploration into the mysteries of life through spirituality and metaphysical subjects can turn your challenges into personal triumphs.
- Ace of Spades individuals can confront you to bring out the best or the worst of your personality. These people can help you to transform old patterns if you rise to the challenge.

The Result of Your Challenge Card is . . .

The 7 of Hearts

- You have the emotional faith in yourself and life to take you into the unknown believing that ultimately everything will work itself out for the best.
- You will accept the responsibilities that come with love to help you transform your insecurities and get rid of negative emotions such as selfishness, jealousy, or suspicion.
- You will be honest with yourself about your true feelings before embarking on relationships with others.
- People who are represented by the 7 of Hearts can light up your life, and your reaction to them often reflects how you are responding to your challenges.

Famous People Who Are the 8 of Diamonds

Ringo Starr, Paul Cézanne, Michael J. Fox, Marc Chagall, Edith Piaf, Janis Joplin, Dolly Parton, Michael Jordan, Cole Porter, Alan Bates, Andrew Jackson, Michael Crawford, Thomas Jefferson, Samuel Beckett, Al Green, Pierre Cardin, Neil Armstrong, John Huston, Charlie Sheen, Alan Ladd, Irving Berlin, Martha Graham, Michelle Kwan, Natalie Portman, Salvador Dalí, Johnny Depp

Birthdays Governed by the 8 of Diamonds

January 19: Capricorn Ruler: Saturn
Your many attributes and charismatic nature suggest that you have the cards stacked up in your favor. According to Saturn, your ruler, being ambitious and determined encourages you to think that hard work and perseverance can only lead to success. Your innate vision and patience are often rewarded with valuable insight that you store in your memory bank. Although you can be persuasive and a good leader or organizer, resist being headstrong or letting frustrations influence your moods or temper. Nevertheless, when you rise up to your challenges your responsible attitude and dependability give you the powers to undertake large tasks.

February 17: Aquarius Ruler: Uranus
Usually a determined and mentally shrewd individual, your quick perceptions and executive skills add to your authoritative demeanor. According to your ruler, Uranus, you usually want the freedom to think for yourself, yet this influence also suggests that change and unexpected events may alter the course of your life. Inspired thoughts and a touch of genius indicate that your unique perspective gives you the edge when solving problems. Although your good sense of values and analytical abilities can help you to succeed in the business world, your originality and mental creativity can find great fulfillment in creative or spiritual interests.

March 15: Pisces   Ruler: Neptune
Receptive and sensitive, your ability to absorb a great deal suggests that underneath your calm exterior you are constantly busy evaluating life's situations. In order to succeed, your vision has to be backed up by patience and decisive actions. Nevertheless, your unique ideas and versatility points out that you can simplify or solve problems. Although adjusting to new plans can open up new opportunities for you, without self-discipline and structure you can become confused about your goals or objectives. Although you may vacillate between being proud and confident to feeling uncertain, you possess a strong self-reliance and desire for self-improvement that will always help you to advance in life.

April 13: Aries   Ruler: Mars
Your vitality usually gives you a head start or adds to the pace of your quick and perceptive mind. Although Mars, your ruler, may be the motivating force behind your drive and ambition, resist being too stubborn or bossy if you want to avoid opposition and tension. Equally, you benefit from slowing down and gathering your thoughts. As a good strategist with a competitive nature, however, you like to think ahead or plan to win. Alternatively, your desire to be enlightened by practical know-how suggests that you are usually well informed and knowledgeable. If you are seeking answers to more profound questions you can gain insight through exploring history, philosophy, or metaphysics.

May 11: Taurus   Ruler: Venus
The potent combination of your inspired thoughts and dynamic emotions indicate that you can achieve a great deal once you have decided what it is your heart desires. According to your ruler, Venus, although you can be fiercely idealistic, you usually have both charm and good business sense. Often sociable with a touch of the dramatic, you may put your talents to the test and find joy through personal self-expression. The ability to overcome obstacles implies that in whatever you do enthusiasm and determination are the keys to your success. Although it may take you some time to figure out your emotional needs or feelings, your innate intuition about people and values grows wiser through the years.

June 9: Gemini   Ruler: Mercury
The potential for success according to Mercury, your ruler, is based on mental self-discipline and acceptance of responsibility. Destined to acquire wisdom and knowledge, your pragmatic approach to mundane issues can help you to quickly develop your awareness and business acumen. One thing you know is, with patience and time all things complete their course. Although your innate intuition and idealistic notions can lift your spirit high, a reluctance to compromise or listen to reason can turn you into an obstinate or bossy individual. Since material issues or other responsibilities will probably fill much of your time, guard against neglecting your emotional needs.

July 7: Cancer   Ruler: Moon
The double influence of the number 7 in your birthday suggests that you are a single-minded individual with an intuitive and receptive mind. Your strong convictions and feelings also confirm that you can be an original and inventive thinker with a unique style. While you can appear confident and determined on the outside, you are often hiding a sensitive ego underneath. Your ruler, the Moon, encourages you to be a caring, imaginative, and creative individual. Being security conscious and possessing natural business acumen implies that you have the brain and the Midas touch to make money and prosper.

August 5: Leo   Ruler: Sun

Determined, instinctive, and restless, the double influence of the number 8 indicates that you are a daring and enthusiastic individual. According to your ruler, the Sun, your resolute nature can help you succeed in competitive situations but warns against taking unnecessary risks. As a pragmatist and a good strategist you quickly learn from past experiences. Your way to the top is based on your ability to develop your leadership and organizational skills. Whatever you do, your productive efforts, versatility, and curious nature suggest that there are rarely dull moments in your life.

September 3: Virgo   Ruler: Mercury

Endowed with shrewd intelligence and quick perception, your communication skills can give you a persuasive manner. In addition, the influence of your ruler, Mercury indicates that your innate business acumen and sensitive awareness can lead to great achievements, especially if they are founded on a good education early in life. As you usually don't like to take orders and possess a natural sense of authority or administrative skills, you are usually better working for yourself or in a position where you have the freedom to do things your own way. Although you can be mentally sharp, emotional insecurities can sometimes cause your innermost feelings to end up being buried under practical considerations. When you blend your pragmatism with your intuition and natural creativity, however, you can empower yourself and find satisfying ways to express your emotions.

October 1: Libra   Ruler: Venus

Your distinctive flair and charismatic nature usually hide your creative talents and purposeful determination. According to your ruler, Venus, you have an engaging personality and charm as well as strong ambitions and a head for business. Even though your pragmatism, foresight, and creative thoughts suggest that you are ideally suited to take the lead, resist being too bossy or egocentric. Since you are likely to be idealistic, Venus's influence also emphasizes the necessity to be more selective and decisive about your objectives. Whether for love or emotional self-expression, avoid becoming bogged down by financial considerations by paying more attention to your inner feelings.

♠ THE 8 OF SPADES ♠

Being a number 8 of the Spades suit, you are a determined and powerful individual with a capacity for hard work. Your clear intent, strong convictions, and staying power can help you achieve your goals and eventually lead to wisdom. It is important, however, not to get involved in power plays along the way that can sidetrack you from realizing your objectives. With the influences of Saturn and Jupiter line in the Earthly Spread, you can be a tenacious strategist with big plans. Be careful, however, that frustration and impatience with limitations does not stop you from persevering with your responsibilities and long-term goals.

Usually, however, people are attracted to the fact that you are straightforward, honest, and capable, with a self-confidence that comes from your drive and strength. With the influences of Saturn and Neptune in the Spiritual Spread you also have vision, sensitivity, and imagination, as well as a natural business sense. This is good for bringing your dreams into reality as long as you are willing to be diligent and self-disciplined. If used negatively these influences suggest escapism from your problems and a dissatisfaction that can lead to dominating others. When developed this Neptune influence can bring compassion and caring for others as well as strong intuition or mystical insights.

Your Two Replacement Cards Are the King of Clubs & the 6 of Clubs.

As the 8 of Spades you share the same planetary position as the King of Clubs in the Spiritual Spread. This signifies that you are mentally smart, so acquiring knowledge is an important part of your life plan. You need to be constantly updating your skills and expertise to put yourself in stronger positions. The King influence here also suggests a dramatic sense and a desire to take the initiative that may naturally place you in leading positions.

As you also share the same planetary position as the 6 of Clubs in the Earthly Spread, you contain within you a combination of idealistic dreamer and ambitious realist. Although you want to achieve recognition and material success, you still need your inner peace and harmony. Your home can become extra important to you as a place to find refuge from your worldly struggles. Any anxieties you may experience around the issues of money or success can be channeled into caring for others, creative pursuits, or making sure that you are leading a well-balanced life.

You have special or karmic links with people who are represented by the King of Clubs and the 6 of Clubs. As you share the same planetary positions you can be soul mates or understand each other very well. Even if you do not get along, you can both see clearly how the other person operates.

Your Mercury Card is . . .

The Ace of Hearts

- Mentally receptive, you are quick to pick up on the emotional repercussions of any situation.

- Your strong need for love and approval influences your thinking and communication.
- Avoid being too self-willed or bossy.
- You do well when pioneering new or original ideas.
- You have an original approach to writing, presentation, or problem solving.
- You can have a good mental rapport with people who are the Ace of Hearts Card. This is a good link for communication and the exchange of ideas.

Your Venus Card is . . .

The Ace of Diamonds

- With your strong desires for money and material success, you are quick to spot financial opportunities.
- Even though you may have the best of intentions you may need to learn not to take over peoples' lives but let them learn through dealing with their own problems.
- You can be very generous and kind with those you love.
- You are attracted to independent and ambitious people of wealth, influence, or power.
- Usually you are drawn to Ace of Diamonds people, especially if they share your creative interests. They are ideal for love and romance as well as close friendships and good business partnerships.

Your Mars Card is . . .

The Queen of Diamonds

- Being intelligent and quick to see the point, you do not always suffer fools gladly. Guard against the tendency for a sharp comment or becoming argumentative.
- You can find ambitious women encourage your drive and desire for action.
- The leadership card here enhances your or-

The 8 of Spades Planetary Card Sequence

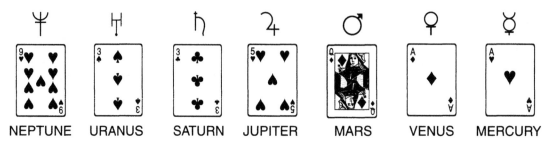

NEPTUNE   URANUS   SATURN   JUPITER   MARS   VENUS   MERCURY

ganizational skills and ability to influence others.

- Queen of Diamonds people can particularly stimulate you to be active and dynamic in the pursuit of your goals and desires. Channel the energy constructively rather than be competitive.

Your Jupiter Card is . . .

The 5 of Hearts

- Your spirit of adventure and love of variety suggest that you find opportunities and benefits come through meeting new people as well as new experiences.
- Travel or moving from your place of birth can be especially good for improving your circumstances.
- Be careful of a restless or impatient streak that can cause you to be too impulsive or emotionally changeable.
- Usually you have a good rapport with 5 of Hearts people, as they can often offer you positive opportunities or possibly even have a spiritual link with you.

Your Saturn Card is . . .

The 3 of Clubs

- Some of your major tests involve decision making. Avoid vacillating between confidence and worry.

- Putting your creative ideas into some form of structure really stimulates your sense of achievement.
- It is important for you to have a plan and finish what you start rather than get scattered.
- 3 of Clubs people can be your guides and help you recognize your shortcomings or need for discipline and responsibility. If you are willing to work on your self-awareness you can learn from your experiences with these people.

Your Uranus Card is . . .

The 3 of Spades

- You possess original and inventive ideas that can inspire and bring happiness.
- Being with friends or in groups can particularly lift your spirits. The lighter you feel, the happier and more detached you become.
- If things go wrong suddenly or unexpectedly avoid taking this personally.
- You possess a sixth sense about business that can help you achieve success.
- 3 of Spades people can help you be more creative, inventive, and impartial due to your Uranus connection. This can be a good link for friendship.

Your Neptune Card is . . .

The 9 of Hearts
- When your defenses are down and you truly care for others you can be extremely loving and giving. This also can represent devotional love of a compassionate or humanitarian type.
- Avoid holding onto frustrations or emotional disappointments from the past.
- You possess innate artistic, dramatic, musical, or healing talents that can bring you remarkable results if you wish to develop them.
- People represented by the 9 of Hearts card have a psychic link with you. You may share the same dreams or ideals, but also stay realistic.

Your Challenge Card is . . .

The 7 of Clubs
- Be more daring and competitive in an enthusiastic and friendly way.
- Do not let a perfectionist streak cause you to be too hard on yourself or others.
- Spend some time alone for self-reflection or to tune into your spirit.
- Use the excellent intellectual abilities at your disposal.
- 7 of Clubs individuals can confront you to bring out the best or the worst of your personality. These people can help you to transform old patterns if you rise to the challenge.

The Result of Your Challenge Card is . . .

The 5 of Diamonds
- You welcome change as an opportunity to be more enterprising, dynamic, and adventurous.
- You channel restlessness or impatience into creating positive change in your life.
- People represented by the 5 of Diamonds can stimulate you to move into action or alter your life. They often reflect how you are responding to your challenges.

Famous People Who Are the 8 of Spades

Mikhail Gorbachev, Jon Bon Jovi, Rosa Parks, Carl Sandburg, Alice Cooper, Benjamin Franklin, Tom Wolfe, Alan Watts, Natalie Imbruglia, Kurt Weill, Betty Friedan, Karen Carpenter, Lou Reed

Birthdays Governed by the 8 of Spades

January 6: Capricorn   Ruler: Saturn
Strong and determined yet idealistic and caring, you are not always what you seem. Underneath your practicality and powerful front you can also be a sensitive visionary if you keep your spirit of compassion and brotherhood alive. If not, there is a danger your strong will can work against you, making you stubborn or domineering. Nonetheless, you possess good people skills and innate creative talent. There is a special emphasis on responsibilities to your home and family, especially on being a good parent.

February 4: Aquarius   Ruler: Uranus
Inventive and straightforward, you are a friendly and determined individual with original ideas. Although independent you often do better in life when working in a group or as part of a team, but avoid being bossy. Freedom is important to you, as is the power that money can bring. Nevertheless, you possess a humanitarian streak that suggests that when everything works well you want to share it with others. Although progressive, clever, and enterprising, a more practical side to your nature can also be businesslike and security conscious.

March 2: Pisces   Ruler: Neptune

An interesting mixture of tough determination, imaginative vision, and emotional consideration, you are an individual with many facets to your personality. If you go to one extreme you could be oversensitive and lose confidence in yourself; if you go to the other you could be strong-willed and domineering. Usually, however, you are charming and caring with a strong character and good people skills. You especially gain from working partnerships and cooperative ventures as well as opportunities to develop your natural insight into true wisdom.

♥ ♣ THE 9 s ♦ ♠

THE NUMBER 9 is the highest number and is therefore usually associated with completion, receptivity, and compassion. With your great sensitivity, you are often susceptible to external influences and your intuitive or psychic abilities usually point to your quick comprehension. You benefit greatly from widening your horizons through travel and interacting with people from all walks of life. Although you are likely to possess inherent talents, you may need to make a real effort in order to achieve your objectives. Impressionable or idealistic, even though you may dislike restrictions make sure your goals are realistic. Without the necessary patience, composure, and self-discipline, hopes or inspired ideals can turn into frustration and disappointments. If you can learn to detach yourself from the past and let go you can surpass many of your limitations. Yet your all-or-nothing attitude can often translate into extreme behavior, such as stubborness, impulsiveness, or emotional outbursts. By developing your tolerance and becoming more impersonal you can express your thoughtfulness and generosity and inspire others.

The following suits further modify the effect of your number:

9 of Hearts

Your sensitivity and need for love imply that you possess powerful and intense feelings. Your success and achievement often come as a result of your creative self-expression and ability to overcome emotional challenges. When you learn to detach yourself you can let go of disappointments and past frustrations. Resist martyring yourself to people or situations that do not deserve your help or emotional power.

9 of Clubs

Your mental capabilities indicate that with your creative thoughts and confident attitude you have the potential to achieve a great deal. Due to a lack of patience, arrogance, or worry, however, you may become mentally stressed or frustrated. Nevertheless, when you feel inspired you can captivate others with your intelligence, innate talents, optimism, and enthusiasm.

9 of Diamonds

Your intuitive understanding about money and values is the key to your success. If you experience financial difficulties or disappointments you may need to reexamine the ratio of your spending against your income. Lack of patience or impulsive enthusiasm suggest that in order to achieve your goals or make your fortunes you need to be poised and resolute. Your generosity and optimism nevertheless usually makes you magnanimous and benevolent.

9 of Spades

Your success is often based on your strong convictions, hard work, and determination to overcome your challenges. Although you may have to be patient in order to see the fruits of your labor, your efforts can produce tangible results. The wisdom and insight you gain along the way can lead to profound understanding or spiritual realization.

♥THE 9 OF HEARTS♥

As a number 9 of the Hearts suit you possess a depth of feeling that most people cannot reach. Your strong emotions, intelligence, and innate charm can make you a caring and compassionate individual with a lot to offer others. Under the double influence of Saturn in the Earthly Spread, you can also be ambitious, practical, and materially shrewd, reflecting a tougher side to your character. Saturn can make you methodical, precise, and hardworking with a strong sense of duty and an ability to take your responsibilities seriously. You may, however, have to work at getting the balance right in your life, especially between work and play or being too generous to others and then withdrawing and appearing cold. By overcoming obstacles and working hard to achieve results you can become very determined, persevering, and self-reliant.

With the double influence of Venus in the Spiritual Spread you have a warm, loving, and magnetic side to your personality. You especially value your relationships and enjoy being of service to others. Many of your life issues may revolve around letting go of personal attachments and past emotional experiences by developing an impersonal attitude or a spiritual approach to love. By being supportive of others but not expecting too much of them you can be realistic and avoid disappointment. Your strong Venus influence also implies you possess an appreciation of beauty and luxury or innate artistic, musical, or creative gifts you may wish to develop. Alternatively, you may use this Venus influence through developing your social skills. Your emotionally generous and humanitarian qualities enable you to mix with people from all walks of life and can spur you on to do much good for others.

Your Replacement Card Is the 7 of Diamonds.

As the 9 of Hearts you are one of the more unusual semi-fixed cards (see page 24), since you share your planetary position in both the Earthly and Spiritual Spread with only one card, the 7 of Diamonds. This signifies that by learning to let go and take life as it comes you are able to trust that it will provide you with everything you need at the right time. The more you live in the moment the more you are able to act spontaneously and build up your faith. If you lose faith, however, a tendency to isolate yourself or fluctuating moods can bring melancholy or a lack of self-esteem. As you are highly intuitive you can listen to your inner guidance and use self-reflection to become more aware and solve your problems. By developing your inner spirituality you can increase your opportunities for inspiration and happiness. Although very sensitive, you can also be mentally analytical and have a strong perfectionist streak.

You have a special or karmic link with people who are represented by the 7 of Diamonds. As you share the same planetary positions you can be soul mates or understand each other very well. Even if you do not get along, you can both see clearly how the other person operates.

Your Mercury Card is . . .

The 7 of Clubs

- Thoughtful, analytical, and precise, you have excellent intellectual skills that are especially good for writing, research, technical problem-solving, or attention to detail.
- You are likely to have experienced conditional love when you were growing up or at times may have felt isolated.
- When confident your communication skills are second to none; when discouraged your communication can seem cold or critical.

You therefore need to develop positive thinking.
- Although you enjoy being well informed, you usually learn best from personal experience.
- Mentally you respond well to a friendly challenge.
- People who are the 7 of Clubs Card are likely to stimulate your desire for knowledge or need to communicate. This is a good link for the exchange of ideas.

Your Venus Card is . . .

The 5 of Diamonds

- Your love life is likely to go through many changes; you can vary from being very enthusiastic to being restless and impatient with your partners.
- Travel and exciting activities, especially with loved ones, can bring you much pleasure.
- A tendency for fluctuating finances suggests you may need to keep some money by for long-term security and investment.
- In relationships avoid victim/rescuer situations.
- Generous and kindhearted, you actively enjoy helping those you care for.
- Usually you are drawn to 5 of Diamonds people, especially if they share your creative interests. They can stimulate your sense of adventure. This link is ideal for love and ro-

The 9 of Hearts Planetary Card Sequence

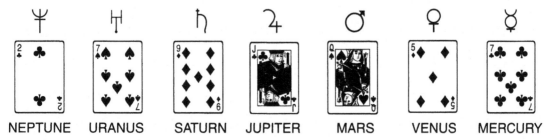

NEPTUNE   URANUS   SATURN   JUPITER   MARS   VENUS   MERCURY

mance as well as close friendships and good business partnerships.

Your Mars Card is . . .

The Queen of Spades
- You possess physical vitality and will work hard when motivated.
- Strong females can actively encourage you to go for your goals.
- When you display courage and drive, the wisdom and dramatic gifts of the Queen of Spades come to your aid. This may place you in a leading role.
- Queen of Spades people can stimulate your enthusiasm and productive activity, but avoid being competitive or argumentative with them.

Your Jupiter Card is . . .

The Jack of Clubs
- Being clever and informed, you enjoy opportunities to share your opinions and ideas with others.
- Your ability to play with ideas creatively may manifest as a lucrative talent for writing, presentation, or entertaining others.
- Although Jacks often do not want to grow up, once you take responsibility for the talent shown here you can make great progress in life.
- You can be fortunate through foreign interests, artists, musicians, and youth in general.
- Jack of Clubs people can be linked with beneficial opportunities. If you are in business or partnership with them you can both be successful, especially if you share the same spiritual values.

Your Saturn Card is . . .

The 9 of Diamonds
- Many of your tests involve being able to move away from old patterns and old situations that no longer nourish you.
- An extravagant streak suggests you may escape from your restrictions or limitations by going shopping.
- You gain much from developing a detached or impersonal attitude.
- Try not to dwell upon fears or frustrations that limit your consciousness or cause you high and low moods depending on the fluctuation of circumstances.
- Learning to successfully conclude both your personal and business relationships can be very rewarding and bring you wisdom.
- When being responsible and dutiful your innate generosity comes to the fore and you often find yourself naturally giving to others.
- 9 of Diamonds people can play an important role in your life, if you are able to learn from them about boundaries, discipline, and responsibilities. Although your relationship with them may not always be easy, their contributions are often very valuable lessons.

Your Uranus Card is . . .

The 7 of Spades
- Although you do need time alone for introspection, you also need positive people contact, especially with groups and friends; otherwise, you could feel isolated.
- Developing your natural humanitarian streak or desire for higher wisdom can take you to places of great personal insight and emotional fulfillment.
- Even though you are often ahead of your time, avoid getting discouraged if everyone else has not caught up with you yet.

- 7 of Spades people can teach you how to be more objective and impersonal. This is a good friendship card, especially if you both share the same interests and value each other's freedom.

Your Neptune Card is . . .

The 2 of Clubs
- You really need another mind to spark ideas, as this opens up your imagination.
- You can protect yourself from becoming oversensitive or dependent on others by using humor.
- Being a sensitive and good psychologist, you can easily pick up on peoples' emotions and be helpful.
- Guard against allowing your imagination to blow your fears out of proportion.
- 2 of Clubs people can have a psychic connection with you. They may link to your dreams and ideals or involve you in spiritual subjects, but remember to stay practical.

Your Challenge Card is . . .

The King of Clubs
- Take the initiative and responsibility for the knowledge and talents you have. The royalty card here suggests you can be in a leading position in some area of your life if you dare to push yourself.
- King of Clubs people may mentally stimulate you or cause you to rise to a challenge. These people can help you to transform your life, but resist power conflicts.

The Result of Your Challenge Card is . . .

The Jack of Diamonds
- You get the balance right between play and taking care of business.

- You are able to sell others your values and talents, or at least keep them entertained.
- Jack of Diamonds people may inspire you to be creative. Your reactions to them often reflect how you are responding to your personal challenges.

Famous People Who Are the 9 of Hearts

Hillary Rodham Clinton, Gwyneth Paltrow, Mahalia Jackson, Bob Hoskins, Henri de Toulouse-Lautrec, Mary Shelley, Billy Connolly, Spinoza, William F. Buckley, Puccini, Brigitte Bardot, Dale Carnegie, Scott Joplin, Maurice and Robin Gibb, Moon Zappa, Cameron Diaz

Birthdays Governed by the 9 of Hearts

August 30: Virgo   Ruler: Mercury
Analytical and practical yet also sensitive and emotional, you enjoy expressing yourself and being helpful to others. As you like to be precise and have a gift with words, you can be good at presenting your ideas or may develop a talent for writing or singing. Since you may also be prone to worry or indecision, it is important to stay detached by remembering life is short and you possess an innate gift for expressing joy and creativity. Friendly and sociable, you are best when you are focused and prepared rather than becoming scattered.

September 28: Libra   Ruler: Venus
Friendly and refined, your strong emotions are sometimes hidden behind a gracious and diplomatic front. At times your need for relationship may be at odds with your desire for independence, but you can still gain much from cooperative ventures. Naturally artistic or creative, you are likely to have natural style whether in your appearance or in your home. When you learn to let go of past disappoint-

ments or frustrations in your relationships you become compassionate and so detached that you can love with no expectations from others. Usually generous and loving, it is vital to keep a balance in partnerships between give and take. You have the potential for great success if you can persevere.

October 26: Scorpio   Ruler: Mars
Powerful feelings can mark you out as a deep, passionate, and receptive individual, yet your mental and analytical abilities are still keen. With your drive to achieve and your inner strength you can go far, especially as you can also be charming and people-aware. You enjoy power and have natural executive abilities, but avoid becoming too material or controlling. Home and family are likely to play an extra strong part in your life agenda. You can especially achieve through working partnerships or cooperative ventures.

November 24: Sagittarius   Ruler: Jupiter
Warm, friendly, and caring, yet willful and determined, you are an honest individual with intense feelings and strong opinions. When positive you are generous and sociable, with a need to express and live your high ideals in a practical way. If you become selfish, however, you may come across to others as being stubborn, bossy, or just a bit too extreme. Clever and informed, you usually enjoy sharing your knowledge with others and are willing to work hard to fulfill your aspirations. Your playful streak and persuasive manner can help endear you to others.

December 22: Capricorn/Sagittarius
Ruler: Saturn/Jupiter
Born on the cusp of Capricorn and Sagittarius, you have the ambition, practicality, and discipline of Capricorn with the warm social skills of Sagittarius. With your natural business acu-

men or strong awareness of work and duty, you may have to take extra care to enjoy life, avoiding becoming overly serious. Nevertheless, you can also be honest, friendly, and kind, with a strong intuitive understanding of others. You particularly gain when you combine your realistic and pragmatic approach with your original ideas, emotional magnetism, and ability to work with others.

♣ THE 9 OF CLUBS ♣

The mental sensitivity associated with your card implies that you are likely to be clever, broad-minded, creative, and imaginative. With your shrewd mentality and natural intuitive abilities, you can grasp situations very quickly. Since the number 9 is usually comparable with completion and high universal vibrations, it demands from the individual self-discipline, patience, and perseverance. Therefore, in order to accomplish your objectives and to tap into the receptive power at your disposal, you need to maintain a positive mental outlook. If you let past disappointments undermine your efforts you can experience worry or frustration.

The planetary influences of Saturn and Venus in your Earthly Spread signify that you can accomplish a great deal if you accept the concept of a labor of love as a challenge. This can involve making sacrifices for others to achieve harmony; you may have to work diligently and be flexible. Although you can be caring and generous, at times you may appear cold. Nevertheless, the Venus influence here also indicates a very sociable side to your character or possible artistic or creative influences you may wish to develop.

The influences of Mercury and Jupiter in your Spiritual Spread indicates that you have an active mind and an interest in world affairs, and so enjoy sharing your ideas with others. Although you like to be direct and speak your mind, you also possess an idealistic, kind, and generous nature. A desire to better yourself can stimulate an entrepreneurial spirit or an interest in literature, law, philosophy, travel, religion, or foreign cultures. Being intelligent, you are likely to enjoy entertaining and expressing your wit and humor.

Your Two Replacement Cards Are the 6 of Diamonds & the Queen of Hearts.

As a 9 of Clubs you share the same planetary position as the 6 of Diamonds in the Earthly Spread. This card signifies that you need to establish a good sense of values and learn to manage your financial affairs well. Creating a strong home base can also be especially important to your overall security and well-being. If you become dissatisfied you may become bossy, interfering, or critical; when positive, however, you are responsible, kind, and caring.

As a 9 of Clubs you also share the same planetary position as the Queen of Hearts in the Spiritual Spread. This royal card signifies your inner sense of the dramatic, emotional power, and need for self-expression. When you combine your cerebral talents with hard work and creativity you can unlock this outstanding potential and achieve success. You usually have special or karmic links with people who are represented by the 6 of Diamonds and Queen of Hearts, as you share the same planetary positions. You can be soul mates or understand each other very well. Even if you do not get along, you can both see clearly how the other person operates.

Your Mercury Card is . . .

The 9 of Spades
- Developing tolerance and mental objectivity can help you to use your natural critical abilities constructively.
- You may have had to overcome some challenging obstacles in your early years, but persisting in the face of adversity strengthened your resolve.
- A natural universal quality to your thinking can help you overcome a tendency for impatience or mentally laziness.
- Finding a positive philosophy in life is essential to your overall mental well-being.
- You should have good mental rapport and special communication with people who represent the 9 of Spades, especially if you share the same interests.

Your Venus Card is . . .

The 2 of Hearts
- Sensitive and receptive, you prefer to work with others rather than be on your own.

The 9 of Clubs Planetary Card Sequence

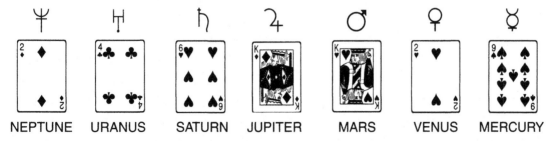

| NEPTUNE | URANUS | SATURN | JUPITER | MARS | VENUS | MERCURY |

- Loyalty and trust in partnerships is essential if you want them to be long-lasting.
- The number 2 in the Hearts suit doubly emphasizes your need for strong emotional ties and close relationships.
- Avoid dependency situations in relationships by getting the balance right between loving and giving to others and your own independence.
- Usually you are attracted to people who are represented by 2 of Hearts, as they are ideal for love and romance as well as close friendships and good partnerships.

Your Mars Card is . . .

The King of Hearts
- You can display your natural leadership qualities through being benevolent and creative.
- This royal card suggests that you gain from harnessing your strong feelings and using them constructively.
- Guard against letting your emotional frustrations turn into selfishness or anger, as it can become a destructive influence.
- Once inspired, your powerful emotions can uplift and heal others or turn you into an enthusiastic and dramatic individual.
- The relationships you have with King of Hearts people can be beneficial if you both share the same aims, ambitions, or creative aspirations. They can stimulate you into action, but avoid being competitive with them or letting them take advantage of your generosity.

Your Jupiter Card is . . .

The King of Diamonds
- The beneficial influence of this royal card increases the opportunities for success, as it relates to your financial resources.

- In order to enjoy your luck and opportunities to achieve prosperity you need to be self-disciplined and hardworking.
- As you do not usually like to take orders you can often succeed when you develop your leadership qualities or work for yourself.
- King of Diamonds people can enhance your life. This is a good link for success, whether through fortunate opportunities or business. Alternatively, these people can inspire you spiritually or stimulate your leadership skills.

Your Saturn Card is . . .

The 6 of Hearts
- The karmic influences suggested by this card indicate the importance of developing a mature and responsible attitude.
- You have an intuitive understanding that can be channeled into healing or being a natural adviser for others.
- You need peaceful, congenial, and secure environments to help you avoid emotional anxieties.
- Caring for others and being responsible for your actions and thoughts can help create harmony in family life and close personal relationships.
- 6 of Hearts people can play an important role in your life, especially if they are close to you. Although your relationship with them may not be easy, their contributions are often very valuable lessons.

Your Uranus Card is . . .

The 4 of Clubs
- Working with your innate pragmatic or constructive mental approach enhances your awareness and ability to solve problems.
- You can express yourself in original and creative ways particularly through writing and the arts.

- If rebellious you can be very stubborn, but sometimes at your own expense.
- Developing an interest in humanitarian work or metaphysical subjects can inspire you or increase your intuitive awareness.
- When you have definite positive plans for the future you usually work best and can be very determined in achieving them.
- 4 of Clubs people can offer you valuable insight or objective advice. In business their knowledge, practical skills, and honesty can help you. This is also a good card for friendship.

Your Neptune Card is . . .

The 2 of Diamonds
- You prefer to work with others rather than on your own.
- Good financial management and fair dealing can create successful partnerships, especially later on in life.
- This card implies that you have a talent for sales and your ideas can appeal to the public.
- Close relationships are often linked with material advantages and cooperative efforts.
- 2 of Diamonds people can help you realize your dreams or ideals. They may also be a spiritual link, but you need to stay realistic.

Your Challenge Card is . . .

The Jack of Spades
- Be patient and work hard in order to express the dynamic and creative power at your disposal.
- Avoid "get rich quick" schemes or dubious characters that can lead to an unethical life style.
- Recognize the spiritual power within you and gain higher awareness.
- Jack of Spades people can fascinate or provoke you. You may need to test them before you can trust them, however. These people may help you to transform your life, but resist confrontations.

The Result of Your Challenge Card is . . .

The 8 of Clubs
- Developing your intellectual sensitivity in practical ways can help increase your brainpower.
- Understanding the need for structure and long-term planning can help you to overcome your challenges.
- When dealing with others you can avoid mental power games and achieve success through your directness, objectivity, and flexibility.
- People who are represented by the 8 of Clubs can help you understand your emotions, and your reaction to them often reflects how you are responding to your challenges.

Famous People Who Are the 9 of Clubs

John Malkovich, Justin Timberlake, Franz Schubert, Jewel, Phil Collins, Philip Glass, Norman Mailer, Ashanti, Carol Channing, Mario Lanza, Jakob Dylan, Mariah Carey, Renée Zellweger, Ja Rule, Prince William, Prince Harry, Robert De Niro, Sean Penn, Joan Collins, Al Pacino, Quentin Tarantino, Demi Moore, Calista Flockhart, Leonardo DiCaprio

Birthdays Governed by the 9 of Clubs

January 31: Aquarius   Ruler: Uranus
Mentally quick and practical, your inventive mind and unique ideas can provide you with a fresh and inspiring outlook. The influence of Uranus, your ruler, indicates that when you discipline your mind, you can assess and sim-

plify situations with your resourceful and objective thinking. By developing your patience and analytical skills you can also overcome your aversion to limitations or a tendency to feel frustrated. Although you love your independence, a desire for peace of mind or a concern for security and stability suggests that you also need a strong foundation or a solid belief system.

February 29: Pisces   Ruler: Neptune

The immense creative potential implied by your master number 11 suggests that if you can add determination, patience, and cooperation to your imaginative ideas you will develop the necessary attributes to make your dreams come true. Your ruler, Neptune, may inspire your intellectual curiosity or lead you to study philosophy and metaphysical subjects. A tendency to feel frustrated or disappointed can be avoided through balancing your checkbook and completing what you have started. Nevertheless, with your intellectual creativity, foresight, and vision you can also turn your inventive ideas into profitable endeavors.

March 27: Aries   Ruler: Mars

According to your ruler, Mars, you have plenty of energy and passion, and the resolve to achieve your goals. Aided by intuitive powers and quick perception you can grasp ideas quickly and show your leadership or unique qualities. Yet before you can claim your success you may need to overcome impatience and learn to utilize your powerful emotions creatively and productively. A tendency to get mentally frustrated can turn into a destructive influence if you let it drain your emotional power. Since your knowledge is often your greatest asset, you benefit from training your mind to creatively analyze and reflect in order to maximize your self-awareness.

April 25: Taurus   Ruler: Venus

Your cerebral power, engaging personality, and creativity indicate that you need to find ways to express your inspired thoughts and self-worth. Venus, your ruler, provides you with charm and a passionate nature as well as good earning opportunities. Although you may have lucky breaks, without the necessary self-discipline and perseverance you may let frustration and indulgence get in your way. Fortunately, your enthusiasm urges you into action and into being productive. Under the influence of the 2 of Hearts, sharing your interests with others or collaborating with a partner is a prerequisite to happy relationships.

May 23: Gemini   Ruler: Mercury

Instinctive and intuitive, you can respond quickly to life's changes. Your ruler, Mercury, indicates that you are a communicative and versatile individual with strong opinions. An inclination to get bored or mentally restless warns that you can scatter your energies on many interests. Although you are quite capable when thinking positive thoughts, a tendency to worry or feel discouraged may become your stumbling block. With confidence and self-esteem, however, there is little that you cannot achieve. In order to succeed you may need to develop your powers of patience and perseverance.

June 21: Cancer   Ruler: Moon

Your emotional sensitivity, according to your ruler, the Moon, indicates that you are a charming, intuitive, and imaginative individual with great scope for mental creativity. Although you often appear cheerful and lighthearted, deliberating or dwelling on past disappointments can become a source of frustration or depression. As a resourceful and idealistic individual, however, with perseverance you can overcome your difficulties and complete projects successfully. In order to find emotional fulfillment and peace of mind, you may need to clarify what your material values are and overcome emotional issues that can separate you from those you love most.

July 19: Cancer   Ruler: Moon

Your powerful yet sensitive emotions are often the motives behind your ambition and need for recognition as a talented individual. Your ruler, the Moon, endows you with imagination, strong intuition, and receptivity. Young at heart, you can be romantic and charismatic. With your psychic abilities you can feel or sympathize with others or perceive inspired thoughts. It unfortunately can also make you susceptible to worry and fluctuating moods. Caring and security conscious, avoid letting negative feelings translate into frustration or over indulgence. Your good fortunes and patience signify that when you combine your business acumen and mental creativity you can achieve success.

August 17: Leo   Ruler: Leo

The dynamic drive and vitality of your ruler, the Sun, indicates that you are a charismatic individual with a touch of the dramatic. Although you have grand plans and creative ideas, you need to back them up with perseverance and attention to detail. Without patience, determination, and inner faith you can let reproach and fixed attitudes obstruct your progress. If you let your pride and sensitive feelings rule your head you may show animosity toward objective criticisms. Nevertheless, your business acumen, leadership qualities, and inspired thoughts can generate enough positive energy to help you overcome your challenges. Alternatively, witty and dramatic, your creativity and adventurous nature can attract you to the world of entertainment.

September 15: Virgo   Ruler: Mercury

Instinctive, mentally quick, and witty, your skills and wisdom usually come through years of experience and practice rather than through theories and hypothesis. Your ruler, Mercury, suggests that you are versatile and persuasive. Although you may take a while to get started in life, resist taking to heart your past difficulties, as they are frequently your best lessons. Your resolute determination to overcome obstacles and to enjoy the luxuries of life usually guarantee your eventual success. However, it warns against being stubborn or uncooperative. Nevertheless, with your friendly and charming manner you can find popularity, and as a perfectionist when you feel inspired by something you will persist until a job is done.

October 13: Libra   Ruler: Venus

Emotionally sensitive and restless, your people skills and creative output signify that you are a charming individual with strong determination. According to your ruler, Venus, you are an excellent networker who can enjoy combining business with pleasure and a busy social life. Indeed, you often prefer close relationships or business partnerships to being on your own. A need to persevere or to be patient suggests, however, that worry and irritability can undermine your great efforts. You usually get good results by using your intuition, intellectual gifts, and diplomacy as tools of persuasion rather than intense emotions.

November 11: Scorpio   Ruler: Mars

Idealistic and passionate, your maverick qualities indicate that you are a sensitive pragmatist. Authoritative and emotionally charged up, you can influence others with your resolute and persuasive demeanor. Although the cards are usually stacked up in your favor, your inspired hopes may be out of reach if you do not add self-discipline and hard work to your plan of action. Capable and motivated, you prefer to follow your own convictions or lead others with your foresight and strategic skills. Since you value your own freedom, guard against being bossy or too critical with other people.

December 9: Sagittarius Ruler: Jupiter
Determined and unyielding, your opportunities for achievement and prosperity under the double influence of number 9 are immense. However, you may first need to understand the laws of values and accept the responsibility of leadership that go with them. When you put your cerebral power to the test, Jupiter, your ruler, can enhance your intellectual capabilities or add to your executive qualities. Since much of your success also depends on your business acumen and positive outlook, resist letting impatience or frustration spoil your confident attitude. Being pretentious or bossy, on the other hand, can lead you to say the wrong things or be too critical. Nevertheless, your remarkable skills and sensitive awareness guarantee to make you someone special.

◆ THE 9 OF DIAMONDS ◆

As a 9 of Diamonds you possess the detachment and universal quality of the 9 combined with the practical and shrewd materiality of the Diamonds suit. When living positively you are friendly, sociable, and detached, always willing to generously be of service to others. When being too self-absorbed, however, you can suffer from frustration and disappointment. Under the influences of Mars and Uranus in the Earthly Spread, you are intelligent and quick on the uptake, so you often appear sharp and confident to others. Straightforward and matter-of-fact, your broadminded attitude also ensures that you are good

at forming objective evaluations of life situations.

As you are also under the influences of Neptune and Saturn in the Spiritual Spread you can be surprisingly sensitive underneath your clever personality. One of your life lessons is to get the balance right between the tough discipline of Saturn and the soft compassion of Neptune. Saturn can also give you focused concentration and clear boundaries. Neptune can give you clear vision. When used positively these influences can suggest you are a practical visionary; misplaced, however, you can be dissatisfied, lacking in confidence, or prone to escape from confronting your problems or responsibilities. You usually perform best when you envision a clear goal, then take action. If your goals have a humanitarian side to them then so much the better.

Your Two Replacement Cards Are the Queen of Diamonds & the 5 of Diamonds.

As the 9 of Diamonds you share the same planetary position as the Queen of Diamonds in the Spiritual Spread. This signifies that you possess natural organizational skills and an excellent ability to quickly evaluate people and situations. With a royalty card as your inner Replacement Card, you can also be dramatic and may display this in your work or with your family. As the Queen of Diamonds can sometimes compromise for material security, you may on occasion encounter a conflict between your ideals and reality. An independent streak suggests that you don't like to take orders.

You also share the same planetary position as the 5 of Diamonds in the Earthly Spread. Your fast mental capabilities indicate that you need a variety of new experiences to keep you excited and stop you from being bored. Physical activity, such as exercise, sport, or travel is particularly good way to transmute an inner restlessness or impatience into a more dynamic you. A tendency to encounter changes in your financial circumstances suggests that you may need to think or save for the long term.

You have special or karmic links with people who are represented by the Queen of Diamonds and the 5 of Diamonds. As you share the same planetary positions you can be soul mates or understand each other very well. Even if you do not get along, you can both see clearly how the other person operates.

Your Mercury Card is . . .

The 7 of Spades

- Clever and analytical, you usually display good communication skills, although if withdrawn you can sometimes appear cold or aloof.
- When inspired you can be fast and competitive, with an ability to express your sharp insight in a spontaneous and creative way.
- You can have an innate gift for writing you may wish to develop.
- Although you can be rational with a perfectionist streak, avoid becoming too critical or skeptical.
- You should have good mental rapport and special communication with people represented by the 7 of Spades, as they activate your Mercury Card. They can stimulate your flow of ideas.

Your Venus Card is . . .

The 2 of Clubs

- You are usually drawn to partners with whom you have a mental rapport or can spark ideas with.
- Being a natural psychologist helps you in all your relationships with others.
- When you lose mental balance or have hidden fears you become argumentative or difficult.
- You find pleasure in using your satirical wit or black comedy sense of humor to ease overly serious situations.
- Usually you are drawn to people represented by the 2 of Clubs Card, particularly if you share the same ideals. This link is good for love and romance as well as friendship and business partnerships.

Your Mars Card is . . .

The King of Clubs

- When active and driven you naturally rise to positions of leadership, especially when you develop your superior intellect and talents.
- Avoid being bossy; people respect you more when you are patient and firmly authoritative.
- When you respond positively to the King of Clubs Card here you can be diligent and de-

The 9 of Diamonds Planetary Card Sequence

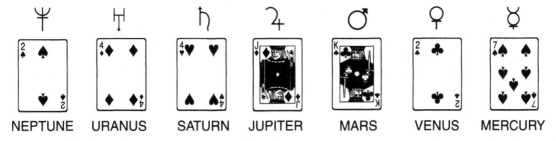

NEPTUNE URANUS SATURN JUPITER MARS VENUS MERCURY

pendable yet still come up with an original approach.

- Competitive situations can bring out your dramatic gifts.
- The relationships you have with King of Clubs people can stimulate your courage, vital energy, and spirit of enterprise. Resist being competitive or argumentative with these people.

Your Jupiter Card is . . .

The Jack of Diamonds
- You are good at selling ideas or concepts you believe in.
- A playful side to your character comes out when you feel optimistic and expansive.
- A taste for luxury and the good life suggests you enjoy quality, but watch a tendency for overindulgence.
- You can be fortunate through links with youth, sales, and entertainment.
- Jack of Diamonds people can bring you beneficial opportunities. You can both stimulate each other to be successful or creative, especially if you both share the same ideologies. This may be a spiritual link.

Your Saturn Card is . . .

The 4 of Hearts
- The heart and marriage card here suggests your major tests in life are mainly emotional and often relate to your relationships.
- You like to build a strong emotional foundation for whatever you do, so you take the responsibilities of marriage seriously.
- By combining patience and perseverance with your willingness to work you can overcome most of your difficulties.
- The number 4 influence here can bring you emotional inhibitions or restrictions, but can also show loyalty.

- 4 of Hearts people can help you if you are able to learn from them about your emotional needs and responsibilities. Although your relationship with them may not always be easy, their contributions are often very valuable lessons.

Your Uranus Card is . . .

The 4 of Diamonds
- Being progressive, you are good at taking theories or new ideas and making them practical and down-to-earth for others to understand.
- You have a very stubborn side that can sometimes be your way of rebelling.
- You can combine organizational skills with humanitarian interests to be either a valued employee or good group leader.
- 4 of Diamonds people can teach you how to be more objective and honest. This is a good card for friendship, especially if you both share the same values.

Your Neptune Card is . . .

The 2 of Spades
- You work well in partnership, team, or cooperative situations, but make sure to also maintain your independence within these relationships.
- Take care to work through your issues with your partners rather than avoid them or pretend they don't exist.
- Your emotional subtlety works particularly well in your one-to-one relationships with others. This can make you a good diplomat or sensitive counselor.
- 2 of Spades people have an almost psychic connection with you. They may link to your visions, dreams, and ideals, but avoid delusions by staying grounded.

Your Challenge Card is . . .

The 8 of Hearts

- Avoid becoming involved in emotional power struggles.
- Use the power of love, charm, and personal magnetism in your relationships.
- Be businesslike yet maintain your ideals.
- 8 of Hearts people can challenge you and provide opportunities for you to transform you life for the better even if the situation with them is confrontational.

The Result of Your Challenge Card is . . .

The 6 of Clubs

- If responding well to your challenge you are leading a well-balanced life and are able to be an adviser for others.
- If you are anxious or stuck in a rut you are not challenging yourself enough.
- Your home will be especially important to you as a safe haven from the world.
- 6 of Clubs people, if positive, can give you good advice and help you bring more peace into your life. They often mirror how you are responding to your challenges.

Famous People Who Are the 9 of Diamonds

Bono, Keanu Reeves, Kevin Costner, Percy Bysshe Shelley, 50 Cent, Albert Einstein, Quincy Jones, Billy Crystal, David Letterman, Herbie Hancock, Fred Astaire, David O. Selznick, Sid Vicious, Frank Lloyd Wright, George W. Bush, Robert Schumann, Joan Rivers, the Dalai Lama, Frida Kahlo, Salma Hayek, Sylvester Stallone, Nancy Reagan, Cary Grant, Danny Kaye, A. A. Milne, John McEnroe, Ice-T, Claire Danes, Michael Caine

Birthdays Governed by the 9 of Diamonds

January 18: Capricorn   Ruler: Saturn

Dynamic, determined, and intelligent, you are an interesting mixture of progressive ideas and friendly sociability. With your shrewd business sense, you enjoy power and understand how to work the system. Ideally, if you can combine this with humanitarian ideals and help others you can get even more emotional fulfillment. Having good communication skills, ambition, and strategic abilities aids your success, although avoid being stubborn or allowing your emotions to get out of your control. Practical as well as astute, a perfectionist streak suggests that when you do a job you like to do it properly.

February 16: Aquarius   Ruler: Uranus

Being both practically minded and psychologically astute, you can quickly assess people and situations. Although stimulated by the world of thoughts and ideas, you also have a strong need for material security. An independent and original thinker, you may be interested in world affairs, humanitarian projects, or simply enjoy arguing your point. Guard against allowing frustration or impatience to spoil your usual detached perspective. Although you require time alone for self-analysis, you also need people to discuss and share your progressive ideas.

March 14: Pisces   Ruler: Neptune

Fast responses, sharp intelligence, and strong imagination all mark you as destined to succeed, providing you persevere and develop your self-discipline. Not only can you think and act quickly, but your strong intuition can guide you successfully. Nevertheless, guard against an innate restlessness and impatience that can bring frustration. Usually, however, you possess the ideal combination of idealism and pragmatism, pride and modesty, determination and humor. With your powerful emotions you need inspiration to keep you feeling productive.

April 12: Aries   Ruler: Mars

Friendly and sociable, with creative ideas, you like to keep active. Being clever and quick off the mark, you usually enjoy a little amicable rivalry. Although independent, you also work well with others, so you gain from teamwork and cooperative efforts. Nevertheless, it is important that you keep some kind of leading role and have the freedom to express yourself. With your strong character you do not like to take orders, but can be generous and kind with those you care about.

May 10: Taurus   Ruler: Venus

Although practical and down-to-earth, you have the ability to inspire others with your ambitions, creative ideas, and big plans. Independent with natural leadership ability, you are clever and broad-minded. Its important never to lose your wonderful sense of humor, as it stops your pride or ego from getting out of line. Although your critical skills are strong and you have an innate business sense, you are still affectionate and gregarious. You particularly gain from being a leader in group situations, as you need mental feedback from others but don't like to take orders.

June 8: Gemini   Ruler: Mercury

Clever and outspoken, your fast reactions combined with your strong views make you a force to be reckoned with. Sociable and creative, you can turn on the charm, but you also enjoy power and have an inborn gift with money or material matters. To avoid being impatient or controlling you need to keep yourself busy, using your many talents. Your

tenacity, willpower, and love of knowledge can provide you with the potential for outstanding success if you are willing to put in the necessary work.

July 6:   Cancer: Moon

Security conscious, you are responsible, kind, and caring and will find people in important positions who want to help you. If you become discontented, however, you may be critical, bossy, or interfering. Home and family will always play a major part in your life script, but you do best if you also develop your innate humanitarianism. You are likely to have an interest in world affairs and strong ideals. Usually the combination of your enterprising spirit, fine mind, and strong feelings gives you a major head start in life.

August 4: Leo   Ruler: Sun

Honest, direct, and kindhearted, you are an individual with a keen intellect and good leadership skills. Your detached and broad-minded viewpoint suggests you can give good objective advice to others or be a natural humanitarian, but avoid a tendency to be stubborn. Dramatic, clever, and people aware, you enjoy an appreciative audience and can be very entertaining. You may particularly succeed through acting, directing, producing, or writing. Your down-to-earth approach can also help you in education or the business world, but whatever you do you usually do best when you are able to put your heart into your work.

September 2: Virgo   Ruler: Mercury

Mentally sharp with a sensitive nervous system, you can be both practical and imaginative. When positive you are considerate, smart, and tactful, with good social skills. If you become negative, however, you may succumb to hypersensitivity, or cynicism, or to being overly critical. Nevertheless, you can be generous, with a desire to be of practical help to others. Your inventiveness and a perfectionist streak ensure that you are usually hardworking and like to do a job properly. You particularly succeed in partnerships or working collaboratively with others.

♠ THE 9 OF SPADES ♠

The symbolic power of the 9 of Spades usually signifies that the path to your success is through self-discipline. Devotion to your work helps you gain wisdom and insight, and when you combine your intuitive understanding with a sense of duty you have the determination to overcome many obstacles. However, a possible sense of frustration or tendency to become overly serious, particularly about your work, warns that you may sometimes feel despondent. As a 9 of Spades you can choose the universal or spiritual dimension over the problems of materialism to help you develop an objective and detached viewpoint. Although your journey in life at times may be challenging, it can also be most fulfilling.

Usually charismatic and gregarious, your natural people skills indicate that you can be very sociable. Self-willed and direct, your leadership qualities shine through when you are confident and idealistic. Under the influences of Uranus and Venus in the Earthly Spread, you are usually independent yet passionate. A tendency to be impulsive due to your powerful feelings suggests, however, that you need to learn to harness your sensitive emotions if you want to avoid delays and disappointments.

The influences of Uranus and Neptune in your Spiritual Spread indicate that you have inner vision, imaginative and original ideas, and creative flashes of inspiration. This planetary combination also denotes that your sensitivity, when disciplined, can give you an interest in music, metaphysical subjects, healing, mysticism, or the arts.

Your Two Replacement Cards Are the 6 of Spades & the King of Hearts.

As a 9 of Spades you share the same planetary position as the 6 of Spades in the Earthly Spread. This card signifies that, although by exercising composure and detachment you can approach your challenges in a calm manner, you need to resist letting inertia or lack of confidence stand in the way of your success. Alternatively, your inspiration and idealism may lead you to occupations that demand dedication and hard work for altruistic rewards.

As a 9 of Spades you also share the same planetary position as the King of Hearts in the Spiritual Spread. This royal card signifies that with your dynamic emotions, noble heart, and charm you are more suited for leadership positions. When you believe in something you will try to move heaven and earth to make your dream come true. Unyielding as you may sometimes be, you win with your love power rather than with a domineering attitude.

You usually have special or karmic links with people who are represented by the 6 of Spades and the King of Hearts, as you share the same planetary positions. You can be soul mates or understand each other very well. Even if you do not get along, you can both see clearly how the other person operates.

Your Mercury Card is . . .

The 2 of Hearts
- Your sensitivity to people suggests that you can be compassionate and caring.
- In youth a close relationship or strong desire to be part of a group suggests that other peo-

The 9 of Spades Planetary Card Sequence

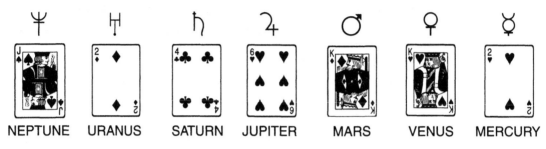

NEPTUNE   URANUS   SATURN   JUPITER   MARS   VENUS   MERCURY

ple had a strong influence on your direction in life.
- The pursuit of knowledge can lead to romantic and loving relationships.
- You usually prefer to work with groups or in partnerships.
- You should have good mental rapport and special communication with 2 of Hearts people, as they activate your Mercury Card.

Your Venus Card is . . .

The King of Hearts
- Generous, you enjoy entertaining and being sociable.
- This royal card reinforces the message that you can succeed in all types of people-related careers, especially if working with the public.
- Males, and especially older males in position of authority, can be of beneficial influence to you.
- You especially realize the dynamic power of your love when you feel inspired or have an important ideal to work toward.
- Usually you are attracted to King of Hearts people, as they are ideal for love and romance as well as close friendships and good business partnerships.

Your Mars Card is . . .

The King of Diamonds
- Success is yours if you believe in yourself and take the responsibility of leadership.
- You can be very competitive and hardworking, especially when the financial stakes are high.
- Making the right career moves is crucial to your success and prosperity.
- Your sense of values and bargaining skills can help you in the financial world.
- Your creative talents can become materially rewarding.
- King of Diamonds people can particularly motivate and stimulate you. If they are on your side their business acumen can benefit you. Avoid being too competitive with this person by channeling the energy constructively.

Your Jupiter Card is . . .

The 6 of Hearts
- When dealing with others, fairness and generosity on your part can be beneficial both personally and financially.
- Fulfillment can be found through creative self-expression or by using your healing powers.

- Guard against letting extravagance, self-indulgence, or strong desires undermine your efforts.
- You can be highly idealistic about love and family.
- Usually you have a good rapport with 6 of Hearts people, as they are often benefactors who can expand and enhance your life or alternatively, may have a spiritual link with you.

Your Saturn Card is . . .

The 4 of Clubs
- You are a practical individual who prefers to deliberate when making decisions.
- Being well informed and well educated can enhance your confidence.
- You benefit from developing your mental capabilities.
- You can succeed particularly when you apply your shrewd common sense and ability to plan with hard work.
- 4 of Clubs people can be your teachers and guides. They may criticize your weaknesses or help you recognize your shortcomings. If you are willing to work on your self-awareness these people can bring valuable lessons.

Your Uranus Card is . . .

The 2 of Diamonds
- Partnerships can be financially rewarding if you share your responsibilities equally.
- You have unusual ideas or talents to make money.
- Unexpected financial rewards or opportunities for employment suggest that you need not worry about money.
- Avoid gambling or acting on impulse when dealing with financial matters.

- People represented by the 2 of Diamonds can help you be more objective about yourself. This is also a good friendship or partnerships link where freedom is valued.

Your Neptune Card is . . .

The Jack of Spades
- The spiritual power of this card indicates that your intuition or inner faith are highly developed.
- Resist offers to attempt crazy schemes or dubious activities, as questionable individuals can come into your life to test your spiritual strength.
- You benefit from studying philosophy or metaphysical subjects as well as artistic and creative pursuits, particularly those that utilize your imagination and vision such as music, art, or photography.
- Jack of Spades people can have a psychic connection with you. They may link to your visions and ideals or help you to materialize your dreams, but stay realistic.

Your Challenge Card is . . .

The 8 of Clubs
- Develop your intellectual power by learning to staying focused and inspired.
- Give structure to your creative ideas.
- Use your ingenuity and positive outlook when facing difficulties.
- Be flexible and not impatient or stubborn.
- Develop your communication skills and avoid misunderstandings.
- 8 of Clubs people can challenge you. They can provoke you to bring out the best or the worst of your personality. Although these people can help you to transform your life, avoid being manipulative.

The Result of Your Challenge Card is . . .

The 6 of Diamonds
- With a responsible attitude you can meet your financial obligations.
- Your sense of values is based on your sound judgment and honesty.
- You are fair and just in all your dealings with others.
- People represented by the 6 of Diamonds card can reflect how you are responding to your challenges.

Famous People Who Are the 9 of Spades

David Niven, Glenn Miller, Alvin Ailey, Norman Rockwell, Gertrude Stein, Paramahansa Yogananda, Harry Belafonte, Robert Duvall, Marilyn Manson, Ron Howard, Morgan Fairchild, Roger Daltrey, Diane Keaton

Birthdays Governed by the 9 of Spades

January 5: Capricorn　Ruler: Saturn
Your shrewd sensibility and desire to transform your life can turn you from a dreamer into a practical visionary. According to your ruler, Saturn, you need to establish a philosophy on life that will give you both structure and freedom, hence overcoming any feelings of being burdened with responsibilities. As an ambitious individual your willingness to endure is remarkable, and usually you want to be proficient and thorough in your work. Although you like to approach issues rationally, resist letting a dispirited outlook or obstinate behavior stand in the way of your progress. If you do not learn to adapt quickly to new situations it may take you longer to achieve your goals and objectives in life. Your birthday has outstanding potential for spiritual attainment if you wish to develop it.

February 3: Aquarius　Ruler: Uranus
The creative and emotional power at your disposal suggests that you can achieve a great deal if you give structure to your thoughts and ingenious ideas. The possibility that you can alternate between ascending to great highs and descending to deeper lows signifies that you need to be decisive and establish harmony. Your ruler, Uranus, indicates that you value your freedom and enjoy mixing with people from different backgrounds. It also implies that your versatility, foresight, or original concepts and even eccentricity can turn into profitable business ventures. Usually your charm and friendly manner can conceal your more dramatic or sensitive nature.

March 1: Pisces　Ruler: Neptune
Your vision and purposeful nature suggest that you are a self-styled individual destined to great achievements if you can avoid dwelling on the past or indulging in self-condemnation. Neptune, your ruler, grants you heightened receptivity and imagination as well as gentle charm and a friendly manner. Although you may possess a noble heart, your principles may be tested before you can rise to positions of influence or leadership. Your foresight and awareness can increase with the passage of time and even lead to altruistic work or service. It is important not to overlook the great spiritual benefits indicated by your birth date by being overly occupied with material matters.

♥ ♣ THE 10 s ◆ ♠

THE NUMBER 10 usually symbolizes initiative, success, accomplishment, and leadership. The auspicious influences that accompany the number 10 also suggest that you have the attributes and opportunities to achieve your objectives. Usually naturally confident, your ambitious spirit can encourage you to travel far afield. Your potentials for success can be minimized, however, if you become too dependent on others or let a lack of self-esteem undermine your initiative. Nevertheless, when you are self-assured you like to be original or ambitious and think big. At these times you are able to impress or influence others with your strong character. As a mark of a true leader you normally stand by your own beliefs even if they differ from others or make you unpopular. Although you can accomplish much when you are being forceful and single-minded, resist being egocentric or dictatorial. In order to accomplish all your grand schemes you need to be resolute and determined.

The following suits further modify the effect of your number:

10 of Hearts

Seeking success and emotional fulfillment, your warm and charismatic personality enables you to find success in all types of people-related activities. Your creativity and idealism can also encourage you to promote the message of love by being compassionate and caring.

10 of Clubs

Seeking success through knowledge or skills, your cerebral power enables you to excel in all types of activities. Your desire to accumulate information and your ability to penetrate to the heart of the matter suggest that you like to think independently and make up your own mind. Watch out that your strong convictions do not make you too stubborn or uncompromising.

10 of Diamonds

Seeking success in the material world, you are a determined, independent, and enterprising individual. Your good sense of values, business acumen, and foresight indicate that although you can be idealistic, you are also a realist. Although you can think big or take charge of large projects, neglecting the small details and being impatient can minimize your efforts.

10 of Spades

Seeking success through your career, usually you have the capacity to work very hard for your objectives. Being ambitious, your achievements are usually very important to you. Alternatively, inspired goals and a desire for wisdom or deeper awareness can lead you to idealistic projects or humanitarian undertakings.

♥ THE 10 OF HEARTS ♥

Motivated by strong feelings and desires, your card suggests that you are an active person with a captivating personality. Belonging to the Hearts suit implies that you are also idealistic and receptive. Since the number 10 is associated with success and accomplishment, you are under a fortunate influence if you are determined to find creative expression for your passions and feelings. Being a Hearts Card you need to emotionally enjoy what you are doing. Being naturally charismatic with a warm charm indicates success in dealing with the public, but avoid emotional excesses or being egocentric. An ability to impress people suggests that, even if you are not keen on taking the lead yourself, when you positively display your talents others may promote you to important positions.

The planetary influences of Mars and Jupiter in your Earthly Spread indicate that you possess pride and enthusiasm and can accomplish much if you develop your enterprising nature. Although you have many opportunities to shine, your impatient or impulsive actions warn that you need to apply emotional self-discipline in order to achieve your objectives. You can make things happen and be successful when you apply your strong will power toward creative and productive activities.

The planetary influences of Venus and Mars in your Spiritual Spread indicate that you are sociable with a warm heart and an attraction for music or the arts. Idealistic and proud, your lively expression and strong feelings can add a touch of the dramatic to your engaging personality. Whether you are expressing your friendly nature or a your innate sensuality, your personal magnetism often makes you attractive to others. Even though you may sometimes be self-indulgent, being amiable, kindhearted, and charmingly assertive you usually do well in all people-related situations.

Your Two Replacement Cards Are the Jack of Clubs & the 5 of Spades.

As the 10 of Hearts you share the same planetary position as the 5 of Spades in the Earthly Spread. Although this signifies that you need to avoid boring or monotonous occupations, your financial or work issues can be subject to fluctuations. This may include changes at work, travel, and important moves. If you do not stay focused on your goals, however, you may scatter your energies by being restless, impatient, or inconsistent. Luckily this card's influence can also provide you with an independent nature, exciting life-style, and many adventures.

As the 10 of Hearts you also share the same planetary position as the Jack of Clubs in the Spiritual Spread. The intelligence and youthful vitality indicated by this card suggests success in intellectual pursuits or different types of mentally stimulating activities. Indeed, when you combine your sharp intellect and creative talents to express the emotional power at your disposal you have a winning formula. Nevertheless, hard work and dedication are essential ingredients to your success story.

You usually have special or karmic links with people who are represented by the 5 of Spades or Jack of Clubs, as you share the same planetary positions. You can be soul mates or understand each other very well. Even if you do not get along, you can both see clearly how the other person operates.

Your Mercury Card is . . .

The 10 of Diamonds
- You have a good sense of values, and with your business acumen and ability to think big you can succeed in large enterprises.
- Although you are ambitious and success-oriented, resist being mentally ruled by money or material affairs.
- You have the potential for gain in your early years.
- You may be extravagant in your thinking and let your spending exceed your earnings.
- You prefer to associate with resourceful and dynamic people who have big plans.
- You should have good mental rapport and special communication with 10 of Diamonds people, especially if you are in business together or share the same goals.

Your Venus Card is . . .

The 8 of Spades
- You can make useful contacts through your work activities and usually you enjoy mixing business with pleasure.
- You have a need for an active and productive life, so life is usually better for you when you are busy.

- Avoid power battles in personal relationships.
- When determined you can influence and even heal others.
- If you love what you are doing you will work hard, even to the point of becoming a workaholic.
- Your Venus link indicates that you are attracted to powerful and dynamic individuals.
- People represented by 8s of Spades are ideal for love and romance. This card can also represent close friendships and good business partnerships.

Your Mars Card is . . .

The Ace of Hearts
- Your idealism and passionate nature suggest that you can dynamic and dramatic.
- Being irrational or emotionally volatile can undermine your charismatic qualities.
- You have a powerful and creative force that needs to be expressed and channeled in a positive way.
- Although your strong desires are often the motivating force behind your aspirations and achievements, resist being selfish or too impulsive.
- Ace of Hearts people can particularly motivate and stimulate you. If you share the same goals you can both be enthusiastic and dynamic in the pursuit of your desires. Avoid being too competitive with this person by channeling the energy constructively.

Your Jupiter Card is . . .

The Ace of Diamonds
- With the dynamic influence of the Ace of Diamonds, you can be lucky financially when you focus your willpower on your goals and ideals.

The 10 of Hearts Planetary Card Sequence

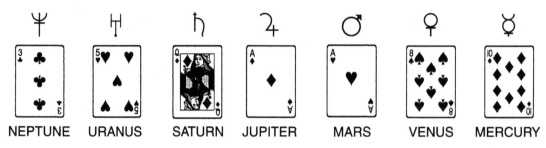

NEPTUNE   URANUS   SATURN   JUPITER   MARS   VENUS   MERCURY

- You are very good at initiating and promoting new projects, ideas, and products.
- Under your nonchalant exterior you can be highly ambitious, especially if you feel inspired by something worthwhile.
- If you want to maximize your chances of success, resist being overly optimistic or impatient.
- Although you can achieve a great deal, remember much of your success is based on your people skills and ability to inspire others.
- Usually you have a good rapport with people represented by the Ace of Diamonds, and often they are benefactors who can bring opportunities to expand and enhance your life. Alternatively, these people may have a spiritual link with you.

Your Saturn Card is . . .

The Queen of Diamonds
- Being too extravagant or managing financial resources poorly can leave you with big burdens or debts you can ill afford.
- Good management of finance and resources can help you overcome periods of economic difficulties and restrictions.
- You may have financial responsibilities toward women, especially those linked to this card.

- If your relationships are based on money and material security you may end up in some restrictive situations that will undermine your freedom-loving spirit.
- Queen of Diamonds people can be your guides and help you recognize your shortcomings. You may have to help or look after someone financially. If you are willing to work on your self-awareness you can learn from your experiences with these people.

Your Uranus Card is . . .

The 5 of Hearts
- Inspired by idealistic notions, you can express yourself in original and creative ways.
- Since your intuition and instincts are usually accurate, you benefit from trusting your sixth sense.
- The emotional restlessness indicated by this card warns that you may experience discontent or frequent changes of feeling.
- Although you want to be cherished or appreciated by other people, you also love your freedom and independence.
- You may also seek to enrich your life through travel and exciting changes.
- 5 of Hearts people can help you be more objective about yourself due to your Uranus connection. This is also a good relationship or friendship link.

Your Neptune Card is . . .

The 3 of Clubs

- Creative activities and intellectual pursuits are highly beneficial, especially in later years.
- Avoid letting uncertainty or indecision undermine your ability to focus on what is important.
- In your dealings with others you need to be clear about your thoughts and feelings in order to avoid misunderstandings.
- Make sure you know all the facts before undertaking important decisions.
- 3 of Clubs people can have a psychic or creative connection with you. You may share the same ideals and dreams, but remember to also stay realistic.

Your Challenge Card is . . .

The 3 of Spades

- Since your Challenge Card is associated with your career and spiritual choices, you need to believe or be inspired by what you do.
- Although you are multitalented and often spoiled for choices, in life you are wise to establish a solid foundation and clear aims and objectives.
- Resist following goals that are good in theory yet are often too impractical.
- Through learning to plan ahead and being responsible you can utilize your innate talents and opportunities for success.
- 3 of Spades people can usually stimulate you to react. Although these people can help you to transform your life, they can also bring out the best or the worst aspects of your personality.

The Result of Your Challenge Card is . . .

The 9 of Hearts

- Your desire to find emotional fulfillment is often reached when you develop self-discipline and overcome your tendency to feel frustrated or disappointed, especially in other people.
- Learning to let go or to forgive can help you find a true expression of love.
- The universal power of this card calls for selflessness, compassion, and emotional detachment.
- You benefit from being realistic in your expectations.
- People who are represented by the 9 of Hearts can inspire you emotionally and creatively. They often reflect how you are responding to your challenges.

Famous People Who Are the 10 of Hearts

J. K. Rowling, Ingrid Bergman, Benjamin Disraeli, Johann Strauss, Harpo Marx, Pablo Picasso, Richard Attenborough, Boris Karloff, Elliott Gould, Dinah Washington, Charlie Parker, Jane Fonda, Frank Zappa, Geraldine Chaplin, Meatloaf, Wesley Snipes, Avril Lavigne, Jon Anderson, Michael Jackson

Birthdays Governed by the 10 of Hearts

July 31: Leo   Ruler: Sun

Idealistic and sensitive, your emotional power and innate talents indicate that you have the potential to achieve a great deal of success in all types of people-related activities. Although you are usually gregarious and sociable, your sensitivity and pride suggest that you can also take things too much to heart. Since your achievements are often based on how well you control and channel your powerful feelings, before you embark on the road to success you need to develop the necessary self-discipline and master some of your wonderful innate talents. Nevertheless, your ruler, the Sun, indicates that your generosity and charismatic personality can attract many admirers and help you to achieve your inspired dreams.

August 29: Virgo   Ruler: Mercury

Your ruler, Mercury, the planet of intellectual insight and discriminative thinking, suggests that your success lies in your ability to articulate your thoughts and feelings well. Your inclination to think on a grand scale is further enhanced by your capacity to pay attention to details or to analyze or refine ideas to perfection. Although you desire excellence, resist undermining other people with your critical views. Your governing card, the 10 of Diamonds, indicates that with your desires and ambition to find material success and emotional fulfillment, very little can stand in your way. Since exercising self-discipline is a prerequisite to your achievements, resist doing things halfheartedly by going after your true objectives or inspired goals.

September 27: Libra   Ruler: Venus

Your ruler, Venus, the planet of love, refined taste, and beauty indicates that, although you usually have a charming personality and enhanced social skills, you also appreciate money and power. Your governing card, the 8 of Spades, further accentuates a career that can link you to the public domain and influential people. Although you usually have the vitality and stamina to pursue your goals, a lack of self-discipline or inability to persevere may undermine your great potential for success. Your popularity and personal relationships are often highly important to you and when you combine your social awareness with your charismatic nature you can charm and impress others.

October 25: Scorpio   Ruler: Mars

Your engaging personality and natural flair for dealing with people usually hides your intense emotions and ambitious drive for success. Your ruler, Mars, urges you to be daring or bold and tenacious. Since your fulfillment can often be achieved through creative self-expression, it can be just the right incentive to push you forward. Your restlessness and lack of persistence, on the other hand, may drive you to look for romance, variety, and excitement instead. If you want to achieve your inspired goals discipline yourself to be decisive and invest your time in developing your intellectual skills, innate talents, and intuitive abilities.

November 23: Sagittarius   Ruler: Jupiter

Creative, sociable and optimistic, your direct and friendly nature indicates that you are a versatile individual with an ambitious personality. Motivated by your strong desire to find emotional fulfillment, you may try different avenues to express yourself. Although you may have numerous opportunities to initiate new enterprises, your restlessness or impatience indicates that you need to resist changing your goals or scattering your energies on too many objectives. Nevertheless, when you finally decide what you want you are able to use your initiative and charm to accomplish your heart's desire.

December 21: Sagittarius/Capricorn
Ruler: Jupiter/Saturn

Sociable, friendly, and idealistic, your outgoing and charismatic personality can easily attract many friends and admirers. Your strong desires usually accommodate noble intentions, yet your acute business sense implies that you can excel in enterprising ventures. Equally, you can be the driving force behind industries relating to the public or the world of entertainment. According to both Jupiter and Saturn your big challenge is how to utilize your emotional power and innate talents for constructive use. A tendency to become impatient or frustrated warns that without the necessary discipline and conviction you can lose interest or scatter your valuable energies on idle pursuits.

♣THE 10 OF CLUBS♣

As the number 10 signifies success you are at your best when fired up with ideas and enthusiasm about achieving your goals or large plans. Being in the Sun line of the Earthly Spread, you can be dramatic and project confidence and resolve. When positive this ability to think and radiate success can bring you worldly recognition and draw people toward you. Independent and strong-willed, you have firm opinions, a penetrating mind, and an ability to think big. The inspired determination that leads to your attainment, however, only works if you are genuinely enthusiastic about what you are doing. You are therefore likely to gain greater benefit from following your interests than from acting purely for material gain. Being an ambitious individual with strong convictions, you usually have a project or purpose that drives you on. You are also helped by your persuasive powers.

Under the influences of Venus and Jupiter in the Spiritual Spread, you possess charismatic qualities and a charm that can make you popular. Despite all your outstanding potential, however, you may have to be careful that hidden insecurities or a lack of self-discipline do not minimize your achievements. Nevertheless, being a 10 of Clubs gives you a natural love of knowledge and a mental edge that can put you in leadership positions.

Your Two Replacement Cards Are the Jack of Spades & the 4 of Spades.

As the 10 of Clubs you share the same planetary position as the Jack of Spades in the Spiritual Spread. This signifies that you possess an inner youthful quality and a spirit of enterprise. Although you are clever, your playful side may sometimes test your maturity and expose your naivete. Nevertheless, you can be very insightful and surprise others with your foreknowledge.

Your card also shares the same planetary position as the 4 of Spades in the Earthly Spread. This indicates that you prefer to be straightforward and direct in your dealings with others. Although the number 4 influence bestows practical and organizational abilities, it also suggests you may need to resist being stubborn. When you use the qualities of the 4

The 10 of Clubs Planetary Card Sequence

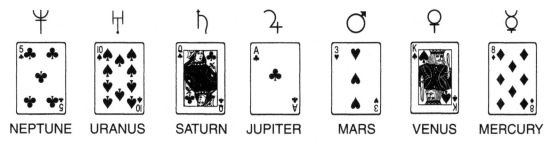

NEPTUNE   URANUS   SATURN   JUPITER   MARS   VENUS   MERCURY

of Spades to your advantage you combine honesty and good planning with the resolution to achieve success.

You have special or karmic links with people who are represented by the Jack of Spades or 4 of Spades. As you share the same planetary positions you can be soul mates or understand each other very well. Even if you do not get along, you can both see clearly how the other person operates.

Your Mercury Card is . . .

The 8 of Diamonds
- Your mental tenacity gives you an advantage over others and suggests that you enjoy power.
- Your thinking is purposeful and strategic, although avoid becoming argumentative.
- You have a good understanding of structure that gives you natural business acumen.
- You like to be frank and speak your mind, yet you benefit from developing patience with those who are less gifted than yourself.
- You should have good mental rapport and special communication with people represented by the 8 of Diamonds Card, as they stimulate your desire to communicate and exchange ideas.

Your Venus Card is . . .

The King of Spades
- As you especially value wisdom and experience, you have high regard for helpful authority figures that can advance your progress.
- Once set on a course of action you can be very focused.
- If a 10 of Clubs man, you can be attracted to strong or forceful women. As a 10 of Clubs woman you may find yourself taking charge when in a relationship, unless you find

someone you really respect, then you will back down.
- You can turn on the charm and possess the ability to take a leading role in social situations.
- You can be especially attracted to people who are represented by the King of Spades. This Venus link is ideal for love and romance. Alternatively, it can indicate close friendships or good business partnerships.

Your Mars Card is . . .

The 3 of Hearts
- You love to be actively creative, although with your many talents, avoid diffusing your energies.
- You possess dynamic drive and quick wit, and can be very entertaining.
- Doubt or indecision in emotional or sexual issues can cause you insecurity, jealousy, or worry.
- You can easily win people over when you are being friendly.
- People who are the 3 of Hearts can motivate and stimulate you due to your Mars link. There is often a great deal of energy in this type of relationship. You may be wise to resist being too competitive with this person, but channel your joint energies constructively.

Your Jupiter Card is . . .

The Ace of Clubs
- You can be full of good ideas and possess the ability to teach or pass on knowledge to others.
- You can be enthusiastic at first, but may become bored easily.
- You grasp ideas quickly and can be a good initiator.

- When inspired you particularly express your originality and strong potential for achievement or material reward.
- Ace of Clubs people can be benefactors who expand and enhance your life. As well as providing opportunities, these people may have a spiritual link with you.

Your Saturn Card is . . .

The Queen of Clubs

- You can be an excellent networker, linking people from different walks of life.
- Although you are highly aware of other people's opinions, you may be too sensitive to their criticism.
- You are at your best when being of service to others, particularly when spreading information or providing advice and opportunities.
- You benefit when not shying away from responsibilities, even though you may sometimes feel imposed upon.
- Queen of Clubs people can act as teachers to help you realize your character flaws. If you are willing to work on your self-awareness, boundaries, or discipline these people can bring valuable lessons.

Your Uranus Card is . . .

The 10 of Spades

- Success can come from your willingness to work with new and untried ideas.
- Your greatest rewards can come through the advancement of your more universal ideals or unified group efforts.
- With your original ideas, you enjoy being different from the crowd.
- Accomplishments are almost guaranteed when you are willing to work hard.
- People represented by the 10 of Spades can help you be more objective about yourself.

This is also a good friendship link where freedom is valued.

Your Neptune Card is . . .

The 5 of Clubs

- Clever and instinctive, you possess fast responses and a daring or adventurous streak.
- New projects or exciting ideas can fire your imagination or take you overseas.
- Developing patience can counteract the restlessness that causes uncertainty or diminishes your resolve.
- A desire for action or travel will bring many stimulating and interesting people into your life.
- You are likely to have many opportunities to travel, especially later in life.
- 5 of Clubs people can have a psychic connection with you due to your Neptune link. They may connect to your visions and ideals or help you to materialize your dreams, but avoid deluding yourself in these relationships.

Your Challenge Card is . . .

The 3 of Diamonds

- One of your challenges is to maintain a stable sense of values.
- When positive you can express joy or creativity, bringing happiness to others.
- Guard against allowing worry or indecision about material matters to undermine your spirit of enterprise.
- 3 of Diamonds people can stimulate your creativity or confront you to bring out the extremes your personality. This person could help you to transform old patterns if you avoid power struggles.

The Result of Your Challenge Card is . . .

The Ace of Spades
- You enjoy initiating new ventures or activities.
- When you accept the challenge of your destiny, you rise to your natural position as a leader and learn to trust your intuition implicitly.
- You should not be afraid to delve deeply into the mysteries of life, as the wisdom it brings can prove to be your greatest asset.
- If you are selfish, bossy, or overly serious you are not responding well to your challenge.
- If your work involves service to others this proves more fulfilling than just work for personal gain.
- People who are the Ace of Spades can stimulate your desire to start new ventures or work and reflect just how well you are responding to your challenges.

Famous People Who Are the 10 of Clubs

Madonna, Nelson Mandela, Nicole Kidman, Tennessee Williams, Sinéad O'Connor, Luciano Pavarotti, Shirley MacLaine, Jim Morrison, Barbra Streisand, Leonard Nimoy, Richard Burton, Tim Rice, Jacob Epstein, Diego Rivera, Sammy Davis, Jr., Morrissey, Lawrence Olivier, Richard Wagner, Arthur Conan Doyle, Robert Frost, Christian Bale, Vin Diesel, Linus Pauling, Franklin D. Roosevelt, Vanessa Redgrave, Brian Wilson, Gene Hackman, Diana Ross

Birthdays Governed by the 10 of Clubs

January 30: Aquarius   Ruler: Uranus
Sociable and a free spirit, you are a friendly and ambitious individual with a rebel streak. With original and progressive ideas you can be enthusiastic and driven when you find a project that fires your imagination. Good with words, you can also pass on your enthusiasm onto others. Being intelligent with many interests and choices suggests that you may have to avoid becoming scattered or indecisive. Although it usually does not come without hard work, you have the potential for large-scale success.

February 28: Pisces   Ruler: Neptune
Ambitious and direct yet idealistic, you are a person who can display a wide range of emotions. Sometimes you are sensitive and caring and at other times strong-willed, forceful, and direct. Your spirit of enterprise and quick intelligence imply that you constantly seek opportunities to improve your circumstances. Valuing knowledge, you appreciate those with wisdom and often succeed through collaborative work. Although you respond fast and possess natural leadership skills, if you become negative be careful these do not degenerate into being impatient or bossy. Nevertheless, you can be persuasive, daring, and progressive, with many creative ideas that can inspire and help others.

March 26: Aries   Ruler: Mars
Strength of will and a need for action mark you out as a friendly and determined individual with business acumen and a sense of purpose. A need to build a good home or be a responsible parent can be as high on your priority list as your worldly ambitions. With your sharp intellect and drive, you should have no problems in achieving tangible results, but you may have to watch a tendency to become materialistic, controlling, or too impulsive. Nevertheless, you are usually, honest, responsible, and very supportive of those in your care. When you express your strong creative gifts you can impress others with your ideas, courage, and talent.

April 24: Taurus   Ruler: Venus
Honest and direct, you are a friendly individual with a strong will. Your warm heart and need for balance and harmony match your determination and desire for knowledge and power. Although you care, you may have to overcome a tendency to be stubborn or controlling. Usually you have the advantage of being able to think on a large scale and can be very focused when you have a goal in mind. Through hard work and discipline you can develop your exceptional talents and win respect and self-mastery. A natural dramatic sense can stimulate an urge to be in the limelight.

May 22: Gemini   Ruler: Mercury
Born on the cusp, you possess the creative mind of Gemini tempered by the shrewd practicality of Taurus. Honest and direct, with a touch of charisma, you have inner strength, but avoid being impulsive or argumentative. With your communication skills and persuasive manner, you can win friends and influence others, but you may have to protect your sensitive nervous system. Highly intuitive, you usually work best when you go on your gut instincts about people or projects. By disciplining yourself to develop your natural talents you have the potential to achieve remarkable results.

June 20: Gemini   Ruler: Mercury
A fusion of opposites, you are a clever and interesting individual. Strong-willed, opinionated, and determined, yet impressionable and kind, you get enthused with new ideas or projects. Although independent, you particularly succeed through partnerships and working cooperatively with others, but you may have to guard against being stubborn or cantankerous. Your quick mind, business sense, and ability to charm others can help you in your quest for success, but it is important to also keep a balance and stand by your own beliefs despite outside interference.

July 18: Cancer   Planetary Ruler: Moon
Strong-willed with determination and drive, you are courageous and enjoy power. With your progressive ideas and emotional sensitivity, you can connect to the person in the street and anticipate trends. With leadership potential, executive abilities, and a dislike of taking orders, you usually fare better when in charge or working for yourself. Be careful, however, of uncontrolled emotions that can cause trouble. A humanitarian side to your nature can be developed to bring fulfillment and emotional satisfaction.

August 16: Leo   Planetary Ruler: Sun
Generous and self-assured, you are an individual with excellent analytical skills, vitality, and drive. With your sharp intellect and thoughtful approach, you grasp concepts quickly. Analytical and reflective, you also possess a strong perfectionist streak. A caring side to your nature implies that your strong quest for individuality may sometimes be at odds with your responsibilities to home and family. Naturally dramatic, your creative ideas, leadership skills, and fine intellect can ensure your material success, but to be really happy you need to find projects that fire your imagination or connect to your spirit.

September 14: Virgo   Ruler: Mercury
Determined and down-to-earth in your thinking, you are an individual with strong opinions and good communication skills. Your work is important and you are usually willing to take care of the detail that others ignore. With your sharp analytical skills and no-nonsense approach, you prefer to be honest and up front with others and have a natural business sense.

Guard against an impatient or stubborn streak, however. Nevertheless, you can still turn on the charm when necessary and win people over with your enthusiasm.

October 12: Libra   Ruler: Venus
The strong influence of Venus in your life indicates that you possess excellent people skills that can help you operate independently or as part of a team. Friendly yet ambitious, you enjoy being sociable and can combine your diplomacy and leadership abilities to achieve success in life. You are also likely to possess a gift with words, whether through writing, speaking, or singing. With your sensitivity for color and style or love of harmony, you have refined taste and an appreciation of the arts. You also have great respect for those that have achieved their goals and mastered self-discipline.

November 10: Scorpio   Ruler: Mars
The combination of your friendly and creative personality with your drive and ambition ensures you are a force to be reckoned with. Success-oriented, you possess natural leadership skills and progressive ideas. With your many talents, however, it is important to stay clearly focused on your goals and not scatter your energies. This is not helped when doubt or indecision regarding your emotional affairs sidetracks you from your mission. Proud and strong-willed, in order to be happy you need to channel your strong emotions into being productive. You have remarkable potential when positively focused.

December 8: Sagittarius   Ruler: Jupiter
Truthful and direct, you an individual with sharp intelligence and inspired ideas. The influence of Jupiter in your life suggests that you think in grand terms and may be drawn to big business or large-scale ventures. Alternatively, your philosophical approach may attract you to religion, education, law, publishing, foreign cultures, or travel. When positive you possess a winning enthusiasm and learn quickly. As you enjoy power, you have natural leadership or executive abilities, but be careful of becoming controlling or bossy. With your strong convictions, you have the moral courage to stand by your beliefs.

♦ THE 10 OF DIAMONDS ♦

The need to accomplish and the desire to excel indicate that by nature you are a determined individual with high goals. Usually you have a head for business and the ability to blend common sense with intuition when it comes to quickly evaluating people or situations. Although you can be ambitious with grand ideas, resist being too materialistic or bossy. The double influence of Jupiter, the planet of expansion, in your Earthly Spread suggests that you are usually very fortunate. The downturn of Jupiter the great benefactor is often carelessness or arrogance. By taking your luck for granted and not knowing when to stop, you can become self-indulgent. To fully capitalize on your great opportunities, therefore, you may need to exercise moderation and self-discipline.

The planetary influences of Mercury and Uranus in your Spiritual Spread indicate that you love your freedom and independence. By relying on your astuteness and inventive thinking you usually gain the edge over others. If you want to lead or inspire people, however, resist being too blunt or acting in a defiant manner. When you apply your natural ingenuity and psychological skills you have the ability to influence people to your way of thinking without causing tension.

Your Two Replacement Cards Are the Queen of Spades & the Queen of Clubs.

As the 10 of Diamonds you share the same planetary position as the Queen of Spades in the Earthly Spread. This royal card signifies that you are highly intuitive and sensitive. Strongly influenced by the need to be of service or to protect others, you may also work for a just cause without recognition. Women can play an important role in your life and usually they are career-oriented or hardworking. Although some women may turn out to be taskmasters, a responsible attitude toward them can minimize conflicts.

As the 10 of Diamonds you also share the same planetary position as the Queen of Clubs in the Spiritual Spread. With your intuitive sensitivity and sharp intellect you can develop your mind and depth of understanding. An idealistic side to your nature, if developed, seeks to transcend the material world by being of service to a higher purpose or to others. The double Queen influence here emphasizes your pride and natural sense of the dramatic.

You usually have special or karmic links with people who are represented by the Queen of Clubs and the Queen of Spades, as you share the same planetary positions. You can be soul mates or understand each other very well. Even if you do not get along, you can both see clearly how the other person operates. It also indicates that women will play an important role in your life, be it a source of irritation or inspiration.

Your Mercury Card is . . .

The 8 of Spades
- Your mental power and practical aptitude imply that you are a shrewd strategist and a clever planner.
- Your vigor and determined mind suggest that you can overcome any obstacle or challenges in life.
- With your resolve and forceful presence, you usually impress other people and achieve what you want.
- If you are not willing to be flexible others will perceive you as a stubborn, bossy, or aggressive individual.
- You should have good mental rapport and special communication with 8 of Spades people, as they activate your Mercury Card. These people can also be friends or business partners.

Your Venus Card is . . .

The Ace of Hearts
- Although you are a realist, the Ace of Hearts indicates that you possess powerful feelings and strong desires.
- Usually idealistic, you hold onto high prin-

The 10 of Diamonds Planetary Card Sequence

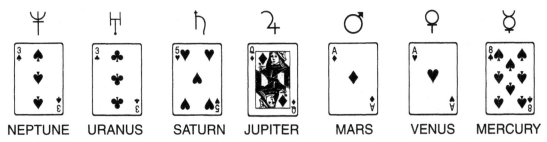

| NEPTUNE | URANUS | SATURN | JUPITER | MARS | VENUS | MERCURY |

ciples when it comes to love, friendship, and close relationships.

- Inspired by noble ideas, you may become a champion for just causes.
- With the creative power of the Ace of Hearts, you are imaginative, sensitive, and artistic.
- Charming and enthusiastic, when in love you are warm and affectionate.
- Usually you are drawn to people represented by the Ace of Hearts, especially if they share your creative interests. They are ideal for love and romance as well as close friendships and good business partnerships.

Your Mars Card is . . .

The Ace of Diamonds
- You can be an initiator of large projects or big business enterprises.
- Your ambitious drive suggests that you have the initiative to succeed and the determination to carry through your material objectives.
- In your resolute drive to succeed monetarily, resist taking risks, being impatient, or bending the rules.
- Your natural leadership abilities indicate that you can rise to the top of your profession or take charge of situations.
- The relationships you have with the Ace of Diamonds people can be financially beneficial or energizing if you both share the same aspirations. Resist being competitive or reckless with these people or they could drain your resources and cause you stress.

Your Jupiter Card is . . .

The Queen of Diamonds
- You can be very generous when supporting a cause or those you love.

- You like to enjoy an extravagant life-style or luxuries, but resist overindulging.
- Benefits come from women, female friends, or partners who are willing to support you or your projects.
- Your people skills and business acumen indicate that you are ideally suited to executive positions.
- People, and especially women, represented by the Queen of Diamonds card can be linked to success or work opportunities. If you are in business or partnership with them you can both be successful, especially as you share the same spiritual values.

Your Saturn Card is . . .

The 5 of Hearts
- To enrich your life you are likely to encounter a wide variety of different emotional experiences.
- The restlessness suggested by this card also implies that you can feel unsettled and doubtful in your close relationships.
- Resist letting mood swings cloud your judgment.
- You have relationships that carry karmic obligations, so do not act on impulse when making commitments as you may later regret your actions.
- 5 of Hearts people can play an important role in your life if you are able to learn from them about emotional issues and responsibilities. Although your relationship with them may not be always easy, their contributions are often very valuable lessons.

Your Uranus Card is . . .

The 3 of Clubs
- Being versatile and clever with words, you can be witty and think inspired thoughts.

- By synthesizing different concepts, you can think progressively or offer fresh ideas.
- Although you can be instinctive, when you are indecisive you can suddenly change your mind or direction.
- Creative thoughts and good communication skills suggest an interest in writing. In your middle years you can develop a unique talent or style of writing.
- Benefits can also come from studying philosophy and esoteric subjects.
- 3 of Clubs people can offer you new ideas or teach you how to be more objective. This is also a good card for friendship, especially if you both share the same intellectual pursuits.

Your Neptune Card is . . .

The 3 of Spades

- You need to be inspired and decisive if you want to fulfill your dreams in later years.
- You can lose your direction by scattering your energies on too many projects or escapism.
- By staying realistic you can be imaginative and creative without letting the ambiguous influence of Neptune delude you.
- In later years you may be drawn to develop your spirituality, especially through your creative activities.
- 3 of Spades people may link to your visions and ideals or have a psychic connection with you, but keep your feet firmly on the ground.

Your Challenge Card is . . .

The 9 of Hearts

- To minimize disappointment you may need to learn detachment when dealing with the affairs of the heart.

- This card calls for a higher level of love, tolerance, and compassion, so resist being self-centered or selfish.
- Emotional disappointments or lack of self-discipline can result in overindulgence and excessive behavior.
- You can find fulfillment if you tap into the expression of universal love.
- You have the task to enrich other people's life or do something for people less fortunate than yourself.
- 9 of Hearts people can captivate you but also challenge you emotionally. They may touch upon your emotional frustrations, but they can also positively help you to transform your life.

The Result of Your Challenge Card is . . .

The 7 of Clubs

- You can achieve faith in yourself and mental victory.
- You can delve into the mysteries of life and gain wisdom.
- If you listen to your inner voice you can minimize your worries and emotional fears.
- 7 of Clubs people can inspire you or help you to develop or refine your intellect. Your reactions to them often reflect how you are responding to your personal challenges.

Famous People Who Are the 10 of Diamonds

Prince, Jim Carrey, Dr. Phil McGraw, Jean Cocteau, Anton Chekhov, Paul Gauguin, Charles Tiffany, Joseph Pulitzer, Al Capone, Galileo, John Barrymore, Candice Bergen, Glenda Jackson, Albert Finney, Liam Neeson, Andy Kaufman, Matt Groening, Jessica Tandy, Lily Tomlin, Muhammad Ali, Tony Bennett, Billy Joel, Barry Gibb, Tom Jones

Birthdays Governed by the 10 of Diamonds

January 17: Capricorn   Ruler: Saturn

Your ruler, Saturn, is the planet of responsibilities and discipline. It also highlights the need to be practical and patient. You can often rise to positions of power or influence by being thoughtful, reliable, and hardworking. Since your Saturn card is the 5 of Hearts you may be prone to emotional fluctuations or mood swings. To achieve the emotional tranquility and stability you desire, resist letting emotional restlessness undermine your objectives. Although you can be friendly, charming, and sociable, your need for variety and change can affect your personal relationships.

February 15: Aquarius   Ruler: Uranus

Your ruler, Uranus, is the planet of sudden change and individualism. Its influence highlights your versatility and ability to think independently and objectively. Being progressive also signifies your capacity to create change by bringing reforms to outdated ideas or systems. A tendency to be indecisive or uncertain can undermine your creative self-expression and cause you to worry unnecessarily. Although you usually love your freedom, you can be impulsive or rebellious at times. As your Uranus Card is the 3 of Clubs your knowledge of human nature makes you intellectually bright and a witty individual who can influence others. Mentally alert with a unique outlook, you can find self-expression through creativity and writing.

March 13: Pisces   Ruler: Neptune

Your ruler, Neptune, the planet of receptivity and imagination, indicates that you are usually more subtle and sensitive than other 10 of Diamonds birthdays. Your intuitive abilities suggest that you have strong sixth sense, and being impressionable can help you to easily identify with others. If you fail to find an inspiring occupation or a vocation you may drift from one job to another not knowing exactly what it is you want to achieve. The influence of your governing card, the 3 of Spades, indicates that you can excel in all types of creative work as long as your goals are based on realistic plans and true aspiration

April 11: Aries   Ruler: Mars

Ruled by Mars, the planet of vitality and drive, indicates that you are an ambitious and motivated individual with strong willpower and the determination to succeed. Your governing card, the Ace of Diamonds, further emphasizes your dynamic personality. As an Ace you are a natural leader, with high ideals and a sixth sense about money or new financial opportunities. Although you are likely to achieve a great deal by being enthusiastic and determined, if you appear too eager or aggressive others may perceive you as pushy or mercenary. By practicing self-discipline and leading people by example, however, you can influence or inspire others and rise to positions of power.

May 9: Taurus   Ruler: Venus

Being ruled by Venus, the planet of love and beauty, indicates that you are a sociable and friendly individual with a strong need to be loved and appreciated. As you are likely to excel in careers that involve working with the public, guard against isolating yourself or working in seclusion. The Ace of Hearts, your governing card, implies that your strong feelings and impulses can make you spontaneous and dramatic. Often your desires are to find emotional fulfillment and love through creative self-expression. Although you can reach emotional highs, your sensitivity can make you vulnerable to hasty actions and criticism. Nevertheless, you can minimize a tendency to fluctuate emotionally by developing a detached view especially with regards to your strong desires or relationships.

June 7: Gemini   Ruler: Mercury

Your ruler, Mercury, the planet of communication and intellect, indicates that you are an independent, intelligent, and versatile individual with common sense. Your analytical ability suggests that usually you like to reserve judgment until you have made up your own mind. Refrain from power struggles, however, as they can accentuate your stubbornness or controlling behavior. Since your governing card is the 8 of Spades, you are likely to be mentally smart, with the vitality to heal yourself or others. As an intelligent and ambitious individual, when you have faith in yourself you can be hardworking and highly productive.

July 5: Cancer   Ruler: Moon

Your strong instincts and impressionable nature indicates that you are a capable yet sensitive individual with dynamic drive. Able to quickly assess people and situations, you can relate easily to others with your sympathetic heart. Although you are usually shrewd, creative, and an enterprising strategist, without the necessary patience or determination you may give up too soon on your ambitious plans. Your ruler, the Moon, suggests that with your versatility, sensitive receptivity, and imaginative ideas you can accomplish a great deal. In order to turn your dreams into reality, however, you need to develop your innate talents and persist.

August 3: Leo   Ruler: Sun

Charismatic and full of vitality, your ambitious nature, versatility, and organizational skills indicate that you possess natural leadership qualities and the aspiration to excel in whatever you do. Although you are usually full of bright ideas, the scope of your possibilities may leave you indecisive as to what to do first. The Sun, your ruler, indicates that your generosity, confidence, and optimism add an auspicious influence to your success story. A need to find an outlet for your creative talents can motivate you to succeed and may even prove to be profitable as well as enjoyable.

September 1: Virgo   Ruler: Mercury

Your ruler Mercury, the planet of communication and intellect, highlights your mental acumen and analytical abilities. Often self-reliant and independent, you prefer to take the lead rather than follow others. Resist becoming involved in power struggles or arguments, however, as they can accentuate your sarcastic or stubborn attitude. Your thrust for knowledge, patience, and pragmatism usually makes you a hardworking and highly productive individual. Although you pay attention to the smallest detail, resist letting your critical voice undermine yourself or other people. Since your governing card is the 8 of Spades, you are likely to have the strength to persevere and the persuasive manner to influence others.

♠ THE 10 OF SPADES ♠

Being a number 10 of the Spades suit suggests that you can be a remarkable achiever if you are willing to identify with the "success through work" element suggested by your card. Under the influences of Jupiter and Mercury in the Earthly Spread, you have the advantage of being clever with the ability to think in large terms. In addition to being kindhearted, honest, and direct you have a wealth of ideas and a natural philosophical bent to your thinking that can help you see the positive side of difficult situations. You may have an interest in a wide range of subjects such as travel, education, literature, religion, philosophy, law, or spirituality. At best you can be an inspired thinker or uplifting conversationalist who enjoys learning and improving your talents and skills. Usually you are good at quickly assessing the heart of a matter, but avoid being self-righteous or arrogant. Generally optimistic, you can combine enthusiasm for your favorite projects with common sense.

As your card has a double Neptune influence in the Spiritual Spread you also have a very vivid imagination that can aid you in your big plans or grand vision. This can provide you with a refined sense of color and sound or creative gifts. Being intelligent and talented, all you need is the willingness to put in the work necessary to fulfill your dreams and outstanding potential. Guard against a tendency toward avoidance, however, that can stop you from confronting issues you would rather not deal with. Benevolent, generous, and a supporter of the underdog, you are helped in life by being amiable and popular in your social group.

Your Two Replacement Cards Are the 4 of Hearts & the Queen of Hearts.

As the 10 of Spades you share the same planetary position as the 4 of Hearts in the Spiritual Spread. This signifies that you usually prefer to be emotionally straightforward in your dealings with others. When positive you can be loyal, caring, and dependable when others need you. Being proud, however, guard against a tendency to be snobbish or self-satisfied. Nevertheless, you have high ideals, and satisfaction comes in giving of yourself to others.

You also share the same planetary position as the Queen of Hearts in the Earthly Spread. This suggests that inside you are sensitive and dramatic, so you need outlets for your natural theatrical abilities. This could be through taking the lead in work situations or in your

social group. Alternatively, you may wish to express this in the arts, music, writing, or drama. Your refined sensitivity and loving nature may also attract you to mystical pursuits, healing, or helping others. Avoid the negative Queen of Hearts influence that could make you moody, lazy, or overly dramatic. Fortunately, you have a strong intuitive sense that can guide you through life if you listen to your inner voice.

You have special or karmic links with people who are represented by the 4 of Hearts and the Queen of Hearts. As you share the same planetary positions you can be soul mates or understand each other very well. Even if you do not get along, you can both see clearly how the other person operates.

Your Mercury Card is . . .

The 5 of Clubs
- With your active mind, you want to improve yourself mentally. You particularly enjoy earning while you learn.
- You have the gift of speech, and with your fast responses can be witty or talk about your pet subject with great enthusiasm.
- Channel any mental restlessness or impatience into problem solving, writing, or exploring new subjects. This stops you from becoming bored.
- People who are the 5 of Clubs can stimulate your intellect and adventurous spirit. This is a good link for mental rapport and exchange of ideas.

Your Venus Card is . . .

The 3 of Diamonds
- Friendly and warmhearted, you attract others and enjoy an interesting social life.
- Avoid worrying or being indecisive about relationships. You usually enjoy your relation-

The 10 of Spades Planetary Card Sequence

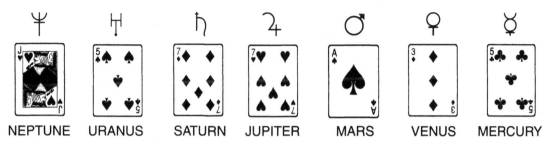

| NEPTUNE | URANUS | SATURN | JUPITER | MARS | VENUS | MERCURY |

ships better when you can keep them light rather than being too heavy going.

- You possess innate creative gifts you may wish to develop. If you do they will bring you much happiness.
- When it comes to money matters you may often find that two opportunities come up at once. Better to make a decision and change it later than stay in a state of anxiety about them.
- When involved in creative activities you like to perfect your craft.
- For you, people represented by the 3 of Diamonds can stimulate your creativity and be especially good for romance, close friendships, or business partnerships.

Your Mars Card is . . .

The Ace of Spades

- When action-oriented or working you can be sharp, innovative, and to the point. You may find yourself naturally taking charge.
- If there is a lack of action in your life or you become too self-absorbed you can be prone to despondency.
- A desire to understand the deeper mysteries of the universe may motivate you to study subjects of a more philosophical nature.
- Pioneering new areas of work can enhance your vitality and drive.
- People represented by the Ace of Spades card

can stimulate your enthusiasm, courage, and productive activity, but avoid being competitive or possible arguments.

Your Jupiter Card is . . .

The 7 of Hearts

- Your high ideals suggest that you respond well to inspiration.
- You enjoy being well informed, and a perfectionist streak suggests you like to improve on existing systems.
- You can be generous and thoughtful.
- Although very sociable, you also need quality time alone for introspection.
- People who are the 7 of Hearts can broaden your horizons and emotionally make you feel more optimistic, although avoid overindulgence together. This link can bring opportunities and be a fortunate or spiritual link.

Your Saturn Card is . . .

The 7 of Diamonds

- Once you have a definite goal in mind you can be resolute, tough, and determined. If these qualities are used for self-discipline then they can prove very productive.
- Regarding your work, you may have to get the balance right between overworking or being too slack.

- Some of your tests may involve overcoming inhibitions or trusting yourself to react spontaneously.
- Although you have an innate understanding of how to achieve material success, you may find that fulfillment comes through work that brings you interesting experiences or wisdom.
- 7 of Diamonds people can act as teachers or help you recognize your own shortcomings. If you are willing to work on your boundaries, discipline, and self-awareness these people can bring valuable lessons.

Your Uranus Card is . . .

The 5 of Spades
- Variety and travel particularly bring out your individuality, sense of inventiveness, and originality.
- If you become restless or impatient you are prone to be obstinate or to do something erratic.
- Instinctive, independent, and freedom loving, your fast reactions ensure that your enjoy new experiences and the autonomy to move freely.
- 5 of Spades people can help you be more active, enthusiastic, and see your own situation more objectively. This is also a good link for friendship or exchanging stimulating and resourceful ideas.

Your Neptune Card is . . .

The Jack of Hearts
- You possess an ability to lose your ego through creative projects or compassion for others. If you develop this ability it will bring you great love and happiness. Alternately, if negative, this influence can suggest an immaturity that leads you to escapism or feeling sorry for yourself.

- Although this card placement indicates you can be very sensitive, it also shows you can be playful and entertaining.
- Jack of Hearts people can help you to keep your sense of fun or vision alive, especially if you share the same dreams and ideas. This is a psychic link, but stay realistic and grounded.

Your Challenge Card is . . .

The 9 of Clubs
- Be constantly expanding your knowledge so that it brings you a universal perspective.
- Build a strong belief system that can help you through times of frustration or disappointment.
- Stand up for your principles enthusiastically.
- Be willing to stay detached and forgive and forget.
- 9 of Clubs people can confront you to bring out the best or the worst of your personality. They can show you where you need to be more mentally detached and help you transform old patterns.

The Result of Your Challenge Card is . . .

The 9 of Spades
- If responding well to your challenge you will be generous and compassionate. You can also be drawn to humanitarian interests.
- If you find yourself becoming overly serious and are disillusioned that you, or others, are failing to live up to your high expectations you may need to become more impersonal or find ways to be more helpful to others.
- People who are the 9 of Spades can reflect how you are responding to your challenges.

Famous People Who Are the 10 of Spades

Michael Stipe, Holly Hunter, Isaac Newton, Ayn Rand, Dyan Cannon, Farrah Fawcett,

Graham Nash, Louis Braille, Floyd Patterson, Jascha Heifetz, Havelock Ellis, Shakira, James Joyce

Birthdays Governed by the 10 of Spades

January 4: Capricorn   Ruler: Saturn
Honest and sincere with a sharp intellect, your sociable nature can hide your ambitions and shrewd practicality. Once you have learned to overcome a sense of reserve, then you can be witty and entertaining and switch on the charm. Proud with a dramatic sense, you may also have artistic or creative gifts, but you are still security conscious and aware of finances. As a practical visionary, your imaginative gifts can also help bring you success, but you accomplish most when you have worked to build a solid foundation for your achievements.

February 2: Aquarius   Ruler: Aquarius
Your interest in people makes you a good psychologist, and your original ideas can help you fulfill many of your ambitions. Receptive and intuitive as well as being an objective thinker, you can be considerate and aware of others. Equally, you can be a free spirit who values your freedom. Although independent, you particularly prosper when working in partnerships or as part of a team. Avoid dependent situations, however, as they can make you oversensitive or lose confidence. Inventive, imaginative, and intellectually creative, you have a gift for writing or presenting new ideas.

♥ ♣ THE JACKS ♦ ♠

USUALLY JACKS REPRESENT individuals who are dynamic, creative, and idealistic. Regardless of gender, you are usually young at heart, with strong convictions and high spirit. Although as a royal card you possess innate talents and leadership qualities, immaturity or a lack of self-discipline may induce an irresponsible attitude that can undermine your efforts. Nevertheless, your vitality and enthusiasm usually inspire you to be innovative and enterprising. Although your highly charged and agile nature can contribute to your outstanding potential for success, guard against becoming overly anxious or too intense. A mixture of self-doubt and confidence suggests that, if you are unsure about your objectives, you can fluctuate from great highs to disheartening lows. Nevertheless, when you learn to take responsibility for your actions you can deal with both sides of your nature and develop a less extremist attitude. The key to success for most Jacks is to become self-reliant and develop their expertise or special talents.

Jack of Hearts

Seeking self-expression through your emotional power, your sensitivity and idealism are usually confirmed by your kindness and generosity. Often romantic and loving, your strength lies in your people skills and ability to assist or support others. Alternatively, you can measure your success by how well you can express your intense feelings or creative talents.

Jack of Clubs

Seeking self-expression through your cerebral power, your success is measured by your intelligence, maturity, or responsible attitude. Capable of quickly understanding concepts and grasping information, you benefit from good education. When inspired your desire is to share your knowledge or expertise with others. Alternatively, you can measure your success by how well you can express your innate talents, especially through writing or teaching.

Jack of Diamonds

Seeking self-expression through your strong sense of values and business acumen, your success is measured by your enterprising ability to sell or promote your ideas. Capable of quickly assessing and utilizing situations, you benefit from all type of activities connected with commerce. Alternatively, you can measure your success by how well you can express your creative and artistic talents.

Jack of Spades

Seeking self-expression through your creative work and productivity, your success is measured by your idealism and ethical conduct. Capable of hard work and dedication, your noble deeds can inspire you to accomplish. Since this card is also called the card of initiation, you can benefit from exploring esoteric subjects and studying metaphysics. Alternatively, you can find fulfillment through expressing your unique or artistic talents.

♥THE JACK OF HEARTS♥

As a Jack Card of the Heart suit you possess strong emotional power, an inner nobility, and personal charisma that can often place you in leadership positions. Nevertheless, you also have a playful heart and a youthful energy that will stay with you throughout life. The dramatic sense that your royal court card bestows suggests that you also enjoy opportunities to display your fast intelligence and good social skills. Equally, you are usually willing to be a responsive audience or sensitive ear for others. At times, however, you may not suffer fools gladly and need patience with those who cannot keep up with your quick mental responses and intuitive understanding. In the past your

card has been identified with the spiritual archetype of Christ's love and sacrifice, so working with the power of love, for example through forgiveness or showing others how to be self-aware, can reveal your strength and idealism. As yours is a Master Card in the deck you often achieve great personal fulfillment through following higher causes.

Under the influences of Jupiter and Venus in both the Earthly and Spiritual spreads, you possess a special gift for dealing with people as well as good organizational skills. You may wish to use your innate charm and charisma to make yourself popular at work or in your social circle. Being warm, caring, and charitable, people usually appreciate your support and understanding. Naturally creative with an appreciation of beauty, you may wish to develop your talents further through art, music, drama, and writing; or your taste for the good life may be seen in your enjoyment of quality and luxury. An alternative side of the youthful Jack influence is that you may just decide to never grow up, spending your life amusing yourself and never taking responsibility for fulfilling your high destiny. Nevertheless, whether you are making the most of your remarkable potential or not, you are kind, proud, and generous, often making magnanimous gestures to help others.

As your card keeps the same planetary position of Jupiter in the Venus line in both the Earthly and Spiritual spreads, it is one of the only three cards in the deck that does not have a Replacement Card but is fixed in the same position (see Fixed Cards, page 24).

Your Mercury Card is . . .

The 9 of Clubs

- Intelligent and articulate, with quick mental responses, you enjoy communicating your opinions, learning new skills, and testing your wits.

- You have a gift for being able to interact with people from all walks of life.
- Avoid dwelling on frustrations or disappointments.
- With your detached perspective you can give others an impersonal view of their situation. This suggests you may end up listening to others' problems or giving advice.
- People who are the 9 of Clubs are likely to stimulate your ideals or desire to communicate. This is a good link for the exchange of ideas.

Your Venus Card is . . .

The 9 of Spades

- By letting go of a tendency to hold onto the past, you open yourself up for new opportunities.
- You have a special gift for being wise and insightful while still being entertaining.
- By developing your ability to love unconditionally or by being of service to others, you can find fulfillment and overcome any frustrations that may occur in your more intimate relationships.
- When positive you can be generous and humanitarian.
- Although you may have to make sacrifices for loved ones, don't play the martyr, try to "save" others, or feel sorry for yourself.
- Usually you are drawn to people represented

by the 9 of Spades, especially if they share your creative interests. They are ideal for love and romance as well as close friendships and good business partnerships.

Your Mars Card is . . .

The 2 of Hearts

- You can be courteous, considerate, and diplomatic when you are actively engaged in work or achieving your desires.
- Although independent, partnerships with others can spur you into action or help you achieve materially.
- A sensitive romantic, a part of you is always looking for the perfect relationship.
- Hidden fears or finding yourself in dependent situations can cause you to become oversensitive or temperamental.
- 2 of Hearts people can particularly motivate and stimulate you. Together you can both be enthusiastic and dynamic in the pursuit of your objectives. Avoid being too competitive with this person, however.

Your Jupiter Card is . . .

The King of Hearts

- Big-hearted and proud, your natural organizational and dramatic gifts usually take you to positions of leadership.
- You have the ability to be in charge yet still

The Jack of Hearts Planetary Card Sequence

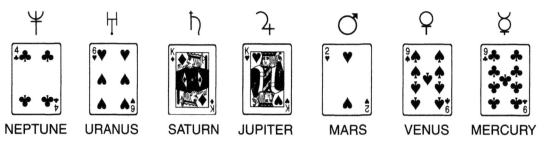

| NEPTUNE | URANUS | SATURN | JUPITER | MARS | VENUS | MERCURY |

retain your emotional warmth, making people feel you care.

- Your idealism and ability to think on a large scale often brings you fortunate opportunities.
- Be careful of an indulgent or arrogant streak that can sap your energy.
- Travel or foreign interests can be especially favorable for expanding your horizons both emotionally and financially.
- Usually you have a good rapport with people represented by the King of Hearts. They can make you more optimistic or be benefactors who can improve and enhance your life. Alternatively, these people can have a spiritual link with you.

Your Saturn Card is . . .

The King of Diamonds

- This second King influence suggests that you possess excellent evaluation skills and are better in positions of authority or working for yourself.
- You possess innate business acumen.
- The more you exercise self-discipline and take responsibility, the more you can empower yourself materially, gaining both money and success.
- You have natural healing abilities that you may wish to develop.
- King of Diamonds people can be your guides and help you recognize your shortcomings. They can show you where you need self-discipline or to be clear about your boundaries. If you are willing to work on your self-awareness you can learn from your experiences with these people.

Your Uranus Card is . . .

The 6 of Hearts

- Your excellent people skills suggest that you are good with groups or working as a team.
- Although you care, particularly for your home and family, if you care too much and become interfering or stubborn, this can bring out negative resistance in those around you.
- Your personal relationships should improve as you get older.
- Guard against a tendency to get stuck in a comfortable rut by developing your fine intellect, creative gifts, or your ability to make this world a better place for others.
- 6 of Hearts people can help you be more objective about yourself due to your Uranus connection. This is also a good friendship link where freedom is important.

Your Neptune Card is . . .

The 4 of Clubs

- The more practical you are about achieving your dreams and ideals the more your intuition will guide and support you.
- Without any form of definite positive planning you can drift or become confused.
- You enjoy a touch of glamour.
- Later in life your opportunities to improve your knowledge and skills increases, bringing you emotional satisfaction.
- 4 of Clubs people can have a psychic link with you. You may share the same ideals or they can stimulate you to think positively or build for the future. In these relationships, however, you may need to stay realistic.

Your Challenge Card is . . .

The 2 of Diamonds
- Keep a balance between your need for independence and your need for others.
- Overcome a fear that you will not receive the resources or money you need.
- Make the most of your relationship skills and ability to make contacts or work cooperatively with others.
- 2 of Diamonds people can usually stimulate you to react. These people can dare you to transform your life if you can rise to the challenge.

The Result of Your Challenge Card is . . .

The Jack of Spades
- The Jack of Spades suggests you can utilize your challenges to gradually develop your insight and wisdom. Alternatively, you can avoid the self-discipline needed to fulfil your high potential and spend most of your life in the pursuit of a good time.

Famous People Who Are the Jack of Hearts

Lisa Kudrow, T. S. Eliot, Henry Ford, Uri Geller, Arnold Schwarzenegger, Goethe, Emily Bronte, Olivia Newton John, Bryan Ferry, George Gershwin, Serena Williams, Martin Heidegger, Ivan Pavlov, Peter Bogdanovich, Terry Gilliam, Henry Moore, Billie Jean King, Boris Becker, Tom Green, Kevin Kline, George Eliot, Shania Twain, Jamie Lee Curtis, LeAnn Rimes

Birthdays Governed by the Jack of Hearts

July 30: Leo   Ruler: Sun
Friendly and sociable with a dramatic sense, you project confidence. When positive you are decisive and creative with a gift for words. You can also be youthful and entertaining and have a flair for dealing with the public. If negative you may be prone to worry and insecurity, or your love of the good life may lead to self-indulgence. Fortunately, your sensitivity combined with your inner strength suggests that you may prefer to lead a noble and productive life where you are able to help or inspire others.

August 28: Virgo   Ruler: Mercury
You can be ambitious and strong-willed as well as sensitive. The extremes of your nature can make you idealistic yet practical and down-to-earth. Similarly, you can be mentally sharp and analytical, yet emotionally impressionable. By developing your tolerance levels you can guard against a tendency to be bossy or impatient with others. Proud and enterprising, you are often daring and broad-minded, but avoid holding onto disappointments from the past. Although independent, you gain much from collaborative ventures or developing your writing skills.

September 26: Libra   Ruler: Venus
Charming and refined, your warm sociability and sensitive emotions belie your inner strength. Naturally dramatic, you are aware of image and style and love a touch of glamour. Although artistic or creative, you have strong business sense and executive abilities. With your need for beauty and luxury you may be prone to vanity or self-indulgence, but generally you are kind and caring with a strong love of home. Although you need to keep your good intellect stimulated, your life usually works best when you are being calm and dispassionate.

October 24: Scorpio   Ruler: Mars
Proud and tenacious, your passionate emotions are hidden beneath a warm and friendly

personality. Intelligent and perceptive, you often have sharp insight into the motivation of others. Although you are usually fair and just, you can also retaliate if others go too far. Being generous and caring, you enjoy sharing your love of the good life with others, although be careful of a domineering or secretive streak. Gracious and social adept, you are an expert at interaction with others, although home and family are highest on your agenda. Creative, with a youthful spirit, you often succeed best in partnerships or when working to fulfill your ideals.

November 22: Scorpio/Sagittarius
Ruler: Mars/Jupiter
Born on the cusp, you have both the tenacity and emotional depth of Scorpio and the broad-minded attitude of Sagittarius. Friendly and honest, your determination and pragmatic approach blends well with your good people skills. Being so sensitive implies that you have a delicate nervous system and often use your strong intuition in your daily life. Although strong-willed, beware of a tendency to sometimes be bossy or stubborn. Nevertheless, a good organizer, you also have a flair for business and will work hard when interested in a project. Being generous, your greatest rewards usually come from helping others.

December 20: Sagittarius   Ruler: Jupiter
Charming and considerate, you have a keen intellect and can exude confidence. Although determined, you are also idealistic and genuinely want to expand opportunities for everyone. At times, however, you may experience a pull between your high ideals and material practicalities. With a love of the good life, you want the best, and can normally be assertive in achieving your goals. Although you are very astute and have strong intuition, beware of being impulsive or oversensitive. With your good

people skills, you particularly gain through partnerships and collaborative efforts.

♣ THE JACK OF CLUBS ♣

Creative with a good mental aptitude, your desire to share your knowledge with others suggests that your strength is usually based on your quick intelligence. As a Jack Card you are also youthful and spirited. Belonging to the Clubs suit indicates that you benefit from broadening your horizons through increasing your knowledge and skills. You usually find problem solving satisfying and are likely to have a natural flair for the written or spoken word. With all your bright ideas, some form of study can often be a cornerstone to your achievements. With so many opportunities for success at your disposal, your challenge is to resist taking the easy route or acting only on financial incentives. By developing a mature and responsible attitude, however, you can rise to your true potential and accomplish many of your objectives.

Under the planetary influences of Uranus and Venus in the Earthly Spread, you can be creative, original, and entertaining. Being sensitive or temperamental, however, implies that you may be prone to impulsive behavior and at times be too willful. Resist allowing these fluctuating conditions to create tension, as they can also impair your thinking or lead to excessive worry. Nevertheless, your warm sociability and ability to radiate personal magnetism can make you very popular with others. Valuing friendship, you have a gift for mixing with people from all walks of life.

The planetary influences of Jupiter and Mars in your Spiritual Spread indicate that your ability to make the right decisions gives you the edge. This is particularly evident if you are self-reliant and motivated. Your enthusiasm, optimistic outlook, and love of enterprise suggest that you can be independent and daring. It warns, however, that your love of freedom may lead you to rebel against restrictions or feel frustrated by limitations.

Your Two Replacement Cards Are the 10 of Hearts & the Jack of Diamonds.

As the Jack of Clubs you share the same planetary position as the 10 of Hearts in the Earthly Spread. This signifies that you can easily impress other people with your engaging personality. Usually you have a great deal of natural charm and charisma as well as a big heart with compassion for others. With your innate people skills, you can achieve success in work dealing with the public or the world of entertainment. The power to impress others, coupled with your quick wit, suggests that you also enjoy socializing and big gatherings.

As the Jack of Clubs you share the same position as the Jack of Diamonds in the Spiritual Spread. The youthful and dynamic influence of these two cards link to an androgynous quality and indicate that you will be active and spirited throughout your life. A material streak associated with the Jack of Diamonds suggests that you may have to watch that your quest for financial security does not stop you from accomplishing the work needed to fulfill your outstanding creative potential. Nevertheless,

with your willpower and strong convictions you can overcome your challenges and are often rewarded for your efforts.

You usually have special or karmic links with people who are represented by the 10 of Hearts and the Jack of Diamonds, as you share the same planetary positions. You can be soul mates or understand each other very well. It also indicates that enterprising or young people will play an important role in your life. Even if you do not get along, you can both see clearly how the other person operates.

Your Mercury Card is . . .

The 9 of Diamonds
- Highly intuitive, you have a sixth sense when it comes to money and business.
- Optimistic and considerate, you can be generous, charitable, and supportive.
- A good sense of values and a responsible attitude toward financial matters can be the key to your success.
- Although you possess the ability to think big, being obstinate or impatient can turn out to be costly.
- Learning to let go can eliminate frustration and worry.
- You should have good mental rapport and special communication with 9 of Diamonds people, as they activate your Mercury Card.

The Jack of Clubs Planetary Card Sequence

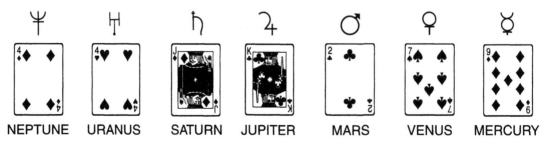

NEPTUNE   URANUS   SATURN   JUPITER   MARS   VENUS   MERCURY

These people can also be friends or business partners.

Your Venus Card is . . .

The 7 of Spades

- Sensitive and idealistic, you usually have strong principles about love and family.
- This card indicates that relationships based on shared work or spiritual values can be highly beneficial for you.
- To avoid emotional disappointment, resist setting your expectations about personal love too high.
- In your relationships you are independent with a strong need for space and freedom. This may attract you to more unconventional relationships.
- This card denotes karmic links to partners and implies that close relationships are usually associated with spiritual lessons.
- You may encounter unusual relationships with mystical influences.
- Usually you are drawn to people represented by the 7 of Spades. They are ideal for love and romance as well as close friendships and good business partnerships, especially if you share the same ideals.

Your Mars Card is . . .

The 2 of Clubs

- Mentally quick and able to retaliate in the right way, you can respond quickly to people or situations.
- Since you are witty and entertaining, resist wasting your powerful thoughts on biting criticism or trivial activities such as fault finding.
- Usually you are stimulated by new ideas, so communicating with others can make you feel motivated.
- Although you are in your element in conver-

sations and discussions, guard against a tendency to argue.
- The relationships you have with 2 of Clubs people can be good if you both positively encourage and motivate each other, but resist being competitive or argumentative.

Your Jupiter Card is . . .

The King of Clubs

- The assimilation of knowledge, whether practical, intellectual, or spiritual, is the key to your well-being or spiritual growth.
- Mature individuals with good knowledge or experience can inspire you, expand your horizons, or help you to succeed.
- This royal card indicates that if you accept the responsibilities of leadership you can rise quickly to positions of influence in your chosen field.
- Your success is often based on what you know and how well you use your analytical skills.
- King of Clubs people and intelligent men can be benefactors who enhance your life or bring lucky opportunities. This can be a spiritual link or you can both be successful together materially, but avoid excesses.

Your Saturn Card is . . .

The Jack of Diamonds

- This royal card implies that in order to achieve material success under Saturn's terms, you need to be patient, hardworking, and self-disciplined.
- A mature approach to career and business can bring good financial rewards.
- Avoid associating with 'get rich quick' schemes, as they can backfire; the safe routes are usually your best option.
- Jack of Diamonds individuals can play an important role in your life if you are able to

learn from them about responsibilities. Although your relationship with them may not always be easy, these relationships often offer very valuable lessons.

Your Uranus Card is . . .

The 4 of Hearts

- This card indicates that in maturity you are more likely to find emotional fulfillment and contentment.
- By being detached, you are able to bring calm and harmony into your life.
- If you rebel against something you can become very stubborn at your own expense.
- If you develop your natural humanitarian streak, you like to do so in a practical way and have much to offer others.
- Creative expression and spiritual or intellectual interests can bring a great deal of satisfaction, especially in later years.
- 4 of Hearts people can offer you more objective views, especially about emotional issues. Their valuable insight can help you see things in a new light. This is also a good card for friendship.

Your Neptune Card is . . .

The 4 of Diamonds

- Benefits and success can come from travel and working in foreign lands.
- The double influence of the 4 of Hearts and the 4 of Diamonds indicates that the later part of your life is likely to be the most rewarding and materially secure.
- You are a practical visionary. You can use this talent in business or for mystical experiences.
- 4 of Diamonds people may link to your plans for the future, dreams, and ideals. Although you may have a psychic connection between, you also stay practical.

Your Challenge Card is . . .

The 2 of Spades

- Learning to balance between give and take in partnerships may be one of your biggest lessons.
- Resist becoming involved in power struggles, as they can deplete your energies and cause you disharmony and stress.
- Cooperation and compromise hold the key to changing the dynamics of your relationships.
- 2 of Spades people can help you to transform your life by challenging you to bring out the best in you, but resist ego conflicts.

The Result of Your Challenge Card is . . .

The 8 of Hearts

- You will get the love and support you need when you show your devotion and loyalty.
- If you are locked into power struggles with others you may not be responding well to your challenge.
- To overcome your obstacles you need to rely on your resolve, emotional strength, and creative output.
- Your personal magnetism and popularity will increase as you apply your love and personal charm on others.
- People represented by the 8 of Hearts can help you to develop your creativity and express your feelings. Your reactions to them often reflect how you are responding to your personal challenges.

Famous People Who Are the Jack of Clubs

Oprah Winfrey, Ben Affleck, Elizabeth Taylor, John Steinbeck, Napoleon Bonaparte, Albrecht Dürer, Eleanor Roosevelt, Sir Walter Scott, Jimmy Cagney, W. C. Fields, Joseph Turner, H. W. Longfellow, Noam Chomsky,

Arturo Toscanini, Roald Dahl, Thomas Paine, Salman Rushdie, Shirley Temple, Roy Orbison, Gloria Steinem, Harold Robbins, Joanne Woodward, Tom Selleck, Anton Chekhov, Princess Anne, Daryl Hall, Michael Bolton, Paula Abdul, Heather Graham, Chelsea Clinton, Notorious B.I.G., Aretha Franklin, Kathleen Turner, Luke Perry, Sarah Jessica Parker

Birthdays Governed by the Jack of Clubs

January 29: Aquarius   Ruler: Uranus
Your warm and friendly manner can conceal your brilliant mind and innate skills. Your ruler, Uranus, suggests that you are intellectually bright with progressive or liberal views. In order to benefit from all your great talents, however, you need to adopt a mature and responsible attitude. Although you may not be very ambitious, your executive skills or leadership qualities can be called upon to help others in worthwhile causes. Alternatively, your natural cerebral capabilities may inspire you to be mentally creative. Whatever you do, use your charm and calm manner rather than eccentric moods to win people over.

February 27: Pisces   Ruler: Neptune
Intuitive and intelligent, your foresight and excellent organizational skills imply that you are highly suited for leadership positions if you are willing to act maturely and be responsible. Although your ruler, Neptune, endows you with imagination and creativity, your common sense and business acumen indicate that you can soon turn your lofty ideas into profitable enterprises. Wanting stability and security, you may find it hard to adjust to changes that are outside your control. Nevertheless, variety can bring a breath of fresh air to your otherwise pragmatic nature. Luckily, your quick perception, good sense of timing, and practical consideration usually indicate that if you are

patient you can achieve success, especially through intellectual pursuits.

March 25: Aries   Ruler: Mars
Your cerebral aptitude and decisive actions suggest that you are an enthusiastic individual with a keen mind and good powers of perception. Your ruler, Mars, usually grants you vitality and leadership qualities, as it urges you to strive toward your objectives. Although your sharp wit and constructive intellect rarely leave you lost for words, resist being too willful or argumentative when entering into discussions or debates. Instead, find creative ways to express your dynamic personality, idealistic thoughts, and astute observations. A strong need to communicate also suggests that you find greater rewards when you share your interests and inspired ideas with others.

April 23: Taurus   Ruler: Venus
Mentally creative, sensitive, and charming, your purposeful nature signifies that you are an instinctive and mentally quick individual with a dry sense of humor. Your ruler, Venus, under the influence of the 7 of Spades, usually accents the spiritual aspects of your innate talents and profound mind. It also warns against fears of being isolated or unloved. Although your ability to grasp information and ideas swiftly can give you the advantage when dealing with others, overindulgence, lack of self-discipline, and fluctuating moods can challenge your health and undermine your efforts. Nevertheless, when you find your inspired goals you can achieve success by mastering your unique talents and empowering yourself.

May 21: Taurus/Gemini
Ruler: Venus/Mercury
Gregarious and charismatic, your friendly personality and youthful nature indicate that you are an intelligent individual with flair and a

good sense of humor. The influences of both Mercury and Venus suggest that your creative thoughts and way with words can make you diplomatic and persuasive. If you let frustration or impatience cloud your judgments your vacillating moods can undermine your great efforts. In order to succeed, you may have to discipline your dynamic mind and master your skills. When you have faith in your inspired goals let your foresight or strong sixth sense guide you to your accomplishments and success.

June 19: Gemini   Ruler: Mercury

Your perceptive and astute mind shows that you are an intuitive and intelligent individual, with ambitious and imaginative ideas. Your charm and friendly manner imply that you can succeed in all type of careers relating to the public. Mercury, your ruler, usually grants you common sense and sound judgment. Able to learn quickly, you can accumulate knowledge and develop your analytical abilities. Being versatile, creative, and clever suggests that you have innate talents worth developing. Although these attributes can help you to rise to positions of leadership or advance your career, guard against letting impatience or an irresponsible attitude toward your financial affairs undermine your efforts.

July 17: Cancer   Ruler: Moon

Your receptivity, inspired ideas, and astute mind suggest that you are a sensitive individual with tremendous potential. Touched by a spark of genius, your sharp intelligence indicates that you can make the most of your talents and opportunities when you trust your intuitive feelings. Although you show your leadership qualities when you combine your enthusiasm with your common sense, a reluctance to listen to advice or criticism can lead to

you behave immaturely. Idealistic and intelligent, however, when you discipline your powerful thoughts and channel your emotions, you can make your dreams come true.

August 15: Leo   Ruler: Sun

Idealistic, instinctive, and mentally quick, your common sense and enthusiastic nature, imply that you are a resourceful individual with creative potential. Your bright and easygoing manner often conceals your vitality, strong willpower, and mental restlessness. Your ruler, the Sun, usually grants you self-confidence, a wealth of ideas, and a touch of the dramatic that you can use in theatrical pursuits or just in keeping others entertained. Although you are usually rational and practical, a stubborn reluctance to listen to advice or an argumentative streak suggests that you learn more from your mistakes and past experiences. When you realize that you have much to gain from collaborating with others you can become a force for good in large groups or enterprises.

September 13: Virgo   Ruler: Mercury

Your ability to turn your knowledge and skills into financial gain signifies that you are a capable and intelligent individual with excellent intuitive power. Full of bright ideas, your ruler, Mercury, indicates that when you develop a mature attitude to values and money you can use your pragmatism and analytical skills to gain success and resolve financial problems. By learning to let go and acknowledging past mistakes, you can also overcome any feelings of frustration or disappointment. Mentally quick, you have an innate talent for writing, research, or business and usually enjoy being of practical help to others. Generous and considerate, your achievement in life often depends on your patience, hard work, and flexibility with people.

October 11: Libra   Ruler: Venus

Idealistic and friendly, your creative mental power needs to find a channel of inspiration in order to manifest your great intellectual abilities and leadership potential. Although you want a great deal of freedom to do as you please, your ruler, Venus, warns that without the necessary self-discipline and innovative planning you can easily scatter your energies on social activities and self-indulgence. Luckily, your desire for knowledge and inspired ideas can provide you with the incentive to work for something worthwhile. Your people skills, inner faith, and youthful enthusiasm can also be the contributing factors to your success and prosperity.

November 9: Scorpio   Ruler: Mars

Sensitive, intuitive, and unyielding, your inner strength and insight suggest that you are a forceful individual with powerful emotions. Mars your ruler signifies that your profound intellect can penetrate to the heart of the matter. Although these planets can make you resolute and determined, your success is often based on your adaptability to situations and willingness to compromise. Your distinctive wit or timed humor can also help you channel your mental creativity in positive ways. Your biting sarcasm or critical views, on the other hand, can highlight your insecurities and fears. By resisting power struggles and learning to overcome frustrations, especially in your close partnerships, you can achieve the equality, harmony, and success you so desire.

December 7: Sagittarius   Ruler: Jupiter

Your decisive actions and inspired ideas indicate that you have the potential to rise to positions of authority and influence. For your success you need to invest time and money in developing your tremendous creative and mental potential. According to your ruler, Jupiter, your search for knowledge and wisdom can bring great rewards. You also benefit from widening your horizons through travel or exploring more lofty concepts. Lack of faith or purpose, on the other hand, can deplete your enthusiasm or cause you to take risks just for the sake of testing your mental agility. Nevertheless, as a persuasive communicator you can excel in all types of intellectual activities that are based on shared information and ideas.

◆ THE JACK OF DIAMONDS ◆

Being a Jack Card, you are friendly and charming with a youthful spirit. As you are also a royalty card of the Diamonds suit you possess a dramatic sense and excellent evaluation skills. The combination of your natural talents, image awareness, and wealth of ideas gives you the potential for much inspiration and success. Under the influences of Neptune and Uranus in the Earthly Spread you are a good judge of public trends due to your intuitive understanding of what people want. Being able to talk to individuals from all different areas of society, you can make an excellent salesperson, whether selling goods, a concept, or an ideal. Your natural talent with people can activate a humanitarian streak that, if developed, can bring you many emotional rewards. At times, however, you may be torn between your high ideals and your need for money or material recognition.

Under the influences of Venus and Uranus in the Spiritual Spread you have a bright personality and are often ahead of your time. Since you can be entertaining you are likely to be popular with others. Your strong individuality stimulates your original ideas, and you usually prefer to do things your own way rather than be dictated to by others. Equally, you need to be given a lot of freedom in other areas of life, including your relationships. The Jack influence of your birthday can bring immaturity, however, if you let other people do all the work for you rather than taking care of your own responsibilities. Usually, though, you are productive and optimistic, with an ability to enchant others.

Your Two Replacement Cards Are the 3 of Spades & the Jack of Clubs.

As the Jack of Diamonds you share the same planetary position as the 3 of Spades in the Spiritual Spread. This signifies that it is important to express your inner creativity, whether through your work or at home. The more creative and light you feel about life, the easier it to be decisive and avoid worry or negative thinking. Since you are likely to have many interests it is important to stay focused.

Since you also share the same planetary position as the Jack of Clubs in the Earthly Spread, you are mentally sharp, learn quickly, and enjoy passing on your knowledge to others. You have a knack for being very amusing while still getting your message across. This enhances your skills in writing or presentation of your ideas. Despite your remarkable potential, avoid letting your need for financial security stop you from taking the risks needed to be more expressive.

You have special or karmic links with people who are represented by the 3 of Spades and Jack of Clubs. As you share the same planetary positions you can be soul mates or understand each other very well. Even if you do not get along, you can both see clearly how the other person operates.

Your Mercury Card is . . .

The 4 of Hearts
- You prefer to be honest and direct in your communication with others.
- Guard against being mentally stubborn or fixed in your ideas.
- You have a gift for communicating in a warm and sociable yet down-to-earth way that others find endearing.
- You fare better when you have a definite plan in mind.
- 4 of Hearts people can arouse your enthusiasm and enhance your communication skills. This is a good link for the exchange of ideas.

Your Venus Card is . . .

The 4 of Diamonds
- Although you value loyalty in your relationships, this can sometimes be at odds with your need for personal freedom.
- It is important to pick partners who allow you to express your free spirit.

The Jack of Diamonds Planetary Card Sequence

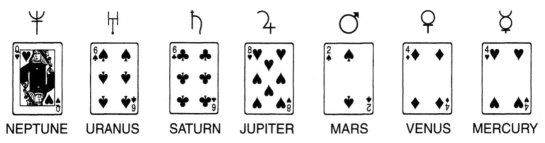

NEPTUNE   URANUS   SATURN   JUPITER   MARS   VENUS   MERCURY

- Being materially shrewd suggests that you can be attracted to partners who are practical, genuine, and sincere. Nevertheless, they can't be boring, as they have to keep up with your quick wit and fast intelligence.
- Although usually friendly, sociable, and expressive, you can also sometimes experience feeling emotionally inhibited or repressed.
- Valuing friendship and often ahead of your time, you may have a more unconventional or open approach to relationships.
- People who are represented by the 4 of Diamonds Card can bring love and friendship into your life. This link is also good for business as well as romance.

Your Mars Card is . . .

The 2 of Spades

- Your cooperative attitude and flair for public relations help you succeed in partnership or teamwork situations.
- If you actively and courageously confront your fears you will discover help comes to you from unexpected sources.
- By working to achieve balanced relationships with others you can avoid arguments or dependent situations.
- 2 of Spades people can stimulate you to be more enterprising, dynamic, or daring. They could encourage you to be productive and you may accomplish much together. Alternatively, you may become competitive or argue with them.

Your Jupiter Card is . . .

The 8 of Hearts

- A love of beauty and the good life suggests you prefer to be surrounded by harmony and luxury. This is good if it spurs you on to accomplish as long as you do not become too self-indulgent.

- You possess an aptitude for combining business with pleasure that can bring you great material benefits.
- The emotional power here suggests you can gain a great deal from travel, philosophy, law, publishing, foreign cultures, higher education, spirituality, healing, or writing.
- People who are the 8 of Hearts Card can stimulate your optimism or be fortunate for you in some way. They can provide opportunities or be a spiritual link.

Your Saturn Card is . . .

The 6 of Clubs

- One of your tests can be to get the balance right between ambition and inertia.
- When disciplined you can be enthusiastic and knowledgeable, making yourself an authority figure in your field of interest.
- Avoid letting your desire for peace and a comfortable life cause you to get stuck in a rut, or you may experience anxiety without really knowing why.
- If you acknowledge and respect your strong intuitive powers you can gain greatly from them.
- People who are the 6 of Clubs can show you where you need to work on yourself. This can be challenging or enlightening. This can be a karmic link.

Your Uranus Card is . . .

The 6 of Spades

- You can be worldly yet home loving, with strong family ties.
- Being practical and able to give an objective opinion, you may find yourself an adviser for others, whether at work or for your friends.
- With your good taste and an eye for style, beauty, and form, you may enjoy creative projects or beautifying your home.

- 6 of Spades people can help you be more impersonal about yourself and your life. They may stimulate your originality or desire for freedom. This is a good link for friendship.

Your Neptune Card is . . .

The Queen of Hearts
- Underneath your confident persona you are sensitive and imaginative.
- Being aware of image, you usually look stylish or enjoy glamour.
- Long journeys overseas can especially bring out your loving, sociable, and theatrical side.
- Your visionary ability and idealism tend to get stronger as you get older.
- The more you positively develop your sensitivity and intuition, the more compassionate you become.
- You may develop a desire to write later in life.
- You can have a strong sensitive or psychic link with people who are the Queen of Hearts. You may share the same dreams or ideals, but guard against unrealistic expectations. Positively, this person could enhance your vision or compassion.

Your Challenge Card is . . .

The 10 of Clubs
- Find people and projects that fire your enthusiasm.
- Think and radiate success.
- 10 of Clubs people can usually excite you or confront you in a daring way. These people can help you to transform your life if you rise to the challenge.

The Result of Your Challenge Card is . . .

The 8 of Diamonds
- You can help others with your strength and strong convictions.
- You are hardworking, determined, and motivated.
- If you are locked into power struggles with others you may not be responding well to your challenge.
- People represented by the 8 of Diamonds can stimulate your resolve and tenacity. They often reflect how you are responding to your challenges.

Famous People Who Are the Jack of Diamonds

Enrique Iglesias, Peter O'Toole, Kate Moss, Harry S. Truman, Sade, Susan Sontag, James Baldwin, James Hoffa, Jack Benny, Liza Minnelli, James Taylor, Jack Kerouac, Gregory Hines, Paul Kantner, Al Jarreau, Joseph Pulitzer, Omar Sharif, Jane Roberts, Sonny Liston, Bjorn Borg, Sandra Bernhard, Gina Lollobrigida, Alan Parker, Steven Seagal, Haley Joel Osment, Aaliyah

Birthdays Governed by the Jack of Diamonds

January 16: Capricorn   Ruler: Saturn
Friendly and mentally sharp, you are reserved and security conscious yet youthful and entertaining. Being practical and responsible, you usually like order and routine in your life. Nevertheless, you can also be inventive, original, and ahead of your time. By developing faith you avoid the pitfalls of negative thinking or becoming too attached to material desires. With your natural creativity and charismatic personality, if disciplined and thinking positively you should have no trouble in achieving success.

February 14: Aquarius   Ruler: Uranus
Sociable and friendly, you are an intelligent individual with a strong love of home and family. As you are also mentally quick and imaginative, you often have many ideas that are ahead of their time. Although amiable, with an ability to get on with everybody, at times you can seem stubborn or aloof. You may need to learn to take chances rather than stay in a comfortable routine. Nevertheless, usually hardworking and original, with a shrewd understanding of human nature, you can be creative and productive. Even though you are practical, you may wish to further develop your dramatic or intuitive gifts through the arts or metaphysical studies.

March 12: Pisces   Ruler: Neptune
Your bright expressive personality and good social skills can often hide your emotional sensitivity. Nevertheless, you can also be determined, strong-willed, and resourceful. Having such fast responses and a spirit of enterprise, you especially respond well to inspiration. Your sense of drama and gift with words can aid you in creative endeavors or in leadership positions. At times you may have to balance your need for self-expression with your desire to please others. By being decisive and cultivating faith, you avoid worry and insecurity, aiding your overall success.

April 10: Aries   Ruler: Mars
Pioneering and action-oriented, you possess a progressive outlook on life. With strong convictions, you really succeed when you add patience and perseverance to your drive and good social skills. Being idealistic, you may sometimes be caught between what inspires you and what is financially lucrative. Although independent and determined, be careful that you do not use your strong will to dictate to others or become selfish. Nevertheless, natu-

rally charismatic, you are likely to be witty and popular. A more serious side to your nature, however, urges you to accomplish and implies it is often through self-mastery that you find the greatest fulfillment.

May 8: Taurus   Ruler: Venus
Down-to-earth and straightforward, yet friendly and personable, you are a determined individual with strong convictions. The combination of your sensitivity and pragmatic approach suggests that you often use your intuition or gut feeling when making everyday decisions. At times you may seem a contradictory mixture of opposites being idealistic, light, and entertaining despite being power conscious with a strong drive for material accomplishment. Mentally quick, you have a talent for writing, analysis, research, or business and may enjoy being of practical help to others.

June 6: Gemini   Ruler: Mercury
You possess fast mental responses and a friendly personality to aid you in the communication of your many creative ideas. Ambitious and enterprising, you have a strong sense of individuality. Although you prefer to be honest and direct in your dealings with others, avoid being critical or too outspoken. Even though you are worldly, you are also home loving and caring. Displaying an interesting mix of idealism and materialism, you have excellent people skills and natural advisory abilities.

July 4: Cancer   Ruler: Moon
Charismatic and emotionally impressionable, you are a fascinating blend of charm, idealism, and practical common sense. Loyal and dependable, you are very protective of those in your charge and usually willing to work hard to achieve results. Equally, you enjoy luxuries, relaxing, and the good things of life. Being car-

ing and security conscious, however, home and family play an especially important part in your life plan. Depending on your mood, at times you are very expressive and at other times you may withdraw and curb your emotions, but it is always wise for you to avoid becoming stubborn or bossy. Creative and talented, you have the potential for prosperity and success, but it is through self-discipline that you achieve the greatest rewards.

August 2: Leo   Ruler: Sun

Dramatic and proud, your warm charm and excellent people skills endear you to others. You enjoy being entertaining and have many creative gifts you may wish to develop, especially in acting or writing. A person of many emotions, you can be both gentle and considerate or bold and dynamic. Being creative suggests that whatever you do you will put your own individual stamp on it. Being especially playful, it is also necessary to develop your discipline and sense of responsibility. Although you can be fiery and independent, you usually gain most through collaborative efforts.

♠ THE JACK OF SPADES ♠

Quick and intuitive, the dynamic influence of this royal card indicates that you are usually a creative and original individual with a youthful or spirited attitude to life. Since this card is also called the entry card to the spiritual realms, it represents choices and morality. On the one hand you can aspire to noble aims and on the other you may be tempted to utilize your ingenious talents incorrectly. Your success and accomplishment therefore depend on how you prefer to live your life and the direction you take. Being associated with the Spades suit suggests that your great achievements are usually based on your hard work and dedication to

your inspired goals. The quicker you become mature and self-disciplined, the faster you reach your objectives.

The planetary influences of Mars and Uranus in the Earthly Spread suggest that you can be a very strong-minded and courageous individual. When motivated you can summon an extraordinary amount of energy in order to achieve your objectives. Your need for freedom and independence, however, implies that you are not likely to be comfortable in restrictive situations or yielding to the will of others. Although your independence is important to you, resist being too willful or rebellious.

The planetary influence of the Sun, and in particular Mars, in your Spiritual Spread indicates that you are a strong individualist whose advancement in life is usually of your own accord. With pride, ambition, and daring, you value achievement and like to keep active and get things moving. With an ability to make fast decisions, you do best when you have a cause to support, are fighting against social injustice, or are actively involved in a creative project. Although you may have to guard against an impatient or competitive streak, if you accept the responsibilities that come with leadership and success, you gain the courage and stamina to take the initiative and the qualities necessary to inspire others.

Your Two Replacement Cards Are the 10 of Clubs & the 7 of Clubs.

As a Jack of Spades you share planetary positions with two cards from the Clubs suit. This emphasizes your desire for knowledge and an innate curiosity about the mysteries of life. In the Earthly Spread you share the same planetary position as the 10 of Clubs. This signifies that you can achieve great success in all types of intellectual pursuits or projects that fire your imagination. Its influence enables you to quickly grasp ideas, assimilate knowledge, and make sound judgments.

As the Jack of Spades you share the same planetary position as the 7 of Clubs in the Spiritual Spread. The influence of this card suggests that with inner faith and trust you can overcome self-doubts and negative attitudes that can undermine your resolve. The challenge of this card is often associated with self-mastery and mind over matter. With the help of this card you may also be able to deepen your spiritual awareness or learn about the metaphysical world.

You usually have special or karmic links with people who are represented by the 7 of Clubs and the 10 of Clubs, as you share the same planetary positions. You can be soul mates or understand each other very well. It also indicates that women will play an important role in your life, be it a source of inspiration or trouble. Even if you do not get along, you can both see clearly how the other person operates.

Your Mercury Card is . . .

The 8 of Clubs
- You like to think constructively, and once you have made up your mind you can be very determined.
- You are highly intelligent, and with little effort you can accomplish much intellectually.

- Although you are a quick learner, you can also be a strong skeptic with a stubborn streak.
- Good education early in life almost guarantees success later on.
- Your creative or spiritual aspirations can elevate you to extraordinary achievements.
- You should have good mental rapport and special communication with 8 of Clubs, people as they activate your Mercury Card. These people can also be lifelong friends or business partners.

Your Venus Card is . . .

The 6 of Diamonds
- You need to choose your partners carefully or build relationships based on shared values.
- Creating harmony and the security of a good home is important in your relationships, but once you find it avoid getting stuck in a comfortable rut.
- Your generosity and kindness are often rewarded by good karma.
- If you are not careful or realistic about your financial responsibilities, debt and obligations can become a challenge.
- In order to overcome financial limitations in your early adult years, avoid taking the easy options as you may regret them later on.
- Usually you are drawn to 6 of Diamonds people, especially if they share your creative

The Jack of Spades Planetary Card Sequence

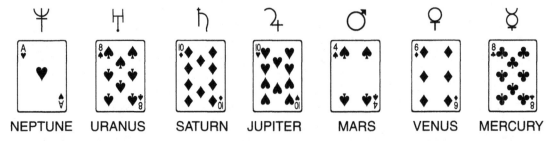

NEPTUNE   URANUS   SATURN   JUPITER   MARS   VENUS   MERCURY

interests. They are ideal for love and romance as well as close friendships and good business partnerships.

Your Mars Card is . . .

The 4 of Spades

- High productivity and good organizational skills indicate that you have very good career prospects if you are willing to work hard.
- Your material success is based on your knowledge, common sense, and business acumen; therefore, you need not accept inferior positions or opportunities that can restrict your freedom or hinder your individual self-expression.
- In order to succeed you need to work with responsible individuals who can stimulate you into action yet be reliable.
- The relationships you have with 4 of Spades individuals can be special or good if you both share the same aspirations. Avoid situations or individuals that are too competitive, especially in your work environment. People who are not pragmatic, direct, and entirely honest can drain your energy or cause you stress or losses.

Your Jupiter Card is . . .

The 10 of Hearts

- You are usually a very generous and helpful individual, with high ideals.
- This card grants you natural charisma, charm, and the ability to influence or inspire other people.
- Avoid getting emotionally carried away. Your emotional power can be channeled successfully into all types of creative endeavors.
- You can enjoy social popularity or prosperity in all type of people or public-related activities.

- You can be a force for good if you are doing humanitarian or charitable work.
- 10 of Hearts people can have a beneficial influence on you. They can help you to express your feelings with greater ease. You may share the same ideals, creative interests, or passions. They can also be linked to new opportunities or success in business. Avoid excesses together.

Your Saturn Card is . . .

The 10 of Diamonds

- Since this planet never gives anything away for free, success is often linked to hard work or carrying the burden of responsibility.
- Although you can be progressive, you achieve more by working with the system than against it.
- You career and success may be connected to large institutions or organizations.
- You may be linked to an inheritance, but it often comes with responsibilities or a price tag.
- 10 of Diamonds individuals can play an important role in your life, if you are able to learn from them about efficiency, accomplishment, and loyalty. Although your relationship with them may not be always easy, their contributions are often very valuable lessons.

Your Uranus Card is . . .

The 8 of Spades

- An interest in reforms, better working conditions, or other humanitarian causes may bring you new career opportunities in your middle years.
- You can become an authority in your field of expertise due to your unique organizational skills and original ways of problem solving.
- You show your inner strength by staying objective and detached.

- You have the power to overcome most health problems and heal yourself as well as others.
- In your middle years you are likely to experience something that will empower you and increase your awareness or ultimately turn you toward spirituality or esoteric subjects.
- 8 of Spades people can help you be more objective about yourself or be good friends. Although 8 of Spades people can offer you a valuable insight into new financial opportunities, resist making financial commitments too quickly.

Your Neptune Card is . . .

The Ace of Hearts

- The emotional power at your disposal is linked to your beliefs and ideals, so make sure your goals are realistic and clear.
- Strong desires for new experiences may lead you to make changes or travel in later years.
- You can utilize your strong vision and imagination to achieve outstanding results in creative projects.
- Dubious notions, too much self-interest, or impulsive actions can lead to unusual emotional experiences.
- Working with compassion and understanding toward others can secure an emotionally rewarding time in later years.
- Ace of Hearts people may inspire you to do something new and exciting or share your dreams and ideals. Although you both may have a psychic connection remain pragmatic.

Your Challenge Card is . . .

The Ace of Diamonds

- You benefit from initiating new concepts that can bring progress and advantages to others.

- You overcome many of your obstacles by balancing your ideals with your material needs.
- Keep your focus and realize your dreams.
- Resist letting your strong desire for material success undermine your integrity.
- Ace of Diamonds people can usually stimulate you to start new projects or transform your life. Although these people can challenge you positively to change, resist becoming involved in dubious enterprises or power struggles.

The Result of Your Challenge Card is . . .

The Queen of Diamonds

- Take your position as a leader or an authority figure.
- Be of service to others by using your organizational skills or business expertise.
- Use your entrepreneurial talents or resources for humanitarian causes.
- People who are represented by the Queen of Diamonds can inspire you to be enterprising or generous and often reflect how you are responding to your challenges.

Famous People Who Are the Jack of Spades

J. R. R. Tolkien, Clark Gable, George Martin, Sherilyn Fenn, Fritjof Capra, Victoria Principal, Don Everly, Brandon Lee, Pauly Shore, Stephen Stills, Lisa Marie Presley, Mel Gibson

Birthdays Governed by the Jack of Spades

January 3: Capricorn   Ruler: Saturn

Although you are an intuitive and emotionally sensitive individual, your ruler, Saturn, indicates that you can be highly successful by being hardworking and dedicated. Usually your friendliness, patience, or relaxed manner can make others feel at ease. Your business acumen or pragmatic outlook imply that even if you have grand and idealistic ideas, you can turn them into profitable projects and earn handsomely from your efforts. Alternatively, your curiosity and desire for higher knowledge may reveal your intellectual acumen and your innate talent for science, philosophy, or metaphysical subjects. Whatever you do, resist taking unnecessary risks, especially when dealing with important financial matters.

February 1: Aquarius   Ruler: Uranus
Being receptive to other people's views suggests that you are usually an objective individual with idealistic beliefs. Your ruler, Uranus, indicates that you love your freedom, and with your innate talents and independent outlook you can also be creative and original. When you feel inspired by a concept or a project you usually show how dedicated and determined you really are. In fact, there is very little you cannot achieve once you exercise self-discipline and focus on your heart's desire. If you choose to rise above mundane existence you may find that exploring philosophy or metaphysical subjects can be empowering and highly rewarding.

♥ ♣ THE QUEENS ♦ ♠

USUALLY CREATIVE AND multitalented, your royal card indicates that you are a sensitive yet highly capable individual. Your authoritative demeanor and good reasoning power indicates that you usually find it easy to promote ideas and influence others. Being determined and resourceful, once you set your mind to accomplish something, very little can stand in your way. Your ability to organize and take charge of situations implies that you are ideally suited for executive positions. Not always in the forefront, however, you can also be highly influential behind the scenes. Although your innate leadership qualities can help you ease your way to the top, you also find personal fulfillment when you are able to support, inspire, or guide others. As a sympathetic, helpful, or friendly individual, your power is found through your optimism and generosity. Since this card represents the female gender, whether you are a man or a woman, you are usually magnetic, amiable, intuitive, and receptive.

Queen of Hearts

Creative and sensitive, you empower yourself through your ability to love and express your powerful emotions. By caring or helping others you also show your compassionate or philanthropic nature. When you translate personal desires into altruistic deeds or creative projects you manifest your real power. You often win the love and admiration you want when you are being kind and thoughtful.

Queen of Clubs

Intuitive and mentally quick, your innate perception and intellectual capabilities indicate that you find your inner strength through your creativity, communication, and knowledge. You also empower yourself when you inspire others with your insightful mind.

Queen of Diamonds

Commanding, practical, and talented, your heightened sense of values and business acumen indicates that you can be highly successful in the material world. In order to find personal fulfillment, however, you need to establish what is really valuable and important in life. You empower yourself when you can combine your material resources with your benevolent spirit in order to benefit yourself and others.

Queen of Spades

Your leadership qualities are often shown by your dedication and hard work. Your astute and discriminate nature can contribute to your success. Your authoritative demeanor and your strong principles usually make you an excellent disciplinarian. You empower yourself when you rise above the drudgery of day-to-day existence and find inspiration in something profound or spiritually enlightening.

♥THE QUEEN OF HEARTS♥

This royal card represents dynamic emotions, sensitivity, and creativity. Your strong need for self-expression and the creative force at your disposal indicate that you are usually dramatic and passionate. Often very attractive, your innate charm can influence or impress other people. Although you can be caring, gentle, and kind, your intense or excitable nature may lead you to act impulsively and show the temperamental side of your character. Your success, therefore, depends on how well you handle your strong feelings.

The double planetary influence of Neptune in your Earthly Spread emphasizes the loving, idealistic, and romantic side of your personality. Neptune's potent impact also implies that you are highly imaginative and receptive. The positive message of this card suggests that besides using your powerful emotions for creative self-expression, you are also able to inspire other people by showing sympathy and compassion. A negative aspect of this planetary influence warns against being too impressionable, as it may lead to mood swings or expressions of negative feelings such as an explosive temper or lack of self-esteem.

The planetary influences of Venus and Saturn in your Spiritual Spread indicates that you can be hardworking, dedicated, and loyal. Unlike Neptune's influence, these two planets can heighten your strong sense of duty and pragmatic outlook. The self-discipline called for by this card also suggests that when you learn to balance your forceful character with tolerance and generosity, you can express your strong feelings and get recognition for your many talents.

Your Two Replacement Cards Are the 9 of Clubs & the 10 of Spades.

As the Queen of Hearts you share the same planetary position as the 9 of Clubs in the Earthly Spread. This signifies that you are highly perceptive and intuitive. Often much of your success depends on your positive mental outlook and how determined you are. Feelings of frustration and disappointment can undermine your efforts if you believe that you can achieve your goals without the necessary hard work. By showing your patience, and perseverance, you can rise to the high calling of this card. The path to your great accomplishment is often found through a positive mental attitude.

As the Queen of Hearts you also share the same planetary position as the 10 of Spades in the Spiritual Spread. This card indicates that you identify with power and achievement. Your potential for accomplishment is immense if you recognize and accept that responsibilities come with success. The key element here is whether you can turn your inspired ideas into something tangible. In order to achieve some of your ambitious plans you need to realize that attainment and higher wisdom are usually gained through constant dedication.

You usually have special or karmic links with people who are represented by the 9 of Clubs and the 10 of Spades, as you share the same planetary positions. You can be soul mates or understand each other very well. Even if you do not get along, you can both see clearly how the other person operates.

Your Mercury Card is . . .

The 10 of Clubs
- Your ability to express your quick intelligence creatively is evident from an early age.
- The mental power of this card also enables you to assimilate information quickly and efficiently.
- You identify with success, particularly if you are mentally enthusiastic.
- Your analytical and inquiring mind suggests that you are usually inquisitive.
- Although you need challenges and mentally stimulating situations, being impatient or headstrong can undermine your great potential for intellectual fulfillment.

- You should have good mental rapport and special communication with people who represent the 10 of Clubs, as they activate your Mercury Card. These people can also be friends or partners.

Your Venus Card is . . .

The 8 of Diamonds
- Charm and natural business sense imply that you can combine your social life with your career.
- You can find financial gains and success through developing innate creative or artistic talents.
- You are attracted to those of power and wealth who can match your own determination and ability to be businesslike.
- Equally you admire hard working individuals who are success-oriented.
- Avoid getting into power conflicts in your relationships.
- You may receive financial support from partners or be rewarded for your creative efforts.
- Usually you are drawn to people who are represented by the 8 of Diamonds card, and especially if they share your material values or creative interests. They are ideal for love and romance as well as close friendships and good business partnerships.

The Queen of Hearts Planetary Card Sequence

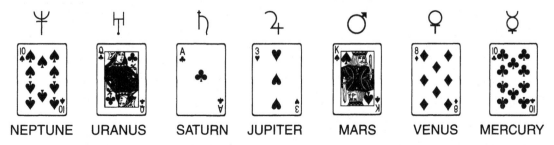

NEPTUNE   URANUS   SATURN   JUPITER   MARS   VENUS   MERCURY

Your Mars Card is . . .

The King of Spades

- Instinctive and independent, your will-power and resolute nature show that behind your gentle or charming expression you can be bold and very determined.
- You can also achieve your goals by letting your common sense and acute intuition guide your actions.
- You have excellent leadership qualities, even though you often play a supportive role.
- Although you can be assertive, avoid being too bossy.
- By developing the steadfast and self-disciplined side of your character you achieve great accomplishments.
- King of Spades people can particularly motivate and stimulate you. Avoid confrontations with these individuals, as both of you can be headstrong. If you can channel your emotional energies constructively you can both achieve a great deal.

Your Jupiter Card is . . .

The 3 of Hearts

- Your charm and engaging personality can attract people from all walks of life.
- Socially active, you enjoy interacting with others.
- You can benefit from all types of creative activities.
- Lack of discrimination on your part can often result in indecision about your love life or relationships.
- Jupiter's expansive influence can increase your emotional sensitivity, so resist being self-indulgent when feeling emotionally unhappy or uncertain.
- Usually you have a good relationship with 3 of Hearts people. You can both enjoy socializing or share the same creative interests.

They can be benefactors who bring opportunities into your life.

Your Saturn Card is . . .

The Ace of Clubs

- Self-discipline and a good education are essential if you want to improve your chances for success.
- If you fail to persevere and focus on serious goals superficial issues may easily distract you.
- When you do persevere your quest for knowledge is justly rewarded.
- Your potential for success can be undermined by negative thoughts or lack of initiative.
- Ace of Clubs people can be your teachers or guides and help you realize your shortcomings. Although these people can bring burdens, if you are willing to work on your self-awareness they can offer you valuable lessons.

Your Uranus Card is . . .

The Queen of Clubs

- This royal card grants you heightened intuitive abilities and quick perception.
- Mentally quick and inventive, your original ideas and progressive views can inspire others.
- Your search for higher knowledge can become more evident in middle years. You can excel in all types of study that relate to metaphysical subjects.
- Learn to trust your gut feelings, as more often than not they are very accurate.
- If positively expressing your good ideas you can naturally become a leader in group or team situations.
- Queen of Clubs people can inspire you or provide you with valuable knowledge. They

can also help you be more detached about yourself due to your Uranus connection. This is also a good relationship or friendship link where freedom is important.

Your Neptune Card is . . .

The 10 of Spades

- Your dreams and aspirations are possible if you are realistic about what you can achieve.
- Your drive and ambition are likely to continue well into old age.
- Your accomplishments in you latter years can also bring you much fulfillment and satisfaction.
- Opportunities and advancement in your career may be linked to distant places or even inspire you to live abroad.
- Your Neptune link indicates that 10 of Spades people can have a psychic connection with you. You may share the same dreams and ideals, but also keep your feet firmly on the ground.

Your Challenge Card is . . .

The 5 of Clubs

- Restlessness, impatience, or changing objectives can cause instability or undermine your accomplishments.
- Words said in haste can complicate situations or create uncertainty, so the less said in emotionally tense situations the better.
- Attention to detail and clear communication can help you to establish a good structure.
- An inability to focus is often as a result of assimilating too much information at once.
- 5 of Clubs individuals can have a strong spiritual link with you or play an important role in your life. These relationships can be influential or intellectually challenging. Although not always easy, their contributions

can help you to transform if you see them as valuable lessons.

The Result of Your Challenge Card is . . .

The 3 of Diamonds

- You enjoy exploring profitable new ideas and meeting new people.
- You use your creativity to overcome fears about financial matters as worry can cause more uncertainty.
- You success is often found in your originality, versatility, and creative abilities.
- People represented by the 3 of Diamonds can help you to establish a good sense of values and eliminate what is not important or viable. Your reaction to them often reflects how well you are responding to your challenges.

Famous People Who Are the Queen of Hearts

Goldie Hawn, Michael Douglas, Catherine Zeta-Jones, Mother Teresa, Edith Piaf, Dmitri Shostakovich, Lyndon Johnson, Bill Forsyth, Benito Mussolini, Beryl Bainbridge, Christopher Reeve, Voltaire, Paul "Pee-wee Herman" Reubens, G. W. F. Hegel, Man Ray, Rene Magritte, Michael Crichton, Pele, Johnny Carson, Barbara Walters, Mark Rothko, William Faulkner, Björk, Will Smith

Birthdays Governed by the Queen of Hearts

July 29: Leo   Ruler: Sun

Creative and full of enthusiasm, your resourcefulness and vitality indicate that you are a multitalented individual with a dynamic personality and high aspirations. Although the emotional power at your disposal can help you shine brightly, watch out that your sensitivity and pride do not turn you into an arrogant or selfish person. In order to fulfill your dreams or grand plans you need to be emotionally disciplined and use your warmth and exuberance to attract admirers. A tendency to fluctuate from great emotional highs to greater lows implies that you need to be constantly occupied in some type of creative endeavor. When you find your ideal goal or vocation, however, your unique talents, dedication, and magic touch can bring you fame and fortune.

August 27: Virgo　Ruler: Mercury

Insightful and intuitive, your charming smile and charismatic personality often conceal your penetrating mind and strong determination. Your ruler, Mercury, indicates that not only do you have the intelligence and good organizational skills needed to succeed, but you also enjoy refining or putting things in order. Although you can be critical or a stickler for rules, the compassionate side of your nature will usually offer practical help and show a willingness to assist others. Since you can excel in almost everything you do, when you invest your analytical skills, time, and enthusiasm into a project you are highly likely to succeed.

September 25: Libra　Ruler: Venus

Your charm and refined manners indicate that you are a receptive individual with quick comprehension. According to your ruler, Venus, you are lucky to possess both the sociable allure and business acumen necessary to make your projects a success. Although you are capable and determined, self-deprecating moods, inner doubts, or a tendency to be skeptical caution against letting your powerful emotions vacillate from great highs to similar lows. Nevertheless, your innate compassion, creative flair, and sociable nature suggest that you can succeed in all types of people-related activities or careers.

October 23: Scorpio　Ruler: Mars

Your innate creativity and intense emotions indicate that you are an energetic individual with a restless nature. A compelling desire to transform your life might motivate you to put your heart and soul into your goals or projects. Versatile and talented, your ruler, Mars, suggests that you are bold with keen insight. Good organizational abilities and practical know-how also confirm your innate ability to take charge and think on your feet. With your mental curiosity and special insight, you can find fulfillment and success in entertainment, the arts, or large organizations where your people skills are needed.

November 21: Scorpio　Ruler: Mars

Sociable and outgoing, your charm and powerful emotions indicate that you are a friendly individual with leadership qualities and strong determination. According to your ruler, Mars, you can be self-assured, tenacious, and pragmatic. Yet at times these attributes can also turn you into an obstinate individual. Although with your mental agility and intuition you are likely to achieve a great deal, guard against attempting to do too much or letting your many interests get in the way of your objectives. Nevertheless, your all or nothing philosophy indicates that when you finally find your ideal goal, you can achieve the impossssible.

December 19: Sagittarius　Ruler: Jupiter

Sociable, receptive, and sensitive, your need for creative self-expression or emotional fulfillment often indicate that you are guided by your powerful intuition or feelings. Although Jupiter, your ruler, and benefactor, usually grants you a cheerful and optimistic perspective on life, it can also incite you to restlessly seek new experiences. In order to meet your card's demands, however, you may need to invest a great deal of time and effort in order to achieve your goals. Since your emotional power is your greatest asset, do not let feelings of frustration get you down. Your individuality and creative power suggest that if you can stay focused and imaginative, you can achieve something inspiring or spectacular.

♣ THE QUEEN OF CLUBS ♣

As a royalty card of the Clubs suit, you are clever and spirited, with a touch of the dramatic. With your quick mind and fast mental responses, you enjoy being well informed. As you usually prefer to give the orders than take them, you often gravitate to positions of leadership or prefer to work for yourself. Under the influences of Mercury and Mars in the Earthly Spread, you have strong persuasive powers and the ability to make decisions quickly. Be careful, however, if you become impatient with those less smart than yourself, as this can cause you to be irritable or obstinate. Usually, however, you are kind and generous, with the courage to fight for your ideals.

Doubly influenced by the planet Jupiter in the Spiritual Spread, you can be enthusiastic and adventurous with the potential to make things happen in a big way. Your desire for honesty can make you outspoken, and being mentally assertive you often enjoy a little friendly competition. The combination of your ambition and strong willpower suggests you like to keep active and productive. Since you find enterprising people mentally stimulating, you are likely to enjoy entertaining or providing occasions for interesting people to meet up. Generally optimistic, you can think in large terms and are independent and self-reliant. Having the ability to spot opportunities and not give up suggests you are often

willing to take a risk in order to achieve your objectives.

Your Two Replacement Cards Are the 3 of Hearts & the 10 of Diamonds.

As the Queen of Clubs you share the same planetary position as the 3 of Hearts in the Spiritual Spread. This signifies that beneath your confident front you are more sensitive than you show. Sometimes this can make you prone to doubt, particularly about your emotional relationships. By finding positive channels for your self-expression, however, you can eliminate worry and feel more free and inspired. When happy your inner creativity naturally shows, whether through your work, play, business ideas, or a rewarding social life.

You also share the same planetary position as the 10 of Diamonds in the Earthly Spread. This signifies that when enterprising and success-oriented you are capable of achieving outstanding results in life. Although you have the power of attainment, you also come to learn that money or status alone do not bring you complete satisfaction. For the best rewards it is important that you fulfill your high ideals and find outlets that can bring happiness into other people's lives.

You have special or karmic links with people who are represented by the 3 of Hearts and 10 of Diamonds. As you share the same planetary positions you can be soul mates or understand each other very well. Even if you do not get along, you can both see clearly how the other person operates.

Your Mercury Card is . . .

The 10 of Spades
• Since a 10 card signifies success, you are mentally keen with a creative edge to your

The Queen of Clubs Planetary Card Sequence

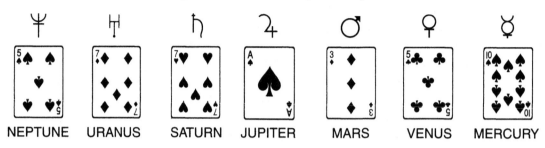

| NEPTUNE | URANUS | SATURN | JUPITER | MARS | VENUS | MERCURY |

mind. This is a success achieved through work, however, so you need to be constantly updating your knowledge.

- Mentally quick, you prefer to be honest and direct with others or possess a gift for being able to assert yourself by retaliating with fast one-liners.
- Ambitious and progressive, your willingness to learn and good communication skills often place you in positions of trust or authority.
- You should have good mental rapport and special communication with 10 of Spades people, as they activate your Mercury Card.

Your Venus Card is . . .

The 5 of Clubs

- As you seek variety and mental stimulation to stop you from getting bored, you need a partner who can keep up with your fast mind and restless spirit.
- Guard against an impulsive streak that can cause you to be too extravagant or act without fully thinking things through.
- You thrive on new learning experiences, so you can increase your enthusiasm and add to your social life through travel, action, variety, and adventure.
- Usually you are drawn to 5 of Clubs people, especially if they share your creative interests. This can be an ideal for love and ro-

mance as well as close friendships and good business partnerships.

Your Mars Card is . . .

The 3 of Diamonds

- Friendly, sociable, and affectionate, you enjoy actively helping others.
- You possess a talent for problem solving or a gift with words that you may wish to develop through writing, drama, or debate.
- With your many interests, avoid becoming scattered or worried about material choices by being decisive and focused.
- 3 of Diamonds people can motivate you and encourage your creativity. If you share the same goals you can both be enthusiastic and dynamic in the pursuit of your desires. Avoid being too competitive with this person however.

Your Jupiter Card is . . .

The Ace of Spades

- The strong Ace influence here indicates that you can use your strong will either selfishly by being bossy and intolerant or selflessly by helping others with your sharp insight and wider mental perspective.
- Your natural business acumen provides you with many fortunate opportunities, although be careful not to take on too much.

- A desire to find work or explore new areas may bring you in contact with foreign interests. Although these may bring extra responsibilities, they can also earn you many emotional or financial advantages.
- A study of higher wisdom, whether through religion, metaphysical subjects, spirituality, or having a personal philosophy can prove highly beneficial to you.
- Usually you have a good rapport with people represented by the Ace of Spades. They can be benefactors who can expand and enhance your life. Alternatively, these people can have a spiritual link with you.

Your Saturn Card is . . .

The 7 of Hearts

- You possess good powers of criticism and a perfectionist streak, particularly in your work or career, although avoid becoming too critical or cynical.
- You need regular time alone for reflection and self-analysis. Meditation can also be an excellent tool for helping you deal with stress.
- Your major tests in life are most likely to be emotional ones. If you find yourself withdrawing from others ask yourself if you are feeling misunderstood or losing faith, in which case you need to communicate your feelings to others.
- 7 of Hearts people can be your guides and help you realize your shortcomings. They can show you where you need self-discipline or to be clear about your boundaries. If you are willing to work on your self-awareness you can learn from your experiences with these people.

Your Uranus Card is . . .

The 7 of Diamonds

- Natural intuition often comes to you suddenly in flashes of insight.
- Although usually kind and accommodating, at times you can be rebellious and separate yourself from others, appearing cold or tense.
- Your interest in people can stimulate you to be charitable and humanitarian.
- Although you can be a very helpful friend and a good adviser to others, be careful that people don't take advantage of your good nature.
- 7 of Diamonds people can help you be more detached and aware of freedom due to your Uranus connection. This is also a good friendship link.

Your Neptune Card is . . .

The 5 of Spades

- Resourceful and imaginative, the clearer the image in your head as to what you want, the sooner it happens.
- If circumstances induce constant impatience and frustration, this can cause you oversensitivity leading to nebulous illnesses, lack of drive, or escapism.
- Naturally psychic with fast instincts, your first impression is usually correct.
- Travel and many changes are highlighted in the later years of your life.
- People represented by the 5 of Spades have a psychic link with you or they may inspire you emotionally. You may share the same dreams or ideals. In these relationships, however, it is important to stay grounded.

Your Challenge Card is . . .

The Jack of Hearts

- Make the most of your natural creativity and playful spirit.
- Avoid being temperamental, playing the martyr, or feeling sorry for yourself.
- Give of yourself in a natural, loving way.
- Jack of Hearts people can usually stimulate you to react. They can, however, bring out the best or the worst aspects of your personality. These people can help you to transform your life, but resist power struggles.

The Result of Your Challenge Card is . . .

The 9 of Clubs

- Be a good networker and pass on your knowledge in a detached and universal way.
- Generously help others and make them feel more positive.
- If you are feeling trapped in frustration and disappointment you may need to reevaluate your challenges and see if you are being daring enough.
- 9 of Clubs people can stimulate your wider mental perspective. You can usually see reflected in your relationship with them how you are responding to your challenges.

Famous People Who Are the Queen of Clubs

Paul McCartney, Jack Nicholson, Isabella Rossellini, Cher, Joe Cocker, Socrates, Mary Baker Eddy, Barry White, Danielle Steel, David Crosby, Erykah Badu, David Lee Roth, Immanuel Kant, Giuseppe Verdi, Magic Johnson, Gary Larson, Jesse Owens, Ben Vereen, Jimmy Stewart, Robert Oppenheimer, Harold Pinter, Ira Gershwin, Steve Martin, Steve McQueen, Jackson Pollock, Mikhail Baryshnikov, Alan Alda, Johnny Cash, Busta Rhymes, Elijah Wood

Birthdays Governed by the Queen of Clubs

January 28: Aquarius   Ruler: Uranus

Intelligent and daring, your natural leadership skills blend well with your common sense and determination. Strong-willed and ambitious, you usually aim straight for your goals, but at times you may be sidetracked by material concerns. With your astute insight into the character of others, you can quickly assess peoples' personalities and motivations but may not tolerate fools gladly. Nevertheless, you are usually friendly and optimistic, with a self-assured front and sharp wit. Guard against a tendency to be bossy or verbally cutting, however. Sensitive as well as clever, you do well when you work hard toward the achievement of your ideals.

February 26: Pisces   Ruler: Neptune

Being both clever and imaginative, you have all the resources you need for success. Nevertheless, a restless or impatient streak may need to be channeled positively so that you can find variety in life and the new opportunities that you seek. Inventive and resourceful, you can be very determined when set on a course of action. Although ambitious, with a desire to travel, you also have a strong love of home and family. Being idealistic and naturally psychic as well as materially aware, you gain much from listening to your intuitive sense about people or situations.

March 24: Aries   Ruler: Mars

Confident and self-assured, your fast mind and sharp insights suggest you do well in situations requiring leadership and creative ideas. Equally, you can be kind and compassionate, with a caring nature. Although naturally dramatic, you also possess pragmatism and a shrewd business sense. When you combine this with the fact that you can also be politically minded, you may often find yourself in an advisory position. Being determined and action-oriented suggests that you can become frustrated or stubborn if events do not move fast enough for you. With discipline and control, you can capitalize on your remarkable potential.

April 22: Taurus   Ruler: Venus
Being confident and charismatic with quick responses usually ensures that you have no problems attracting others. Nevertheless, you can also become bored easily, and an inner restlessness can sometimes lead you into trouble. When you discipline yourself, however, and add the magic of your excellent mental abilities and psychological insight, you can achieve miracles. Usually you are friendly and optimistic, with an ability to win people over. This does not detract from your practicality and good business sense, which can help your overall achievements. An artistic or creative flair can be developed to add to your many skills and talents.

May 20: Taurus   Ruler: Venus
Honest and sincere, with quick mental responses, you are a confident individual with charm and a down-to-earth approach. Being considerate, you value the opinions of others, but remember to also stay independent. Your ruling card, the 5 of Clubs, suggests that you possess a quest for knowledge and excitement so will always be adding to your learning skills and many talents. Usually friendly and caring, relationships figure high in your priorities, but beware of a tendency to become touchy or oversensitive. Ambitious, with innate leadership ability, your sharp intelligence and natural business sense ensure you can excel in anything you undertake as long as you persevere.

June 18: Gemini   Ruler: Mercury
Youthful, friendly, and smart, you are an independent individual with original ideas. Mentally quick, your clever and witty personality often conceals your ambition and determination. Being strong-willed and success-oriented, you frequently seek to be in leadership positions but avoid being too competitive or stubborn. Nevertheless, you respond well to challenges, as they force you to be enterprising and progressive. If ever you are feeling indecisive or insecure about emotional affairs you can turn the energy around by reconnecting to your strong natural creativity. The more you develop your innate humanitarian streak the more fulfilled you become. Direct, honest, and multitalented, you have a gift with words and a strong business sense.

July 16: Cancer   Ruler: Moon
Intelligent and analytical, yet emotionally impressionable, you are a fast-thinking individual with a sympathetic nature. Naturally psychic, you pick up on the feelings of others. At times this can lead to your being pulled between your own needs and the needs of those around you. You can still be ambitious and businesslike, however, and may use your advisory skills in leadership positions. Avoid becoming oversensitive, as this can cause you anxiety or to withdraw. With your sharp insight you can have a talent for writing or for helping others.

August 14: Leo   Ruler: Sun
Active and creative, you are an individual with natural leadership skills and an attractive personality. Warm and sunny, with an exceptionally quick mind, you have a strong sense of drama. Being ambitious with a need for achievement implies that you particularly value your work. Although determined and strong-willed, avoid becoming bossy or obstinate. Usually courageous, however, you can

think in large terms and enjoy a challenge. Your versatility and need for need for variety can make you resourceful and encourage you to seek new experiences. Developing patience can especially help you in your climb to the top.

September 12: Virgo   Ruler: Mercury
Friendly but dignified, you are an intelligent individual with ambition and drive for material success. With good analytical skills, you have sharp insight, a practical outlook, and clear thinking. Equally, you possess a sense of the dramatic and a need to express yourself. You may decide to integrate this with your gift for words, whether through writing, speaking, or singing. If you avoid worry or anxiety you have good mental application and are thorough in whatever you do. When you combine your level of competence with hard work you often find yourself in leadership positions. Being generous, you particularly enjoy helping others.

October 10: Libra   Ruler: Venus
Creative and proud, your sharp mind and original ideas can often take you to leading positions. Usually friendly and sociable, you can also be persuasive and forceful. Independent, with an interest in relationships, you are a shrewd judge of character. With a need for change and diversity you seek new experiences to keep your interest and may wish to develop your innate talents for drama, writing, music, or art. Although you have a talent for dealing with people and can be popular, you still prefer to be in charge.

November 8: Scorpio   Ruler: Mars
With your powerful emotions and quick intelligence, you are an individual who does not put up with hindrance from others. Ambitious and productive, you strive for accomplishment and

material security. You also have high ideals and a strong sixth sense, though you may keep them hidden from others. By developing patience and tolerance you can overcome a tendency to be controlling and find your life runs easier. With strong imagination, good intelligence, and a natural business sense you only need to stay positively focused in order to succeed.

December 6: Sagittarius   Ruler: Jupiter
Generous and sociable, you are a mentally bright individual with an independent attitude. Usually you like to be truthful and direct even if your words can sometimes be interpreted as too frank. A desire to expand your horizons may include a love of travel, but you have an equally strong love of home. Although caring and protective, especially toward family members, you can also be assertive with strong convictions, but avoid being bossy. Broadminded, you are likely to have a wide interest in worldly affairs but still retain an idealistic stance. With your sharp insight, you gain much from the study of metaphysical or philosophical subjects.

♦THE QUEEN OF DIAMONDS♦

As a royal card from the Diamonds suit you possess the creative and practical skills needed to achieve material success or to rise to positions of leadership. As well as being able to organize and plan, your strong sense of worth and resourcefulness allow you to quickly assess people and situations. Nevertheless, a slow but sure advancement in life and especially in monetary matters is recommended. Although you have the Midas touch, your generosity or strong desire to enjoy the best of what life can offer inevitably leads to one question: How well do you manage your finances? A failure to control your income can lead to a cycle of debts or worry caused by bad management of money. Since Diamonds also represents values, once you realize your true worth as a ruler of this suit you are able to help others with your diligence, hard work, and special insight.

The planetary influences of Mercury and Saturn in your Earthly Spread indicates that you are usually a reliable and rational person with a critical mind. Although pragmatic by nature with good concentration, you may need to be careful that your realistic outlook does not turn to pessimism. Nevertheless, your tenacity and endurance suggest that you are a strong and determined individual who does not give up easily. Even though you are not the type to quit, you become your own worst enemy if your approach is too obstinate or uncompromising. Fortunately, your industrious nature and natural talents ensure your certain advancement in life.

The planetary influences of Mars and Uranus in your Spiritual Spread indicate that you are courageous and confident. A strong urge for freedom or a love of independence implies that you can summon up an unusual amount of energy in order to achieve your purpose in life. If you develop an inclination to rebel or argue with others, however, this can lead to conflicts and strong emotional tension. By taking actions based upon objective and progressive thinking, you can use this powerful influence to lead others, bring reforms, or invent new methods of work. If you develop your innate humanitarian streak you may also fight for the rights of others and obtain much satisfaction.

Your Two Replacement Cards Are the 9 of Diamonds & the 3 of Diamonds.

As the Queen of Diamonds you share the same planetary position as the 9 of Diamonds in the Earthly Spread. This powerful universal card symbolizes the importance of values in personal and material matters. By staying broadminded in all your affairs you are able to show your more generous nature and avoid dwelling on disappointments or frustrations from the past. By being productive and utilizing your inspired ideas and natural business acumen, you have the ability to promote concepts that are enterprising or creative.

As the Queen of Diamonds you also share the same planetary position as the 3 of Diamonds in the Spiritual Spread. The influence of this card suggests that you are versatile, gregarious, and multitalented with a strong inner need for self-expression. With your original ideas you are often ahead of your time and can be witty or entertaining. Although indecisiveness can cause you to worry, when you are focused on a goal you can be highly motivated with the potential for exceptional prosperity.

The Queen of Diamonds Planetary Card Sequence

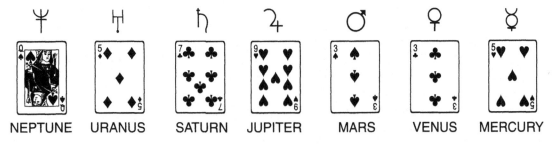

NEPTUNE   URANUS   SATURN   JUPITER   MARS   VENUS   MERCURY

You usually have special or karmic links with people who are represented by the 3 of Diamonds and the 9 of Diamonds, as you share the same planetary positions. You can be soul mates or understand each other very well. Even if you do not get along, you can both see clearly how the other person operates.

Your Mercury Card is . . .

The 5 of Hearts
- You are likely to change your mind and direction a number of times before you find your true goals.
- An ability to learn quickly and make progress indicates that you are versatile and talented if you are willing to persevere with one goal for long enough.
- Intuitive and instinctive, the foundation for your thinking is often focused on emotional security.
- By developing patience you avoid fluctuating emotions, restlessness, or a tendency for cutting remarks.
- You should have good mental rapport and special communication with people represented by the 5 of Hearts, as they activate your Mercury Card. They are also good partners for travel and shared creative interests.

Your Venus Card is . . .

The 3 of Clubs
- You can be bright, charming, and amusing, with a natural talent for words.
- Uncertainty or indecisiveness may lead to delays or disappointments in close relationships.
- By developing your communication skills and learning to compromise, you will be able to avoid misunderstandings and confusion with partners and loved ones.

- You have a natural talent for expressing your feelings through writing, music, or drama that if developed bring you much emotional satisfaction.
- Your Venus link signifies that you are attracted to people represented by the 3 of Clubs. This card is good for romance, close friendships, and good business partnerships.

Your Mars Card is . . .

The 3 of Spades
- The creative force of the number 3 in both your Venus and Mars cards indicate that you can be a highly talented person.
- The message of this card suggests that you benefit far more from vocational careers than mundane jobs.
- Difficulties in deciding exactly what your goals are may slow down your progress.
- You are likely to try different types of career before you finally find your ideal vocation.
- People represented by the 3 of Spades can particularly motivate and stimulate you. If they are on your side their business acumen can benefit you. Avoid being too competitive with this person by channeling both your energies constructively.

Your Jupiter Card is . . .

The 9 of Hearts
- The universal message of this card implies that you find emotional fulfillment by surrendering your ego to a higher purpose.
- In your search for emotional satisfaction and happiness, resist being overindulgent or extravagant, as it may end up being too costly.
- You can show your compassion by being very generous and giving.
- Usually you have a good rapport with people represented by the 9 of Hearts, as often they

are benefactors who can expand and enhance your life. Alternatively, these people can have a spiritual link with you.

Your Saturn Card is . . .

The 7 of Clubs

- The mystical influence of this card suggests that a positive outlook is essential to your success and well-being.
- Good education and learning to structure your analytical skills can change insight into higher wisdom and refine your mental competence.
- Mental pressure or excessive worry can cause you to become pessimistic.
- You do well in life, and especially in your career, when you have the faith in yourself to act spontaneously.
- People represented by the 7 of Clubs may help you recognize your responsibilities and shortcomings, or be a source of worry. If you are willing to work on your self-awareness these people can bring valuable lessons.

Your Uranus Card is . . .

The 5 of Diamonds

- Your need for variety and freedom of movement indicates that you enjoy making changes and trying new challenges.
- You may need to avoid taking impulsive actions that can affect your material circumstances.
- Fluctuations in your financial situation are often sudden or unexpected.
- Your unique ideas and talent for business can bring you new opportunities and luck.
- 5 of Diamonds people can help you be more objective about yourself. As business associates, resist rushing into making the wrong commitments. This can be a good friendship link where you can both value freedom.

Your Neptune Card is . . .

The Queen of Spades

- This royal card is associated with dedication, hard work, and wisdom gained from experience; therefore, your opportunities to take the lead, or your significant achievements, are likely to take place in the second part of your life or later years.
- Through self-discipline and willingness to be of service you can make your ideals come true.
- Learn to trust your intuition and gut feelings, as they are very often highly accurate.
- The influence of a strong woman in the latter part of life is likely to be more evident.
- Your Neptune link signifies that people represented by the Queen of Spades can have a psychic connection with you. You may share the same dreams and ideals or they may inspire you but stay grounded.

Your Challenge Card is . . .

The Jack of Clubs

- Your transformation and success are often achieved by the development of a mature attitude toward your responsibilities and financial management.
- One of your challenges is to further develop your sharp intelligence and creative potential.
- Stay open-minded to new ideas or learning new skills.
- Honesty and truthfulness can also help you to overcome spiritual tests that can appear from time to time.
- People represented by the Jack of Clubs can usually stimulate you to react. Therefore, they can bring out the best aspects of your personality, but avoid becoming drawn into power struggles.

The Result of Your Challenge Card is . . .

The 9 of Diamonds
- By staying detached you can become free from frustrations and less concerned with material issues.
- Your prosperity and material success are usually linked to your broad understanding of values, maturity, and a responsible attitude.
- Your high ideals are achieved if you overcome a tendency to waste or scatter your resources.
- People who are represented by the 9 of Diamonds can inspire you and often reflect how you are responding to your challenges.

Famous People Who Are the Queen of Diamonds

Martin Luther King, Robert Browning, Aristotle Onassis, Charles Baudelaire, Rupert Murdoch, Hugh Hefner, Johannes Brahms, Eva Peron, Gary Cooper, Yves Saint Laurent, Tom Stoppard, Laurie Anderson, George Segal, Dennis Quaid, Dom DeLuise, Jerry Springer, Ken Russell, Robbie Williams, Jerry Garcia, Peter Gabriel, Mark Wahlberg, Tom Cruise

Birthdays Governed by the Queen of Diamonds

January 15: Capricorn   Ruler: Saturn
Analytical, pragmatic, and sensitive, your intuitive understanding and good sense of values indicate that you can accomplish a great deal. Although your ruler, Saturn, grants a rational mind and executive abilities, under the influence of the 7 of Clubs it also suggests that at times you can be skeptical or too concerned about your finances. The mystical influences linked to your card signify that when you gain knowledge or feel inspired by new ideas your quick comprehension and foresight can turn you into a dynamic leader. As a versatile and efficient individual you usually like to maintain a high standard and take pride in your work.

February 13: Aquarius   Ruler: Uranus
Although you are usually hardworking and practical, as an idealist and sensitive individual you may act on the impulses of your restless nature. The influence of the 5 of Diamonds can also indicate career changes and travel. Although Uranus, your ruler, can make you independent and freedom loving, resist showing your self-ruling stubborness instead. The creative potential indicated by your card suggests that when you develop a responsible attitude and apply self-discipline to your inspired ideas your executive skills become evident. You get most satisfaction when you are able to utilize your natural leadership qualities for the good of others.

March 11: Pisces   Ruler: Neptune
Instinctive and intuitive, your quick perception and innate wisdom suggest that your inspired ideas can lead to great success. When you combine the idealistic nature of your ruler Neptune to your innate common sense, your ingenious mind can make you excel or lead others. Being motivated by inspired or ambitious plans, you usually take pride in your work and are hard working and productive. Alternatively your grand dreams and creative talents may inspire you to find a vocation in arts, music or drama. When you rise to the spiritual challenge of your card you may chose to be of service to a noble cause.

April 9: Aries   Ruler: Mars
As a sensitive, receptive, and purposeful individual you have the vitality, willpower, and determination to overcome obstacles and make

headway. According to your ruler, Mars, you have natural executive skills and a great deal of enthusiasm or drive. An inclination to feel frustrated or impatient can arise when conflicting principles or indecisiveness can steer you from your objectives. In order to stay focused, resist scattering your energies in too many directions. Nevertheless, when you combine your practical instincts with your idealistic schemes, your versatility, innate creativity, and spiritual awareness can lift you to the heights of your success.

May 7: Taurus   Ruler: Venus

As an independent and resolute individual your single-mindedness and practical intuition can make you a highly productive and successful individual. Venus, your ruler, endows you with mental creativity, charm, and an attractive demeanor. As you often possess many hidden talents, all you need do is discipline your mind to stay focused and let your shrewd perception dissolve your constant inner doubts and worries. Indeed, when you turn your tendency to be obstinate into decisive actions, there is little to stop you from achieving your goals. You may also find that by developing your intellectual aptitude you can use your versatility to gain the recognition and admiration you desire.

June 5: Gemini   Ruler: Mercury

Instinctive, mentally quick, and resourceful, your cerebral power and shrewd perception can help you to transform your life and achieve success. Your ruler, Mercury, indicates that your curiosity and quick grasp of fast-changing situations makes you adaptable and versatile. Under the influence of the 5 of Hearts, however, Mercury also warns against a low threshold of boredom, moodiness, or mentally restlessness. When you are willing to put the effort in, your intellectual and creative output can be both entertaining and highly profitable. Success often comes after you learn about self-worth and the values or the cost of being extravagant.

July 3: Cancer   Ruler: Moon

Charismatic, dynamic, and creative, your versatility usually conceals your many diverse talents. Your ruler, the Moon, accents your sensitivity and innate perception. It also suggests that an innate concern for material security may prompt you to work hard and accomplish. Luckily your natural executive abilities and business acumen can go a long way to secure your finances. Good at evaluating others, you have an intuitive sense about people and the ability to excel in careers dealing with the public. Alternatively, a touch of the dramatic indicates that you may dedicate your time to developing your artistic or musical talents.

August 1: Leo   Ruler: Sun

Your number 1 birthday in the Sun sign of Leo implies that you usually believe you are someone special. Your pride and self-assured demeanor rarely leaves others in doubt of who should be in charge. Your ruler, the Sun, grants you vitality, creative talents, and a resolute nature. Being independent and daring, your life can be quite eventful, yet lack of responsibility on your own part can put challenges in your path. In order to back up your claims you need to be accountable for your actions and develop your innate talents. Indeed, with a strong sense of the dramatic and the willingness to work hard for your ideals you can achieve success and shine brightly.

♠ THE QUEEN OF SPADES ♠

As a Queen Card of the Spade suit you possess shrewd practicality and a sharp insight into others. Although very clever, you usually learn best by experience or working things through. As a royalty card you have natural leadership ability and the potential to help others with the combination of your intuitive perceptiveness and practical common sense. Wisdom can be gained if you apply the necessary self-discipline to your many natural talents. Under the influences of Mercury and Uranus in the Earthly Spread, you have many original ideas and are a good psychologist. You learn quickly and have the ability to go straight to the heart of a matter. Being outspoken with strong convictions suggests powerful individuality, although be careful of a rebel streak that can cause you to become obstinate.

As you also are under the influences of the Sun and Jupiter in the Spiritual Spread, you possess natural dramatic gifts and the ability to think in large terms. If you are working in a low position beneath your talents and high calling you may need to identify more with the positive faith, optimism, and leadership shown by your life card. This indicates that you can rise to influential positions through self-mastery and by using your astute intelligence for the good of all.

Your Two Replacement Cards Are the 10 of Diamonds & the 8 of Diamonds.

As the Queen of Spades you share the same planetary position as the 10 of Diamonds in the Spiritual Spread. This signifies that you have an excellent ability to turn your many inventive ideas into hard cash. It is especially important, however, that you do not get too involved in just making money for its own sake. With your card's strong emphasis on work, you may easily get caught up in the rat race for material gain. To obtain inner satisfaction as well as outer success, there is a need for activities you consider to be of real value.

Since you also share the same planetary position as the 8 of Diamonds in the Earthly Spread, you can be determined and ambitious. You enjoy power, which you can use positively for achievement and personal transformation. Alternatively, if you become too controlling you may be involved in power struggles with others. Through using your natural authority wisely, being responsible, and following your inner guidance you can attain remarkable results in life.

You have special or karmic links with people who are represented by the 10 of Diamonds and 8 of Diamonds. As you share the same planetary positions you can be soul mates or understand each other very well. Even if you

The Queen of Spades Planetary Card Sequences

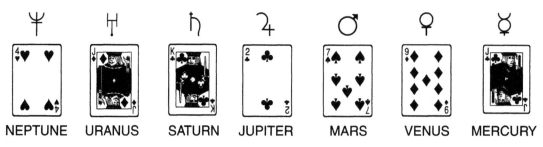

NEPTUNE   URANUS   SATURN   JUPITER   MARS   VENUS   MERCURY

do not get along, you can both see clearly how the other person operates.

Your Mercury Card is . . .

The Jack of Clubs

- This royalty card indicates superior mental abilities and a gift for presenting your ideas.
- If negative, you can be nervous, restless, or argumentative.
- You can excel in passing your knowledge on to others, particularly through education or writing.
- You possess fast responses and a talent for problem solving.
- Jack of Clubs people can stimulate your communication skills and bring you good ideas.

Your Venus Card is . . .

The 9 of Diamonds

- You can be generous and altruistic, especially with loved ones.
- Avoid hanging on to frustrations or disappointments with others, as this can cause problems within your relationships. It is better to utilize your natural detachment.
- You appreciate quality things, so you may have to curb an extravagant streak.
- By developing your innate humanitarian streak, you improve the quality of your close personal relationships.
- People represented by the 9 of Diamonds card are ideal for love and romance. This card can also represent close friendships and good business partnerships.

Your Mars Card is . . .

The 7 of Spades

- When driven, you will work very hard, even to the point of overwork.

- If you combine faith with positive action you will find your life just falls into place at the right time.
- Avoid a tendency to be overly critical or perfectionistic with yourself or others.
- Your desire for self-improvement, acquiring knowledge, and developing your mind can bring you greater awareness, material success, and spiritual fulfillment.
- People who are the 7 of Spades can motivate and stimulate you or you may both be enthusiastic in achieving shared goals. Avoid being too competitive by channeling the energy constructively.

Your Jupiter Card is . . .

The 2 of Clubs

- Being clever, you enjoy partnerships that involve witty quips and quick smart retorts. This can keep you on your toes and bring out your sense of humor.
- If your ego gets inflated this can lead to you becoming antagonistic, quarreling about money, or making provocative comments.
- Cooperative efforts and teamwork situations can be especially beneficial for you. You have a flair for public relations that you can utilize for material gain.
- Usually you have a good rapport with 2 of Clubs people, as they often bring opportunities to expand and enhance your life. These people may have a spiritual link with you.

Your Saturn Card is . . .

The King of Clubs

- This powerful intellectual card suggests the potential for outstanding achievements and leadership through taking responsibility and self-mastery.
- Although you usually prefer to give the or-

ders than take them, be careful of being bossy.

- Intelligent male authority figures are likely to act as teachers or play a strong part in your life agenda.
- King of Clubs people or intelligent men can be your teachers or help you recognize your shortcomings. If you are willing to work on your self-awareness these people can bring valuable lessons.

Your Uranus Card is . . .

The Jack of Diamonds

- You possess strong individualism and many inventive ideas. This may especially manifest through creative projects such as writing, drama, music, or the arts.
- If you give way to an immature streak or too great a love of the good life you can become rebellious, tense, or obstinate.
- You are often ahead of your time with your values.
- You particularly gain from friends or group and team situations.
- Jack of Diamonds people can help you become more original, objective or humanitarian. They can stimulate your sense of freedom or desire to be playful. This is a good friendship link.

Your Neptune Card is . . .

The 4 of Hearts

- You are a practical visionary. You can utilize this gift in business or for mystical experiences.
- Long-distance travel overseas can be especially favorable for finding emotional satisfaction.
- When you open your heart you are honest and direct yet sensitive to others.
- 4 of Hearts people can have a psychic con-

nection with you. They may link to your ideals or help you to materialize your dreams. Fortunately, this 4 influence suggests you can also both be practical in this area.

Your Challenge Card is . . .

The 4 of Diamonds

- Be methodical and build a strong foundation for whatever you want to achieve.
- Transform a tendency to be stubborn into listening and being more flexible.
- Develop your vision or spiritual potential and apply it practically in your life.
- 4 of Diamonds people can dare you to react and bring out the best in you. Although these people can help you to transform your life, resist becoming involved in power struggles.

The Result of Your Challenge Card is . . .

The 2 of Spades

- Have good working relationships with others.
- Transform self-indulgence or feelings that life is too much of a struggle into a desire to work constructively, be of service, and cultivate your self-awareness.
- Utilize your diplomatic and social skills and lead a well-balanced life.
- People represented by the 2 of Spades could be good working partners or reflective if you are lost in unreality. They can mirror how well you are responding to your challenges.

Famous People Who Are the Queen of Spades

Isaac Asimov, Roger Miller, Christy Turlington, Jim Bakker, Cuba Gooding, Jr., Saint Therese de Lisieux, David Bailey, Taye Diggs

Birthdays Governed by the Queen of Spades

January 2: Capricorn   Ruler: Saturn

Although your determination and pragmatic approach singles you out as a hardworking individual, your intuitive and receptive awareness indicates that you aspire to more in life. Indeed, you can discover your true potential if you decide to employ your sensitive intellect and develop your analytical abilities. Through the knowledge you gain you can find that important or meaningful goal you were looking for. Although you are independent by nature, your people-related activities are often your great source of joy as well as trouble. With your sharp intelligence and practical knows how, resist letting constant worry or indecisiveness undermine your efforts. Saturn, your ruler, usually endows you with the perseverance and the responsible attitude needed to meet your challenges.

♥ ♣ THE KINGS ♦ ♠

AMBITIOUS AND HARDWORKING, Kings are usually confident, resourceful, and enterprising. As you are commonly associated with leadership and creative self-expression you prefer to be independent rather than dependent on others. Your royal card also indicates that you are often proud, multitalented, and enthusiastic. A tendency to want to be in control indicates that you need to overcome an inclination to be bossy or egocentric. Nevertheless, your unique and innovative approach inspires new and exciting ideas, which frequently result in your ability to impress others. Since your royal card represents the masculine principle, the women under this influence often have strong character.

The following suits further modify the effect of your number:

King of Hearts

Your royal card indicates that you have the charisma or emotional strength to lead others through the power of love and compassion. Whatever you choose to do, with your author-

ity you also acquire responsibilities that may require some sacrifices. If you invest in developing your unique talents you can stand out as someone special. As you may need to learn to distinguish between true love and strong desires, avoid using your powers for selfish reasons.

King of Clubs

Astute, well-informed, and perceptive, your royal card signifies that through knowledge and intellectual pursuits you have the intelligence and resolve to lead others. Whatever you may choose to do, you can achieve great success with your analytical capabilities, organizational skills, and authoritative manner. As you often have the upper hand intellectually, resist using your power to dominate or criticize others. Nevertheless, confident and persuasive, with patience and tolerance you can gain the respect you desire and achieve success.

King of Diamonds

Your ability to assess people and situations quickly indicates that you have excellent perception and a good sense of values. Your royal card also suggests that you possess the power and determination to be highly productive. Although you often have the ability to influence people, avoid being too bossy or stubborn. With your business acumen and authoritative manner, you can achieve great material success in whatever you may choose to do.

King of Spades

Your royal card indicates that, although you may have to work very hard for your success and accomplishment, the knowledge you gain along the way can culminate in self-mastery. Usually independent and authoritative, resist letting the hidden wisdom linked to your card to set you apart from others. Although your innate common sense can help your career advancement, investing your time in developing or exploring spiritual or esoteric subjects can be also highly beneficial.

♥ THE KING OF HEARTS ♥

Being a King of the Hearts suit indicates that you are warm, sociable, and naturally dramatic. Friendly and kind, you are often at your best when entertaining others. With the influences of Mercury and Mars in the Earthly Spread, you are mentally sharp and quick on the uptake. You can use this skill in humor and usually enjoy fast quips or banter with your friends. With your brain power and big emotional range, you can achieve in almost any field that you choose, but you can particularly excel at working with people, in management positions, or in drama, writing, music, and the arts. If in a contrary mood, however, your natural leadership may deteriorate into bossiness or stubborn resistance.

With the influences of Uranus and Venus in the Spiritual Spread, you have natural creative talent and can mix well with all different types of people. Your freedom is important to you and you usually wish the same freedom for people in general. This humanitarian streak can be developed further for the good of others. Although your royalty card puts you in a leading position, avoid allowing self-indulgence or emotional excesses to stop you from fulfilling your outstanding potential. When being self-sacrificing and utilizing your powerful ability to love and charm others you can be a dynamic force for transformation.

Your Two Replacement Cards Are the 2 of Clubs & the 9 of Spades.

As the King of Hearts you share the same planetary position as the 2 of Clubs in the Spiritual Spread. This signifies that you are a good psychologist who can see the irony of life. You realize that you want your independence, yet you also need the help, support, and feedback of others. If you find yourself being especially argumentative or frustrated, you may need to ask yourself if you have unexpressed secret fears or are in dependent situations. Being proud, it is important that you find somebody who you trust enough to expose your inner vulnerability.

You also share the same planetary position as the 9 of Spades in the Earthly Spread; this implies that when you express your true noble and humanitarian nature, you can be very magnanimous and loving. This higher unconditional love comes from having no selfish motivation behind your actions and is usually achieved through learning to let go of the past, being honest with yourself, and staying detached.

You have special or karmic links with people who are represented by the 2 of Clubs and 9 of Spades. As you share the same planetary positions you can be soul mates or understand each other very well. Even if you do not get along, you can both see clearly how the other person operates.

Your Mercury Card is . . .

The King of Diamonds

- An excellent observer and shrewd judge of character, you respect clever people who can match your wits or outdo you.
- Mentally confident, you have good communication skills and a latent talent for writing that, if developed, could bring you much success.
- The King of Diamonds card here indicates a skill in evaluation or natural business acumen.
- You should have good mental rapport and special communication with people represented by the King of Diamonds, as they activate your Mercury Card. These people can stimulate an exchange of ideas.

Your Venus Card is . . .

The 6 of Hearts

- Magnetic, charming, and sociable, you have no trouble attracting friends and relationships, although you may find that you need recognition from others.
- As you especially value your home as a haven of escape from harsh reality, you may be willing to make compromises or sacrifices for family or the comforts of a secure base.
- Although you may mean well, in your desire to help those you care for, avoid becoming interfering or dominating.
- You can be a loyal and generous friend.

- Usually you are drawn to people who are represented by the 6 of Hearts, especially if they share your material aspirations or creative interests. This link is ideal for love and romance as well as close friendships and good business partnerships.

Your Mars Card is . . .

The 4 of Clubs

- You are stimulated by the quest for knowledge so usually enjoy creative problem solving and lively debates.
- Frank and to the point, you often like to confront people with the truth.
- Be careful of an impatient streak that may cause you to neglect taking care of the detail.
- You usually work best when you have a definite plan before moving into action.
- 4 of Clubs people can positively motivate and stimulate you into action, but avoid being too competitive or confrontational with these individuals.

Your Jupiter Card is . . .

The 2 of Diamonds

- You usually gain from public relations or making contacts.
- When optimistic and expansive you have a gift for sales. Whether a concept or a product, you can be very convincing, but it has to be something you really believe in.
- Do not allow a busy social life to distract you from the discipline needed to achieve your goals.
- Business or working partnerships can prove especially beneficial for you.
- Usually you have a good relationship with 2 of Diamonds people. You can both enjoy socializing or share the same interests although avoid overindulging together. These people can bring opportunities.

The King of Hearts Planetary Card Sequence

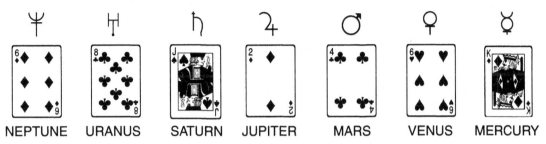

| NEPTUNE | URANUS | SATURN | JUPITER | MARS | VENUS | MERCURY |

Your Saturn Card is . . .

The Jack of Spades

- The high potential represented by this "spiritual initiate" card indicates that many of your life tests involve displaying honesty and integrity in all your actions, or "walking your talk."
- Overindulgence and excess can prove especially detrimental to your physical and psychological health.
- It is important to keep a clear focus and steadily persevere toward your main life goals.
- Avoid harboring an immature streak that would encourage you to take the easy way out or mix with bad company.
- People represented by the Jack of Spades can be your teachers or guides and help you recognize your shortcomings. Although these people may sometimes bring burdens or responsibilities, if you are willing to work on your self-awareness they can also offer you valuable lessons.

Your Uranus Card is . . .

The 8 of Clubs

- You gain much from mentally exploring new areas of interest and experimenting with fresh ideas or discoveries.
- Ego attachment or rebelliousness can cause you to become mentally controlling or manipulative.
- The mental power card here signifies that you can be highly inventive and inspired when you connect to your higher knowledge. This may attract you to humanitarian interests, social reform, or the study of philosophical, spiritual, or metaphysical subjects.
- People who are represented by the 8 of Clubs Card can provide you with valuable insight or help you be more detached due to your Uranus connection. This is also a good friendship link.

Your Neptune Card is . . .

The 6 of Diamonds

- Your home and family emphasis gets even stronger in your later years. How responsible you have been, and continue to be, attests to how much your can relax and enjoy the fruits of your labors.
- Be careful that inertia or too great a desire for an easy life does not cause you to avoid putting your dreams into action.
- With your eye for color and style, you usually enjoy beautifying your home.
- You can use your powerful imagination and vision for creative purposes, such as writing, film, acting, music, or other artistic pursuits.

- Your Neptune link indicates that 6 of Diamonds people can have a psychic connection with you. You may share the same dreams or ideals, but guard against self-delusion.

Your Challenge Card is . . .

The 4 of Spades
- Build a strong foundation for whatever you want to achieve.
- Be totally honest with yourself as well as with others.
- Have a plan as to how you are going to establish your goals.
- Ensure your relationships are on a sure footing.
- 4 of Spades individuals can confront you to bring out the best or the worst of your personality. This person could help you to transform old patterns if you rise to the challenge.

The Result of Your Challenge Card is . . .

The 10 of Hearts
- You will be using your charismatic appeal and natural talents to create success for yourself and to inspire others.
- If too self-oriented and living far beneath your natural potential you may need to reevaluate your Challenge Cards.
- You are a progressive leader with strong ambitions and a magnanimous personality who is born to work with the power of love.
- People represented by the 10 of Hearts can help mirror back to you how you are dealing with your emotions and your challenges.

Famous People Who Are the King of Hearts

Brad Pitt, Christina Aguilera, Christopher Isherwood, F. Scott Fitzgerald, Marcel Duchamp, Paul Klee, Steven Biko, Jacqueline Kennedy Onassis, Geraldine Ferraro, Macaulay Culkin, Linda McCartney, Jim Henson, Beatrix Potter, Keith Richards, Branford Marsalis, Timothy Leary, Doris Lessing, Derek Jacobi, Jeff Goldblum, Franz Liszt, Robert F. Kennedy, Duane Allman, Nadine Gordimer, Steven Spielberg

Birthdays Governed by the King of Hearts

June 30: Cancer   Ruler: Cancer
Friendly and sociable, with a charismatic personality, your dynamic emotional power can prove to be one of your greatest assets. When positive you are loving and expressive with a need for achievement. If negative your natural pride may turn to conceit or your caring nature can turn to worry. Nevertheless, you are usually creative and dramatic with a kind heart. Home and family play a large part in your affairs and you will be protective and supportive of those you love. With a natural gift for words, you enjoy entertaining others.

July 28: Leo   Ruler: Sun
Proud and self-assured, with a warm heart, your natural dramatic gifts ensure you are usually the life and soul of the party. As you usually do not like to take orders, you are best working for yourself or in positions of authority. Often you can be daring and creative and succeed through sheer determination and will. Guard against becoming domineering or selfish, however, as this can spoil your winning charm. Nevertheless, you are usually kind, magnanimous, and entertaining, with quick responses and a way with people. By applying self-discipline to your remarkable potential you can achieve amazing results.

August 26: Virgo   Ruler: Mercury
Practical and determined, you are a person who can be both humble and self-effacing yet

proud, dramatic, and self-willed. Ambitious, if not for yourself then for family, you like life to run smoothly and efficiently. Your loving, caring nature and strong love of home mixes peculiarly with your desire for power and control. A good organizer and communicator, you have a strong sense of values that you stand by. You may wish to develop your innate writing skills or work with your natural leadership ability to be of service to others.

September 24: Libra   Ruler: Venus

Honest, friendly, and straightforward, you are a strong individual who believes that actions speak louder than words. Sociable and kind, you are a caring individual. Home loving and responsible, your family plays an especially vital role in your life story. Equally, you can be idealistic but usually take a pragmatic approach to getting things done. As you have an appreciation of beauty you like to be surrounded by luxury or attractive surroundings. With your strong artistic or creative streak, you often experience inspired ideas and wish to put them into form.

October 22: Libra   Ruler: Venus

Sociable and charming, with a magnetic personality, you are an intelligent idealist with a gift for communication. With your special psychological insight, you can be influential in changing others. You place a high price on the security and peace of home and can be caring in a practical way. Although usually generous and kind, beware of a tendency to become stubborn or egotistical, especially if frustrated. Generally, your broad-minded attitude, leadership skills, and emotional sensitivity ensure your success. Proud and aware, you can be the perfect host or hostess and have a gift for dealing with people.

November 20: Scorpio   Ruler: Mars

Although sensitive and charismatic, you are also a strong-willed individual with dynamic emotions. Spurred by a love of knowledge, you enjoy expanding your skills and experience. Being strong-willed and sensitive, you can be friendly and entertaining and mix with people from all walks of life. Although a natural leader, you can also be diplomatic and benefit from partnerships and collaborative efforts. A person of extremes, guard against becoming impatient or moody. Generally, however, you are a positive thinker and planner who is willing to work to accomplish your desires. When disciplined you gain from good social contacts and can attract positions of power.

December 18: Sagittarius   Ruler: Jupiter

Warm, friendly, and charismatic, with a sharp intellect, you can project confidence. With an innate understanding of how to make social contacts or negotiate yourself a deal, you can do well through associating with people who can be helpful to you. Underneath your winning smile you are determined and assertive, with a strong drive and a need to rise to positions of authority. Proud and idealistic, you like to follow your own path or set of beliefs. Although usually good-humored, at times you may have to avoid becoming overly serious or stubborn. Generous and kindhearted, however, when disciplined your ambition and excellent people skills can help you achieve outstanding results.

♣ THE KING OF CLUBS ♣

As a ruling card of the Clubs suit you are a leading player when it comes to intelligence. Your King Card signifies that you prefer to be in charge rather than in a subservient position and are not afraid to take the initiate. An interesting mixture of conservatism and rebel, you can appear sincere and down-to-earth while making smart quips that many people cannot even comprehend. If a woman with this card, you often think like a man, even though you have the emotions and body of a woman. This means if something needs doing you are not afraid to take the first step and get things done. This is usually good as long as you are careful not to be bossy. Under the double influence of Uranus in the Earthly Spread, you value your freedom and are often ahead of your time. Independent but group aware, you can be inventive and progressive, with a strong sense of individualism. With your highly sensitive nervous system, however, it is important to learn to stay calm, otherwise, tension and impatience can spoil some of your appeal.

Under the influences of Jupiter and Saturn in the Spiritual Spread, you are an excellent strategist who can be tenacious in pursuit of your goals. As you are fully aware that the attainment of your long-term plans takes hard work and persistence, you have only to apply the necessary drive and dedication to really succeed. Whatever you do, being a King Card implies that you have a responsibility to help others with your superior knowledge, emphasizing the importance of developing your many natural talents.

Your Two Replacement Cards Are the 2 of Spades & the 8 of Spades.

As the King of Clubs you share the same planetary position as the 2 of Spades in the Spiritual Spread. This signifies that working partnerships and cooperative ventures can play a big part in your life. This 2 influence also suggests a need for you to keep balanced between your overconfidence and self-doubt, as well as your independence and need for part-

nership. If you lose this balance you may be prone to hidden fears. Usually on the right path, however, you can impress others with your clear thinking or objective and unbiased views. At these times you show your consideration for others and often take a protective attitude toward people around you.

You also share the same planetary position as the 8 of Spades in the Earthly Spread, which indicates that you enjoy power and can be resolute and authoritative with strong convictions. With this 8 influence, you usually seek security, accomplishment, and material success. Being proud and capable with good organizational skills, when you display your steadfast and unshakable certainty and determination, you are often given management positions. Although very competent, you may have to develop your patience and tolerance through being understanding and taking others people's weaknesses into consideration before passing judgment.

You have special or karmic links with people who are represented by the 2 of Spades and 8 of Spades. As you share the same planetary positions you can be soul mates or understand each other very well. Even if you do not get along, you can both see clearly how the other person operates.

Your Mercury Card is . . .

The Jack of Diamonds
- Able to learn subjects quickly, you particularly value knowledge and freedom of thought. By continually educating yourself you can develop your outstanding potential.
- With your fast mental responses and ability to stand your ground, you usually enjoy the witty retort or controversial discussion.
- You have innate writing ability or can present your ideas in an interesting way.

The King of Clubs Planetary Card Sequence

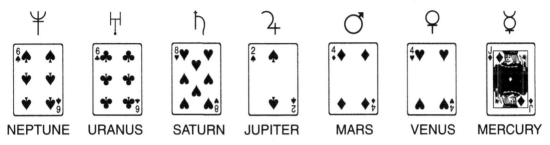

| NEPTUNE | URANUS | SATURN | JUPITER | MARS | VENUS | MERCURY |

- Friendly and clever, you are particularly attracted to people who can keep you entertained or who have a youthful spirit.
- You can have a good mental rapport with people who are the Jack of Diamonds and find them creatively stimulating. This is a good link for communication and the exchange of ideas.

Your Venus Card is . . .

The 4 of Hearts

- In relationships you prefer to be honest and direct, and as security is also important to you, you value loyalty.
- Although usually sociable and loving, at times in relationships you can be strict and emotionally undemonstrative, especially if you feel people are not being honest with you.
- A practical side of you likes to create stability in your dealings with others. This card is a good indicator for a strong marriage.
- You value strong family links and can be an excellent parent, often sacrificing for the sakes of your children.
- Usually you are drawn to people represented by the 4 of Hearts, especially if they share your creative interests. They are ideal for love and romance as well as close friendships and good business partnerships.

Your Mars Card is . . .

The 4 of Diamonds

- You are usually willing to work hard to achieve your desires.
- Since for you stubbornness or being too frank can lead to arguments, it may be necessary to be more flexible.
- A pragmatic and sensible side of you shows that you will very rarely be without money. Even when things look difficult you will find some plan to make things happen.
- 4 of Diamonds people can particularly motivate and stimulate you into action. Avoid confrontations, however, especially if you are both stubborn. By channeling your energies constructively you can achieve a great deal.

Your Jupiter Card is . . .

The 2 of Spades

- Although independent, partnerships and teamwork efforts can pay off in a big way both emotionally and materially.
- You may swing between arrogance and oversensitivity.
- Travel or getting away every so often can be especially good for you.
- Be careful of dependency situations or overindulgence, which could prove to be weak spots and sap your energy.

- Your inner idealist likes to include others in your big plans.
- Usually you have a good rapport with 2 of Spades people, as they are often benefactors who can bring opportunities and expand or enhance your life, especially as they are also your Replacement Card.

Your Saturn Card is . . .

The 8 of Hearts

- Although you can possess uncompromising determination, a tendency to relax and enjoy the good life suggests you may still need to develop your self-discipline in achieving your goals.
- Your powerful emotions show that you are not afraid to stand up for yourself, but be careful not to go too far and get embroiled in power challenges.
- You possess good organizational or executive abilities that can help you succeed.
- With this Heart Card influence, your major tests in life are often emotional ones. You do have, however, the strength and capabilities to overcome any difficulties.
- 8 of Hearts people can be your guides and help you recognize your shortcomings if you are willing to work on your boundaries and self-awareness. Although it may not always be easy, you can learn from your experiences with these people.

Your Uranus Card is . . .

The 6 of Clubs

- You value freedom and do not like to be restricted.
- A humanitarian side to your nature suggests you may be interested in reforms or changing and bettering circumstances for others.
- A contrary streak or emotional tensions and inhibitions can cause anxiety. You need a harmonious environment and to keep educating yourself in self-improvement, as this helps you to stay detached.
- Your powerful mental intuition can be developed to guide both your life and help others.
- 6 of Clubs people can help you be more objective about yourself due to your Uranus connection. This is also a good friendship link.

Your Neptune Card is . . .

The 6 of Spades

- Although peace is an important ideal for you, if this causes you to get stuck in a comfortable routine, you may not stretch yourself to your full potential.
- You possess an innate understanding that you do not get anything for nothing or that whatever you put out you get back.
- Much more sensitive than you show people, you can guide your life through your inner vision and deeper emotional insight if you listen to it and trust it.
- Even though your old age can be a contented time for you, you are still likely to want to keep busy with some type of work.
- People represented by the 6 of Spades have a psychic link with you. You may share the same dreams or ideals but also stay realistic.

Your Challenge Card is . . .

The Queen of Hearts

- Share your feelings and emotional needs with those close to you, especially partners.
- Transmute a tendency to be lazy or too laid-back to working on achieving your ideals.
- The royal card here signifies your leading part in influencing others. Being a Hearts Card particularly emphasizes the power of love in this process.

- Queen of Hearts people can usually provoke you to react. They can bring out the best or the worst aspects of your personality. Although these people can help you to transform your life, resist becoming involved in power struggles.

The Result of Your Challenge Card is . . .

The 10 of Clubs
- You find work or projects to be enthusiastic about, especially ones where you feel you are learning.
- You can think "success."
- You feel spirited and alive rather than stuck in a comfortable routine.
- People represented by the 10 of Clubs can stimulate your natural talents. They often reflect how well you are responding to your challenges.

Famous People Who Are the King of Clubs

John Lennon, George Harrison, Frankie Muniz, Walt Disney, Marie Curie, Queen Elizabeth II, Fritz Lang, Malcolm X, Leon Trotsky, D. H. Lawrence, Jessica Mitford, Sean Ono Lennon, Little Richard, Fidel Castro, Rembrandt, Robert Hand, Jackson Browne, Barry Manilow, Pete Townshend, Alfred Hitchcock, Joey Ramone, Meher Baba, W. A. Mozart, G. F. Handel, Joan Crawford, Christina Rossetti, Joni Mitchell, Otto Preminger, Moby, Dean Martin, Renoir, Sharon Osbourne, Lewis Carroll, Venus Williams

Birthdays Governed by the King of Clubs

January 27: Aquarius   Ruler: Uranus
As an original and independent thinker you enjoy new ideas and progressive ways of doing things. Being friendly, you love to socialize and share your many ideas with others; this can be extended to developing your innate humanitarianism. Even though you rely on your fast intelligence, you can also be sensitive and idealistic. With a desire for harmony, you are home loving and may be musical, but at times you can become highly strung or anxious. Usually responsible and inventive, however, you can display remarkable strength in achieving your goals.

February 25: Pisces   Ruler: Neptune
An intelligent person with strong vision, your idealism urges you to seek harmony and perfection. Mentally analytical yet imaginative and sensitive, you have a wide emotional range. With your quick wit and sharp insight into human nature, you can be popular and successful. Sensible and judicious, you also possess a nonconformist streak that is more experimental or rebellious. Although responsible, avoid a tendency to sometimes be moody or impatient. The more you trust your exceptional intuition or develop your natural humanitarianism the happier you will be. You can particularly excel by using your fine brain power combined with your strong intuition or compassion. You may especially value your home as a special haven of retreat from the harsh world.

March 23: Aries   Ruler: Mars
Strong and commanding, you are a dynamic personality with keen intelligence. Although you can be daring, you never lose your practicality. Honest and direct with others, you often find yourself naturally taking charge. As long as you stay disciplined and tolerant this is fine, and you are able to help or inspire others with your original ideas and creative power. If you become selfish, however, you may be impatient or too tough and cause resentment. Usually you are spirited and adventurous with

a need to channel your drive into exploring new experiences.

April 21: Aries/Taurus
Ruler: Mars/Venus

Born on the cusp of Aries and Taurus, you have both the leadership skills of Aries and the solid practicality of Taurus. Intelligent, proud, and resolute, you like to present a strong front. Honest and direct with others, you enjoy company and are likely to have many social connections. Capable and hardworking, your inner sense of power can make you firm and uncompromising, which can work for you when being courageous and disciplined or against you if you become too controlling. An appreciation of beauty and nature may inspire a love of art and music that you may wish to develop further.

May 19: Taurus   Ruler: Venus

Proud and mentally bright, you like to be seen as open and straightforward. Besides your frank manner you can be friendly and people-oriented, with a need for a strong purpose in life. A naturally creative thinker, your progressive attitude can take you to the top. With your strong convictions it is important to stay positive and focused, as otherwise an egotistical or self-indulgent streak may sidetrack you from your high ideals. You may have to get the balance right between your own self-development and your desire to help others.

June 17: Gemini   Ruler: Mercury

Friendly and thoughtful, your superior intelligence and strong-willed disposition usually become clearly evident. As well as being analytical you also have original ideas and like to think things through. Nevertheless, at times you may be hasty or impatient. Determined with a perfectionist streak, you particularly benefit from your communication skills, such

as, in writing, law, or education. Equally, your youthful spirit implies you can be creative or musical. Always wanting to learn, you gain from sharing your knowledge with others.

July 15: Cancer   Ruler: Moon

Spirited, intelligent, but sensitive, you are a person of opposites. Although you are highly imaginative, sympathetic, and impressionable, you usually let your keen intellect make the decisions. You are likely to have an interest in education or philosophy and can make a good writer. With your fast instincts, you pick up on situations very quickly and have many creative ideas. Although you have a strong love of home you are also adventurous and independent with remarkable potential. You need projects that challenge you in order to stop from becoming restless.

August 13: Leo   Ruler: Sun

Ambitious and intellectually bright, you are a strong-willed individual with innovative ideas. Your natural dramatic sense blends well with your determination and need to accomplish. Proud and courageous, you can be especially successful as a leader in business, education, acting, directing, producing, or as a writer. Your innate rebel streak can even work for you as long as you do not become too stubborn and uncompromising. Whatever you do, your natural executive abilities, creative ideas, or good organizational skills are sure to come to the fore.

September 11: Virgo   Ruler: Mercury

With your keen mental abilities, practicality, and sensitivity you have everything you need to reach the top in life. You learn fast, and when you do a job you like to do it well. Although you possess a sharp mind and can be articulate and precise, you may have to avoid being too critical. Your excellent analytical skills, however, may serve you fine in research or writing. Although you have a playful side, ideally you should be in a position of authority. Goal-oriented, you benefit from applying your strong intuition to your practical plans.

October 9: Libra   Ruler: Venus

Honest and frank, you are an original and idealistic person with keen intelligence and a friendly personality. An interesting blend of pragmatist and rebel, you benefit from projects that involve you emotionally. At times you can be romantic and sensitive, yet at others you may seem undemonstrative. Nevertheless, you also possess a humanitarian side to your nature that can bring much satisfaction if developed. Guard against a stubborn or selfish streak, however. Naturally artistic or creative with excellent people skills, you are usually popular and forward thinking in your views.

November 7: Scorpio   Ruler: Mars

Emotionally sensitive yet highly intelligent, you have an analytical and forthright approach to life. With your penetrating insight and natural psychic ability you can often get straight to the heart of a matter, though be careful of a tendency to withdraw and appear cold or too self-absorbed. Imaginative, resourceful, and smart, you can be a natural leader in almost any field you choose. If positive you are likely to have broad-minded humanitarian beliefs. The extremes of your nature suggest you need regular time alone for reflection. Although practical, you may be attracted to philosophy or metaphysical knowledge.

December 5: Sagittarius   Ruler: Jupiter

Independent, clever, and strong-willed, you are a person who likes to be in charge. Equally, you realize the importance of others and so place a special value on your partnerships and collaborative efforts. Honest and frank, you

have strong convictions and like to be direct, although avoid becoming tense or impatient. As you need freedom and mental stimulation, travel, education, or large projects are good catalysts to arouse your sense of adventure and progressive ideas. Broad-minded, idealistic, and intelligent, you can be protective and a pillar of support for others.

◆ THE KING OF DIAMONDS ◆

As a King of Diamonds you usually possess a forceful character, good business acumen, and strong ambition. Determined to succeed, you may have to work hard for your material success and recognition, but you often prosper through your enterprising spirit or by finding expression for your idealism and creativity. Although you can be an astute judge of character, if you are too impatient or competitive, you may create conflict or tension. The royal influence of this card also implies that as a proud and single-minded individual, you do not feel at ease in low or subservient positions. You are more inclined to seek your independence or be your own boss. Although your card suggests that you are destined to rise to positions of authority or influence, you first need to recognize the responsibilities that come with such a high position. One of the key rules is that a good king shares his wealth with others.

The planetary influences of Venus and Mars in your Earthly Spread indicates that you are courageous, motivated, and creative. When inspired your need for self-expression can become a strong incentive for work and productivity. Although you can be kind and understanding with good social skills, a lack of tact can sometimes cause intense situations. With your dynamic charm and need to be popular, however, your relationships often prove especially important to you.

The planetary influences of Jupiter and Uranus in your Spiritual Spread signifies that you can rise above the material world. Usually you are progressive and open to experimenting with new ideas, religions, or philosophies. Strong urges to break away from convention suggest that you have a rebel streak or may be far more interested in the unconventional than the ordinary. Your love of freedom and the ability to intuitively sense good ideas suggests that you can have many fortunate opportunities to realize your objectives.

Your Two Replacement Cards Are the 7 of Spades & the 3 of Clubs.

As the King of Diamonds you share the same position as the 7 of Spades in the Earthly Spread. As this card is often associated with spiritual victory, finding an expression for your talents is essential to your inner faith and sense of self-worth, otherwise, you can become cynical. You have the potential, however, to become a channel for higher spiritual expressions that can inspire or bring wisdom to others. There is a great deal you can achieve with your conviction and perseverance.

As the King of Diamonds you share the same position as the 3 of Clubs in the Spiritual Spread. Since this card is often linked to intellectual creativity and versatility, you are likely to have many interests or be involved in the pursuit of knowledge. This influence also suggests you can have a gift with words, whether through presenting your ideas or writing. The indecisiveness and worry linked to this card implies, however, that unless you focus on your aims and objectives you are in danger of scattering your energies in too many directions.

You usually have special or karmic links with people who are represented by the 3 of Clubs and the 7 of Spades, as you share the same planetary positions. You can be soul mates, understand each other very well, or be a source of inspiration. Even if you do not get along, you can both see clearly how the other person operates.

Your Mercury Card is . . .

The 6 of Hearts
- Sociable and sensitive, your direct yet sympathetic approach toward others can help you win many friends.
- Your creative ideas and artistic expression can attract you to writing or the arts.
- Highly intuitive, your sixth sense or gut feeling are often accurate.
- Your home and family are especially important to your well-being.
- You should have good mental rapport and special communication with people represented by the 6 of Hearts, as they activate your Mercury Card. These people can also be lifelong friends or business partners.

Your Venus Card is . . .

The 4 of Clubs
- You like to be well informed, since the knowledge you gain is usually utilized in practical ways.
- Your positive mental attitude can help you to overcome emotional tensions or mental restlessness.
- Ideally you like to mix your social activities with learning new skills, intellectual interests, or favorite pursuits.
- In relationships guard against being bossy, stubborn, or arrogant.
- A desire for knowledge or curiosity about people may influence you to explore subjects such as astrology or psychology.

The King of Diamonds Planetary Card Sequence

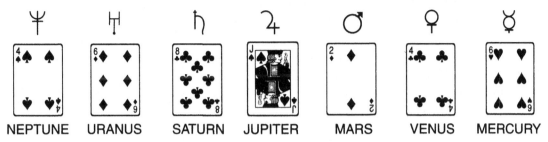

| NEPTUNE | URANUS | SATURN | JUPITER | MARS | VENUS | MERCURY |

- Usually you are drawn to people who are represented by the 4 of Clubs, and especially if they share your creative interests. They are ideal for love and romance as well as close friendships and good business partnerships.

Your Mars Card is . . .

The 2 of Diamonds

- Your financial dealings often benefit from your people skills and ability to network socially.
- The masculine influence of Mars indicates that you can be daring and quite assertive in your business dealings.
- Resist using power tactics as they may backfire and cause arguments in your relationships.
- Successful partnerships can be an important key to material prosperity.
- You gain in relationships when you balance assertively standing up for yourself with being diplomatic.
- People, and especially males, who are represented by the 2 of Diamonds card can particularly enthuse and motivate you. If they are on your side their business acumen can benefit you. Avoid being too competitive with this person, by channeling the energy constructively to get a great deal done.

Your Jupiter Card is . . .

The Jack of Spades

- Your sense of adventure may inspire you to travel for pleasure or for career opportunities. The spiritual message of this card indicates that if you want to succeed honesty and integrity are essential.
- Self-discipline and a mature acceptance of responsibilities will also help you to achieve your lofty goals.
- An interest in metaphysical subjects can inspire or transform your life.
- To avoid harmful relationships with dubious characters use your discerning mind and trust your instincts.
- Usually you have a good rapport with Jack of Spades people, as often they can bring positive opportunities into life or make you feel more optimistic. Alternatively, these people can have a spiritual link with you.

Your Saturn Card is . . .

The 8 of Clubs

- As Saturn is your taskmaster, you benefit from developing your intellectual abilities and long-term planning.
- Resist a tendency to be stubborn or fixed in your views, as it can lead to misunderstandings.

- Although you can be very determined, you need to be self-disciplined if you want to master your craft or give structure to your thoughts.
- Your intelligence and good organizational skills can elevate you to positions of authority.
- You may have to overcome a fear of being controlled or manipulated by others. Alternatively, if you become fearful, avoid being controlling yourself.
- The mental power shown here indicates you have excellent healing abilities and the strength to overcome obstacles.
- 8 of Clubs people can be your teachers or criticize your weaknesses. If you are willing to work on your self-awareness these people can bring valuable lessons.

Your Uranus Card is . . .

The 6 of Diamonds
- Your intuition, objectivity, and patience can lead to good luck or financial opportunities.
- Unexpected financial expenses or gains are indicated by your past actions.
- Resist getting stuck in a rut, either in a desire for an easy life or in low-paying jobs that have no scope for growth.
- A responsible attitude toward money can minimize the threat of debts.
- You can get much satisfaction from developing and utilizing your innate humanitarian streak.
- 6 of Diamonds people can help you be more objective about yourself. This is also a good friendship or partnerships link where freedom is valued.

Your Neptune Card is . . .

The 4 of Spades
- Your later years can be very productive, so your retirement may be delayed. You are also likely to enjoy an active life and good health.
- Your work can be linked to distant places or involve travel.
- If you develop your spirituality this can be a source of joy and contentment, especially in your old age.
- 4 of Spades people may positively link to your ideals and visions for the future, but also guard against escapism or delusion

Your Challenge Card is . . .

The 10 of Hearts
- Recognize the power of love and the emotional fulfillment it can bring.
- Guard against getting emotionally carried away.
- Present your creative talents in the public domain.
- People represented by the 10 of Hearts card can provoke you to bring out the best or the worst of your personality. Although these people can create intense emotional situations, they can also help you to transform your life.

The Result of Your Challenge Card is . . .

The 10 of Diamonds
- You can judge your material success on the basis of the values that you set for yourself.
- Your financial success and grand plans can be achieved by expressing your high ideals and creative talents.
- Prosperity and fulfillment comes from understanding the value of love.
- People who are represented by the 10 of Diamonds can reflect how you are responding to your challenges.

Famous People Who Are the King of Diamonds

George Clooney, Abraham Lincoln, Sharon Stone, Tony Blair, Charles Darwin, Albert Schweitzer, LL Cool J, Franz Kafka, Orson Welles, Sigmund Freud, Dr. Ruth, Franco Zeffirelli, Imelda Marcos, Betty Ford, Rudolph Valentino, Faye Dunaway, Mary Pickford, Julian Lennon, Prince Edward, Jerry Hall, Dennis Weaver, Willie Mays, Michelle Phillips, Christina Ricci, Angelina Jolie, Kofi Annan

Birthdays Governed by the King of Diamonds

January 14: Capricorn Ruler: Saturn

Determined, talented, and ambitious, your resolute nature is usually hidden under your friendly charm. Often practical and hardworking, with your leadership qualities and perseverance you can achieve recognition and status in your chosen profession. Your ruler, Saturn, under the influence of the 8 of Clubs emphasizes that you can empower yourself through your special talents and skills or the knowledge you gained. Although your pragmatic nature and good sense of values can help your business plans, lack of discipline or restlessness can undermine your efforts or creativity. When you utilize your wisdom in a practical way you usually succeed.

February 12: Aquarius Ruler: Uranus

Your friendly approach and quick perception indicate that you are a charismatic person with common sense. Although you may not make it evident, you usually tend to take the lead once you know that others are supporting you. According to your ruler, Uranus, you are usually progressive, spontaneous, and independent. Although you want the freedom to enjoy different experiences and to make your own decisions, resist spending your money or scattering your energies in too many directions due to restlessness. Luckily, your good sense of values and the need for material security will give you the incentive to focus on your goals and achieve success out in the big world.

March 10: Pisces Ruler: Neptune

Your grand and ambitious plans are often based on your imaginative ideas and intuitive understanding of money and values. Your ruler, Neptune, indicates that you are an idealistic and sensitive individual with strong feelings. According to your ruling card, the 4 of Spades, when your inspired ideas are backed up by your pragmatic reasoning and hard work you can succeed admirably. Although your friendly charm and mild manner attracts other people, being endowed with executive attributes also suggests that your independent nature can at times make your bossy or stubborn. Nevertheless, your great potential to achieve success rests on your ability to be both practical and inspiring.

April 8: Aries Ruler: Mars

Energetic and ambitious, your determination and willingness to work hard for your objectives signify that sooner or later you rise to positions of power and influence. According to your ruler, Mars, you are usually strong-willed and full of vitality. Although you can be forceful and dynamic, at times others can interpret your assertive manner as controlling, bossy, or too aggressive. Luckily, the influence of the 2 of Diamonds also makes you aware that there are great benefits or financial rewards to be gained from diplomacy and collaborating with others. Nevertheless, in order to maintain good partnerships resist power struggles and insist on equality.

May 6: Taurus   Ruler: Venus
Idealistic and mentally quick, your direct approach blends well with your charm or friendly demeanor. Your ruler, Venus, endows you with a charismatic personality, a head for business, and a taste for rich living. Able to apply your pragmatic and analytical skills to problem solving indicates that you are insightful and discerning. Although you may be inspired by lofty ideas, as a royal card you can excel in almost anything you want to do. Nevertheless, if you want to rise up to the challenge of your card, you may find that establishing a good philosophy on life and perfecting your cerebral power can turn out to be one of your best investments.

June 4: Gemini   Ruler: Mercury
Your friendly and easygoing manner often disguises your determination and ambitious nature. According to your ruler, Mercury, you are an intuitive thinker and a sympathetic communicator. Your self-reliant attitude and analytical abilities can also make you independent and persuasive. Having an inquisitive mind and a compelling need to express yourself creatively implies that you can be preoccupied with subjects that can help you gain greater self-awareness. Alternatively, being creative and versatile, you may want to express your idealism and talents by working on projects close to your heart. Under the influence of your Mercury Card, the 6 of Hearts, many of your personal relationships and especially family ties are linked to past karma.

July 2: Cancer   Ruler: Moon
Possessing inner strength and powerful emotions implies that, although you may appear unassuming or reserved, you are often disguising your dynamic nature and special talents. Your ruler, the Moon, indicates that usually you are a caring, friendly, and receptive indi-

vidual. Being able to intuitively assess people, others are often drawn to your sympathetic or charming demeanor. Although your comfort and security are essential to your well-being, your restless emotions can cause mood swings or emotional fluctuations. With the right incentives, however, your creativity and business acumen can help you excel in financial enterprises and partnerships. In fact, activities relating to the public may prove to be both financially rewarding and emotional fulfilling.

♠THE KING OF SPADES♠

As the King of Spades you are not only a royal card, but in the unique position of making only one appearance in the year and in the card system. Unlike most cards, your positions in both the Earthly and the Spiritual spreads is unchangeable; therefore, you do not have any Replacements Cards. Being associated with this dynamic card suggests that your potential for achievement is immense if you are willing to transcend the prospect of a mundane existence and follow your inspired ideals. In order to achieve your goals, however, you need to be self-disciplined and autonomous. Alternatively, you can develop your leadership abilities and show your unflagging determination. Indecision, lack of motivation, and failure to see your golden opportunities may leave you disappointed or frustrated at your own failures. Although you are by nature pragmatic and realistic, resist letting a pessimistic outlook undermine and repress your vitality and idealism. Capable of enduring and persevering, your inner strength and wisdom usually increase with time and experience.

The powerful influence of Saturn and the Sun indicate that you enjoy power and usually an older or hardworking male played an important role in shaping your personality or future. This could even be a teacher or guide who inspired you or helped you to get started, if not your father. The particular energies of the number 1 associated with your card indicate that in your life you will be forced to learn about being independent and self-reliant. For this reason you will gain a great deal of insight from learning to stand on your own two feet. As you are also likely to want freedom from mundane existence, you may encounter spiritual issues concerning your inner faith and self-mastery.

Your Mercury Card is . . .

The 3 of Hearts

- Your mental sensitivity signifies that you think creatively and often let your feelings influence your thoughts.
- Your charm and subtle ways can make a strong impression on other people.
- Mixed emotions can often bring uncertainty and even confusion to your early relationships and family ties.
- Often mature beyond your years, your vulnerability, sensitivity, or need for affection may go unnoticed by others.
- You should have good mental rapport and special communication with people represented by the 3 of Hearts, as they activate your Mercury Card. These people can also be lifelong friends or business partners.

Your Venus Card is . . .

The Ace of Clubs

- Your intellectual pursuits or quest for knowledge may link you to important relationships or friendships.
- Your enthusiasm and passion for modern ideas can inspire you to initiate new projects or enterprises.
- Your appetite for mentally stimulating experiences suggest that although you have a fast mind you may also have a tendency to be abrupt with individuals less clever than you.
- Attracted to sharp and intelligent individuals, you are usually drawn to people who are represented by Ace of Clubs, especially if they share your creative interests. They are ideal for love and romance as well as close friendships and good business partnerships.

Your Mars Card is . . .

The Queen of Clubs

- This royal card gives you exceptional intellectual powers and heightened intuitive abilities.
- Your work may involve writing, serving the public through teaching, or guiding others to greater knowledge.
- Usually you have excellent organizational skills and a commanding presence due to

The King of Spades Planetary Card Sequence

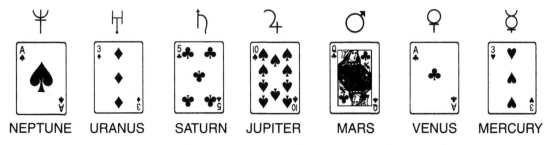

your ability to make sound judgments and act quickly upon your decisions.

- Women can play a significant role in your path to success.
- A certain reluctance to listen to criticism suggests that you prefer to make up your own mind.
- The relationships you have with Queen of Clubs people can be special or good if you both share the same aspirations. Resist arguments or being competitive with these people, as they can drain your mental energy or cause stress.

Your Jupiter Card is . . .

The 10 of Spades
- Jupiter, the great benefactor, often rewards your determination and willingness to work hard for your goals.
- The ability to think on a grand scale or visualize the whole suggests that you have exceptional talents for undertaking large projects.
- The mystical powers of this card imply that you are success-oriented or that you have high aims and objectives regarding your career.
- Your ambition to succeed may lead you to work in the public domain.
- 10 of Spades people can be your benefactors, bringing opportunities to expand and enhance your life. Alternatively, these people can have a spiritual link with you.

Your Saturn Card is . . .

The 5 of Clubs
- Versatile and multitalented, your ability to make progress depends on how quickly you can adapt to changing situations.
- The alternating nature of this card also indicates that one of your challenges will be to

resist scattering your energies on too many objectives by disciplining your mental restlessness.

- Learning to persevere and maintain continuity can help you cope with fluctuating circumstances.
- Important changes in middle years can bring insight or valuable lessons to increase your spiritual awareness.
- 5 of Clubs people can be your teachers or show you your need for discipline and responsibility. Although these people may bring uncertainty or burdens, if you are willing to work on your self-awareness they can offer valuable lessons.

Your Uranus Card is . . .

The 3 of Diamonds
- Use your ingenuity and versatility, especially if you want to benefit from fresh opportunities or new business ventures.
- In order to avoid worry and uncertainty you have to be very clear about your career direction and your financial circumstances.
- When taking a detached and objective view on life you can come up with many creative ideas.
- Indecision and mental restlessness can undermine your efforts and achievements.
- 3 of Diamonds people can help you be more objective about yourself. With regard to business dealings they can be beneficial yet unpredictable. This is, however, a good link for friendship.

Your Neptune Card is . . .

The Ace of Spades
- This card indicates that you have a highly developed sixth sense that will come into its own in latter years.

- Your curiosity or a desire for greater awareness can lead you to explore mysticism or metaphysical and philosophical subjects.
- Your leadership abilities may inspire you to teach or be of service to others.
- Ace of Spades people can help you materialize your dreams. If they are wise and knowledgeable they can inspire you spiritually. In these relationships, however, you may need to stay grounded.

Your Challenge Card is . . .

The 7 of Hearts

- Develop your inner faith and live up to your ideals.
- Practice emotional detachment in your close relationships.
- Stand on your own two feet rather than feel let down by those who cannot live up to your expectations.
- Learn to love unconditionally and not withdraw and appear cold or cynical.
- Express yourself emotionally honestly in the moment even if you feel vulnerable.
- 7 of Hearts people can fascinate you but also challenge you. Although they may force you to express yourself they can also touch upon your insecurities or the worst aspects of your personality. These people can, however, help you to transform your life if you can resist power conflicts.

The Result of Your Challenge Card is . . .

The 7 of Diamonds

- The mystical power of the number 7 in both your Challenge and Result cards indicates that a higher power is at work and, therefore, your faith is constantly tested.

- Through perseverance and inner faith you can overcome financial difficulties and turn potentially challenging situations into success stories.
- Your financial or material success depends on you and not on others.
- If you can maintain a positive outlook and think abundance you also have the power to manifest your dreams.
- 7 of Diamonds people can help you understand your inner thoughts or insecurities and your reaction to them often reflect how you are responding to your challenges.

Famous People Who Are the King of Spades

J. Edgar Hoover, Paul Revere, Betsy Ross, J. D. Salinger, Verne "Mini-Me" Troyer, Barry Goldwater

Birthdays Governed by the King of Spades

January 1: Capricorn   Ruler: Saturn

Idealistic and practical, the unique attributes associated with your card indicate that you possess great initiative and innate leadership qualities. Your ruler, Saturn, also suggests that you are likely to be ambitious with strong views. Even though you can sometimes have a restless nature, your quick perception and sharp insight often provides you with the incentive to be independent. In order to achieve the great potential indicated by your card, however, you need to develop the necessary patience and self-discipline to make your great goals a reality. When inspired by knowledge and wisdom your sound judgment and responsible attitude can put you in positions of authority.

♥ ♣ THE JOKER ♦ ♠

CLEVER AND PRAGMATIC, with a strong dramatic streak, you are usually a unique individual with natural charisma. Being hardworking and organized with forceful opinions, you often have a practical way of approaching life. Yet you are also creative and possess a powerful need for self-expression that may take you into working with music, art, writing, or drama.

The Joker card belongs in the crown line and has no set planetary position, number, suit, or Personal Card Sequence. This gives you special talents and a certain freedom, with the result that you can often be a law unto yourself. Although you can adapt to any card in the system, you may find that operating under the influence of either the King of Spades or the Ace of Hearts relates to you the most.

Just as the jester in the courts acted out "the fool" archetype, you have the ability to keep others entertained and act from outside the usual order or conformity. At times this can give you powerful projection, profound insight, or great inner strength. If operating negatively, however, you might cleverly disguise your motives or give up your principles in the quest for money or material gain.

Having different sides to your personality can sometimes make you an enigma and hard for others to figure out. Nevertheless, to obtain the respect you desire, you are usually reliable and dependable and take your work very seriously. Independent and proud, at these times you also prefer to be in control or take charge, giving the orders rather than being told what to do. Ambitious and goal-oriented with natural business sense, you can be enterprising and multitalented. Although you are strong-willed and want to excel at whatever you do, avoid a tendency to be obstinate or too demanding. Dramatic, sensitive, and creative, you can be attracted to the theater. Your talent for words, whether through speaking, writing, or presenting your ideas can also help in your overall success. Often you are blessed with strong intuitive gifts that you can develop further through listening to your inner guidance.

At your best you can be dynamic, gifted, and humble, willing to help others with your insight and talents. You may have to avoid, however, giving way to anxieties or melancholic and pessimistic moods. Equally, resist exaggerating negative experiences into tragedies. With your bold charm, you like to be the center of attention, possessing a childlike innocence and youthful quality that will stay with you throughout life. Although you can be persistent in obtaining your objectives, when you combine your creative streak with self-discipline and practical determination you are able to make the most of your potential and unique talents.

FAMOUS PEOPLE WHO ARE THE JOKER

Ben Kingsley, Henri Matisse, Elizabeth Arden, Val Kilmer, Sarah Miles, Barbara Carrera, John Denver, Donna Summer, Joey McIntyre, Odetta, Anthony Hopkins

PART III

Your Destiny Years

A Card for Every Year of Your Life

THE CARD SYSTEM also provides you with a unique opportunity to see the whole of your life through the symbols of the cards. Each year is represented by one card, and it influences you from one birthday to the next. For example:

When an Ace of Hearts person has their twenty-seventh birthday, they are strongly affected by the 2 of Hearts Card. This means that there is a strong influence of emotional relationships all that coming year. A person may find a deep love partnership in that year or be more emotionally aware of others. They may learn to balance being emotionally independent with a need for partnership. This is a strong love card.

Alternatively, when a 4 of Clubs person turns 50 the 9 of Diamonds becomes influential. Since the number 9 signifies the end of a cycle, and Diamonds can refer to money and very practical affairs, it is often a year of concluding old business and letting go of the past in order to move on. This can vary from leaving homes to just clearing out all the old junk in our cupboards and houses. The Diamonds influence of values here also suggests that with all this clearing, the 4 of Clubs individual is likely to process and transform their previous values, hence experiencing the positive 9 quality of broad-mindedness.

Find the cards governing each and every year of your life from the Birth Card list that follows:

THE HEARTS SUIT

Ace of Hearts

Age 0 to 7: Ad, Qd, 5h, 3c, 3s, 9h, 7c

Age 7 to 14: 9d, 5c, Kd, Jd, 7d, Js, 3c

Age 14 to 21: 4s, 8c, Jd, 10s, 4d, 8d, 2d

Age 21 to 28: 8s, 3s, 10s, 10c, Ks, Qs, 2h

Age 28 to 35: Qs, 10d, Kd, 3d, 7h, 5s, 9h

Age 35 to 42: 5h, 3s, 3d, Ad, 9s, Qc, 2d

Age 42 to 49: 6s, 10d, Ad, 10h, 6d, 10s, Ks

Age 49 to 56: 5s, 3s, Qh, Ks, 10c, 2h, 4s

Age 56 to 63: 2h, Ad, 6s, 8h, 7s, 7c, 3s

Age 63 to 70: 2s, 7h, 8h, Js, Jd, 8c, 4c

Age 70 to 77: 8s, Qd, 4d, Kd, Qs, 6c, Js

Age 77 to 84: Ad, 9h, Kd, Jh, 6h, 10d, Ac

Age 84 to 90: 7d, 7s, Jh, 3d, Qs, 2h, 10d

2 of Hearts

Age 0 to 7: Kh, Kd, 6h, 4c, 2d, Js, 8c

Age 7 to 14: 10d, Qh, 4c, Qd, 2c, As, 9h

Age 14 to 21: 6s, 8h, Qd, 3d, Ah, 4s, 8c

Age 21 to 28: 8d, 6d, 3d, 5d, 9s, Kh, 9h

Age 28 to 35: Kc, As, 5d, 9d, Qc, 10s, 8c

Age 35 to 42: Js, Jd, 9d, Kd, 2s, 6s, 9h

Age 42 to 49: 6c, Kh, Kd, 3c, Qs, 9c, 8c

Age 49 to 56: 4s, 10h, 3c, 8h, 8s, Kc, 9h

Age 56 to 63: Ad, 6s, 8h, 7s, 7c, 3s, 8c

Age 63 to 70: 10s, 4d, 7s, As, 2d, 6c, 9h

Age 70 to 77: 3h, Kc, As, 7h, 10c, Jc, 8c

Age 77 to 84: 9c, 5c, 7h, Kh, Ah, Ad, 9h

Age 84 to 90: 10d, 6c, Kh, 2c, 4h, 5s, 8c

3 of Hearts

Age 0 to 7: Ac, Qc, 10s, 5c, 3d, As, 7h

Age 7 to 14: Ah, 9d, 5c, Kd, Jd, 7d, Js

Age 14 to 21: 4h, 8c, Jc, Qh, 5h, 7c, Ad

Age 21 to 28: 6c, Jd, Qh, 4s, Ks, 8d, Ac

Age 28 to 35: 8d, Qs, 7s, Qd, As, 4d, 7d

Age 35 to 42: 8d, Qs, 7s, Qd, As, 4d, 7d

Age 42 to 49: 5c, Jd, Qd, Ah, 6s, 10d, Ad

Age 49 to 56: 2s, Qs, Ah, 5s, 3s, Qh, Ks

Age 56 to 63: 4d, Jd, 9c, Ks, 4s, Ac, 4h

Age 63 to 70: Ac, Ah, 2s, 7h, 8h, Js, Jd

Age 70 to 77: Kc, As, 7h, 10c, Jc, 8c, 6h

Age 77 to 84: 7c, 9d, 5h, 7s, 8d, 2d, 10c

Age 84 to 90: Ah, 7d, 7s, Jh, 3d, Qs, 2h

4 of Hearts

Age 0 to 7: 4d, 2s, 8h, 6c, 6s, Qh, 10c

Age 7 to 14: 5s, Qs, 6c, 3h, Ah, 9d, 5c

Age 14 to 21: Js, Ks, 10d, Ac, Qs, 9c, 6h

Age 21 to 28: 8c, Jc, Qh, 5h, 7c, Ad, 10d

Age 28 to 35: 8h, 10c, 5h, 7s, 2c, 2s, Ad

Age 35 to 42: Ks, 7c, 2h, Js, Jd, 9d, Kd

Age 42 to 49: 4c, 7h, 9s, 8s, 3h, 5c, Jd

Age 49 to 56: 10d, Js, 7c, 7h, 5d, Kh, 5c

Age 56 to 63: 5s, Kd, 7h, 6c, 8s, 7d, 9d

Age 63 to 70: 2h, 10s, 4d, 7s, As, 2d, 6c

Age 70 to 77: 4s, Kh, 7s, 2s, 3d, 9h, Jd

Age 77 to 84: 9s, 8h, Kc, Qd, 7d, Jc, 2s

Age 84 to 90: 5s, 8c, Qd, 5h, Kd, 3s, 10c

5 of Hearts

Age 0 to 7: 3c, 3s, 9h, 7c, 5d, Qs, Jc

Age 7 to 14: Kc, 7h, 2d, 2s, 9c, 4s, 7c

Age 14 to 21: Jh, 3s, 2s, 2h, 6s, 8h, Qd

Age 21 to 28: 7c, Ad, 10d, Qc, 3c, 6d, 8h

Age 28 to 35: 7s, 2c, 2s, Ad, 4d, 6d, 6h

Age 35 to 42: 3s, 3d, Ad, 9s, Qc, 2d, Jc

Age 42 to 49: 9h, Qh, As, 4h, 4c, 7h, 9s

Age 49 to 56: Jd, 3d, 4h, 10d, Js, 7c, 7h

Age 56 to 63: Ah, 2h, Ad, 6s, 8h, 7s, 7c

Age 63 to 70: Jc, 6d, Ks, 4h, 2h, 10s, 4d

Age 70 to 77: 8h, 2c, Ad, 2d, 7d, 3c, Jh

Age 77 to 84: 7s, 8d, 2d, 10c, Qs, 4c, 5s

Age 84 to 90: Kd, 3s, 10c, Qh, 10s, 6s, 7h

6 of Hearts

Age 0 to 7: 4c, 2d, Js, 8c, 6d, 4s, 10h

Age 7 to 14: Ad, 10c, 8c, 3s, 4h, 5s, Qs

Age 14 to 21: 9d, Kh, 2c, 7d, 5h, Jh, 3s

Age 21 to 28: 8h, 10h, 7d, 4s, 7s, Js, 4d

Age 28 to 35: 2d, Kh, 3h, 6c, Jd, Qh, 4s

Age 35 to 42: Jh, 10h, 6c, Ac, 8s, 2c, 3c

Age 42 to 49: 4s, Qc, 7c, 8d, 8h, 9d, 2c

Age 49 to 56: As, 6s, 6c, Qc, 4c, Jc, 9d

Age 56 to 63: 10h, 5d, Qc, Kc, 8d, 3h, 4d

Age 63 to 70: 7d, 3s, 9s, 9c, Qd, Kh, Kc

Age 70 to 77: 5s, 5d, 9c, 7c, 4h, 4s, Kh

Age 77 to 84: 10d, Ac, Qc, 8s, 2c, As, 4s

Age 84 to 90: 4d, Jc, Ks, 9c, Ac, 6d, 4c

7 of Hearts

Age 0 to 7: 7d, 5s, Jh, 9c, 9s, 2h, Kh

Age 7 to 14: 2d, 2s, 9c, 4s, 7c, Ks, Qc

Age 14 to 21: 9s, 6c, 10h, Qh, 5c, 8s, As

Age 21 to 28: 9d, Qd, 3h, 4h, 8c, Jc, Qh

Age 28 to 35: 5s, 9h, 4h, 8h, 10c, 5h, 7s

Age 35 to 42: 4s, 5c, 8h, Kh, Kc, Ah, 5h

Age 42 to 49: 9s, 8s, 3h, 5c, Jd, Qd, Ah

Age 49 to 56: 5d, Kh, 5c, 7d, 9c, 2c, 10s

Age 56 to 63: 6c, 8s, 7d, 9d, Jh, 5h, Ah

Age 63 to 70: 8h, Js, Jd, 8c, 4c, 10h, 9d

Age 70 to 77: 10c, Jc, 8c, 6h, 5s, 5d, 9c

Age 77 to 84: Kh, Ah, Ad, 9h, Kd, Jh, 6h

Age 84 to 90: 8s, 9d, 9h, 10h, Kc, Jd, 3c

8 of Hearts

Age 0 to 7: 6c, 6s, Qh, 10c, 8d, Ks, 3h

Age 7 to 14: Kh, 8s, Jc, 10s, 5h, Kc, 7h

Age 14 to 21: Qd, 3d, Ah, 4s, 8c, Jd, 10s

Age 21 to 28: 10h, 7d, 4s, 7s, Js, 4d, Kd

Age 28 to 35: 10c, 5h, 7s, 2c, 2s, Ad, 4d

Age 35 to 42: Kh, Kc, Ah, 5h, 3s, 3d, Ad

Age 42 to 49: 9d, 2c, 5h, 9h, Qh, As, 4h

Age 49 to 56: 8s, Kc, 9h, Qd, Jh, 4d, Ad

Age 56 to 63: 7s, 7c, 3s, 8c, 5c, Jc, Qd

Age 77 to 84: Kc, Qd, 7d, Jc, 2s, 3s, 5d

Age 84 to 90: 7c, Ad, 4s, 8d, 6h, 4d, Jc

9 of Hearts

Age 0 to 7: 7c, 5d, Qs, Jc, 9d, 7s, 2c

Age 7 to 14: 4d, Jh, 6d, 6s, Ac, 9s, 7s

Age 14 to 21: 10c, Kd, 7c, 5s, 3c, 7h, 9s

Age 21 to 28: 5c, Jh, Jd, Kc, Ac, 2s, 7h

Age 28 to 35: 4h, 8h, 10c, 5h, 7s, 2c, 2s

Age 35 to 42: 6h, Jh, 10h, 6c, Ac, 8s, 2c

Age 42 to 49: Qh, As, 4h, 4c, 7h, 9s, 8s

Age 49 to 56: Qd, Jh, 4d, Ad, Ac, 2d, 9s

Age 56 to 63: 6d, Kh, Qh, 3d, 2c, 2s, 2d

Age 63 to 70: 5d, Jh, 5c, 3h, Ac, Ah, 2s

Age 70 to 77: Jd, 6s, 6d, 9d, 9s, 8s, Ah

Age 77 to 84: Kd, Jh, 6h, 10d, Ac, Qc, 8s

Age 84 to 90: 10h, Kc, Jd, 3c, 2s, 2d, Qc

10 of Hearts

Age 0 to 7: 10d, 8s, Ah, Ad, Qd, 5h, 3c

Age 7 to 14: 5d, 8h, Kh, 8s, Jc, 10s, 5h

Age 14 to 21: Qh, 5c, 8s, As, Ad, Kc, 6d

Age 21 to 28: 7d, 4s, 7s, Js, 4d, Kd, As

Age 28 to 35: 9c, 5c, Js, Ah, Qs, 10d, Kd

Age 35 to 42: 6c, Ac, 8s, 2c, 3c, 5d, 10d

Age 42 to 49: 6d, 10s, Ks, Js, Ac, 10c, Jc

Age 49 to 56: 3c, 8h, 8s, Kc, 9h, Qd, Jh

Age 56 to 63: 5d, Qc, Kc, 8d, 3h, 4d, Jd

Age 63 to 70: 9d, Qh, 8d, 4s, 10c, 2c, Kd

Age 70 to 77: 3s, Ks, 10s, Ac, Qh, 5h, 8h

Age 77 to 84: 8c, 3d, 4d, 3c, 6d, Js, 10s

Age 84 to 90: Kc, Jd, 3c, 2s, 2d, Qc, Js

Jack of Hearts

Age 0 to 7: 9c, 9s, 2h, Kh, Kd, 6h, 4c

Age 7 to 14: 6d, 6s, Ac, 9s, 7s, 3d, 6h

Age 14 to 21: 3s, 2s, 2h, 6s, 8h, Qd, 3d

Age 21 to 28: Jd, Kc, Ac, 2s, 7h, 9d, Qd

Age 28 to 35: Jc, 8s, 2h, Kc, As, 5d, 9d

Age 35 to 42: 10h, 6c, Ac, 8s, 2c, 3c, 5d

Age 42 to 49: 5s, 2d, 2h, 6c, Kh, Kd, 3c

Age 49 to 56: 4d, Ad, Ac, 2d, 9s, 7s, Kd

Age 56 to 63: 5h, Ah, 2h, Ad, 6s, 8h, 7s

Age 63 to 70: 5c, 3h, Ac, Ah, 2s, 7h, 8h

Age 70 to 77: 4c, Qc, 2h, 3h, Kc, As, 7h

Age 77 to 84: 6h, 10d, Ac, Qc, 8s, 2c, As

Age 84 to 90: 3d, Qs, 2h, 10d, 6c, Kh, 2c

Queen of Hearts

Age 0 to 7: 10c, 8d, Ks, 3h, Ac, Qc, 10s

Age 7 to 14: 4c, Qd, 2c, As, 9h, 4d, Jh

Age 14 to 21: 5c, 8s, As, Ad, Kc, 6d, 4h

Age 21 to 28: 5h, 7c, Ad, 10d, Qc, 3c, 6h

Age 28 to 35: 4s, Ks, 8d, Ac, 7c, 3s, Qd

Age 35 to 42: 8c, 5s, 6d, 4c, 10c, 3h, 8d

Age 42 to 49: As, 4h, 4c, 7h, 9s, 8s, 3h

Age 49 to 56: Ks, 10c, 2h, 4s, 10h, 3c, 8h

Age 56 to 63: 3d, 2c, 2s, 2d, 10d, 6h, 10h

Age 63 to 70: 8d, 4s, 10c, 2c, Kd, 6s, 6h

Age 70 to 77: 5h, 8h, 2c, Ad, 2d, 7d, 3c

Age 77 to 84: 2h, 9c, 5c, 7h, Kh, Ah, Ad

Age 84 to 90: 10s, 6s, 7h, 8s, 9d, 9h, 10h

King of Hearts

Age 0 to 7: Kd, 6h, 4c, 2d, Js, 8c, 6d

Age 7 to 14: 8s, Jc, 10s, 5h, Kc, 7h, 2d

Age 14 to 21: 2c, 7d, 5h, Jh, 3s, 2s, 2h

Age 21 to 28: 9h, 5c, Jh, Jd, Kc, Ac, 2s

Age 28 to 35: 3h, 6c, Jd, Qh, 4s, Ks, 8d

Age 35 to 42: Kc, Ah, 5h, 3s, 3d, Ad, 9s

Age 42 to 49: Kd, 3c, Qs, 9c, 8c, 4d, 3s

Age 49 to 56: 5c, 7d, 9c, 2c, 10s, 6h, As

Age 56 to 63: Qh, 3d, 2c, 2s, 2d, 10d, 6h

Age 63 to 70: Kc, Ad, Qs, 3d, 5s, 3c, 10d

Age 70 to 77: 7s, 2s, 3d, 9h, Jd, 6s, 6d

Age 77 to 84: Ah, Ad, 9h, Kd, Jh, 6h, 10d

Age 84 to 90: 2c, 4h, 5s, 8c, Qd, 5h, Kd

THE CLUBS SUIT

Ace of Clubs

Age 0 to 7: Qc, 10s, 5c, 3d, As, 7h, 7d

Age 7 to 14: 9s, 7s, 3d, 6h, Ad, 10c, 8c

Age 14 to 21: Qs, 9c, 6h, 9d, Kh, 2c, 7d

Age 21 to 28: 2s, 7h, 9d, Qd, 3h, 4h, 8c

Age 28 to 35: 7c, 3s, Qd, 3c, 6s, 9s, 7d

Age 35 to 42: 8s, 2c, 3c, 5d, 10d, Qh, 8c

Age 42 to 49: 10c, Jc, 5d, 7s, Kc, 2s, 7d

Age 49 to 56: 2d, 9s, 7s, Kd, 8d, 6d, 8c

Age 56 to 63: 4h, 5s, Kd, 7h, 6c, 8s, 7d

Age 63 to 70: Ah, 2s, 7h, 8h, Js, Jd, 8c

Age 70 to 77: Qh, 5h, 8h, 2c, Ad, 2d, 7d

Age 77 to 84: Qc, 8s, 2c, As, 4s, 10h, 8c

Age 84 to 90: 6d, 4c, As, 9s, 3h, Ah, 7d

2 of Clubs

Age 0 to 7: Kc, Jd, 4h, 4d, 2s, 8h, 6c

Age 7 to 14: As, 9h, 4d, Jh, 6d, 6s, Ac

Age 14 to 21: 7d, 5h, Jh, 3s, 2s, 2h, 6s

Age 21 to 28: Ah, 8s, 3s, 10s, 10c, Ks, Qs

Age 28 to 35: 2s, Ad, 4d, 6d, 6h, 2d, Kh

Age 35 to 42: 3c, 5d, 10d, Qh, 8c, 5s, 6d

Age 42 to 49: 5h, 9h, Qh, As, 4h, 4c, 7h

Age 49 to 56: 10s, 6h, As, 6s, 6c, Qc, 4c

Age 56 to 63: 2s, 2d, 10d, 6h, 10h, 5d, Qc

Age 63 to 70: Kd, 6s, 6h, 7d, 3s, 9s, 9c

Age 70 to 77: Ad, 2d, 7d, 3c, Jh, 4c, Qc

Age 77 to 84: As, 4s, 10h, 8c, 3d, 4d, 3c

Age 84 to 90: 4h, 5s, 8c, Qd, 5h, Kd, 3s

3 of Clubs

Age 0 to 7: 3s, 9h, 7c, 5d, Qs, Jc, 9d

Age 7 to 14: 8d, 10h, 5d, 8h, Kh, 8s, Jc

Age 14 to 21: 7h, 9s, 6c, 10h, Qh, 5c, 8s

Age 21 to 28: 6h, 8h, 10h, 7d, 4s, 7s, Js

Age 28 to 35: 6s, 9s, 7d, 4c, Jh, Jc, 8s

Age 35 to 42: 5d, 10d, Qh, 8c, 5s, 6d, 4c

Age 42 to 49: Qs, 9c, 8c, 4d, 3s, 6h, 4s

Age 49 to 56: 8h, 8s, Kc, 9h, Qd, Jh, 4d

Age 56 to 63: 9s, 4c, 9h, 6d, Kh, Qh, 3d

Age 63 to 70: 10d, 8s, 7c, Qc, 5h, Jc, 6d

Age 70 to 77: Jh, 4c, Qc, 2h, 3h, Kc, As

Age 77 to 84: 6d, Js, 10s, 4h, 9s, 8h, Kc

Age 84 to 90: 2s, 2d, Qc, Js, 5d, 5c, 8h

4 of Clubs

Age 0 to 7: 2d, Js, 8c, 6d, 4s, 10h, 10d

Age 7 to 14: Qd, 2c, As, 9h, 4d, Jh, 6d

Age 14 to 21: 7s, Jc, 9h, 10c, Kd, 7c, 5s

Age 21 to 28: 6c, 2c, Ac, 8s, 3s, 10s, 10c

Age 28 to 35: Jh, Jc, 8s, 2h, Kc, As, 5d

Age 35 to 42: 10c, 3h, 8d, Qs, 7s, Qd, As

Age 42 to 49: 7h, 9s, 8s, 3h, 5c, Jd, Qd

Age 49 to 56: Jc, 9d, 3h, 2s, Qs, Ah, 5s

Age 56 to 63: 9h, 6d, Kh, Qh, 3d, 2c, 2s

Age 63 to 70: 10h, 9d, Qh, 8d, 4s, 10c, 2c

Age 70 to 77: Qc, 2h, 3h, Kc, As, 7h, 10c

Age 77 to 84: 5s, Jd, Ks, Qh, 2h, 9c, 5c

Age 84 to 90: As, 9s, 3h, Ah, 7d, 7s, Jh

5 of Clubs

Age 0 to 7: 3d, As, 7h, 7d, 5s, Jh, 9c

Age 7 to 14: Kd, Jd, 7d, Js, 3c, 8d, 10h

Age 14 to 21: 8s, As, Ad, Kc, 6d, 4h, Js

Age 21 to 28: Jh, Jd, Kc, Ac, 2s, 7h, 9d

Age 28 to 35: Js, Jh, Qs, 10d, Kd, 3d, 7h

Age 35 to 42: 8h, Kh, Kc, Ah, 5h, 3s, 3d

Age 42 to 49: Jd, Qd, Ah, 6s, 10d, Ad, 10h

Age 49 to 56: 7d, 9c, 2c, 10s, 6h, As, 6s

Age 56 to 63: Jc, Qd, 10s, Qs, 10c, Js, As

Age 63 to 70: 3h, Ac, Ah, 2s, 7h, 8h, Js

Age 70 to 77: 10h, 3s, Ks, 10s, Ac, Qh, 5h

Age 77 to 84: 7h, Kh, Ah, Ad, 9h, Kd, Jh

Age 84 to 90: 8h, 7c, Ad, 4s, 8d, 6h, 4d

6 of Clubs

Age 0 to 7: 6s, Qh, 10c, 8d, Ks, 3h, Ac

Age 7 to 14: 3h, Ah, 9d, 5c, Kd, Jd, 7d

Age 14 to 21: 10h, Qh, 5c, 8s, As, Ad, Qc

Age 21 to 28: 2c, Ah, 8s, 3s, 10s, 10c, Ks

Age 28 to 35: Jd, Qh, 4s, Ks, 8d, Ac, 7c

Age 35 to 42: Ac, 8s, 2c, 3c, 5d, 10d, Qh

Age 42 to 49: Kh, Kd, 3c, Qs, 9c, 8c, 4d

Age 49 to 56: Qs, 4c, Jc, 9d, 3h, 2s, Qs

Age 56 to 63: 8s, 7d, 9d, Jh, 5h, Ah, 2h

Age 63 to 70: 9h, 5d, Jh, 5c, 3h, Ac, Ah

Age 70 to 77: Js, 10d, 5c, 10h, 3s, Ks, 10s

Age 77 to 84: 3h, 7c, 9d, 5h, 7s, 8d, 2d

Age 84 to 90: Kh, 2c, 4h, 5s, 8c, Qd, 5h

7 of Clubs

Age 0 to 7: 5d, Qs, Jc, 9d, 7s, 2c, Kc

Age 7 to 14: Ks, Qc, 2h, 10d, Qh, 4c, Qd

Age 14 to 21: 5s, 3c, 7h, 9s, 6c, 10h, Qh

Age 21 to 28: Ad, 10d, Qc, 3c, 6h, 8h, 10h

Age 28 to 35: 3s, Qd, 3c, 6s, 9s, 7d, 4c

Age 35 to 42: 2h, Js, Jd, 9d, Kd, 2s, 6s

Age 42 to 49: 8d, 8h, 9d, 2c, 5h, 9h, Qh

Age 49 to 56: 7h, 5d, Kh, 5c, 7d, 9c, 2c

Age 56 to 63: 3s, 8c, 5c, Jc, Qd, 10s, Qs

Age 63 to 70: Qc, 5h, Jc, 6d, Ks, 4h, 2h

Age 70 to 77: 4h, 4s, Kh, 7s, 2s, 3d, 9h

Age 77 to 84: 9d, 5h, 7s, 8d, 2d, 10c, Qs

Age 84 to 90: Ad, 4s, 8d, 6h, 4d, Jc, Ks

8 of Clubs

Age 0 to 7: 6d, 4s, 10h, 10d, 8s, Ah, Ad

Age 7 to 14: 3s, 4h, 5s, Qs, 6c, 3h, Ah

Age 14 to 21: Jd, 10s, 4d, 8d, 2d, Qc, 3h

Age 21 to 28: Jc, Qh, 5h, 7c, Ad, 10d

Age 28 to 35: 9d, 5d, 3c, Kd, 7s, 8h, 7h

Age 35 to 42: 5s, 6d, 4c, 10c, 3h, 8d, Qs

Age 42 to 49: 4d, 3s, 6h, 4s, Qc, 7c, 8d

Age 49 to 56: 5h, Jd, 3d, 4h, 10d, Js, 7c

Age 56 to 63: 5c, Jc, Qd, 10s, Qs, 10c, Js

Age 63 to 70: 4c, 10h, 9d, Qh, 8d, 4s, 10c

Age 70 to 77: 6h, 5s, 5d, 9c, 7c, 4h, 4s

Age 77 to 84: 3d, 4d, 3c, 6d, Js, 10s, 4h

Age 84 to 90: Qd, 5h, Kd, 3s, 10c, Qh, 10s

9 of Clubs

Age 0 to 7: 9s, 2h, Kh, Kd, 6h, 4c, 2d

Age 7 to 14: 4s, 7c, Ks, Qc, 2h, 10d, Qh

Age 14 to 21: 6h, 9d, Kh, 2c, 7d, 5h, Jh

Age 21 to 28: 4c, 6c, 2c, Ah, 8s, 3s, 10s

Age 28 to 35: 5c, Js, Ah, Qs, 10d, Kd, 3d

Age 35 to 42: 4h, Ks, 7c, 2h, Js, Jd, 9d

Age 42 to 49: 8c, 4d, 3s, 6h, 4s, Qc, 7c

Age 49 to 56: 2c, 10s, 6h, As, 6s, 6c, Qc

Age 56 to 63: Ks, 4s, Ac, 4h, 5s, Kd, 7h

Age 63 to 70: Qd, Kh, Kc, Ad, Qs, 3d, 5s

Age 70 to 77: 7c, 4h, 4s, Kh, 7s, 2s, 3d

Age 77 to 84: 5c, 7h, Kh, Ah, Ad, 9h, Kd

Age 84 to 90: Ac, 6d, 4c, As, 9s, 3h, Ah

10 of Clubs

Age 0 to 7: 8d, Ks, 3h, Ac, Qc, 10s, 5c

Age 7 to 14: 8c, 3s, 4h, 5s, Qs, 6c, 3h

Age 14 to 21: Kd, 7c, 5s, 3c, 7h, 9s, 6c

Age 21 to 28: Ks, Qs, 2h, 8d, 6d, 3d, 5d

Age 28 to 35: 5h, 7s, 2c, 2s, Ad, 4d, 6d

Age 35 to 42: 3h, 8d, Qs, 7s, Qd, As, 4d

Age 42 to 49: Jc, 5d, 7s, Kc, 2s, 7d, 3d

Age 49 to 56: 2h, 4s, 10h, 3c, 8h, 8s, Kc

Age 56 to 63: Js, As, 3c, 9s, 4c, 9h, 6d

Age 63 to 70: 2c, Kd, 6s, 6h, 7d, 3s, 9s

Age 70 to 77: Jc, 8c, 6h, 5s, 5d, 9c, 7c

Age 77 to 84: Qs, 4c, 5s, Jd, Ks, Qh, 2h

Age 84 to 90: Qh, 10s, 6s, 7h, 8s, 9d, 9h

Jack of Clubs

Age 0 to 7: 9d, 7s, 2c, Kc, Jd, 4h, 4d

Age 7 to 14: 10s, 5h, Kc, 7h, 2d, 2s, 9c

Age 14 to 21: 9h, 10c, kd, 7c, 5s, 3c, 7h

Age 21 to 28: Qh, 5h, 7c, Ad, 10d, Qc, 3c

Age 28 to 35: 8s, 2h, Kc, As, 5d, 9d, Qc

Age 35 to 42: 9c, 4h, Ks, 7c, 2h, Js, Jd

Age 42 to 49: 5d, 7s, Kc, 2s, 7d, 3d, Jh

Age 49 to 56: 9d, 3h, 2s, Qs, Ah, 5s, 3s

Age 56 to 63: Qd, 10s, Qs, 10c, Js, As, 3c

Age 63 to 70: 6d, Ks, 4h, 2h, 10s, 4d, 7s

Age 70 to 77: 8c, 6h, 5s, 5d, 9c, 7c, 4h

Age 77 to 84: 2s, 3s, 5d, 6s, 6c, 3h, 7c

Age 84 to 90: Ks, 9c, Ac, 6d, 4c, As, 9s

Queen of Clubs

Age 0 to 7: 10s, 5c, 3d, As, 7h, 7d, 5s

Age 7 to 14: 2h, 10d, Qh, 4c, Qd, 2c, As

Age 14 to 21: 3h, 5d, 4c, 7s, Jc, 9h, 10c

Age 21 to 28: 3c, 6h, 8h, 10h, 7d, 4s, 7s

Age 28 to 35: 10s, 8c, 10h, 9c, 5c, Js, Ah

Age 35 to 42: 2d, Jc, 9c, 4h, Ks, 7c, 2h

Age 42 to 49: 7c, 8d, 8h, 9d, 2c, 5h, 9h

Age 49 to 56: 4c, Jc, 9d, 3h, 2s, Qs, Ah

Age 56 to 63: 8d, 3h, 4d, Jd, 9c, Ks

Age 63 to 70: 5h, Jc, 6d, Ks, 4h, 2h, 10s

Age 70 to 77: 2h, 3h, Kc, As, 7h, 10c, Jc

Age 77 to 84: 8s, 2c, As, 4s, 10h, 8c, 3d

Age 84 to 90: Js, 5d, 5c, 8h, 7c, Ad, 4s

King of Clubs

Age 0 to 7: Jd, 4h, 4d, 2s, 8h, 6c, 6s

Age 7 to 14: 7h, 2d, 2s, 9c, 4s, 7c, Ks

Age 14 to 21: 6d, 4h, Js, Ks, 10d, Ac, Qs

Age 21 to 28: Ac, 2s, 7h, 9d, Qd, 3h, 4h

Age 28 to 35: As, 5d, 9d, Qc, 10s, 8c, 10h

Age 35 to 42: Ah, 5h, 3s, 3d, Ad, 9s, Qc

Age 42 to 49: 2s, 7d, 3d, Jh, 5s, 2d, 2h

Age 49 to 56: 9h, Qd, Jh, 4d, Ad, Ac, 2d

Age 56 to 63: 8d, 3h, 4d, Jd, 9c, Ks, 4s

Age 63 to 70: Ad, Qs, 3d, 5s, 3c, 10d, 8s

Age 70 to 77: As, 7h, 10c, Jc, 8c, 6h, 5s

Age 77 to 84: Qd, 7d, Jc, 2s, 3s, 5d, 6s

Age 84 to 90: Jd, 3c, 2s, 2d, Qc, Js, 5d

THE DIAMONDS SUIT

Ace of Diamonds

Age 0 to 7: Qd, 5h, 3c, 3s, 9h, 7c, 5d

Age 7 to 14: 10c, 8c, 3s, 4h, 5s, Qs, 6c

Age 14 to 21: Kc, 6d, 4h, Js, Ks, 10d, Ac

Age 21 to 28: 10d, Qc, 3c, 6h, 8h, 10h, 7d

Age 28 to 35: 4d, 6d, 6h, 2d, Kh, 3h, 6c

Age 35 to 42: 9s, Qc, 2d, Jc, 9c, 4h, Ks

Age 42 to 49: 10h, 6d, 10s, Ks, Js, Ac, 10c

Age 49 to 56: Ac, 2d, 9s, 7s, Kd, 8d, 6d

Age 56 to 63: 6s, 8h, 7s, 7c, 3s, 8c, 5c

Age 63 to 70: Qs, 3d, 5s, 3c, 10d, 8s, 7c

Age 70 to 77: 2d, 7d, 3c, Jh, 4c, Qc, 2h

Age 77 to 84: 9h, Kd, Jh, 6h, 10d, Ac, Qc

Age 84 to 90: 4s, 8d, 6h, 4d, Jc, Ks, 9c

2 of Diamonds

Age 0 to 7: Js, 8c, 6d, 4s, 10h, 10d, 8s

Age 7 to 14: 2s, 9c, 4s, 7c, Ks, Qc, 2h

Age 14 to 21: Qc, 3h, 5d, 4c, 7s, Jc, 9h

Age 21 to 28: 5s, 9c, 4c, 6c, 2c, Ah, 8s

Age 28 to 35: Kh, 3h, 6c, Jd, Qh, 4s, Ks

Age 35 to 42: Jc, 9c, 4h, Ks, 7c, 2h, Js

Age 42 to 49: 2h, 6c, Kh, Kd, 3c, Qs, 9c

Age 49 to 56: 9s, 7s, Kd, 8d, 6d, 8c, 5h

Age 56 to 63: 10d, 6h, 10h, 5d, Qc, Kc, 8d

Age 63 to 70: 6c, 9h, 5d, Jh, 5c, 3h, Ac

Age 70 to 77: 7d, 3c, Jh, 4c, Qc, 2h, 3h

Age 77 to 84: 10c, Qs, 4c, 5s, Jd, Ks, Qh

Age 84 to 90: Qc, Js, 5d, 5c, 8h, 7c, Ad

3 of Diamonds

Age 0 to 7: As, 7h, 7d, 5s, Jh, 9c, 9s

Age 7 to 14: 6h, Ad, 10c, 8c, 3s, 4h, 5s

Age 14 to 21: Ah, 4s, 8c, Jd, 10s, 4d, 8d

Age 21 to 28: 5d, 9s, Kh, 9h, 5c, Jh, Jd

Age 28 to 35: 7h, 5s, 9h, 4h, 8h, 10c, 5h

Age 35 to 42: Ad, 9s, Qc, 2d, Jc, 9c, 4h

Age 42 to 49: Jh, 5s, 2d, 2h, 6c, Kh, Kd

Age 49 to 56: 4h, 10d, Js, 7c, 7h, 5d, Kh

Age 56 to 63: 2c, 2s, 2d, 10d, 6h, 10h, 5d

Age 63 to 70: 5s, 3c, 10d, 8s, 7c, Qc, 5h

Age 70 to 77: 9h, Jd, 6s, 6d, 9d, 9s, 8s

Age 77 to 84: 4d, 3c, 6d, Js, 10s, 4h, 9s

Age 84 to 90: Qs, 2h, 10d, 6c, Kh, 2c, 4h

4 of Diamonds

Age 0 to 7: 2s, 8h, 6c, 6s, Qh, 10c, 8d

Age 7 to 14: Jh, 6d, 6s, Ac, 9s, 7s, 3d

Age 14 to 21: 8d, 2d, Qc, 3h, 5d, 4c, 7s

Age 21 to 28: Kd, As, 6s, 2d, 5s, 9c, 4c

Age 28 to 35: 6d, 6h, 2d, Kh, 3h, 6c, Jd

Age 35 to 42: 7d, 10s, 7h, 4s, 5c, 8h, Kh

Age 42 to 49: 3s, 6h, 4s, Qc, 7c, 8d, 8h

Age 49 to 56: Ad, Ac, 2d, 9s, 7s, Kd, 8d

Age 56 to 63: Jd, 9c, Ks, 4s, Ac, 4h, 5s

Age 63 to 70: 7s, As, 2d, 6c, 9h, 5d, Jh

Age 70 to 77: Kd, Qs, 6c, Js, 10d, 5c, 10h

Age 77 to 84: 3c, 6d, Js, 10s, 4h, 9s, 8h

Age 84 to 90: Jc, Ks, 9c, Ac, 6d, 4c, As

5 of Diamonds

Age 0 to 7: Qs, Jc, 9d, 7s, 2c, Kc, Jd

Age 7 to 14: 8h, Kh, 8s, Jc, 10s, 5h, Kc

Age 14 to 21: 4c, 7s, Jc, 9h, 10c, Kd, 7c

Age 21 to 28: 9s, Kh, 9h, 5c, Jh, Jd, Kc

Age 28 to 35: 9d, Qc, 10s, 8c, 10h, 9c, 5c

Age 35 to 42: 10d, Qh, 8c, 5s, 6d, 4c, 10c

Age 42 to 49: 7s, Kc, 2s, 7d, 3d, Jh, 5s

Age 49 to 56: Kh, 5c, 7d, 9c, 2c, 10s, 6h

Age 56 to 63: Qc, Kc, 8d, 3h, 4d, Jd, 9c

Age 63 to 70: Jh, 5c, 3h, Ac, Ah, 2s, 7h

Age 70 to 77: 9c, 7c, 4h, 4s, Kh, 7s, 2s

Age 77 to 84: 6s, 6c, 3h, 7c, 9d, 5h, 7s

Age 84 to 90: 5c, 8h, 7c, Ad, 4s, 8d, 6h

6 of Diamonds

Age 0 to 7: 4s, 10h, 10d, 8s, Ah, Ad, Qd

Age 7 to 14: 6s, Ac, 9s, 7s, 3d, 6h, Ad

Age 14 to 21: 4h, Js, Ks, 10d, Ac, Qs, 9c

Age 21 to 28: 3d, 5d, 9s, Kh, 9h, 5c, Jh

Age 28 to 35: 6h, 2d, Kh, 3h, 6c, Jd, Qh

Age 35 to 42: 4c, 10c, 3h, 8d, Qs, 7s, Qd

Age 42 to 49: 10s, Ks, Js, Ac, 10c, Jc, 5d

Age 49 to 56: 8c, 5h, Jd, 3d, 4h, 10d, Js

Age 56 to 63: Kh, Qh, 3d, 2c, 2s, 2d, 10d

Age 63 to 70: Ks, 4h, 2h, 10s, 4d, 7s, As

Age 70 to 77: 9d, 9s, 8s, Ah, 8d, Qd, 4d

Age 77 to 84: Js, 10s, 4h, 9s, 8h, Kc, Qd

Age 84 to 90: 4c, As, 9s, 3h, Ah, 7d, 7s

7 of Diamonds

Age 0 to 7: 5s, Jh, 9c, 9s, 2h, Kh, Kd

Age 7 to 14: Js, 3c, 8d, 10h, 5d, 8h, Kh

Age 14 to 21: 5h, Jh, 3s, 2s, 2h, 6s, 8h

Age 21 to 28: 4s, 7s, Js, 4d, Kd, As, 6s

Age 28 to 35: 4c, Jh, Jc, 8s, 2h, Kc, As

Age 35 to 42: 10s, 7h, 4s, 5c, 8h, Kh, Kc

Age 42 to 49: 3d, Jh, 5s, 2d, 2h, 6c, Kh

Age 49 to 56: 9c, 2c, 10s, 6h, As, 6s, 6c

Age 56 to 63: 9d, Jh, 5h, Ah, 2h, Ad, 6s

Age 63 to 70: 3s, 9s, 9c, Qd, Kh, Kc, Ad

Age 70 to 77: 3c, Jh, 4c, Qc, 2h, 3h, Kc

Age 77 to 84: Jc, 2s, 3s, 5d, 6s, 6c, 3h

Age 84 to 90: 7s, Jh, 3d, Qs, 2h, 10d, 6c

8 of Diamonds

Age 0 to 7: Ks, 3h, Ac, Qc, 10s, 5c, 3d

Age 7 to 14: 10h, 5d, 8h, Kh, 8s, Jc, 10s

Age 14 to 21: 2d, Qc, 3h, 5d, 4c, 7s, Jc

Age 21 to 28: 6d, 3d, 5d, 9s, Kh, 9h, 5c

Age 28 to 35: Ac, 7c, 3s, Qd, 3c, 6s, 9s

Age 35 to 42: Qs, 7s, Qd, As, 4d, 7d, 10s

Age 42 to 49: 8h, 9d, 2c, 5h, 9h, Qh, As

Age 49 to 56: 6d, 8c, 5h, Jd, 3d, 4h, 10d

Age 56 to 63: 3h, 4d, Jd, 9c, Ks, 4s, Ac

Age 63 to 70: 4s, 10c, 2c, Kd, 6s, 6h, 7d

Age 70 to 77: Qd, 4d, Kd, Qs, 6c, Js, 10d

Age 77 to 84: 2d, 10c, Qs, 4c, 5s, Jd, Ks

Age 84 to 90: 6h, 4d, Jc, Ks, 9c, Ac, 6d

9 of Diamonds

Age 0 to 7: 7s, 2c, Kc, Jd, 4h, 4d, 2s

Age 7 to 14: 5c, Kd, Jd, 7d, Js, 3c, 8d

Age 14 to 21: Kh, 2c, 7d, 5h, Jh, 3s, 2s

Age 21 to 28: Qd, 3h, 4h, 8c, Jc, Qh, 5h

Age 28 to 35: Qc, 10s, 8c, 10h, 9c, 5c, Js

Age 35 to 42: Kd, 2s, 6s, 9h, 6h, Jh, 10h

Age 42 to 49: 2c, 5h, 9h, Qh, As, 4h, 4c

Age 49 to 56: 3h, 2s, Qs, Ah, 5s, 3s, Qh

Age 56 to 63: Jh, 5h, Ah, 2h, Ad, 6s, 8h

Age 63 to 70: Qh, 8d, 4s, 10c, 2c, Kd, 6s

Age 70 to 77: 9s, 8s, Ah, 8d, Qd, 4d, Kd

Age 77 to 84: 5h, 7s, 8d, 2d, 10c, Qs, 4c

Age 84 to 90: 9h, 10h, Kc, Jd, 3c, 2s, 2d

10 of Diamonds

Age 0 to 7: 8s, Ah, Ad, Qd, 5h, 3c, 3s

Age 7 to 14: Qh, 4c, Qd, 2c, As, 9h, 4d

Age 14 to 21: Ac, Qs, 9c, 6h, 9d, Kh, 2c

Age 21 to 28: Qc, 3c, 6h, 8h, 10h, 7d, 4s

Age 28 to 35: Kd, 3d, 7h, 5s, 9h, 4h, 8h

Age 35 to 42: Qh, 8c, 5s, 6d, 4c, 10c, 3h

Age 42 to 49: Ad, 10h, 6d, 10s, Ks, Js, Ac

Age 49 to 56: Js, 7c, 7h, 5d, Kh, 5c, 7d

Age 56 to 63: 6h, 10h, 5d, Qc, Kc, 8d, 3h

Age 63 to 70: 8s, 7c, Qc, 5h, Jc, 6d, Ks

Age 70 to 77: 5c, 10h, 3s, Ks, 10s, Ac, Qh

Age 77 to 84: Ac, Qc, 8s, 2c, As, 4s, 10h

Age 84 to 90: 6c, Kh, 2c, 4h, 5s, 8c, Qd

Jack of Diamonds

Age 0 to 7: 4h, 4d, 2s, 8h, 6c, 6s, Qh

Age 7 to 14: 7d, Js, 3c, 8d, 10h, 5d, 8h

Age 14 to 21: 10s, 4d, 8d, 2d, Qc, 3h, 5d

Age 21 to 28: Kc, Ac, 2s, 7h, 9d, Qd, 3h

Age 28 to 35: Qh, 4s, Ks, 8d, Ac, 7c, 3s

Age 35 to 42: 9d, Kd, 2s, 6s, 9h, 6h, Jh

Age 42 to 49: Qd, Ah, 6s, 10d, Ad, 10h, 6d

Age 49 to 56: 3d, 4h, 10d, Js, 7c, 7h, 5d

Age 56 to 63: 9c, Ks, 4s, Ac, 4h, 5s, Kd

Age 63 to 70: 8c, 4c, 10h, 9d, Qh, 8d, 4s

Age 70 to 77: 6s, 6d, 9d, 9s, 8s, Ah, 8d

Age 77 to 84: Ks, Qh, 2h, 9c, 5c, 7h, Kh

Age 84 to 90: 3c, 2s, 2d, Qc, Js, 5d, 5c

Queen of Diamonds

Age 0 to 7: 5h, 3c, 3s, 9h, 7c, 5d, Qs

Age 7 to 14: 2c, As, 9h, 4d, Jh, 6d, 6s

Age 14 to 21: 3d, Ah, 4s, 8c, Jd, 10s, 4d

Age 21 to 28: 3h, 4h, 8c, Jc, Qh, 5h, 7c

Age 28 to 35: 3c, 6s, 9s, 7d, 4c, Jh, Jc

Age 35 to 42: As, 4d, 7d, 10s, 7h, 4s, 5c

Age 42 to 49: Ah, 6s, 10d, Ad, 10h, 6d, 10s

Age 49 to 56: Jh, 4d, Ad, Ac, 2d, 9s, 7s

Age 56 to 63: 10s, Qs, 10c, Js, As, 3c, 9s

Age 63 to 70: Kh, Kc, Ad, Qs, 3d, 5s, 3c

Age 70 to 77: 4d, Kd, Qs, 6c, Js, 10d, 5c

Age 77 to 84: 7d, Jc, 2s, 3s, 5d, 6s, 6c

Age 84 to 90: 5h, Kd, 3s, 10c, Qh, 10s, 6s

King of Diamonds

Age 0 to 7: 6h, 4c, 2d, Js, 8c, 6d, 4s

Age 7 to 14: Jd, 7d, Js, 3c, 8d, 10h, 5d

Age 14 to 21: 7c, 5s, 3c, 7h, 9s, 6c, 10h

Age 21 to 28: As, 6s, 2d, 5s, 9c, 4c, 6c

Age 28 to 35: 3d, 7h, 5s, 9h, 4h, 8h, 10c

Age 35 to 42: 2s, 6s, 9h, 6h, Jh, 10h, 6c

Age 42 to 49: 3c, Qs, 9c, 8c, 4d, 3s, 6h

Age 49 to 56: 8d, 6d, 8c, 5h, Jd, 3d, 4h

Age 56 to 63: 7h, 6c, 8s, 7d, 9d, Jh, 5h

Age 63 to 70: 6s, 6h, 7d, 3s, 9s, 9c, Qd

Age 70 to 77: Qs, 6c, Js, 10d, 5c, 10h, 3s

Age 77 to 84: Jh, 6h, 10d, Ac, Qc, 8s, 2c

Age 84 to 90: 3s, 10c, Qh, 10s, 6s, 7h, 8s

THE SPADES SUIT

Ace of Spades

Age 0 to 7: 7h, 7d, 5s, Jh, 9c, 9s, 2h

Age 7 to 14: 9h, 4d, Jh, 6d, 6s, Ac, 9s

Age 14 to 21: Ad, Kc, 6d, 4h, Js, Ks, 10d

Age 21 to 28: 6s, 2d, 5s, 9c, 4c, 6c, 2c

Age 28 to 35: 5d, 9d, Qc, 10s, 8c, 10h, 9c

Age 35 to 42: 4d, 7d, 10s, 7h, 4s, 5c, 8h

Age 42 to 49: 4h, 4c, 7h, 9s, 8s, 3h, 5c

Age 49 to 56: 6s, 6c, Qc, 4c, Jc, 9d, 3h

Age 56 to 63: 3c, 9s, 4c, 9h, 6d, Kh, Qh

Age 63 to 70: 2d, 6c, 9h, 5d, Jh, 5c, 3h

Age 70 to 77: 7h, 10c, Jc, 8c, 6h, 5s, 5d

Age 77 to 84: 4s, 10h, 8c, 3d, 4d, 3c, 6d

Age 84 to 90: 9s, 3h, Ah, 7d, 7s, Jh, 3d

2 of Spades

Age 0 to 7: 8h, 6c, 6s, Qh, 10c, 8d, Ks

Age 7 to 14: 9c, 4s, 7c, Ks, Qc, 2h, 10d

Age 14 to 21: 2h, 6s, 8h, Qd, 3d, Ah, 4s

Age 21 to 28: 7h, 9d, Qd, 3h, 4h, 8c, Jc

Age 28 to 35: Ad, 4d, 6d, 6h, 2d, Kh, 3h

Age 35 to 42: 6s, 9h, 6h, Jh, 10h, 6c, As

Age 42 to 49: 7d, 3d, Jh, 5s, 2d, 2h, 6s

Age 49 to 56: Qs, Ah, 5s, 3s, Qh, Ks, 10c

Age 56 to 63: 2d, 10d, 6h, 10h, 5d, Qc Kc

Age 63 to 70: 7h, 8h, Js, Jd, 8c, 4c, 10h

Age 70 to 77: 3d, 9h, Jd, 6s, 6d, 9d, 9s

Age 77 to 84: 3s, 5d, 6s, 6c, 3h, 7c, 9d

Age 84 to 90: 2d, Qc, Js, 5d, 5c, 8h, 7c

3 of Spades

Age 0 to 7: 9h, 7c, 5d, Qs, Jc, 9d, 7s

Age 7 to 14: 4h, 5s, Qs, 6c, 3h, Ah, 9d

Age 14 to 21: 2s, 2h, 6s, 8h, Qd, 3d, Ah

Age 21 to 28: 10s, 10c, Ks, Qs, 2h, 8d, 6d

Age 28 to 35: Qd, 3c, 6s, 9s, 7d, 4c, Jh

Age 35 to 42: 3d, Ad, 9s, Qc, 2d, Jc, 9c

Age 42 to 49: 6h, 4s, Qc, 7c, 8d, 8h, 9d

Age 49 to 56: Qh, Ks, 10c, 2h, 4s, 10h, 3c

Age 56 to 63: 8c, 5c, Jc, Qd, 10s, Qs, 10c

Age 63 to 70: 9s, 9c, Qd, Kh, Kc, Ad, Qs

Age 70 to 77: Ks, 10s, Ac, Qh, 5h, 8h, 2c

Age 77 to 84: 5d, 6s, 6c, 3h, 7c, 9d, 5h

Age 84 to 90: 10c, Qh, 10s, 6s, 7h, 8s, 9d

4 of Spades

Age 0 to 7: 10h, 10d, 8s, Ah, Ad, Qd, 5h

Age 7 to 14: 7c, Ks, Qc, 2h, 10d, Qh, 4c

Age 14 to 21: 8c, Jd, 10s, 4d, 8d, 2d, Qc

Age 21 to 28: 7s, Js, 4d, Kd, As, 6s, 2d

Age 28 to 35: Ks, 8d, Ac, 7c, 3s, Qd, 3c

Age 35 to 42: 5c, 8h, Kh, Kc, Ah, 5h, 3s

Age 42 to 49: Qc, 7c, 8d, 8h, 9d, 2c, 5h

Age 49 to 56: 10h, 3c, 8h, 8s, Kc, 9h, Qd

Age 56 to 63: Ac, 4h, 5s, Kd, 7h, 6c, 8s

Age 63 to 70: 10c, 2c, Kd, 6s, 6h, 7d, 3s

Age 70 to 77: Kh, 7s, 2s, 3d, 9h, Jd, 6s

Age 77 to 84: 10h, 8c, 3d, 4d, 3c, 6d, Js

Age 84 to 90: 8d, 6h, 4d, Jc, Ks, 9c, Ac

5 of Spades

Age 0 to 7: Jh, 9c, 9s, 2h, Kh, Kd, 6h

Age 7 to 14: Qs, 6c, 3h, Ah, 9d, 5c, Kd

Age 14 to 21: 3c, 7h, 9s, 6c, 10h, Qh, 5c

Age 21 to 28: 9c, 4c, 6c, 2c, Ah, 8s, 3s

Age 28 to 35: 9h, 4h, 8h, 10c, 5h, 7s

Age 35 to 42: 2c, 6d, 4c, 10c, 3h, 8d, Qs, 7s

Age 42 to 49: 2d, 2h, 6c, Kh, Kd, 3c, Qs

Age 49 to 56: 3s, Qh, Ks, 10c, 2h, 4s, 10h

Age 56 to 63: Kd, 7h, 6c, 8s, 7d, 9d, Jh

Age 63 to 70: 3c, 10d, 8s, 7c, Qc, 5h, Jc

Age 70 to 77: 5d, 9c, 7c, 4h, 4s, Kh, 7s

Age 77 to 84: Jd, Ks, Qh, 2h, 9c, 5c, 7h

Age 84 to 90: 8c, Qd, 5h, Kd, 3s, 10c, Qh

6 of Spades

Age 0 to 7: Qh, 10c, 8d, Ks, 3h, Ac, Qc

Age 7 to 14: Ac, 9s, 7s, 3d, 6h, Ad, 10c

Age 14 to 21: 8h, Qd, 3d, Ah, 4s, 8c, Jd

Age 21 to 28: 2d, 5s, 9c, 4c, 6c, 2c, Ah

Age 28 to 35: 9s, 7d, 4c, Jh, Jc, 8s, 2h

Age 35 to 42: 9h, 6h, Jh, 10h, 6c, Ac, 8s

Age 42 to 49: 10d, Ad, 10h, 6d, 10s, Ks, Js

Age 49 to 56: 6c, Qc, 4c, Jc, 9d, 3h, 2s

Age 56 to 63: 8h, 7s, 7c, 3s, 8c, 5c, Jc

Age 63 to 70: 6h, 7d, 3s, 9s, 9c, Qd, Kh

Age 70 to 77: 6d, 9d, 9s, 8s, Ah, 8d, Qd

Age 77 to 84: 6c, 3h, 7c, 9d, 5h, 7s, 8d

Age 84 to 90: 7h, 8s, 9d, 9h, 10h, Kc, Jd

7 of Spades

Age 0 to 7: 2c, Kc, Jd, 4h, 4d, 2s, 8h

Age 7 to 14: 3d, 6h, Ad, 10c, 8c, 3s, 4h

Age 14 to 21: Jc, 9h, 10c, Kd, 7c, 5s, 3c

Age 21 to 28: Js, 4d, Kd, As, 6s, 2d, 5s

Age 28 to 35: 2c, 2s, Ad, 4d, 6d, 6h, 2d

Age 35 to 42: Qd, As, 4d, 7d, 10s, 7h, 4s

Age 42 to 49: Kc, 2s, 7d, 3d, Jh, 5s, 2d

Age 49 to 56: Kd, 8d, 6d, 8c, 5h, Jd, 3d

Age 56 to 63: 7c, 3s, 8c, 5c, Jc, Qd, 10s

Age 63 to 70: As, 2d, 6c, 9h, 5d, Jh, 5c

Age 70 to 77: 2s, 3d, 9h, Jd, 6s, 6d, 9d

Age 77 to 84: 8d, 2d, 10c, Qs, 4c, 5s, Jd

Age 84 to 90: Jh, 3d, Qs, 2h, 10d, 6c, Kh

8 of Spades

Age 0 to 7: Ah, Ad, Qd, 5h, 3c, 3s, 9h

Age 7 to 14: Jc, 10s, 5h, Kc, 7h, 2d, 2s

Age 14 to 21: As, Ad, Kc, 6d, 4h, Js, Ks

Age 21 to 28: 3s, 10s, 10c, Ks, Qs, 2h, 8d

Age 28 to 35: 2h, Kc, As, 5d, 9d, Qc, 10s

Age 35 to 42: 2c, 3c, 5d, 10d, Qh, 8c, 5s

Age 42 to 49: 3h, 5c, Jd, Qd, Ah, 6s, 10d

Age 49 to 56: Kc, 9h, Qd, Jh, 4d, Ad, Ac

Age 56 to 63: 7d, 9d, Jh, 5h, Ah, 2h, Ad

Age 63 to 70: 7c, Qc, 5h, Jc, 6d, Ks, 4h

Age 70 to 77: Ah, 8d, Qd, 4d, Kd, Qs, 6c

Age 77 to 84: 2c, As, 4s, 10h, 8c, 3d, 4d

Age 84 to 90: 9d, 9h, 10h, Kc, 2d, 3c, 2s

9 of Spades

Age 0 to 7: 2h, Kh, Kd, 6h, 4c, 2d, Js

Age 7 to 14: 7s, 3d, 6h, Ad, 10c, 8c, 3s

Age 14 to 21: 6c, 10h, Qh, 5c, 8s, As, Ad

Age 21 to 28: Kh, 9h, 5c, Jh, Jd, Kc, Ac

Age 28 to 35: 7d, 4c, Jh, Jc, 8s, 2h, Kc

Age 35 to 42: Qc, 2d, Jc, 9c, 4h, Ks, 7c

Age 42 to 49: 8s, 3h, 5c, Jd, Qd, Ah, 6s

Age 49 to 56: 7s, Kd, 8d, 6d, 8c, 5h, Jd

Age 56 to 63: 4c, 9h, 6d, Kh, Qh, 3d, 2c

Age 63 to 70: 9c, Qd, Kh, Kc, Ad, Qs, 3d

Age 70 to 77: 8s, Ah, 8d, Qd, 4d, Kd, Qs

Age 77 to 84: 8h, Kc, Qd, 7d, Jc, 2s, 3s

Age 84 to 90: 3h, Ah, 7d, 7s, Jh, 3d, Qs

10 of Spades

Age 0 to 7: 5c, 3d, As, 7h, 7d, 5s, Jh

Age 7 to 14: 5h, Kc, 7h, 2d, 2s, 9c, 4s

Age 14 to 21: 4d, 8d, 2d, Qc, 3h, 5d, 4c

Age 21 to 28: 10c, Ks, Qs, 2h, 8d, 6d, 3d

Age 28 to 35: 8c, 10h, 9c, 5c, Js, Ah, Qs

Age 35 to 42: 7h, 4s, 5c, 8h, Kh, Kc, Ah

Age 42 to 49: Ks, Js, Ac, 10c, Jc, 5d, 7s

Age 49 to 56: 6h, As, 6s, 6c, Qc, 4c, Jc

Age 56 to 63: Qs, 10c, Js, As, 3c, 9s, 4c

Age 63 to 70: 4d, 7s, As, 2d, 6c, 9h, 5d

Age 70 to 77: Ac, Qh, 5h, 8h, 2c, Ad, 2d

Age 77 to 84: 4h, 9s, 8h, Kc, Qd, 7d, Jc

Age 84 to 90: 6s, 7h, 8s, 9d, 9h, 10h, Kc

Jack of Spades

Age 0 to 7: 8c, 6d, 4s, 10h, 10d, 8s, Ah

Age 7 to 14: 3c, 8d, 10h, 5d, 8h, Kh, 8s

Age 14 to 21: Ks, 10d, Ac, Qs, 9c, 6h, 9d

Age 21 to 28: 4d, Kd, As, 6s, 2d, 5s, 9c

Age 28 to 35: Ah, Qs, 10d, Kd, 3d, 7h, 5s

Age 35 to 42: Jd, 9d, Kd, 2s, 6s, 9h, 6h

Age 42 to 49: Ac, 10c, Jc, 5d, 7s, Kc, 2s

Age 49 to 56: 7c, 7h, 5d, Kh, 5c, 7d, 9c

Age 56 to 63: As, 3c, 9s, 4c, 9h, 6d, Kh

Age 63 to 70: Jd, 8c, 4c, 10h, 9d, Qh, 8d

Age 70 to 77: 10d, 5c, 10h, 3s, Ks, 10s, Ac

Age 77 to 84: 10s, 4h, 9s, 8h, Kc, Qd, 7d

Age 84 to 90: 5d, 5c, 8h, 7c, Ad, 4s, 8d

Queen of Spades

Age 0 to 7: Jc, 9d, 7s, 2c, Kc, Jd, 4h

Age 7 to 14: 6c, 3h, Ah, 9d, 5c, Kd, Jd

Age 14 to 21: 9c, 6h, 9d, Kh, 2c, 7d, 5h

Age 21 to 28: 2h, 8d, 6d, 3d, 5d, 9s, Kh

Age 28 to 35: 10d, Kd, 3d, 7h, 5s, 9h, 4h

Age 35 to 42: 7s, Qd, As, 4d, 7d, 10s, 7h

Age 42 to 49: 9c, 8c, 4d, 3s, 6h, 4s, Qc

Age 49 to 56: Ah, 5s, 3s, Qh, Ks, 10c, 2h

Age 56 to 63: 10c, Js, As, 3c, 9s, 4c, 9h

Age 63 to 70: 3d, 5s, 3c, 10d, 8s, 7c, Qc

Age 70 to 77: 6c, Js, 10d, 5c, 10h, 3s, Ks

Age 77 to 84: 4c, 5s, Jd, Ks, Qh, 2h, 9c

Age 84 to 90: 2h, 10d, 6c, Kh, 2c, 4h, 5s

King of Spades

Age 0 to 7: 3h, Ac, Qc, 10s, 5c, 3d, As

Age 7 to 14: Qc, 2h, 10d, Qh, 4c, Qd, 2c

Age 14 to 21: 10d, Ac, Qs, 9c, 6h, 9d, Kh

Age 21 to 28: Qs, 2h, 8d, 6d, 3d, 5d, 9s

Age 28 to 35: 8d, Ac, 7c, 3s, Qd, 3c, 6s

Age 35 to 42: 7c, 2h, Js, Jd, 9d, Kd, 2s

Age 42 to 49: Js, Ac, 10c, Jc, 5d, 7s, Kc

Age 49 to 56: 10c, 2h, 4s, 10h, 3c, 8h, 8s

Age 56 to 63: 4s, Ac, 4h, 5s, Kd, 7h, 6c

Age 63 to 70: 2h, 10s, 4d, 7s, As, 2d

Age 70 to 77: 10s, Ac, Qh, 5h, 8h, 2c, Ad

Age 77 to 84: Qh, 2h, 9c, 5c, 7h, Kh, Ah

Age 84 to 90: 9c, Ac, 6d, 4c, As, 9s, 3h

About the Authors

Geri Sullivan is a professional astrologer and writer who has researched this card system for over twenty-five years to find it a powerful tool for self-development and understanding others. In addition to running a successful astrological practice, she travels internationally to give lectures and workshops. Her science degree combined astrology with psychology and included study of the unconscious, dreams, and mystical experience.

You can contact Geri at her website: www.gerisullivan.com

Saffi Crawford, M.A., is a professional astrologer and numerologist with twenty years of experience. She runs a successful astrological counseling practice in London and gives workshops in astrology, numerology, and the playing card system. Her master's degree in social sciences combined the history and philosophy of Western civilization with the history of astrology. Her research focused in particular on holistic paradigms, hermeneutics, and reflexivity.

E-mail: SCraw99301@aol.com